Flame
in the
Snow

Flame
in the
Snow

THE LOVE LETTERS
OF ANDRÉ BRINK
& INGRID JONKER

FRANCIS GALLOWAY (ED.)

TRANSLATED INTO ENGLISH BY
LEON DE KOCK AND KARIN SCHIMKE

UMUZI

Published in 2015 by Umuzi
an imprint of Penguin Random House South Africa (Pty) Ltd
Company Reg No 1953/000441/07
Estuaries No 4, Oxbow Crescent, Century City, 7441, South Africa
PO Box 1144, Cape Town, 8000, South Africa
umuzi@penguinrandomhouse.co.za

The first portrait of Ingrid Jonker in the photo section is by Anne Fischer.
The red jersey is by Izak de Vries.

First edition, first printing 2015
9 8 7 6 5 4 3 2 1

ISBN 978-1-4152-0878-6 (Print)
ISBN 978-1-4152-0879-3 (ePub)
ISBN 978-1-4152-0880-9 (PDF)

Cover and text design by mr design
Cover photography by André Brink
Set in Garamond
Printed and bound in South Africa by CTP Books

Damning Blue Words on Paper

In one of her earliest letters to André Brink, Ingrid Jonker concludes with the following statement:

> I still want to tell you so, so much more, when we are alone and without damning blue words on paper between us – they look so banal, so crass, so unaccounted for.

On the following day (that is, before he receives this communication), Brink expresses a similar frustration with words in letters:

> But letters and words are becoming more fraudulent by the day. I can't remember ever experiencing the insufficiency of words as agonisingly as in the past while.

If the letters presented in this volume were as unreliable and painfully deceptive for their authors as these quotations suggest, then how much more fraudulent and painful might they not appear to us, decades later? For contemporary readers, the likelihood that the words in these letters will appear banal and crass is far greater than for the writers themselves. At the time, Jonker wrote that genuine communication without actual physical presence was impossible: "Everything enlarged and out of context, because there are only words, without facial expression or the touch of a hand."

WITHOUT FACIAL EXPRESSION OR THE TOUCH OF A HAND
Reading the letters today, with merely the words on paper before us, it is even more difficult to grasp the context, for two reasons in particular: firstly, we do not have access to their telephone conversations, or to the tape recordings they sent each other, containing information about the times they spent together and the situations in which they sat down to write their respective letters. All we have are scraps – scattered references to such details. And secondly, we read these letters today

in the knowledge of how the rest of their lives played out. Readers are likely to be familiar with certain details of Jonker's life, which came to an end surrounded by seawater and kelp. At the time, Brink was still in the early stages of his career as a writer. When the two met for the first time, Brink's important early novel, *Lobola vir die Lewe* [Dowry for Life], had just appeared, and Jonker had published a single volume of poetry called *Ontvlugting* [Escape]. Today we think of Brink as a celebrated, prize-winning author with twenty-four novels to his name, and as a highly regarded academic. We view Jonker as an iconic poet whose reputation has grown to almost mythical proportions. In 1994, her poem "The Child Who Was Shot Dead by Soldiers in Nyanga" was recited by Nelson Mandela during his oration at the opening of South Africa's first democratic parliament. Brink published a comprehensive autobiography, *A Fork in the Road* (2009), in which he devoted an entire chapter to his relationship with Jonker. Petrovna Metelerkamp's biography, *A Poet's Life* (2003), was enthusiastically received. There has also been Louise Viljoen's pocket biography of Jonker (2012).

Despite the authors' dissatisfaction with the inadequacy of words on paper, their correspondence was in fact a major part of the relationship, a love affair that lasted just under two years. The physical distance between Grahamstown, where Brink was a lecturer at Rhodes University, and Cape Town, where Jonker worked as a proofreader, meant they had very limited time to actually *be* together, to supplement a relationship that consisted of mere words. For the most part, the lovers had to rely on correspondence to conduct their relationship. The often fiery exchange of letters began immediately after they met at the home of Jan Rabie and Marjorie Wallace on 18 April 1963, when Brink was on a short visit to Cape Town. In the two days before Brink returned to Grahamstown, they fell passionately in love. Following this encounter they periodically spent "stolen" time together: no more than a handful of weekends, or whenever Brink visited Cape Town to give lectures or attend meetings. On one occasion, they were able to spend ten days together. In addition, they undertook a disastrous tour of Europe that was cut short after a disagreement.

Apart from the fact that their correspondence constitutes a very large part of the relationship between the lovers, and opens a window onto it, their exchange of letters also provides a fascinating perspective on a particular period and on the daily routines and experiences of two literary figures, including their personal and literary insights, not to mention their own work as writers. The letters contain frequent references to the literary scene at the time, as well as bits of gossip about other writers. In addition, Brink and Jonker give voice to their deepest beliefs with regard to religion and politics, and they frequently refer to their most intimate sexual experiences. Ironically, despite the lovers' despair concerning the efficacy of words, their writing displays a unique ability to communicate, and a remarkable facility with language.

AN "EPISTOLARY NOVEL"

The apparently insatiable appetite for literary material relating to the near-mythical figure of Ingrid Jonker will no doubt entice many readers to read *Flame in the Snow*, especially because of speculation concerning the role of her relationship with Brink in her suicide. While these letters may, on the one hand, satisfy readers' curiosity about the enigmatic figure of Jonker, they will also transport the reader in the manner of a gripping epistolary novel. One is likely to be captivated by the head-over-heels love affair, with its insider-view, and the perspective provided by a poet and also a novelist. The language in which these two authors lay bare their feelings, and by means of which they learn to know each other – across vast distances and with revealing candour – lends the correspondence a lyrical quality, with references to planned encounters creating a sense of suspense.

The first letter begins with flashbacks to a meeting that swept them both off their feet. This event is described as mutually life-changing. Frequently, suspense builds up as they anticipate their next meeting, and their letters urgently express their longing to be together. Opportunities have to be planned with great circumspection within a conservative community (even hotels were reluctant to accommodate unmarried couples in shared rooms), and in conditions where the lovers have to avoid provoking gossip, even among friends and acquaintances.

About the time they spent together little is disclosed. Subsequently, it is only in the first letter after each such meeting, with the mutual expression of rapture in the afterglow of intimacy, that readers can begin to draw conclusions concerning the nature of the relationship. On some occasions, inferences may be drawn from expressions of regret, along with confessions of guilt, or attempts to put misunderstandings aside. The actual details of their tempestuous fights, and of their intimacy, are left to the reader's imagination. The two letter-writers' varying versions and interpretations of the same events come across much like the inner workings of an adroit narrative technique adopted by a novelist. Suspense builds up via misunderstandings, and especially the frustrations that arise with delayed postal delivery, unhappy telephone calls, and when the lovers' precious trysts are tainted by arguments that must then be patched up in subsequent letters.

The correspondents are caught up in the daily grind of work obligations, child care, and labouring to earn enough income – Jonker just to survive, while Brink seeks to earn additional funds to finance a middle-class life, to buy the many books he needs, and to send his lover money every now and again. The letters voice the discontent and frustration that flows from the tedium of daily existence, and articulate the lovers' loneliness and longing, as well as their mutual admiration, in moving prose (and sometimes verse, too). At times the prose tends towards the purple, and there are also frequent sexual references.

Structurally, too, *Flame in the Snow* reads compellingly as an epistolary novel: it traces the course of a love affair, from its breakneck beginning, with lengthy, eloquent letters that gradually alter in content and tone as the correspondents describe the more mundane details of their daily existence, detailed narrations that are attempts to get to know each other better. Later still, the letters are dominated by practical arrangements, and there are many references to repeated clashes, along with efforts to repair matters. At times their romantic dreams hold sway, bolstered by hopes of a more satisfying mode of mutual existence, until the relationship eventually unravels. Very few of Brink's letters in the final months of the affair have survived (significantly, he no longer kept copies during that time, while certain letters were torn up, resulting in a lacuna). This means that Jonker's increasing loneliness and desperation are accentuated as her letters follow one upon the other in rapid succession, with apparently fewer letters from her lover.

There is no overarching narrator's voice in the letters, and so the reader relies entirely on two, sometimes divergent, interpretations of events. The effect of this is an awareness that no final truth is possible regarding events that are perceived from different perspectives; there is no access to a "reality" that lies beyond the words – either for the two correspondents at the time, or for the readers of this book, many years later.

A WORLD IN WHICH NOTHING WOULD EVER AGAIN BE CERTAIN OR SAFE

Flame in the Snow is of course *not* fiction, and this correspondence bears witness to a relationship that had a far-reaching influence on the lives of both of these famous writers. Brink writes, in *A Fork in the Road*, that his life after meeting Ingrid Jonker would never be the same again. He was a mere twenty-seven years old at the time, had already obtained two MA degrees at the University of Potchefstroom, and had written a handful of novels that drew on the heritage of realism in Afrikaans literature. His first genuinely innovative novel, *Lobola vir die Lewe*, had just appeared. Brink had recently returned from a two-year period in Paris (1959–1961), where he studied at the Sorbonne on a scholarship, and had taken up a lectureship in the Department of Afrikaans-Nederlands at Rhodes University. In a letter to Jonker, he refers to three events that radically influenced his life – his residence in Paris, the birth of his son (Anton), and his encounter with her. More than forty years later, as he coolly assesses his long life, he retains the same sense of being breathlessly swept off his feet as he had expressed in his very first letter to Ingrid Jonker:

It was in the late afternoon of a blue and golden late summer's day, Thursday 18 April, 1963, that Ingrid walked into my ordered existence and turned it upside down. Until that moment I was ensconced in an

ultimately predictable life as husband and father, lecturer in literature
[...] And afterwards? A world in which nothing would ever be sure
and safe again, and in which everything, from the most private to the
public, from love to politics, was to be exposed to risk and uncertainty
and danger. (*A Fork in the Road*, 91–92)

Jonker was at the time employed as a proofreader in Cape Town.
She was divorced from her husband and lived with her daughter in
a flat. At this point, Jonker was just twenty-nine years old. She had
published several poems while still in high school, and her first volume,
Ontvlugting, made its appearance in 1956. She had an extensive circle of
friends among writers and artists in Cape Town, and had, since 1961,
been involved in a complex relationship with the much older writer
Jack Cope. During her two-year relationship with Brink she repeatedly
broke off and resumed her affair with Cope, and this became a source of
conflict between her and Brink. Some time before her fateful meeting
with Brink, she had received treatment at Valkenberg, a psychiatric
hospital.

As the letters clearly show, Jonker was engaged in a constant battle
merely to survive. She frequently complained that the employment she
was able to find (as a proofreader) was soul-destroying, and she worked
in difficult circumstances (in what she called the "Grey Pit"). As a single
mother, she was also involved in an exhausting struggle to arrange her
daughter's care. Time and time again, she thanks Brink for financial
support. However, Jonker makes it clear to Brink from the start that
she refuses to be possessed by anyone, and that he must not labour
under any illusion that he can ever pin her down or fully understand
her. This freedom, upon which she prides herself and for which she so
stubbornly fights, is precisely the quality that Brink finds irresistible –
yet it also frustrates him.

Jonker's death by drowning occurred on 19 July 1965 at Three
Anchor Bay, Cape Town. The tragic end to her tempestuous life
has, over the years, led to comparisons with, among others, the poet
Sylvia Plath. Despite the fact that Jonker's oeuvre is far from extensive

(consisting of three volumes of poetry, a play, and a handful of short stories), her poetry had an immediate and overwhelming impact on readers. Her deceptively simple poems capture something about the human condition that found favour very widely, as attested to by the translations of her verse into multiple languages, as well as the setting of her work to music (Chris Chameleon in two albums, *Ek Herhaal Jou* and *As Jy Weer Skryf*). The enigma that is Ingrid Jonker continues to hold readers' attention and has given rise to several films, as well as a play, about her life.

When Brink first met Jonker, he was working on his novel *Die Ambassadeur* (later translated as *The Ambassador*). He heeded her comments on the manuscript and made changes on the basis of her recommendations (like Jonker, the character Nicolette is not "have-able"). Brink altered the second edition of *Lobola vir die Lewe* as a result of Jonker's influence. Furthermore, their relationship serves as the basis for *Orgie* [Orgy], published in 1965, which is presented as a dialogue between a man and a woman; from the correspondence between Brink and Jonker, it becomes clear that *Orgie* was the product of their collaboration (in one letter, he refers to it as "our novel"). It emerges from the letters that *Orgie* is in fact an (auto)biographical work. This opens up an alternative approach to reading the novel, which has often been regarded by critics as merely an experimental, modernistic work. The fact that Brink's tone is noticeably more detached after the publication of *Orgie* suggests that the completion of this novel signalled, for him, something akin to an end of their relationship.

THE OPIATE OF BOURGEOIS LIFE

From the very first letter that Brink writes to Jonker, the enormous impact of their sexual relationship, not only on his life but also on his work, begins to emerge. When he reflects on their encounter, he resorts to a register of religious language – for him, their sex is "a sort of holy Mass, in which transubstantiation is complete". Brink then rhetorically asks whether sex might not perhaps be "the most pure religion for us 'non-believers'". Jonker, too, writes in quasi-religious language about sex when she mentions that she is suffering hunger on a "spiritual-sexual level".

For the young Brink, exploring sexuality is crucially important. His and Jonker's sexual relationship, and his experience of her permissiveness, but also her refusal to be bound, had a liberating influence on him. It was a liberation on the intimate level of love that worked its way through to every aspect of his existence. From this moment onwards, the power of sex to liberate, to break established patterns, and to call into question restricted, bourgeois values, plays a central role in Brink's novels. Sex is often a subversive plot device that challenges social boundaries – across colour and class, and between slaves and masters. Significantly, sex serves as a means of communication when no other avenue exists. It is an act of freeing the self, surrendering to the other, and becoming one with this other in a manner that extends beyond words. Apart from the role of sex in Brink's novels, his relationship with Jonker liberated him from the suffocating confines, the "respectability", of the middle-class existence in which he found himself.

Brink's ideological and literary convictions seem, at this stage, to have been moulded by everything he had thus far read and thought about. He was already in a state of rebellion against social exclusion and political and sexual repression, but he hadn't yet *lived out* this rebellion in his own life. He hadn't yet escaped his own middle-class comfort zone. Indeed, he explains to Jonker that his writing, up until this early stage, has remained "conformist", and that his rebellions have occurred within the bounds of acceptability. It is only when he gets to know her, along with her absolute contempt for parochialism and her own form of personal sexual freedom, that he realises how boxed in he himself is, how comfortable he has become in his own life as a lecturer, a spouse and a father. He tells her he admires her for the fact that she will never have to resist middle-class values. This, he says, is because she runs no risk of becoming bogged down in that particular morass. He explains that he needs her to continue liberating him from the "opiate" of bourgeois life.

The extent to which Brink was dependent on Jonker to make him aware of his own, established patterns, is apparent, inter alia, from the manner in which he describes, in one letter, an idyllic dream-existence for the two of them. He writes how he, after sitting and working the entire day in their little house, would get up and meet her in the afternoons on her way back from work. In writing this, he shows no awareness at all of the attitudes that underlie his dream. Jonker then confronts him about the fact that *she* is expected to go work while *he* sits at home writing.

Jonker's liberating influence on Brink, which he finds alluring and values very highly, does not, however, imply that he is able to throw off all his bonds instantaneously. From this point onwards, though, his writing became increasingly fearless, until his novel *Kennis van die Aand* (translated as *Looking on Darkness*) was eventually banned in 1973. From then on, he used the banning as an opportunity to conduct, in an even more scathing register, his struggle against the oppressiveness of Afrikaner nationalism, petit-bourgeois religion, and small-minded thinking. Eventually his critique broadened to include the consequences of not only colonialism, but also racial as well as gender discrimination. He was nevertheless careful, in this phase of his affair at least, not to jeopardise his marriage – partly for the sake of his young son, but also out of consideration for his aged, ill father, whom he did not wish to distress. He also felt sorry for his wife.

The affair was not merely a case of Brink finding Jonker enchanting. Her admiration for him is equally clear. She describes him as a "magician", and is especially admiring of his wide reading and broad insight. She often asks his advice on what to read. When *Rook en Oker* [Smoke and Ochre] appears, she relies entirely on Brink's judgement to make changes for the volume's second printing, which he does directly with the publisher and about which he mostly just informs her. What is especially revealing about the two writers is the self-doubt that they frequently confess to each other. She often expresses doubt about her own talent, while Brink wonders aloud whether he will ever be able to write anything that really matters.

During the course of the correspondence, the reader is privy to much information about the habits and lifestyle of the lovers. Brink's work rate is astonishing. Outside of the relationship, which plays such a large role in his life, he finds time to translate 6 000 words a week (from French and English into Afrikaans) in order to earn extra money. He does these translations while lecturing full-time, putting together new courses on aspects of literature he has never taught before, and marking student essays. At the same time, he edits the journals *60* and *Sestiger*, and mentions at one stage that he is preparing two articles for these. He comments, too, that between all this he gets up several times a night to see to his baby son, and that he is caught up in all manner of domestic and administrative duties. Throughout, however, he continues to read, quoting liberally from world literature and local writers, and delving into various theoretical works. Then, almost in passing, he writes that he is working on a new novel, or play.

The letters of Jonker, the poet in the relationship, are generally not as prolix as the familiar prose of Brink. Although her letters are shorter, she often makes particularly sharp observations about people's actions, and displays a special sensitivity to political prejudice and the exclusion of people on the basis of colour or class. In contrast to Brink, she refrains for the most part from engaging in lengthy philosophical discourse. Instead, she often gives a brief description of an event or uses a few powerful words that vividly demonstrate her political awareness. These letters make it clear that she was no social butterfly who flitted from one artist's party to the next, almost incidentally writing a few good poems in the process. It becomes obvious, from certain brief references, that she takes immediate action (on a bus, at one point) to prevent injustice; moreover, resistance for her is not merely a theoretical matter (as it is, to a certain extent, for Brink), but something that must be actualised in one's personal life.

CENSORSHIP

The factor that brought Brink and Jonker together in the first place was their shared resistance to the growing threat of censorship regulations at the time. This is a matter to which they frequently return in their letters. Jonker mentions several court cases she is attending – including the one where Wilbur Smith's *When the Lion Feeds* was banned. She and Brink frequently discuss complaints concerning *Lobola*, along with the possibility that Brink's novel might have to face a possible banning. They also often refer to sensational reports in the media following comments made by Brink about censorship – and they express disappointment about fellow writers who distance themselves from these opinions. (Brink mentions at one point that his mother has urged him to stop trying to explain his point of view in the media, since his friends understand him in any case while his enemies will refuse to give him his due – a rare moment that reflects positively on Brink's family.)

By the time Brink and Jonker met in 1963, the struggle against censorship in South Africa already had a long history; this resistance intensified in the early 1960s. In the 1940s, the main Afrikaans churches had requested that the government act against "pornography". Shortly after the National Party came to power in 1948, a commission was established to investigate "undesirable publications". Such matter was defined as any publication that was "indecent or obscene or offensive or harmful to public morals", or merely damaging to "the feelings or convictions of Christians". In practice, this might include any criticism of Christianity or its practices or any questioning of the policy of apartheid.

The commission set up by government to look into the matter of censorship, under the chairmanship of Geoff Cronjé, had recommended in 1956 that a publications board be set up and that all publishers, printers and distributors of publications be required to have licences that could be withdrawn if they published material that did not have the prior approval of the publications board.

The Cronjé commission recommended, inter alia, that the Prohibition of Mixed Marriages Act (1949) and the amended Immorality Act (1950) be made applicable to publications also; accordingly, any depiction of racial mixing would constitute a violation of those laws. The alarming powers that would thereby be given to the publications board were strongly resisted by opposition parties as well as many organisations and individuals: freedom of speech would be curtailed, and any criticism of the country's race policy would be outlawed. Established poets such as N.P. Van Wyk Louw and D.J. Opperman joined younger "Sestigers" such as Brink and Jonker in their opposition to censorship. In 1960, discussions about censorship were still ongoing, but after the Sharpeville massacre that year (which gave rise to Jonker's poem "The Child Who Was Shot Dead by Soldiers in Nyanga"), the Verwoerd government declared a State of Emergency and instituted draconian censorship measures – not only for books and films, but also for the press. Despite much protest, the Publications and Entertainments Act was passed in 1963 and the Publications Control Board brought into being.

Jonker and Brink were clearly united in their struggle against censorship. Their political convictions also come to the fore in these letters. Jonker often sharply articulates her impatience with exclusions under apartheid legislation, now bitterly, now satirically (such as when she describes her father's attempts to connect his surname to European forefathers while in fact Jonker could be traced back to a slave from Indonesia). Brink's fighting spirit is evident when he writes: "The charge against *Lobola* has been withdrawn. I am sorry it didn't go ahead. I so badly wanted to remove the taint from the book – and conduct a nice little fight."

The early 1960s were also years in which the government was increasingly taking action against the African National Congress (ANC): it was the time of the infamous Rivonia trial. Brink and Jonker make reference in their letters to the Park Station bomb, John Harris, Stephanie Kemp and Adrian Leftwich. Jonker is ruthless in her judgement of other writers' political views. At one point, she remarks that Etienne Leroux's politics are "a little off the mark, like Bartho's".

New literary journals came into being during this period since there was no place in the older, more conservative journals for the new group of writers. In contrast with many other Afrikaans writers, Brink and Jonker were in the same camp as several English-speaking writers in their opposition to censorship. Both were aware of what was being written and published in English at the time (Jonker via Cope and the journal *Contrast*, which he edited, and Brink as part of his voracious general reading in many languages). Jonker occasionally published in *Contrast* and sometimes in *60*, and it is obvious that neither she nor Brink wished to be restricted by the increasing polarisation between English and Afrikaans.

SENSATIONALISM

A publishing venture such as *Flame in the Snow* is a risky one, since it is open to accusations of sensationalism and prurience, feeding the apparently insatiable public appetite for juicy "scandal". It might be accused of being a tasteless exposé of personal details about the lives of two famous writers. Indeed, the letters undeniably contain material that the media might be eager to report in a sensational manner. There are many intimate descriptions and details that might make some readers cringe. Examples include Brink's nickname for Jonker, "Kokon" ("Cocoon"), "Kokontjie" or "Kontjie", while she in turn uses the endearment "papie" (pupa) to describe his penis. There are also Brink's frequent enquiries as to whether a "vlindertjie" (little butterfly) has yet taken residence inside her. Ejaculate is referred to as "secrets" that he leaves behind in her (at one point, Brink even puts a spot of semen on a page that he posts off to Jonker). Jonker's genitals are referred to as a "chick". The lovers discuss abrasions resulting from intercourse – in fact, in one letter Jonker notes that they had sex thirty-six times during a ten-day period. However, to excise this kind of detail from their correspondence would constitute bowdlerisation: it would be a betrayal of their joint struggle against censorship.

Though certain readers may experience a degree of discomfort, it is important to realise that these two illustrious literary figures were ordinary flesh-and-blood human beings with the same desires, urges, needs and failings as the rest of us. For them, sex was an intense spiritual experience, and they were reluctant to conform to social expectations; their frankness in this regard was in itself an act of defiance against bourgeois values. In one particular letter, Brink recalls a question Jonker had put to him on a tape: "Why are people so afraid of passion? Why do they treat us like children?"

Despite Jonker's elevated status, and the passing of the decades, readers will experience that warm blood flowed through the hand that composed her poems. The words of poets and writers, especially those who are held in high esteem, can too easily be seen as bloodless and "exalted". These letters remind the reader, however, of the passion and the ordinary human experiences from which their work arose.

The fact that André Brink himself, fully aware of the risks involved, offered the correspondence to the publisher, may ease the qualms the reader may experience. Moreover, it is significant that, from the start, Brink kept carbon copies of his letters, thereby ensuring that he had in his possession a record of almost every letter he wrote to Jonker. One can only speculate about his reasons for doing so. Perhaps he anticipated that the material might be useful to him in his novel-writing, though he may also have believed that there might at some future point be public interest in the correspondence. When one examines the original letters, it is noteworthy that neither writer deleted or corrected much. Their style and word choice apparently hit the mark, without requiring revision, although Jonker's style is often telegrammatic.

Brink remarks in one of his letters that he is busy reading the correspondence between Lawrence Durrell and Henry Miller. He describes the letters as "a hefty collection that reads wonderfully. Personal insight into other peoples' lives is always more 'significant' than that which has been turned into objective literature!"

Flame in the Snow offers a very personal glimpse of two remarkable people during a specific period, thereby providing insight into their lives and their work. Even if these words are all the reader has, without the advantage of facial expression or touch, they nevertheless offer an experience that is "significant".

In the final analysis, the letters offer not only a peek into a phase of the lives of two exceptional people, they also serve as an articulation of life in its entirety: from falling in love and the experience of the enchanting, almost mystical liberation that can be found in intimacy with another human being, to shared idealism and candid exchanges of opinions, to hurtful clashes, and light-hearted fun. The age-old themes of forbidden love, betrayal and loyalty, of social pressure on individuals and reckless rebellion against propriety, not to mention the inexorability of death, are all uniquely considered and vividly expressed in the correspondence of the courageous young novelist and the sun-loving poet.

Willie Burger
UNIVERSITY OF PRETORIA

WORKS CITED

Brink, André P. 2009. *A Fork in the Road*. Cape Town: Human & Rousseau.

Metelerkamp, Petrovna. 2003. *Ingrid Jonker: Beeld van 'n Digterslewe*. Hermanus: Hemel en See.

Viljoen, Louise. 2012. *Ingrid Jonker: A Jacana Pocket Biography*. Auckland Park: Jacana.

Grahamstown
Sunday, 21 April 1963

Delightful little creature,

I needed some neutral "in transit" days between the Cape and being back again, just to make the transition more gradual. After the week – and especially those three days – of change, I feel very averse to enduring, all over again, that old threat of a settled, "safe", bourgeois life. Respectability. Predetermined reactions to predetermined stimuli. There are people for whom such an existence will never be a threat because they're too free *within* themselves ever to get caught up in it; but I must constantly resist this opiate precisely because it would be so easy just to let it take me. During the week in the Cape you at least provided something of an antidote. Should I politely say "thank you"? That would make it too banal. Especially "our" night. [T.S.] Eliot's line – "poetry can communicate before it is understood" – also applies, in a certain sense, to people who come together, freely, through sex. It is precisely an act of communion that, thank God, remains beyond words. I mean, what would I include in my little inventory – especially in the clear light of day?: a scent; memories of your hands, hair and breasts; your voice; tears; cynicism; game-playing; red wine; two double brandies; eyes: mocking, saying no, cursing, showing contempt, playing with me, saying yes, sweet and happy, or the-hell-in and huffy …! All of this gets one nowhere. Luckily, however, these things are just starting points. Memories and bodies are mere titles of long poems; and our "sleeping together" is a sort of holy Mass, in which transubstantiation is complete. (Is this perhaps the most pure religion for us non-believers? Otherwise, why exactly would a person say "Lord God in heaven"? – Giuseppe di Lampedusa's loveliest girl character does in fact say "Gesùmaria!")

Is a body itself capable of remembering? I think its recollection is better than unreliable "memory". My body remembers yours. And it's not because of those few strategic little pains or the mark on my shoulder. Also not – I hope! – because I have now become "part of your sorrow"; it's more positive. The body's memory, as opposed to the brain's, is like imagery in the midst of matter-of-fact words.

Okay, go ahead and say: "What nonsense!" Or worse. I'm not busy with a Simone de Beauvoir dissertation here. I'm actually just busy saying in a roundabout way what I've already said: thank you.

Until such time as I get to see you again, I shall have to make do with your manuscript. (And please let me know when you think it's time for it to be returned!) Luckily there is the unexpected prospect that my seeing you again might occur sooner than expected. Some or other study group in Stellenbosch has asked me to deliver three lectures there later this semester. Then I'll be able to come and visit you on their account! This kind of lecturing gives me the shits. William Styron (have you read his *Lie Down in Darkness*?) said something like: "One thing I can't stand is that a young writer, after having written one book, starts lecturing and giving pompous interviews on all sorts of subjects about which he knows nothing." Long live Styron! But sometimes a collar is more precious than the dog that wears it.

Christ Almighty, and this morning a ceremonious telegram arrives here announcing that it pleases the South African Academy of "Art" and Science to award me with a "Eugène Marais Encouragement Prize for Drama". Now that my hilarity at hearing this news has died down, I find myself in quite a pickle: first of all, I don't have a clue (and neither, apparently, does anyone else) what kind of an animal this prize is; I don't even know on what grounds it's being awarded, or what it's worth. And now? Must I reply: deposit the prize up your anus? Or should I accept it tongue-in-cheek because I could use a few extra rands and don't in any case have too many illusions about my abilities as a dramatist? Or would that be "dishonest"? You see, I have long hoped that the Kakkademy would award me a Hertzog Prize one day so I can refuse it on the grounds that they're incapable of making any decisions about literary merit. (Or would that be ridiculous?)

Meanwhile, my biggest task – and headache – right now is typing up *Die Ambassadeur / Die Ongedurige Kind* [The Ambassador / The Restless Child]. I want to finish it now – if there hadn't been so many changes to add in the retyping process, I would have hired you as a professional typist. Now I'm sucking it all up myself – and there's no use moaning about mistakes. I want you to meet Gillian and Nicolette. (Fortunately I know you won't mince your words!) At least a fragment will be appearing in the second *60*. But when will that be? Bartho [Smit] in fact sounded quite half-hearted about the journal's financial prospects in his most recent letter. He's arriving here in the next few days; I'll be able to learn more at first hand then.

I saw Rob [Antonissen] this morning, and without my asking, he referred to your poems in *60* (which he seems only now to have read). He says he's "very taken" with them. You've told me you don't care much what critics say, but maybe this will warm your heart a little. You've been through enough wintery things as it is. I know we relate as free individuals, hold each other to nothing, and don't commit each other to any bonds, but I do wish I could be with you; and help a bit. Not only to find a place to live and share every day's finicky little tasks with you, but maybe also to save you from the thought that "the cure for loneliness is solitude".

Please – for God's sake, Ingrid – don't do what you wanted to do in Jan [Rabie]'s house. No reasonable grounds exist for my being able – or willing – to persuade you otherwise. Maybe my insistence is based on purely selfish considerations. But *don't*. You must still make things like "Begin Somer" ["Early Summer"], "Dood van 'n Maagd" ["On the Death of a Virgin"], "Bitterbessie Dagbreek" ["Bitter-Berry Daybreak"], "L'Art Poétique", the series of "intimate conversations"; and we must once again make, together, what Afrikaans itself can't: love.

The sun's calling me outside (it's already fully winter here); I want to go sit in the garden and read [Paul] Éluard, and Jonker.

Write, Ingrid. And allow me to do anything I possibly can to help. In whatever way.

Send my regards to Chris [Lombard], and thank him again. And write – for us – a poem about: "The memory of evening is like an apple";

find a way to relate it to Adam and Eve's apple; when you're done, eat the apple; and then ask: what now? You will know how. I'm not a poet.

With love,
André.

Monday, 29 April 1963

LETTER FLOWERS RECEIVED STOP THANK YOU FOR EVERYTHING AND FOR YOU ANSWER FOLLOWS LOVE = INGRID

Dept. of Afrikaans
Rhodes
Grahamstown
Tuesday, 30 April 1963

Ingrid, my dearest little child,

I know I probably "ought" not write yet again, but why would I pay any attention to "shoulds" and "should nots" when I'm talking to you? I was thinking about the fact that you're moving out of your flat today, and that you probably have no refuge after Jan, so I'm sitting here feeling frustrated that mere physical *distance* makes it impossible to help. God, and it also won't help for me to tell you that I'm *thinking* about you. What else have I done this week? I've been *forcing* myself to work, but in the quieter moments in between I'm busy with you; at night I remember you, and I lie awake feeling happy about you.

And – "oh, what nonsense!" you will say – but you have opened up something unsuspected in me and got me writing poetry! This is not a "high and compelling duty" – but perhaps a kind of emergency valve

24

attesting to our few but precious little things, allowing them to endure. And I'm reckless enough to send you a few of these attempts – in the hope that you'll also be reckless enough to tell me honestly if you think they're rubbish. You would find it boring if I were to write above each of them, "For Ingrid"; but that's how they were meant ("fire of my loins"!).

I'm busy typing up the book [*Die Ambassadeur*] – 200 pages done. The few days with you meant a lot for this work; much of it now suddenly seems prophetic! You must decide for yourself when, in ten days' time, you are saddled with it.

But this isn't a letter. I await yours first before I write another. This is just a note for the accompanying verses; a tiny effort to convince you that I want, especially in this current period, to be with you and nowhere else.

Until later, with love,
André.

Oh, what I wanted to say right from the start: thank you for your telegram, which arrived at a very depressing moment, and changed much for me.

1. As Ek Sê [When I Say]
2. Jong Digteres [Young Poet]
3. Ek Kan Sê [I Can Say]
4. Deur die Spieëlglas [Through the Looking Glass]
5. Slegs [?] [Only] [?]
6. Meisie [Girl]

Citadel Press
145 Bree Street
Cape Town
Wednesday, 1 May 1963

My dear André,

I started writing to you on Sunday, but after five interruptions I gave up and went for a walk up the mountain, then an ice-cold swim at Clifton, a warm bed and a drink, and in the meantime I've sent you a telegram. I want to thank you again for your lovely letter – so open and honest and innocent! I'm already looking forward to the next one! But first I have to scold you. Why did you accept the Eugène Marais Prize? André, André! That easily you must not compromise, and I'm not going to congratulate you on it. Are you also glad about the fuss over the "stance" of the writers? A whole lot of new names have been added, including Ina Rousseau. F.L. Alexander said that no artist with any self-respect would allow himself to be associated with the [Publications Control] Board. Did you see all of that? Also, the editorial in *The Friend*?

I'm glad you'll soon be coming to Cape Town again – you must see my beautiful flat (with garden) in Green Point; such a cosy and intimate little home. At the moment I'm staying (till 15 May) in Jan and Marjorie's [Jan Rabie and Marjorie Wallace] house. The two of them left for a holiday in Hangklip today. Everything still good, or same as usual. My friends still make me bitterly angry, and then I miss your calm protection. Chris is the same. Of course, he sends you his regards – last night we had a meal together at 191; he took me home at about eleven o'clock and I still had to pack ... But tell me, when are the lectures?

Right now I'm writing from godforsaken Citadel Press, which dulls my imagination ... I'll write more from home tonight. I remember some of your questions: whether a body can remember? There are more things in heaven and earth, Horatio, than are dreamt of in our philosophy ...

No, André, I would really like to see you one more time before, screaming and cursing like [J.] Slauerhoff, I leave this life.

I'm sorry that on the weekend you were there stuff like that had to hit me. But I've always had a surprising capacity to recover, and your friendship is healing and cleansing too.

Thank you for the news about Rob. I am of course happy that he liked some of my poems in *60*. One can rely on his judgement and it looks as though a few new horizons have also opened up for him in the last while.

Went and poured tea now. Still at work.

Just after you left, I heard from "reliable sources" that my former (always sounds like deceased) husband has no intention at all of returning Simone to me. I received a highly upsetting letter, wrote back to him immediately – no answer – and, just now, a registered letter in which I demand Simone back. I hope this mess turns out well and that he and I don't have to see one another in court again.

I haven't written a single word in the past two weeks with all these things. How is it going with *Die Ongedurige Kind* [The Restless Child] …? The poem is beautiful. You must please not call the book *Die Ambassadeur.* No one will buy it … it's such a fusty old title. *Die Ongedurige Kind* is poetic and light and ephemeral … You're welcome to send me the first chapters … I'll also pick up any typing errors.

Oh yes, with regard to the people, the citizenry, you're a little muddled in the way you speak. They are *precisely* not free, it is their bondage that grieves me and bores me into the abyss.

But apart from that, I bought myself a lovely new coat (Chris says it looks absolutely French) and I'm already beginning to pamper myself for the coming winter … went to sleep with Simone's teddy bear last night, it's so wonderfully warm and woolly, and yellow as a Bantry Bay summer.

Have you seen May's *Drum* yet? I haven't. I hope you get it in Grahamstown. It should be on sale somewhere today.

Do you know George Barker's "News of the World: 3"?

... before
The serried battalions of lies and the organizations
of hate
Entirely encompass us
...
Lie one night in my arms and give me peace.

Write soon, you hear!

Love ... Godspeed ... gratitude,
Ingrid.

{Sorry about the typing – am perpetually in a hurry! What I said about
the Marais Prize is not because I don't believe in your talent as a play-
wright, you hear; also, I've *again* read *Lobola vir die Lewe*.}

———————

Dept. of Afrikaans
Rhodes University
Grahamstown
Friday, 3 May 1963

Feather-fluff-girl,

While an apathetic U.E.D. [University Education Diploma] class sat and
wrote a test (the best solution when one doesn't feel like lecturing), I
read your letter. God! Here I am, fretting about your accommodation
problems and your other daily tribulations – and then your letter steals
in and mocks me! Perhaps it was a bit bold of me to think (or to hope)
that I could "know" you *after* getting to know you in a biblical sense!
And then yesterday I also went and bought a copy of *Drum* and read
your poem – which, like "Die Kind" ["The Child Who Was Shot Dead
by Soldiers in Nyanga"], grows on me more and more. I read the note

about you and looked at your picture, slotted in most tastefully amid Tennis Biscuits, Edblo mattresses, Powa Pills for Men, Sunbeam Polish and Mum. Theatre of the absurd without any words, this particular little combination; and in itself a commentary on the *comédie humaine*? But what I actually wanted to say about all this is the following: I sat and looked at the photo and didn't recognise you; it was "the poet Ingrid Jonker". And I read your own declamation or declaration ("sweet" – for a Mum-public?) and noticed, among other things, that you were born in Douglas where, Christ Almighty, I also lived for seven years; and realised all over again: what minuscule little piece of you do I really *know*? (I don't even dare ask: which minuscule little piece do I even *have*? Can you, of all people, be "have-able"?) Which almost makes it a matter of necessity to come back to you and learn *more* about your beautiful land.

This is why it's quite some consolation that the lectures in Stellenbosch have been arranged for earlier than I'd thought: the week beginning Monday 20 May. In 2½ weeks' time. Things are still being ironed out right now. If they can see their way clear to paying at least half of my air ticket, I'll be arriving in Cape Town on Friday the 17th, and leaving again the following Friday morning. The lectures themselves will keep me busy for just three days: Monday morning ("Experimental Novels"); Tuesday evening ("Novel and Taboo"); Wednesday afternoon ("Theatre of the Absurd"). Plus, somewhere in between, a small party. If it can be so arranged, I'll need to be in Stellenbosch for only a minimum of the time. And Thursday, a public holiday, we'll have all to ourselves. The only complication in this whole business is the back-and-forth travelling between Stellenbosch and Cape Town, for which the South African Railways and Harbours doesn't really make modern provision.

Otherwise I'll come down by car: in that case, it'll be Sunday afternoon the 19th; and then I'll stay until the following Sunday morning – leaving very early! Either way, I'll let you know. That's assuming you want me there, and have space for me.

I'm happy about your nice flat. Where you found the time to arrange that on top of everything else, I don't know. Is it your own – just for you? And Simone's? In the picture she looks just like her lovely, petite mother. And for me you will – once again – be a new "you". I hope it won't be necessary to go through all the misery of a court case. Is there any way I can help?

I must type-type-type; and try to keep my usual work going, too. Thank god I have no "social conscience" forcing me to pay back and forth visits to people I want nothing to do with, or to attend things I have no interest in. And so the MS is at least coming along, slowly; I think it will be done by next Wednesday. I know *Die Ongedurige Kind* is the nicer title. But first read the MS and see if it *fits*. That's the main issue. Maybe you'll come up with something completely different, a better suggestion.

We can talk about it when I'm there. In the meantime you can – and must – please mark up the MS wherever you find it necessary; please be merciless. (Not that I doubt you will.) You'll in any case be the first to receive it. And it's probably best that, if surgery is needed, it be deep and clean and quick. For me *this* is always the most bitter thing about a writing life: during the joy and sorrow of the process itself, *and* afterwards, you have the words all to yourself, virginal, completely untouched. But then the work calls out to the world; and the first set of eyes that looks upon it, whether approvingly or otherwise, disturbs that inviolate state. Or is this just that very old line that something magical cleaves to everything young and new?

I did not mean, in my first letter, that your average civilian, or the public, are themselves free. I myself have a phobia for the bourgeoisie; pattern-people. What I meant was simply this: some people (like me) find the masses a bigger *threat* than others do, because they have an inner tendency to go along with things, and to settle for a life of home and wife and child and servant ... I find that, to remain free, I have to live in a continuous state of *conscious* rebellion against such a life. Others (you?) have within themselves so much freedom that they remain untouched despite living in a bourgeois environment. The masses don't threaten them, they're invulnerable. But I must also admit – and this is not to be sentimental, just honest – that, after you, I feel freer in relation to the world than ever before. Let me acknowledge, in addition: I have had only two singular experiences in my life that completely, and in an instant, scorched me open – the first was the birth of my son, Anton, seven months ago (or: the almost 24 hours that I had to be there, present but powerless, until a Caesarean put an end to it); and the second was: *you*. Maybe there was a third, though it wouldn't have been a single experience, but a long series of events that rendered true Henry Miller's words, "There is only one adventure, and that is inward, towards the self" – and this was Paris.

For me it's hard to remember, and to believe, what came before Paris. A life of friendly, adventureless obedience to a pattern. Oh, I was constantly in a state of rebellion; in my second year already I was thrown out of the synagogue of the Christian Nationalists – but even this revolt was a kind of play with the pattern; properly breaking loose was something I would never really do. I still needed my religious opiate; I knew – unavoidably, after seven years at university – that I had been "accepted". Nobody found it necessary any longer to judge anything I did on its own merits. It was done according to a particular public "image" that created a series of "achievements" in advance. A model boy. I even attended intervarsity along with a textbook from which I would study during breaks. My only real release was writing. But even that was conformist. God, the most daring image in anything I wrote before Paris was: "The crowing of a cock rips through morning's mystical hymen." And then – serves me right – even that was cut by the publisher! See? You read my palm correctly, little diviner-star. This sweet youth of mine: only *now* do I recognise and appreciate all those frustrated attempts at rebellion. And then came Paris. Nobody knew me. Nobody took me at face value. The fact that I existed meant precisely zero to the rest of the world. And so on. The congregation will find it written up in *Lobola*. That's why [W.E.G. Louw]'s reaction was so adolescent (and maybe old Fransie [Malherbe] was not quite so wrong in this respect?).

Well, then: next thing I had to come home, after just two years – which was too short. It did give me the chance, though, to start dismantling everything I'd previously accepted. And I mean *everything*. But there wasn't time to start something new; to seek and find a "new myth", as Stephen [Etienne] Leroux would put it. For that reason, my first reaction back in SA was fairly hysterical. I wanted to write letters to newspapers about all the things that filled me with disgust; and just about everything did. Don Quixote and his windmills. [J.D.] Salinger's young boy, in *The Catcher in the Rye*, who wants to remove all the dirty words from all the world's lavatory walls – but finds that one can never actually do this. Even my reply in DH [*Die Huisgenoot* magazine] to Prof. Fransie [Malherbe] was a little along these lines: an attempt to hold forth against stupidity and pig-headedness. But does one achieve anything by doing that? Does one actually *wipe out* stupidity and ignorance? Or must one rather learn, not to "accept" that which is supposedly "mature" (in that case I don't ever want to be mature), but to "live ironically" – with justness, a little pride, and much love.

And it was about this time that you, with your lovely blouse and your green slacks and your little feet and beautiful eyes, entered Jan's house and said "hello", setting everything in motion. You will understand: it's not something for which one can *say* thank you. It's a thank you that has to be lived.

The Eugène Marais Prize. I have a knack for doing the wrong thing. Bartho put it with such nice irony: "The day the Akademie awards you a prize, you must know that you're on the wrong path." But this is something I myself knew very soon after the publication of *Caesar*. And it is without the least shred of illusion that I'm accepting the thing. I won't attempt to justify it. It's done now, beyond the range of regret. All I'm allowed to be happy about is that it will bring me back to Stellenbosch on 29 June!

Meanwhile there is something else on its way, too, which you will find equally unappealing: *Sempre Diritto*, an Italian travel journal. I have only just been through the proofs; Bartho has promised to have it out by my birthday on the 29th. This one is literally just my diary during the journey. And I'm beginning to realise more and more: people say things in a diary that are personally valuable as a result of associations, but which decidedly don't make interesting reading for others. Unless it's in the nature of [W. Somerset] Maugham or others' "Writer's Notebook", but that's a different kettle of fish. I told Bartho at the time I felt sceptical about the whole business, but he insisted it be published. Now it's coming out, and I'll have to play father to it. {So be it, then.}

~~("Play father"? *Remember.* It might sound crazy: but I would love to make a little daughter!)~~

I'm sending you another verse or two. ("Dearest auntie, I bring you some roses.") Laugh if you like. All that remains for me now, following [Friedrich] Schiller, is to write an "Ode to Joy". {I wrote to Bartho asking him if he might be interested in a little volume. That is to say: if I can be convinced that it shouldn't, like *Caesar*, etc. etc., actually have remained unpublished.}

My love to you. And send my regards to Simone's teddy bear, which I'm currently more jealous of than Chris! (But send him my regards, too.) ~~And a kiss for the "little garden of Eros".~~

André.

ps: I think I'll send you the section of the book that has already been typed. The rest next week. Okay?

My Wilder Kind [My Wild Child]
Die Uiltjie [Little Owl]
Hy Het met Goeie Bedoeling Gesê [He Said, with Good Intentions]
Selfs Heiliges [Even Saints]

André, my dear little heart,

I write you quite a lot more than I actually post – an old habit. Thank
you for your letter of Tuesday, which you "shouldn't have" written! I
hope you will never again feel that you "should" this or that with me – I
particularly like your open, honest, spontaneous reactions. And so your
letter was actually a delightful surprise and I let a mistake through on
the front page of the *Strydkreet.* But I told the foreman it was actually
only 50% my fault, which confused him a little until I could think of a
better excuse.

Guess what? My child arrived by plane yesterday and she is now
sleeping nice and warm in the next room. She's grown to be so cute and
when I can't bring myself to reprimand, I just have to laugh, especially
when she calls me "little mommy"! I'm sitting here now at Jan's table
where we read Richard Rive's letter, do you remember? Last night, with
Richard – sorry – thought for a moment about Richard's letter and won-
dered why I wasn't intuitively "warned"! Last night I had a meal with
Dan [Daniel] Kunene, such a civilised soul with an impressive kind of
dignity and a quick mind. He is a lecturer in African languages at the
University of Cape Town and at the moment head of the faculty. I am
eager to introduce you to him when (when?) you come down to Cape
Town. He is also the translator of the African poems in the Penguin
edition of South African poetry. Trying to go overseas for a year for a
study tour, but what a mess … it's almost impossible for him to leave
the country because of all the suspicion …

Did my last letter depress you terribly? I am not a prose writer – but,
as you say, there are a few things in life for which, thank God, no words
are necessary. I'd also love to speak to you, but heaven knows, not with
words on a piece of paper. Also want to tell you about my new poem
based on the Dutch hex-text "You put a spell on me, magician …" then
the poem moves in a kind of a dream atmosphere, I mow everything
down and stand naked, all alone and happy, until the "spell" is broken

and I must go "back to my blood relations / back to my kin / back to the pre-birth-death / where I belong" ["terug na my bloedverwante / terug na my naasbestaandes / terug na die voorgeboort-e-like dood / waar ek hoort"].

André, you speak about renouncing things, is this an indication that they are being lost already, because "what is actual is actual only for one time / and only for one place / I rejoice that things are as they are and I renounce the blessed face …" Allowing something to endure, will you find a charm for that, Magician? Child, I feel frustrated and so I went off to look for your little portrait in *Die Huisgenoot* so that I could, at the very least, see how your "declared" face looks … it is rare to discover someone so suddenly and completely, and afterwards the *physical distance* as you call it, which everything now rests upon and where it happens …! In the meantime, I swim in the ice-cold water of Clifton and I work, and I receive, it seems, hundreds of people … and sleep so terribly much!

The poems you sent me are once again proof of your astonishing receptiveness and high emotional tempo – which is of course absolutely essential to the whole complex organisation of an artist's tools. What this poem still lacks is the *technical expertise,* which will come later (if you kept it up and I know you should and now you must keep it up). Poetry lies just under the surface of your highly lyrical prose in *Lobola* and *Caesar.* I'm looking greatly forward to *Die Ongedurige Kind,* you will in no way burden me with it, I await its arrival with joy, to which I also have a right. To get back to the poems … Most of them are successful, "Through the Looking Glass" and especially "the earth" that drifts away "like a dandelion seed" ["die aarde wat soos 'n sydisselsaadjie" wegdryf]. (The two people I showed the poems to in confidence – Freda Linde and Chris – both said almost without hesitation in the same words, although they didn't see the poems as successful *as a whole:* "But there's no doubt; he's our man." I also like "Meisie" ["Girl"] from: "*you*: you play with the sky" and especially "little Midas-child / under your fingers / everything becomes poetry …"

Also "come and sleep with me" and some of the words that play like naughty children in dark rooms.

I hope you will continue, long, very long, after the original inspiration has dwindled … Send me everything you write, and when we are together again, I would like to examine everything, line by line, also because I, I already know this, can learn so much from you.

But now I'm not writing another word. Soon you'll believe that I am in love with you! But call me one night (when you get this letter).

Fixed time and Personal. Then I will hear your voice and see whether this is true!

Until then, darling,
Ingrid.

ps: What is your second name? IJ.

Grahamstown
Monday, 6 May 1963

Dear Ingrid,

Perhaps you know what it feels like to have typed up a book of 341 pages? I'd rather be with *you* to share it. Meanwhile, all I can do is send you the last bunch of pages and start chewing my nails, hoping it won't be too much of a trial for you. Please don't keep me in the dark for too long (but you should also not neglect more important things for my sake!).

I would like it especially if you could look out for certain things:

a) The consciously heavy, semi-official style of Part One – which gradually dissolves during heartfelt talk as Keyter pulls himself out, against his better judgement, from behind his mask: is this perhaps too "heavy"? Do the first 10 pages make too hard a read?

b) The adaptation of Dante: the *Inferno* in para. 2 of the section entitled "Ambassador"; the *Paradiso*, no more than synoptically in the visit to the Champs-Élysées on 322 et. seq.; and Canto {26 of the *Purgatorio*} in the conclusion – is this once again a case of a "poster comparison", or is it unobtrusive enough here?

c) Are all the episodes in the section "Ambassador" necessary? (I have some doubt especially about the visit to the fashion boutique.) Otherwise: anything you can put your finger on.

I worked myself half to death to finish the job by today. In the process, my weekend went down the drain. But maybe this was a good thing: on weekends I suffer too much longing. Meanwhile, life here is not without its own crises. I feel a need to get away, go sit somewhere and *think*, sort things out and seek answers to many questions.

Write to me. I await your letters. And please send me the title of that lovely anthology of modern American poetry; I must get a copy. Thank you for the beautiful quotation the other day ("Before the battalions …").

And love,
André.

———————

Citadel Press
145 Bree Street
Cape Town
Tuesday, 7 May 1963

André, my fiery, rebellious thing!

What on earth does your remark about my modest little journalistic article specially written for *Drum* mean? You call it "a note, a declamation etc!" Of course, I didn't write the captions – I'd be more precise if I had to do anything like that! I did indeed give them the photo … and why don't you recognise me? Because my hair is done up? You frighten me with that "I'll have to get to know you anew" or something like that. I hope you aren't disappointed! And above all, do not make me *"a thing with one face … Like water held in the hands would spill me / Otherwise kill me …"*

Just back from work – received your letter and poems last night – thank you for everything – and also for the MS, which is lying here on the table next to me. The house is untidy; I am terribly tired. May I tell you what a "normal" day is like for me – wake at 6.30, rush to feed Simone, get dressed, both of us – wait for the bus – five drive past, all full – catch one, drop her at nursery school – wait for another bus – another five drive past, all full, clock in at eight o'clock and read non-stop for ten hours. Back, fetch Simone, another bus, home, a drink, and then quite busy again till ten, eleven or twelve o'clock. Child, one could go mad from it! And on top of that, someone tried to steal my poor purse on the bus – got it back from him, then the conductor asked what was going on, everyone making a noise, I said I simply fell against the man, got off, tired, amused, and yet … it's probably part of life!

And did you get my other letter? And was it at least better received?

We must go and see Douglas again, I left there when I was about three and can only remember a little. There's a river, isn't there? I have a photo of us children, naked, on the riverbank and I have a swallow's nest in my hand.

I'm very happy to hear you're coming down soon; let me know if it'll be the 17th or the 19th – there's a complication in terms of my flat – I can only move in after the 25th. From the 15th I want to go to a boarding house here in Green Point – near the nursery school – I can reserve a place for you there too. Good heavens, André, I just *had* to find time to look for a flat – I'm convinced that your concern about it and about me was an inspiration to get such a lovely place – besides, I plan to entertain you there! And on top of that I managed to get my little daughter back! And of course you can help, you already help through your at times almost physical nearness, all your books, letters, poems, thoughts.

Now it's time again for Simone's bath and the whole evening's organisation, before I can continue to write calmly.

11:30: Do you see how long it takes to get little children into bed and to chat and eat with Erik ~~Laubser~~ Laubscher and Claude [Bouscharain]. Darling, hello – have since Sunday, I think, picked up some or other infection and already have a rising fever which I must take (if they will allow me at the Press) to my Dr Katz. Congratulations on your Italian volume – was at Uys [Krige]'s last night to fetch your letter – then told him about it and almost killed myself laughing – he was so wonderfully indignant because his travel sketches have been lying around for twenty years waiting to be published – I actually laughed at both of you then – your wonderful drive and his ... fear?

Busy reading your France sketches and find them highly readable – not sure when I'll get to *Oupa en Ouma se Boererate* [Grandpa and Grandma's Traditional Remedies] – or are you cross with me again?

The one I like most (now speaking about your poems) is "Even Saints" so far ... a lot ... maybe because my own feelings connect so closely to it ... "small forgettable futile signs" ... It screams to high heaven! If only it wasn't that way, Magician! Don't you know, some nights I pace up and down, raging, crazy from loneliness ... precisely because of the small forgettable futile signs ...! (Still, you must be careful of the influence of [N.P.] Van Wyk Louw!) (Sometimes it looks as if my whole life is made of exclamation marks – there are so many ways one can use them – mockery, irony, teasing, lies, happiness ...! Etc. Etc.) I especially also like: "the way in which your little dove breasts nestled / in my hands."

André! Good night, until the day after tomorrow? Or when will you write again? I still want to tell you so, so much more, when we are alone and without damning blue words on paper between us – they look so banal, so crass, so unaccounted for.

Love, darling,
Ingrid.

Grahamstown
Wednesday, 8 May 1963

Lovely, much needed Ingrid,

Forgive the technicolour-effect of the bladdy typewriter ribbon; it's
unintended, and should not be used as a Rorschach test. Typing has
actually been a kind of last resort today. You should see the pile of
scored and scribbled paper I've already produced this morning. Anton,
meanwhile, has begun chomping the things, licking and devouring
them – little understanding how incriminating is the corpus delicti he's
chewing over! But I find I no longer manage to say, with a ballpoint
pen, what I want to say (in so far as I *ever* get to say what I want to
say!). For that reason, please excuse my recourse to typing. A rose will
smell as sweet in any print, to mix my metaphors. (At least I'm in good
company: keeping in mind Abel [J.] Coetzee's mug of sour milk!)

Thank you for your letter: for *you*, behind the letter (a very unliter-
ary approach!) and for all the gladness the letter awakened in me (a very
psychologistic approach!). All the more because it arrived here in the
midst of the day's ordinary, unavoidable, chronological things: a student's precious "appreciation" of "Oom Gert Vertel" ["Uncle Gert's
Stories"]; buying meat, along with yet another comment about getting
a piece pasella; making sure the gardener is doing what he's supposed to
be doing (something he knows much better than I, who alas am by no
means a "boer in heart and spirit", failing to tune in to agricultural radio
shows); marking essays; forgetting to put petrol in the car.

I wanted to sit down and write back immediately. But letters and
words are becoming more fraudulent by the day. I can't remember ever
experiencing the insufficiency of words as agonisingly as in the past
while. (But the more I despair about the gulf between what I want to
say and what I do say, the more luminous and precious your words-on-
paper become. "Little Midas-Child …"?!) Perhaps, also, it's wrong to
try saying things; one should just *say* them. As Henry James once said:
Do not describe what is happening: Let it happen!

But writers are of course mad, sick beings who will not rest just *knowing* things – sometimes deliciously, at full throttle; they must go and contaminate the experience with words, too, *say* it. One wants to signify the synaesthetic sensation.

{Or is it a case of: How can I know what I want to say until I see what I've said?}

(In service of an invisible fellow person? Nonsense. One doesn't think about fellow people when one writes.) One should learn to make peace with the meditative experience of a thing itself, in and of the moment, far beyond reason and reasoning. The *unquestioning* happiness with which we lay together at six on our Sunday morning, for example, you in your white pyjamas with their open little fly. Outside of this kind of knowing one another in the essence of being (and it happens so *seldom*), everything else is incidental: a mere accumulation of givens; statistics (birth dates; youth; all the little segments of a person's "history"; all one's judgements and prejudices and opinions). These are at most mere symptoms of a deeper life. How sad – scandalous, actually – that such superficial things so often act as *replacements*; that for the masses it even confuses the issue of sex – which is in fact the only pure meeting place where the whole I-as-I encounters the whole you-as-you. (A result of civilisation? – Henry Miller said: "To be civilised is to have complicated needs; and a man, when he is fullblown, should need nothing" … i.e.: nothing but this essence-of-life itself.)

I'm *happy* about Simone. I look forward to seeing her. One of my biggest yearnings in life has always been to have a daughter. The Stellenbosch business has now been arranged in such a way that I'll be coming down by car; so, expect me at about four on the afternoon of Sunday (the 19th … still ten days away!). If I don't come alone, there will be other complications, but nothing insoluble (in that case I'll still stay with you at least from Wednesday evening until Friday morning). I think, however, that I'll come alone. For several reasons, it's become necessary for me to get out again, go somewhere; I need space in which to add things up and see if I still come out as myself. I will in any case let you know in good time what the final decision is.

Phone you? Have you any idea how often I've walked up to the telephone? But what holds me back is knowing all too well that few things on god's earth are more frustrating than a telephone conversation. ("How are things going?" "Is the weather there also good?" "What did you do today?" "I'm working my fingers to the bone." "I miss you." "Have you written anything since last time?" Three minutes go by. Or six, nine or twelve, as the case may be.) And as our telephone is situated in the middle of the house, everywhere audible, such a conversation will be limited to precisely those things in which we have no interest. But that doesn't mean I won't maybe phone you, on impulse! Will you, by the way, have a phone in your new flat?

And so you had to use the little *Huisgenoot* photo (that same loathsome, know-it-all picture) to supplement your memory? Like I have to rely on the picture in *Drum*: in itself it's actually very pretty – I wasn't trying to be "rude" the last time, I promise! It's just so *unsatisfying*. Luckily I sometimes see you again, at night – your smile or your being unhappy – and then I can lie half-awake and reminisce. But I think I'll bring my own bundle of apparatus along with me this time (photography's actually one of my favourite occupations), and see if I can improve on the *Drum* picture. Will you model for me?

Please send me the *whole* of your magician poem. The incantation effect of the repetitions "back to ... back to ..." is excellent. Meanwhile, I dip into your little pile of papers all the time. The cyclicality of "Bitterbessie Dagbreek", where the echo in the poem itself *becomes* an echo, grows ever more charming to me. I know there are even better poems in the collection, but my favourite remains "Begin Somer". (Its only dull spot is the phrase "people like ants" which, among the novel, clear imprints of the other "images" – they're actually more concrete than images – doesn't *radiate* quite enough.)

Went to see *The Quiet American* [Graham Greene] on Monday evening; and I'm now rereading the novel – disappointing. He now lacks the subtlety of works like *The Heart of the Matter* and *The Power and the Glory*.

Thank you for your candid comments about the first few poems. Now that a little distance has come, I am beginning to feel that they don't have sufficient substance; a little thin. Here and there some nice lines. But *poetry*? No, my Ingrid, I'm not a poet. *You* are. I also don't know whether I shall continue. ("I won't be rhyming for very long / my words are too few / and there's too much / still waiting in the queue".) It's not something I can predict in advance. It must either *happen* – or not.

I'm sending one or two more; but I will only know with any certainty whether I'm likely to carry on after the Cape trip. Is it "original inspiration that might wane" that you're talking about? I know it might; everything might; *must*, perhaps. But that's for later. For now, what is, *is*. And that's more than "inspiration"! I really don't know what to think any more; and I don't know how to continue. ~~You've said to me repeatedly you have no faith in promises; and you yourself have experienced the proof of this all too often, and all too bitterly. I don't want to contribute to it as well. But if I say that I love you, then it's true – now.~~ All I know is that it's been a long time since I've experienced such a state of clarity as in recent times; and it's not just the quietude of autumn, either.

My reaction to the seemingly endless labour on the novel seems to have caught up with me in the last two days only. (I got the idea end Nov. – it split off from a different book I was about to get working on –; began writing end Jan.; finished mid-March; then revised; and retyped.) And the reaction is: profound, heartfelt depression. Like a great vacuum coming down over me. You're like a little shoot in the dark, quite unprotected. Something has run its course; come loose from you. Is this the way it felt when Simone was born and was no longer inside you, not part of you any more? Or was that different? All I know is that I won't be writing anything in a hurry – not such a long thing. It's too unbearable; it overextends one. Maybe poetry is different: each in its own right a rounded-off piece of feeling and experience. A drop of water rather than a drainpipe.

Speaking of sewage brings me – naturally – to Abel Coetzee. (Have

43

you demanded your money from him yet? You *must*.) I see the *Sunday Times* is once more splashing out the fact that he might become the chief bigwig of the Kakkademy. Bill [W.A. de Klerk] told me in his most confidential (!) manner about the interview and the implications of Abel's presence (in the waiting room, not at the interview, I deduced) – but it was all presented as such a big secret that I had to blink twice. Is this another of [Maish] Levin's loathsome (but in its own way inimitable!) stunts? Or did Bill or someone else talk out of turn? Meanwhile I feel very happy about the additional names. We did achieve *something*. It stands, and it's undeniable. Now we must engage in our work ever more in the manner of *acte de défi*.

I'm counting the days until *Rook en Oker* [Smoke and Ochre] appears. If it appears too soon before my arrival, rather keep it there with you – otherwise I might miss it in the post. *Lobola*'s second imprint should be out this week; with a new ending. I await it with greater equanimity and je m'en foutisme about the reception than before. W.E.G. L[ouw] is apparently going to write a notice, again. Making the most of his little talent.

I don't have all that much time to relax after *Die Ambassadeur*: now I must get going with translation again to earn R300 before 31 May, otherwise I might have to go into liquidation. I am *always* bankrupt. This time it's all those "respectable" things like property tax and insurance premiums and stuff that has got the better of me. It makes me MAD that one should be so trapped in the mere struggle to keep one's head above water; it's humiliating, actually. But just listen to me, complaining like this! You have to endure all those days at the Citadel. For me, it's an unbearable thought. Particularly *you*. And the Citadel! Please don't work yourself to death. Look after yourself. And be happy.

With love,
André.

Ek is Een v/Jou Minnaars [I Am One of Your Lovers]
Jy's Nooit Gedoop Nie [You Were Never Baptised]

Proefleser [Proofreader]
Nooi Hom [Invite Him]

{The P. stands – against my will and lifelong protest – for the sturdy name Philippus. And with that, the worst has been said between us! (Or do you still have a Petronella or a Fransiena somewhere?)}

{Oh my God, you should come and lie here with me on the grass in our enormous garden. One can *smell* the sun.}

———————

Citadel Press
145 Bree Street
Cape Town
Thursday, 9 May 1963

My dear André,

So, what happened to you last night? I understand you called earlier but at the moment it's quite a thing to reach the house … probably difficult for you in the evening? After the last part of your MS yesterday and your note I wanted more than ever to chat to you and perhaps explain what looks to you "incomprehensible" and "cool". Or is that in the past now? Thank you, dear heart, for your telegram today – yes – I know maybe what you're talking about but not actually what you mean. You'll have to educate me! Will you? I'm still reading your *Pot-Pourri*, which I am thoroughly enjoying – I'm now near "nothing for a sixpence" – and have not started the new MS yet – don't be disappointed – the weekend lies ahead and I can go through it at leisure, something I'm looking forward to greatly – just because it's also a part of you.

   And thank you very much for the assignment – and yet it connects – I mean the "restlessness", to a trusted friend's heated remark today, which has left me in a state of dismayed shock! It was so unexpected,

45

and we weren't talking about the topic at all – "Loyal!" she says. "You've never been loyal to anyone in your life!" Now I wonder whether this is true, and if it is indeed true, is it a terrible attack on my integrity as a person and a writer? What does it actually mean? I didn't wait for an explanation, but left immediately, without saying goodbye to her, and went for a cup of tea in a café … "This above all: to thine own self be true …"

And I honestly try to be that, seeking, investigating, experiencing, analysing, but scared to death especially for people I may learn to love or whom I already love. Touchiness? Selfishness? Fear of isolation, or actually just a fight for self-preservation and contact?

So if I sometimes sound remote, may I tell you that this is already grounded in a feeling of responsibility towards you, in a certain sense "loyalty" too? That I also consider your family life; that I don't want to deny you, as a writer, any disappointment (!) and that as a person, I still want to protect you against it … (?) Does that make any sense?

You know, my little heart, this poem "Even Saints" is the most successful one so far. Already told you: the end resembles Van Wyk Louw too much: I want to suggest that you limit it and work around these lines:

Even saints
Must leave behind signs to be remembered

Etc. but more poetic: Then:

but you are remembered only by my body

And:

the way in which your little dove breasts nestled
in my hands;
and your virginal still sweet sleep with me afterwards.
But now that you are gone

46

And I your only archive
Who will rely on the word …
… small futile forgettable signs …

One could cry, reading that line – I also agree with you and [Lawrence] Durrell: "Love is a form of metaphysical enquiry." No, child, I feel that this poem already has a hold on your unconscious, that it is planted squarely in your imagination; just shorter, sharper, more patience, darling, the "patience that can carry so much" and of which you (true or not?) do not have much!

Chris came here last night, a little sick, a little gloomy, and sends his regards and looks forward to your arrival. We'll have to organise a party immediately. I hope you'll give me a date.

Do you perhaps know David Lytton – [C. Louis] Leipoldt's cousin? *A Place Apart* or *The Paradise People* or *The Goddamn White Man*? He once said to me: "Never pretend what you don't feel or overestimate what you do feel." And now I feel so unsure again, and I wish you'd come back: "And I wished that he would come back, my snake … I felt so honoured." D.H. Lawrence: "Snake". Or, as my ouma would say: Ecc. 1. v. 13. But now I'm going to "bath immediately" and get into bed with your sketches, and try to believe … in myself, in something … in you?

Love, darling,
Ingrid.

ps: Which American collection do you want: the big *Modern American Poetry* or the smaller paperback *New American Poetry 1945–1960*?

Your letter, 3 May: Try to come by car – the flat is my own, yes, and Simone's; I have an aversion to people knowing all my business! I don't think you, especially, need to have a fear of the bourgeoisie – although it's a healthy fear; break loose – about the "single experiences" the two of us will chat – about the stupidity and idiocy – Uys said "it's the century of the glorification of the asinine" – André, I'm not answering your letter curtly now, trust me. I read your letters often and often again – if I say I appreciate everything it sounds weak and it actually says nothing – with poems I will always help and support and encourage you – how do you manage in any case to do everything that you do?

You say, "dearest auntie I bring you roses", to which, in the first place, I object emphatically – at the moment I am still your little girl – in the second place – I hope I do indeed have a sense of humour, but this sentence is inappropriate as it exists in terms of earnestness and honesty and beauty – as is the case with you.

Are we going to Paris together one day?

Ingrid.

ps: What is the crisis? IJ.
pps: Just thought: "How long will it take / moment of reality / without the insanity / and in touch with the dream?"

IJonker.

——————

Grahamstown
Friday, 10 May 1963

Lovely, beloved dear,

Just a note to set your mind at ease. (Heavens, it seems each time one has to say again afterwards what one actually *wanted* to say in the first place! The purest commentary yet on human communication is surely to be found in Hamlet's "Words, words, words"!) Therefore: please don't imagine for a moment that I wanted to run you down about your piece in *Drum*! It was meant with a twinkle in the eye. And the photo is

48

indeed *lovely*. (I said this yesterday, too.) All I meant in my comment about the "strange" you, was this: I suddenly realised how exceedingly much *more* of you there was, is, than the little fragment that's "mine". I was therefore speaking precisely about your "infinite variety", or trying to do so. (God, it was *this*, among other things, that so disturbed me for a while that night at Chris's place: the astonishing way in which you are so different in *every* moment, so deliciously different!) My only reason for dismay is: I would so very much like to understand and know *all* of you and – ? – *have* it as my own? But that's impossible, simply because I have met you only now, instead of 28 years ago. Or rather 27 years and 11½ months ago, when I first saw the light of day (or the dark? I no longer remember). Once again, purely "physical" reasons, thus.

Ag *no*, no, man, Ingrid! The flat only on the 25th? I am totally shocked. I was *hoping* so much – but very well, then. I keep learning the lesson: don't count your chickens before they hatch. In that case, please would you book a place for me at your boarding house, *near* to you. Otherwise we can go and stay at Lanzerac in St'bosch for a few days (e.g. from Wednesday through to Thursday, a holiday) and the weekend. But I think I should phone and see what you say, tomorrow, from the university if possible (though it's a little side connection there – several phones all over the building using the same number). Last night I had a call booked because I was meant to be alone in the house – but then plans changed and I quickly had to cancel the call. With a gnashing of teeth.

This accursed pen-and-paper business. I want to be with *you*. Talk. And – then stop talking and *be* with you.

Don't be ill. Did you go see the doctor after all? What *was* it in the end? You're far too precious to be overcome by illness.

Thank you, also, for the vignette of you, or the lot of you, at the river in Douglas, naked, and the swallow's nest. Perhaps we can do something as bourgeois as look at all your photos when I'm there.

I must go and mark more essays now, with a head that's fit to burst. Since January I haven't had a single day without sinus – except for those few days in the Cape. Allergic to the climate. Etc. Perhaps it's mere hypochondria.

Lonely little thing: just ten days; by the time you get this letter: only a week. We have much to say and still more to do, to *be*.

My record player has come back after months at the electrical shop. That's why I felt compelled to send the telegram this morning. There is indeed still Brahms, and many other things that make me mad with joy. I just had to send news about the Sanctus, because last night I closed my study door and sat alone in the dark, listening, with a glass of wine, and with memories for which you, despite your best intentions, were responsible.

And then that also had to come to an end because it was Anton's bath time. He and I always bath together in the big tub; I wish you were able to see this. It's the highlight of his day. But afterwards I'm exhausted. I want to help you put Simone to bed. Or is she very particular about strange men?!

And this was supposed to be a "note", did I say? A hell of a mixed bag, I fear. And maybe I've said a whole lot of stuff that I'll have to explain later, again! I don't want to explain things any more. I want, once more, to "climb down your little rock pool and find the anemone".

Love,
André.

———————

Friday, 10 May 1963

My dear André,

Thank you for today's letter – tried to read it between all the work and sent Anne out a few times for all kinds of trivial little things; this afternoon a lovely rain started in Cape Town and now it is pouring out there and everything is cosy inside: Simonetta over there, drawing, and talking to herself – I've just finished Jan's mail and I'm drinking a glass of red wine. Child, your letter has something of a threat – so much "our house" and "our garden" and "maybe I won't come alone" – the days when you "will stay with me" I will be working in any case …! The "cock that crows" is of course also a denial (!) and that's also why it doesn't flow and I think you know why:

En al ons dade, al ons denke selfs,
Bind ons lewensgang aan bande …

Quote from "Bonds" by Abr[aham] H. Jonker … You don't know if the "inspiration" can, will or must fade. It's all very logical and honest, but Lord! And it looks as if everything depends on your "Cape Town detour". And it *scares* me. I hate it when people expect something of me that I may not be, and I hate having to put on an act to ensure their approval (love?). And perhaps on top of it all you think I am "clever" or learned – I've got a 2nd class matric and that's all. Afrikaans Lower, because I was at an English school that I hated; and besides, the circumstances at home were anything but good: but there was at least the Child Life!

I think your second name is nice. André Philipus. Brink? Is that Dutch or maybe German? We on the other hand are from Java. Our family name is Adolph Jacobus Jonker, and the first guy with this name was a Javanese slave, who today, of course, would not qualify as a white or as a human.

In any case, my dear heart, I would *die* if I had to live in a house like that with a garden and insurance. I tried it in Johannesburg's suburbia, until we departed, raging, for Hillbrow's slums.

My next address (I am apparently terribly "elusive", especially to creditors) I'll *call* through to you, if needs be. It will be third class at best – the boarding house, because, like you, I am always bankrupt and don't care much for "filthy lucre", if it weren't for my child, I probably would never "work" – because, as you say, it is, to put it nicely, at the very least degrading to be bound to this sort of existence.

When do you actually sleep? Seems to me you keep writing and teaching and reading, and going out, and then sometimes you lie awake at night too!

And now, must I find you accommodation with me for the week, or will it be a hell of a lot of sneaking around, which I have an aversion to?! Don't worry, I'm actually in an excellent mood, have been all day.

Now I'll make us some food and have a bath, and then I'm expecting people. Will write to you again tomorrow – if I don't – I might become "Dear Ingrid" – more businesslike than my publisher, from whom I heard, by the way, that my little volume is appearing this month – goodnight, darling.

Babsie (that's my family nickname). That was when my father was still UP [United Party].

ps: Anne says your photo in *Die Huisgenoot* is nice. But she doesn't like the one in *Pot-Pourri*, she says it looks like a girl. (While I've been writing to you, Simone came and stood behind me and combed my hair – now she's got a cup of water here and it's wet – excuse the drops if they land here.)

Your poem "You Were Never Baptised" (how'd you know that?), at least I was baptised at five years of age, is good: especially

never a wedding dress
but naked dressed in light …

Do you know what [D.J.] Opperman said about "Begin Somer": "insignificant" and "could perhaps be accepted as a small visual sketch". Are you also so "visual"? I am. Till tomorrow … I.

Ek wil nie meer alleen slaap nie
Ek wil nie meer alleen wakker word nie
Sonder om die lig en die lewe
Opslag te herken.
(Éluard)

Good night! I. Jo.

Can also never sleep. (Just wanted to tell you how much I appreciated your phone call yesterday morning – what did we actually say?) I went to look at a boarding house here in Green Point this evening – the R10 per week – double room (for me and Simone!) with eavesdropping old people everywhere – lots of annexes and "small sitting rooms" and a suspicious middle-aged woman who said she might have to put my cousin in a room inside the building … when I asked whether she had a single room near mine for my country cousin!!! Child, I'm really going to enjoy myself! Florals everywhere, little cupboards, and washbasins and washstands – as if these are the chief desire of humankind … doilies and little ornaments and vulgar furniture …

Had a lovely day with Uys – read about forty pages of your MS which I don't want to say anything about quite yet: must see how it develops, you know how it is.

Look forward to your promised letter tomorrow. Look after mine nicely, will you, there's no getting away from it.

Find that terrible!

Sweet dreams. Till later.
Jo.

PS: That's my new name at the Press. Derived from Jonker and especially for you and the Press. I love changing my name and will be duty-bound to marry –
J.

PPS: Will you let me know *soon* where and how and from when you want a place?
I Jonker.

Grahamstown
Saturday, 11 May 1963

God, my dearest Ingrid,

Nowadays futility is calculable in small doses of three minutes each. And I can't even claim that I didn't know this in advance. It wasn't the phoning itself that frustrated me so mightily, but mainly the fact that I could hear almost nothing you said. And, time and time again, the little bits that I did hear – precisely because I heard it out of context – sounded vaguely upsetting. Something "not proper" in connection with the boarding house. Something to do with being angry or afraid about a letter. Etcetera.

So then I rushed off to the university to get the anticipated letter. Nothing! And immediately after the confrontation with my empty postbox I had to deliver *two* lectures. (At least I compensated for my misery by finding a minor pretext in [C. Louis] Leipoldt to recite your "Die Kind" and discuss it with the third-year students! Good for them, too. In this way they get something lovely and I get some relief.) After this I had to go and buy meat, milk, and vegetables. Only then could I sit down to write. Committed about eight letters to paper; threw them all away, and had something to eat; now I can talk to you more calmly.

Ingrid dear: *don't* seek out bogeymen in my letters! I'm sure I didn't ever say I have to learn to know you "all over again". At the most – and this is surely forgivable – I said I wanted to learn *more* about you. Never stop drinking from your fountain.

As far as my coming down alone is concerned: there's nothing to be afraid of. It *will* happen that way. Let's rather not talk about it in disembodied words, or about the future. Let's wait until we're together again and everything's clear; rather that than one-dimensional words on paper or words in the mouthpiece of a telephone.

Just to confirm the arrangements: as I understand it, you'll be booking accommodation for me, too, together with you, from Sunday to

Sunday; *send me the address* (please also leave it with Jan). I should be there between three and five in the afternoon, I hope (leaving here Saturday afternoon and staying over somewhere). Is it *impossible* to get the flat earlier? In any case, insist on the 25th – the Saturday; then I can at least help you move, and wet the roof with you.

I'm glad to hear you're no longer ill. I felt quite trapped this week after you wrote to say you weren't feeling well. Look after yourself.

If my calculations are correct, you would have known by this week whether your little search in the wardrobe that night had the desired (?) outcome. Poor me, I got such a roasting about it that night; so I now deserve to know, at least!

I heard from Bartho yesterday that he's quite eager to see a volume of my poems. (I sent him two or three.) But in the past I've too often been overeager to publish, and now I'm sitting with a long row of books that should rather have remained in the bottom drawer; I don't want to make the same mistake again. Luckily, this time I can rely on you. Perhaps it will become a practically valuable thing between us over time: that *one* of us remains clear while the other is hot-headed.

Child of love, here I sit again, putting words on paper! All the while, I want to be with you. Do you know John Donne's "The Ecstacy"? – even in that austere, loquacious time they sometimes came up with beautiful lines. He talks about bodies in love:

They are ours, though they are not we, we are
The intelligences, they the sphere.

We owe them thanks, because they thus,
Did us, to us, at first convey.

Lobola has appeared for a second time – and they actually went and set the title page in capital letters *again* instead of using lower case, as I requested. One always has to cut back on expectations and ideals – right down to the smallest things. The past few weeks have delivered their full measure of disenchantment. Except for one big difference: you, the neverending you.

Dearest, dearest creature, just one more week.
André.

Sunday.

Strange – it's a new discovery every time! – how in the final analysis one is influenced, in fact determined, in one's reactions by physical things such as time and distance. Today, just because a lovely sleep and a happy Sunday morning lies between now and yesterday, I can hardly understand why that silly phone call frustrated me so! Everything seems so certain and "undoubtable", as our ministers would say. I hope your Sunday morning was similar. I slept late, with a quiet sun after last night's unexpected thunderstorm. Anton tumbling around on the double bed like a washing machine, clambering and playing. Then slowly getting dressed – and driving for twenty miles through beautiful countryside where the aloes are just beginning to flame. Return, nibble at Sunday papers; make food. (I love playing chef! As long as I can do it when *I* want to.) And while it's all cooking up, I can sit here and converse with you, my little penny from heaven.

I look forward to the lovely open road next week, because you'll be waiting for me at the other end. Do you know what part of me remembers you the most, in the nicest way? Not my ears or eyes or mouth, but my hands. Actually more than just my hands, but everything that can experience you in a tactile way. Every day at dusk I take an hour to myself and walk along a hilly pathway, taking pleasure in my memories.

From the sublime to the more normal – I remembered with a shock that I didn't give you (and Lena [Oelofse]) money for the calls I made from your flat. Must be about R3 altogether. I wanted to send it along with my first letter, but it just seemed too banal to include a cheque. I'll bring it with me. And forgive the lapse! I didn't mean to sponge.

Just today I began a translation that I must finish off this week if I want to get my cheque from John Malherbe: a children's book about archaeological activities in Egypt (Leonard Cottrell). Quite interesting, although I could surely spend my time more "fruitfully". Meanwhile I've read [William] Golding's *Lord of the Flies*: a terrifying, special novel. Do you know it? Starts deceptively – a group of boys who find themselves alone on an island. Then they develop into a primitive community that gradually disintegrates for fear of the Unknown. And, if you think about it, it's the primitive being with whom we have the greatest affinity – rather than a Greek or Roman or Renaissance man or whatever.

I am glad you like *Pot-Pourri* – a little. Weglouw[W.E.G. Louw]'s wife [Rosa Nepgen] gave me a regular tongue-lashing about it last time around. But I have a soft spot for it, for non-literary reasons. It's in any case just *reportage*. One can't, and doesn't want to, always be in a state of high tension when "creating".

I am so afraid you won't like the novel! Precisely because it's so important to me that you do!

Meanwhile I have dug out *Ontvlugting*. There are more good things in there than a lot of people think. And I suddenly found myself wondering: Freda [Linde] is surely also going to make one of those HAUM records with you? Maybe we can "wangle" it in such a way that both of ours come out together – I've only just done my recording. Ask her.

Now there's really no choice: I must stop writing (and wasting your time?).

With love,
André.

Have I asked you yet – or was it during your drug-coma?! – if you know these lines by [J.H.] Leopold? –

O nachten van gedragene extasen
en diep gedronkene versadiging,
als elk met zijn geluk te rade ging
en van alleenzijn langzaam wij genazen.

Dearest little girl,

I'm very tired tonight. Spent the whole day fiddling with the Stellenbosch lectures – which are still far from done – and then did another shift of translation. It's such soulless work. And even though the book is in English, it's still the kind of style that translates very laboriously. I'll take French any day. But if one has no choice in the matter, complaining won't help. I simply need the money. And in the meantime I must prepare a lecture for my second-year class tomorrow.

Amid all this, however, one lovely thing happened today. I received a letter, seven pages long, which I stood and read in the Common Room among all the learned, qualified gentlemen drinking their tea, "an island entire of myself". Just a missive from a light-haired girl with whom I am in love. Her name is Ingrid. It's a pretty name, isn't it? But she's even more lovely than her name. And even though she kept on saying "Hm-hm, Chris, *no* Chris", she did allow me to *see* how lovely she is. And then one night, in the hours after midnight, actually – but you won't in any case believe me. Besides, one isn't allowed to write such things, because there's a Publications and Entertainments Act.

There were some other good moments too: the education department will be making a special appointment from July for someone to teach the diploma students grammar – and then it'll finally be off my back. (It was always my greatest hell, even though it's only been two periods a week this year.) In addition, our department's going to get a typist and Rob said I can give her all my manuscripts for typing if I like. Thirdly, we had to decide on prescribed books for next year. Because I'm the one who deals with prose, Rob said that I couldn't myself include *Lobola* – but he then offered to take over some of my lectures so that *he* can discuss it.

Usually I prescribe the third-year poetry volumes during the course of the year. I'm very tempted to find a place for *Rook en Oker* this year.

Do you realise that as far as poetic form and character are concerned, it's actually completely new in Afrikaans? I'm so impressed with you, and proud – as if it's my own achievement!

Girl, what on earth do you mean by "loyalty", or: "not being loyal"? I don't know *who* said that to you. But either she doesn't *really* know you, or she doesn't know what "loyal" really implies. If it means that you must always "protect" someone you love, or a friend, or an acquaintance, because you don't want to hurt them by being honest – then you should *never* be loyal. I said to you on our first night already (what does "first" or "second" or "third" night mean to us? – it was one moment that made three days timeless) that above all you are *honest*, and *free*. You must stay that way. But not in loneliness. I want – even though it must frequently be on paper only, from a distance – to wrap myself up in you: not to smother you, but to protect, and to shield you from the Southeaster.

For this reason you should also not be afraid that you, in the *true* words that you quoted from Lytton, will "pretend what you don't feel or overestimate what you do feel". Your honesty will not allow it. Just remember: one can also "underestimate"! And it's just as wrong to underestimate a feeling or experience as to exaggerate it. I know how precious this lucid *angoisse* is with which I've been living over the past three weeks. (*And you?*) I know, too, that you won't allow me to live in a state of illusion out of pity or consideration if things are no longer what they used to be – just as little as I would do this to you.

I can very well understand your hesitation after the many hurts you've suffered. "To love is to give a hostage to fate" goes one facile maxim which, like all sayings, announces a truth but also oversimplifies it. But getting hurt happens so often because one creates a particular image of, or for, the future, as if this trajectory, this "one day" is the most important thing of all. It is not. *This* is what seduces people into being false to each other, making promises for a "one day" over which they have no control. And that's why what I offer – God, it's very little, I know, but it's so precious to me – is *now*. It's not the fatalism of hedonism or whatever "ism", maybe not even realism. But isn't this, in the final analysis, all that we, as humans, can be certain about? And it's a "now" that actually makes time less important. It might be days, or weeks, or years, or "for ever and ever".

Why am I even writing this? You know it just as well as I do, don't you? And isn't that which we do have, can have (and, I *hope*, *will* have next week), not on its own wonderful enough? Precisely: wonder-ful, "in the shape of a wonder". As people, we are an insect race upon the surface of the earth, my little Ingrid; we have so little; and we have little about which to feel proud. But what we do have – God, how beautiful it is. "There is only one thing that matters," goes a quotation I remember vaguely, "and that is being together".

Good night, my Ingrid. And allow me to do in my thoughts what the *whole* of me would like very much to do tonight.

Tuesday morning.

What does one do when a first-year comes and asks: "Sir, I have to go to class in a minute, but can you please tell me *quickly*: what is existentialism?"!

That, however, is more or less how my day began.

I held this letter back, in case the "severe"(?) letter you spoke about on the phone arrived this morning. But my postbox was quite empty. Miserere mei!

Meanwhile, yesterday's lovely, lustrous letter is more than enough to keep me going.

I hope your work today isn't as claustrophobic as usual. I'm living within such an open, free happiness today that it wouldn't be *right* for you to feel alone or depressed.

Love to you, my fleet-footed child,
André.

THANK YOU FOR LETTER DUNCE PHONE ME TONIGHT LOOKING FORWARD TO
SUNDAY LOVE = INGRID

Wednesday, 15 May 1963

Lovely little thing,

Your funny, moody, dearest jumbled-letter arrived today, at last.
Thank you! From the inaudible telephone conversation, I'd expected
much worse. And your fears, in any case, are unfounded. First of all,
I'm coming alone, as you already know (and I do hope your backveld
cousin's room is close to yours). Secondly, the poem about the red
rooster has nothing to do with *us*. I wanted mainly to protest against
the fact that the church as an institution renders a life of passion powerless. Third: now you're lashing me because I say "inspiration" might
wane – while my words were simply an answer to *your* reference to
"one day when the original inspiration has waned": and I also said: it's
a lot *more* than "inspiration". And it doesn't all depend on my "Cape
detour": all I said was that this visit may determine whether or not I
will continue writing *poetry*.

Beloved little minx, I don't come to you because I expect certain
things from you or because I've formed a certain image of you and
want to "test" you! I come unquestioningly, because I love you, and
because I want to leave it to the visit itself to determine what will happen. Satisfied?

The suspicious old aunties must just not undermine our plans. But
that, in itself, might become quite a fun little game!

I don't agree about my second name (which you spell incorrectly
each time). "Brink" is actually Danish, apparently; but my original
ancestor Andries came from Germany, somewhere around 1730. How,

no one knows. All that's known is that he was in fact here and took a wife and began his contribution to population growth. I like to imagine he was a stowaway who came hidden in a vat – and then sneaked out at night in his striped shirt and big bare feet, stealing an enormous joint of ham or a tin of rusks and a pitcher of water.

I feel a bit bleary-eyed this morning: had to get up four times last night for Anton, who sometimes absolutely *refuses* to sleep at night; then I had a class at eight. In the meantime I need to finish preparing the St'bosch lectures. The most important one, at least, is complete – for Tuesday evening. By the way, would you be able to drive with me to St'bosch on Tuesday after work? There might be a party afterwards. Then we can return together afterwards. Or do you have an aversion to such hoity-toity stuff? We can discuss this in one of the floral lounges, or in our single room, or in Simone's double room. (So there!)

Rob will tell me tomorrow what he thinks about the book. Meanwhile, your silence – even though I know it isn't intended as such – is ominous!

After our lovely autumn weather it began to get miserable today, with little gusts of wind, dry leaves, and occasional rain. It hems me in. I want to hit the road and come to your little spot of sun.

By the way – and please forgive the fact that this letter is jumping around so much – do you know this lovely poem by Erich Fried ("Traum vom Tod")?:

Traum
Traum aus der Nacht
Traum aus der Nacht vor dem Tod
Traum aus der Nacht vor dem Tod einer Welt
einer Welt aus Angst vor dem Traum

Angst
Angst vor dem Traum
Angst einer Welt vor dem Traum
Angst einer Welt vor dem Traum vom Tod
vor dem Traum vom Tod aus der Nacht.

Talking about poems: do I still need to *say* what I think of Opperman's opinion about "Begin Somer"? Opperman also rejected [Peter] Blum's *Enklaves van die Lig* [Enclaves of Light] at one point. You're in very good company! In his best work O. is brilliant, and he's apparently an excellent lecturer. But as a *critic* I've never had much time for him.

"Visual sketch"? God! Eyes are becoming ever more important for artists. The most modern French novelists are *above all* concerned with eyes. For me, one of the nicest compliments on *Lobola* was when someone said it was overwhelmingly visual. And it's one of the purest qualities of your work.

Padmini – *that*'s your name. It's a Lotus girl. Or, if you will: it's *one* of your names because naturally you should have many. Do you know the lovely start to *Lolita*? –

Lolita, light of my life, fire of my loins. My sin, my soul. Lo-lee-ta: the tip of the tongue taking a trip of three stops down the palate to tap, at three, on the teeth. Lo. Lee. Ta.

She was Lo, plain Lo, in the morning, standing four feet ten in one sock. She was Lola in slacks. She was Dolly at school. She was Dolores on the dotted line. But in my arms she was always Lolita.

And, whether you like it or not, your "central" name, for me, is "Ingrid". Because, in the irrational manner of such things, I have always felt it to be a most beautiful name; it has a certain strangeness to it, a sense of distance that invites one always to want to find out more.

I'll rather send this letter to Uys – because if it arrives there on Saturday, you'll only get it on Monday. And then, soon after, I'll also be arriving. As I've already said, I ask for nothing, demand nothing, set no conditions. I simply want to be with you. Because, little Padmini, I love you.

André.

Grahamstown
Thursday morning, 16 May 1963

Deeply loved Ingrid-Babsie-Jo!

It's the crack of dawn and I'm sitting here writing to you. I.e. not yet nine o'clock. In fact, I sat myself down last night already to do so, but the thought of words on paper gave me cold feet after our quarter-hour on the phone. *Thank you*, my little child. (And then I still forgot to ask you who the "dunce" in your telegram refers to!)

I'm sorry you're somewhat overwhelmed by people until you move in, tomorrow, with the ancients. I hope you don't end up sleeping uncomfortably. You work so hard that you should at least get some rest at night.

I think I'll just send the money in cash so you won't have to deal with the problems of depositing and cashing a cheque etc. Don't pay the old *padrona* the whole week's fee (unless of course she insists on it) – just give her a deposit. Because if we do decide on a different course of action, as both of us more or less agreed last night – from Wednesday through to the weekend – it won't be necessary to commit ourselves in advance. Before you get me wrong (!): I have nothing against the board-ing house but if you have the day off on Thursday, it might be a lovely little escape for us if I could find us a place somewhere in St'bosch – or near the sea, outside Cape Town itself. Then I could bring you back in time for work on Friday and drop Simone (the French would say: Sisi) at her nursery school. If the weather's good we must drive around, just for the hell of it, and get you some fresh air for a change. Ag man, I'm *so* looking forward to seeing you.

For this reason I'm sorry that you've now been burdened with wor-ries about *me* – re gossip etc. Don't let it upset you. God, my dear thing, there's nothing that restricts one as much as other people's opinions. I promise to be discreet. But I never want you to think we have no choice but to spend our time together like furtive crooks. Our lasting moment is too pure and valuable for that.

A weak little winter sun has made an appearance today but it's still very cold. You must come with me, one day, and get a taste of Paris's crystal-clear, brittle winter air. I'm glad you're finding *Pot-Pourri* pleasant company – even if it means lying awake at night to read. One of my friends, who was reading it in hospital a while ago, had to stop because one of his stitches apparently popped out. (Now maybe your judgement of *Die Koffer* [The Suitcase], the one-hander based on *'n Reël Is 'n Reël* [A Rule Is a Rule], will be less damning.)

Please regard this as just another of my "notes" – I have to dash off to the bank now if I want to get to Rob's in time for feedback on my book; then, two classes – and only after that, breakfast. And finish typing the remaining half of a St'bosch lecture. Also, work on translating that book; it now seems I *won't* be able to finish it off this week. And finish reading [Alain] Robbe-Grillet's *Voyeur* (magnificent piece of work). Never a dull moment. But as you can see: not the kind of life in which much "happens" – except in one's inner reactions, and these are subjective; to remain healthy, they need external nourishment. For this reason you mean what you do to me; and that's why my little Cape escape is like an intake of air, a chunk of *life* that's more than mere "existence".

Till Sunday, darling,
André.

––––––––––

Grahamstown,
Monday, 27 May 1963

My darling little thing,

Dare I think about the fact that – and in what way – I was still with you yesterday afternoon this time (three-thirty)? Although I have "proof" enough (!), it makes no difference to the ache of *longing*. The drive yesterday afternoon wasn't too bad, I was full of your presence and I couldn't really believe I was "on my way". This fact only hit me – very suddenly – when I arrived in Albertina last night at eight and discovered I was the only guest in the hotel. It wasn't a Franschhoek kind of quiet – where there were at least some crickets outside, and your voice, or your deliciously sweet breathing in the crook of my arm; this was the absence of sound or life, pure and simple. There was only one solution – switch off the lights at nine and go to sleep. (Didn't even take a bath, as I was reluctant to rid myself of your secrets.) And you? Did you sit and translate? Answer Simone's questions? Skip supper and then get hungry for chocolate or bananas? Or was Chris there? I hope so.

This morning I hit the road at six. Despite the long sleep, I became so drowsy that for a while I had to stop every ten or twenty miles and do a quick jog or swing my arms around, just to shake off the tiredness and the sleepiness. But even so I was home by one. And then, with great dedication, I opened the Beckett and transplanted your beautiful little curl, along with the other strands of hair, into your big American book.

(My dearest, dearest thing, I can never say thank you enough for this book, not only because it's so lovely in its own right but even more so because I *know* just how much it meant to you. It is the most precious gift I have ever received.)

I don't yet want to begin "processing" our week together. At the moment I just want to feel completely happy, irrational, with everything still unsorted in my subconscious – words, sensory impressions, the look in your eyes, the movements of your delightful little body, your voice, promises, little games, tears, and all manner of "secrets". This much I have never had. (Poor old Jan Cilliers [Jan F.E. Celliers] … he will never know what hit him.)

My god, girl, the two poems I brought back with me yesterday are among the very best in *Rook en Oker*. I've only just booked a call to Bartho to find out exactly when our books are appearing. I should have come to visit in early June after all – then we could have thrown a big party in your neat little flat.

And talking of that: as I arrived home I encountered a letter from the Akademie with news that, at first glance, took me by surprise. They've decided not to make the prize-giving coincide with the AGM, and so I no longer "have to" come to St'bosch on 29 June. But I quickly decided I would come down in any case – because by then I'll have to finalise things with Koos [Human] about the MS. Perhaps the visit will be a week or so later than we first thought, but in that case there's a good chance I might be able to stay a few days longer. Okay, loveliest being?

(Damn! The exchange just phoned to say the call will only come through at five-thirty, and by then Bartho's no longer in his office. I'll try again tomorrow.)

And now, will you have to deal with buses and things again from today on? Did you eventually find a nanny for Simone? Please take good care of our girl. She's a cute little thing.

Lovely little tortoise, my head's bursting. I must go take some pills and sit down so I can think about you. And about a time when we can be together; prise ourselves loose from constant bondage to time and haste; be *peaceful* – both of us writing, reading, conversing, or just being together in the many wonderful ways that will be open to us.

I'm sending you the only photo I have available. Looks a little sad, but beggars can't be choosers. Hopefully I'll be able to get the other ones within a week or two. Meanwhile, I await the little swallow's nest and anything else you can dig up. The past week's shots must first go off to Port Elizabeth for developing – but I'll be sending some of them before too long. The one or two "personal" pictures among them I'll develop myself, along with Christie [Roode], when I go to Potch in two or three weeks' time. I should get the colour photos back in about two weeks.

Meanwhile … you probably know the enchanting letter that Mellors writes at the end of *Lady Chatterley's Lover*:

You can't insure against the future, except by really believing in the best bit of you, and in the power beyond it. So I believe in the little flame between us. For me now, it's the only thing in the world … It's my Pentecost, the forked flame between me and you … And if

I can't put my arms round you, yet I've got something of you. We fucked a flame into being. But it's a delicate thing, and takes patience and the long pause.

So I love chastity now, because it is the peace that comes of fucking. I love being chaste now. And when the real spring comes, when the drawing together comes, then we can fuck the little flame brilliant and yellow, brilliant. But not now, not yet! Now is the time to be chaste, it is so good to be chaste, like a river of cool water in my soul.

Thank you, thank you, darling. For your fire *and* your quiet, your restlessness *and* your rest, for your maturity and for the child that lives inside you.

I'm sending a little kiss for my naked little purse.

And I love you.
André.

———

Monday, 27 May 1963

My André,

I had a genuine longing this afternoon to walk in the Gardens, as all good (female) Afrikaans writers have done before. Went and lay flat on my back on one of the lawns in the winter sun and I can't describe to you the feeling of happiness, consciousness and *revelation* that possessed me – as if for 28 (?) years I was kept small and bright and intact against all the attacks and all the compromises I had to ward off – that there was a meaning in it (maybe temporary? But still!) and that I am so glad now – the feeling that a virginal bride should have! And I thought about your *generosity* and I really would not have been surprised if you were next to me and asked me for a cigarette. Unfortunately neither a person nor life itself is that simple … Thank you for your telegram, my love … Anne nodded approvingly when she read over my shoulder … "Saved by grace …" So where did you sleep and was it horrible? What time did you arrive in the Athens of the North?

The doctor visited yesterday afternoon – Simone is in tip-top health and I could take her to school (my/our landlady, by the way, is very kind and was accommodating when I told her Simone was sick, etc.). Funny, hey? She almost died laughing. Then she said she would look after Simone. It ended up not being necessary – we left in the drab dawn – laughing and stumbling – and the old "dame" at the school said this afternoon I only have to pay for one week – so I paid for her for 1½.

Simone told the people here in the small sitting room: Fee fo … fum … I smell the blood of an Englishman … They asked her whether she knows what an Englishman is and she said: "Yes, Jack [Cope] …" This child!

So, Chris came yesterday afternoon – we sat in the sitting room and had tea with all the old people: then went and bought a chocolate cake on this dreary day; sliced some of it and ate but I couldn't tell him … didn't want to … maybe later. He sends his regards. We chatted about you and later I read your lecture again and also some of *Die Ambassadeur.* Had a bath, slept … for ten solid hours.

I pick up not a book and see not a thing, but everything speaks to me even for e.g. "die huis waar Hans en Grietjie by die heks / voorloping argloos en luilekker woon". But I *miss* you, blindly too.

Love darling,
I.

Good night. Just got back from Jan and company – do the thing you dream – he, especially, hints and teases – also as if I am a man-eater – but friendly, actually – hot from running, had to go back in my blue pyjamas (with a jersey over them) to fetch my coat, which I'd left behind.

... die bloed gestort op ons mooiste oomblikke,
Die bloed van die vrygewigheid,
Dra jou met verrukking.

...

ek het jou lief om te sing
Van die geheim waar die liefde my skep en homself bevry.

Jy is rein, jy is nog reiner as ekself.

I get out of the unholy bath and now *all* the "secrets" are definitely gone!
I.

―――――――

Grahamstown
Wednesday, 29 May 1963

Dearest darling,

The sun is soundlessly lovely and clear today; autumn leaves aflame everywhere. I'm sending you one of them. But in the midst of all this quiet I feel lost, aware of the very different space and stillness in which you and I spent time together. Following our week I've begun to look at everything in my "normal" life with X-ray vision – and often feel compelled to admit, à la Hamlet: "How weary, stale, flat and unprofitable seem to me the uses of this world." Or, otherwise, in [Walt] Whitman's words (and these of course come from your book, now my only source of daily alleviation):

> Stop this day and night with me and you shall possess the origin of all poems,

You shall possess the good of the earth and sun, (there are millions
    of suns left,)
You shall no longer take things at second or third hand, nor look
    through the eyes of the dead, nor feed on the spectres in books,
You shall not look through my eyes either, nor take things from me,
You shall listen to all sides and filter them from yourself.

(*That*'s where I placed your fragrant curls of hair!)

I should actually return to *Die Ambassadeur* and start revising, but
I'm so tired of working on it, and on top of it all I'm having to work like
crazy to catch up with last week's lectures, mark a whole pile of essays,
and complete articles on Rome and Paris for *Die Huisgenoot* – along
with the never-ending translation work.

I phoned Bartho yesterday. It would seem our books have been
delayed yet again (naturally). But they're apparently working overtime
to get copies ready for the typographic exhibition in the Cape that
begins this coming Monday (3 June). Will you go have a look? The rest
of the print run should be ready a week or ten days later.

I haven't written any more poems, it's still "too deep for tears". But
there's a lot on the brew that should start emerging one of these days.
In the meantime I selected about six or so of the old ones, reworked
them here and there, and sent them all off to *Standpunte* under the joint
heading "For Ingrid".

I can't articulate any longer. The best I can do is to go lie on my back on
the grass, look at the sun, and rest assured in the knowledge of you. Know
how involved we have become with one another, *and*: know that I *wanted*
to become involved, and still do, as you said with such faultless honesty.
I live in a kind of daily agony – which is *also* lucidity, *also* ecstasy: a time
in which I need your love and trust more than anything else. Nothing
is simple, but everything's clear. (You: my singular flame that separates
light from dark so inexorably; *poet*. Me, working in prose, having to seek
out my authentic formulations more slowly, more carefully.)

In the past I used to think, as I said that night at the foot of the big
fire, that the unquestioning state I initially set up as an ideal was actually

a kind of lasting, *eventual* condition. Now I know that – because we are in the first instance *people* – we also have to *live* the words, beyond mere acceptance. Perhaps people need "grace" for that. But what if you don't believe in "grace"? Then, inevitably, the only consolation I dare allow myself is loving and being loved.

My precious, precious thing: through all the waiting of these days, and the necessary learning of patience, for both of us – though neither of us is at all very patient! – we must simply continue believing, continue trusting, keep on loving. I hope I'm not asking too much in any of these areas.

Meanwhile, my exquisite darling, I'm already comforting myself with the thought of returning to you in four weeks' time. We'll isolate ourselves splendidly from the world, read a lot, go for walks, in good weather and on rainy days, and sleep, sleep, sleep.

A well-meaning colleague phoned me, supposedly to wish me happy birthday, and then boringly began speculating about "everything that could happen in a year … you might even become a father again." And I smiled quietly into the mouthpiece, thinking, with as much "hearty enjoyment" as Jan F.E. Celliers's piggie: Dear bourgeois people, if you only *knew* …!

Have you talked to Chris yet? And? Was Uys nasty to you? I wish I could always be there to protect you from the bile, so you could hide away safely in my arms and your gorgeous eyes would stay happy.

I'm sending this letter to your flat – or to Jan (I'll decide when I write the address) – because otherwise you'll only get it on Monday.

Please write back soon, little tortoise. It's miserable existing without any letters from you!

Before I forget: I include a small "commentary" on the few sections of the book based on Dante. So you can evaluate the perspective better. Don't hesitate to be candid. Koos and company have already disabused me about the book! Whatever you say, will be *meaningful* to me.

I must return to my marking. I'll have to take care that I don't write "with love" under each essay instead of the more usual, cutting commentary.

But for you, darling, indeed: with love,
André.

Evening.

Having a guest here tonight eased the conclusion of a long, empty birthday. From my mother I got a marvellously bulky, thick jersey in autumn colours – and unavoidably thought back to our dress-buying on Friday; that hideous green thing the woman tried to pass off on us as an autumn hue. I also found myself thinking about the lovely dress that fits so beautifully over your petite little breasts. And everything else, too. Your formal dressing up, with handbag and coat, whenever you go to the toilet; all the things we can laugh about together, be happy about, get mad about. The changing shades of light on the mountain, and your eyes, with that beguiling little smile playing around your mouth, the defenceless surrender of your skin to my hands, the taste of your hair and shoulders, and everywhere, *you*.

This is all just reminiscence, and a very incomplete way of saying I love and miss you unbearably. Take good care of yourself; give our little girl a kiss from me, and be with me tonight. Last night I kept waking up and stretching out my arm to touch you, only to discover it wasn't you; my sleep for the rest of the night was very lonely.

One of these days I'll have to send you a little tape.

With love – once again, always,
André.

Grahamstown
Thursday, 30 May 1963

Precious love, my little thing,

Thank you for your glorious letter about sun and grass and longing. I left my tea – which was meant to be my breakfast – just where it was and withdrew into my office at the university, to a sunny corner of the table, and read, and read again. This is happiness: this reading, this assurance about being in love, this joy, inside of which one can wander for the rest of the day.

My virginal little bride! In a certain sense you are the most virginal person I know. And even in this separateness there is a kind of value, maybe a new means of purification?

I hope the small accompanying photo is useful for the exhibition. I simply don't have any bigger ones, and I'm still struggling to get the negatives out of Mrs [Hilda] Brinkman. I just hope it's not too late. Friday being a public holiday messes a bit with our correspondence – although I'm glad you'll have a chance to rest for a change. Make sure you have a restful break!

Actually I wish you were able to grow little wings so you could come visit this weekend, because Estelle and her mother are leaving early tomorrow to visit the family of a friend who died last week; I'll be on my own until Sunday night. I'll try to phone, but must still work out which number to use. By the time you get this letter, it will all be old news in any case. (I hope the other one, which should be with Mrs Oxley on Saturday, reaches you.)

Bartho has written to say he's planning an anthology of "younger writers" for next year, and he wants to include the two of us. I hope this plan works out – although I can hardly imagine when I'll ever write again. (Prose.) I might distil something poetic during the long weekend that lies ahead – though I have a string of classes again on Saturday.

I'm glad to hear Jan and his crowd are at least not unpleasant, although the spectre of Uys still looms. Perhaps that will also go off surprisingly well. I don't *want* them to make you unhappy.

74

Where do those lovely Hansel and Gretel lines come from?

My letters jump around so! It's because with every sentence I think of a hundred other things I want to say at the same time – and eventually I never finish anything I start. Fortunately you won't misunderstand me any more. We know each other too well for that, each and every pore. Have I ever known anyone in the way I know you? Besides: all the "secrets" I've ever possessed – in whatever way – are now in you. And you're wrong: they don't wash out that easily! Somewhere, who knows, one of them still hides, biding his time. I'm starting to get used to the pretty name Deirdre. (Do you know [Roland] Holst's version of the beautiful Celtic myths about Cú Chulainn and Conchobar? *That's* where Deirdre comes from, or am I wrong?) But I also like Heloïse. *And* Ingrid. Or shall we make a serene little Nicole, or an audacious Brunhilde? "Other names are still slumbering"!

(Do you have a copy of *Tristia* [N.P. Van Wyk Louw], or must I send you one?)

I walked into both bookshops here today and asked them – actually, *demanded* – that they each order six copies of *Rook en Oker*. And I gave the third-years notice that we're definitely going to discuss it this year. (No one will be able to say we're not "up to date"!)

All of this, still! – ways of longing.

Do you know Jacques Prévert's little portrait, "Alicante"? Forgive my imperfect translation:

An orange on the table
Your dress on the rug
And you in my bed
Sweet gift of the present
Freshness of the night
Warmth of my life.

Today I encountered the letters of [Lawrence] Durrell and Henry Miller: a hefty collection that reads wonderfully. Personal insight into other people's lives is always more "significant" than that which has been turned into objective literature! And a few new [Georges]

Simenons arrived. Where will I find the time to read them all, on top of my schedule? And this while every so often I simply walk away from everything, lean back, with or without music, and sit thinking, longing for you.

Forgetful little femina! (Referring to the jacket that you had to go and retrieve from Jan's in your blue sleep suit.) Light-footed deer, fragrant wisp of memory, sleep with me and be happy. Time is no longer of any importance.

I am *happy*. I long for you. I love you more than ever before,
André.

Entièrement à toi!

Grahamstown
Saturday morning, 1 June 1963

Little darling,

Greetings, my "morning bride"!

Never have you been so keenly with me, despite our state of separateness, than in my night of sleeping alone in this big, empty house. I woke up just now with thoughts of you, and now I'm sitting here writing in the early morning, while you're still in your sweet Saturday slumber, and Simone's busily zipping around somewhere, buzzing like a bee.

I wasn't able to work alone in the house last night, so I took my marking to a friend and sat myself down in her flat. She's a very *understanding* kind of person – the matron at one of the university's residences, in fact. She can be quite embarrassingly superficial in company – but very different in one-on-one conversation. (Her husband left her a few years ago and is now married to Louise Conradie, someone you might know?) And so I told her about everything. I'm *glad* I did. She understands and appreciates things so well; she's able to be *happy* about it, too, *and* she understands how complex everything actually is.

I got home at about midnight, laboured until almost two o'clock on diary-work, and only then went to sleep. This morning I felt a slight tristesse seeping into my day after reading the lead story on the dying pope. I've actually been aware of it all week. Why does it affect me so? One day we must convert to Catholicism, together. It's another one of the wide range of things that bind us: we connect so *precisely* in almost every area. In this case: both of us agnostic, sceptical, and yet – am I right? – both with a kind of need to believe in something nonetheless, even if it's just a greater sense of meaning or coherence; and the enchantment (for lack of a better word) of Catholicism. It's just the idea of a large, organised *system* that always makes me feel uneasy.

Darling, demonic little angel, if I'd slept in the same bed as you last night, neither of us would have gotten much sleep. And it would have been the whole sonata, the glorious fire of the ecstasy, the more languid, restful togetherness *con sordino*, the playful light happiness, *and* then the quiet, the space, eventually, in which everything becomes bigger and one feels small and reverent towards the other, and the night.

I shouldn't write so much! You're doing the tape-thing today, aren't you? But how can I do otherwise, once I start conversing with you?

I marked the tape to indicate which is side 1; let Erik put it on – and then push off. There's a little period of silence before I begin. Then, at the end, he can turn it around and play side 2. Tell him it plays at *standard* speed; 3¾. And ask him if his recorder has three speeds, then you can record your answer at the slowest speed (it plays twice as long).

I must have a glass of milk now and then dash off to class.

But here – since I've already put so much of [Paul] Van Ostaijen's poetry on the tape! – is one more poem, a piece that you yourself might almost have composed:

NIEMAND
     verstaat mij
mijn spel is zó eenvoudig

>   niemand kan het raden
> Mijn handen voelen
>   al mijn voelen dat zij nooit wisten
> en mijn borsten
>   sidderen
>   om de streling die komen moet
>   geen wet
>   maar
>   LOT

I'll write again tomorrow, maybe tonight even, or maybe I'll phone tonight.

With all my love, and a soft little kiss, you-know-where,
Your André.

———————

Grahamstown
Sunday afternoon, 2 June 1963

My little bride-child, mine,

"The blind head butting at the dark" – that is what this weekend of being alone feels like. But in the midst of my minor descent into hell, I have *you*; you are the "blaze of light along the blade". Yesterday's telephone conversation, and your dear voice, your happiness and your love, meant such a lot to me. You must know the lovely epigraph that Graham Greene uses to introduce one of his books: "Man has places in his heart which do not yet exist, and into them enters suffering in order that they may have existence." Like all births, this one is not without its share of suffering. But it's indispensable; and despite how paradoxical it might sound, I wouldn't want it any other way; there's a kind of

78

primeval happiness, pristine and unraffinated, in this clear light; I shall always be thankful for it.

You asked yesterday: "But what still needs to be thought about?" And yet you *know*. Now is the time for finding words, for confrontation, for standing up implacably to the chaos in one's own heart. I am too endlessly tired, stripped too bare by two nights and a day of this kind of "being" to want to keep anything from you. And yet it's actually unnecessary to say it: you *know*. I have to decide to shake myself loose from everything: not from someone I despise or hate or about whom I feel neutral, but someone I do love, after all, someone who has shared many essential moments with me; a soft person, and a vulnerable being. And is there any greater cruelty than that against the defenceless?

If I were to break my ties too easily, just shake off everything I have taken on and try to deny its value, I would break down something inside me – and you would be the first to abhor me for that.

This is the hell that I must get through this weekend. To put it humorously, in the words of a wise old lady (read it with a bit of a brrr-aay):

Die lewe is 'n brakwal:
hy kalwer uit
hy kalwer uit
tot hy in sy dônner val!

[Life is a brackish embankment
it hollows out
it hollows out
until it collapses completely!]

But I know I'm getting closer to the light. What remains is still more exhaustion. I haven't really slept the past two nights. Or: it was a jig-saw puzzle of sleep and wakefulness, thoughts, dreams, associations, memories, expectations.

Many scraps of poetry emerged from all of this. It's actually strange how often I wake up with a cadence in my head, a series of loose words; then, one by one, they start slotting into a rhythm until a line emerges – which I forget unless I write it down immediately. One more or less finished fragment goes like this:

Kom ons weeg: jý links jý regs
maar die hand bewe met die gewiggies
en niks lê roerloos op die klein agaatkant nie:
die siel weeg in die donker teen 'n veer.

[Let us weigh things up: you left, you right
but the hand with the weights trembles
and nothing lies motionless on the agate-surface:
The soul balances in the dark against a feather.]

(Should we call it "Osiris"? He's the one who weighed people's souls, after all. And in ancient Egypt the feather was a symbol of truth.)

Another one, which grew longer:

Kon mens maar sonder sê
van liefhê liefhê
wéés
sodat niks gemeet hoef te word
aan die tyd nie
want hoe lank duur duur?
is is?
moet ek my voortdurend gysel aan die lot
prakseer, bereken, uitsorteer
iewers-heen "word"
op Francesca se donker wind
of die son en die ander bewegende sterre
in plaas van net
die klein prikkie is

te is
wat nie geheue of verwagting het nie
wat niks doen op grond van gister
of in hoop op môre nie
wat selfs vry kan wees van my en jou
en dergelike toevallighede:
'n onverbonde
ongebroke
is?

[Can one exist
without ever saying
"I love you", "I love you"
so nothing has to be measured
against time
because how long does time last?
how long is is?
must I constantly make myself a hostage to destiny
devise, calculate, sort out
somewhere "becoming"
on Francesca's dark wind
or the sun and the other moving stars
instead of just being
the little dab of is
without memory or expectation
that does nothing on the basis of yesterday
or in the hope of tomorrow
that can even be free of me and you
and similar incidentals
an unbounded
uninterrupted
is?]

(Are the three concluding lines necessary?)

And the other one is still just a few scraps. Like:

> Wie-weet-waar in die wilde lewe
> woon jy, kind,
> met jou heilige sonderlinge oë.

> [Who knows where in this wild life
> you live, child,
> with your holy, singular eyes.]

And:

> Slaap, poësie, 'n berg, en jy. [Sleep, poetry, a mountain, and you.]

Etcetera! (I want to work the final one in the manner of a fugue: develop all four elements one by one; mix them up, switching their roles, and then eventually reunify them. Easier said than done!)

Last night I did a little translation work – not too much – and now I want to continue; but first I feel like lying in the sun a bit, perhaps to sleep, perchance to dream, and be with you, deliciously, and *happy* – as Van Ostaijen (him again!) says in his poem:

> IK LACH
> ik lach niemand
> zelfs niet mijzelf
> mijn lach is zó
> ik lach
> ik ben gelukkig
> om
> het wonder mijn lacht niet te begrijpen

Heavens, this letter is becoming an anthology. Forgive me! How else can I think about you, though, except through poetry? When I simply write your name, it becomes the title of a poem.

Girl with the little feet and big eyes. Last week this time, at three in the afternoon, my last "secret" disappeared deep inside your wonderful darkness. And even in that banal, uncomfortable environment, it was beautiful and delicious. Because I *love* you. I *need* you endlessly. And I want to be needed by you.

Thank you for listening to my talk-on-paper all this time. It's such a mercy to know in advance that you understand, because you are in love. Don't ever stop being in love. Don't ever stop being yourself. You are, like St Francis's "Sister Water" – "molto utile et humile et pretiosa et casta" ("very needed and humble and precious and chaste").

And I am yours, darling,
André.

Evening.

Thank you, again, for your dear voice. But don't be sad. Because "you are one-and-all breath and sun". And what I said is *true*: this afternoon's few verses – after I wrote the previous part of my letter – and the quiet, cool walk through the bush, brought a new sense of repose in me. Perhaps it *cannot* last, but I'm thankful for the comfort as long as it does. And I'm happy. If I have to say how much I long for you, I won't have sufficient words for the task. Our little time of "sleeping together" last night at nine-thirty was also so lovely, so replete with longing.

I have never yet felt so whole and so aware of life as in the past six weeks, and especially this past week.

I hope your meeting up with Jack [Cope] again, when he brings the lamp, won't create a difficult situation. I think about you all the time, and nothing happening here can disturb my thoughts enough to pre-vent my constant concern for your happiness.

A few days ago I managed to translate your "The Child", as I promised I would, into English. I did so without looking at Jack's version – taking a peek only afterwards out of curiosity. Unavoidably, the greater part of the translations is exactly the same – the poem's short, gritty words lend themselves to this – but I'm perverse enough to think that my version, where it does deviate, is better! In any case, it's for you to decide. I'm sending it along, as well as one or two of the pieces I composed this afternoon (including the one I read to you over the phone).

Damn, I keep forgetting to send you these two clangers from my first-year students' essays. One writes: "Erns van Heerden was deeply pressed into everything he saw in America." Another writes about Paris: "Picasso, Renoir, Chopin, Mendelssohn and Mona Lisa all lived there."

Things like this make the slog worthwhile, after all!

Now I have to switch back to translation. Haven't done a stitch of work all day. Luckily I don't have any lectures tomorrow, so I can catch up then.

I am happy, and I love you. Sleep sweetly tonight, my darling, and don't let your naked little chick get cold!

Love, love,
André.

———————

Castella
Wessels Street
Green Point
Sunday, 2 June 1963

My dearest André,

In about a quarter of an hour you will phone – I am here in my little cubicle, where, last night after your phone call, I also tried to write to you. Why are you sad? Ag, when you are not happy, I am not happy! Just look at Simone, how happy she is – she's singing in the bath next door – I forbade her to say nigger, so now she sings: Eeny, meeny, miny, moe, catch the niggerball by his toe …

And now you called, and I was "quiet" – as I told you, I wrote you a hell of a long letter last night after your call: I quote: "Will it help if I give you up?" No, my precious André, and maybe I am also a "part of your development, and I will accept that also, should the time for that come …"

In the kitchen, four children are trying to fix my leaking tap – everything here is so homely, and Mrs Oxley is really kind: brought me a tray with tea yesterday morning, she's Catholic and next Sunday Simone and I are going to Mass with her, which I have no particular reason or need for. In any case, Simone should also go.

It gets dark quickly now, and at this time, around seven o'clock, it is so quiet, and of course we can't hear the sea. It's like a real house on its own and Marjorie [Wallace] is very impressed with it, they all promise to come and help me paint it, and moan about the Terrible Child [Uys Krige?], much to their enjoyment, and I just let myself be lulled and scolded – "as if nothing moved him".

Precious child, I miss you so much and I wish I could give you more support at this time – but I dare not influence you – I feel so powerless! I am glad you've decided to tell Estelle tomorrow, it's better than living with this tension and, in the long run, also more fair. Just remember that I am with you and will stay with you, that you will and must trust me – and trust in the ultimate moral right that you owe yourself (and others). I will go MAD if Lena [Oelofse] doesn't come this evening. She should have been here at five o'clock and was supposed to stay over: and I can't go and phone her until Simone is asleep – Mrs Oxley's telephone is for *you* alone (!).

But now we must be happy – and that is an *order*. Your poem in tonight's call was beautiful, really polished. My beautiful, tender man. Tomorrow our books are going on display and on Wednesday they're putting our photos in the APB's window together – I suppose one just mustn't be afraid! And that brings us again to faith and grace – in your last (changeably moody) letter, you ask: what if one doesn't believe in grace? You, my dearest god-graced! Graced in all your generosity and compassion, graced in the depth and intensity of your experiences, graced in your ability to love, graced as an artist! And that's why I told you at the fire (the big fire of Saturday evening, sleepy man): You are a precious human being. And not just to me.

I told you that Marjorie was here when your beautiful flowers (which light up the whole house) arrived, and when Mrs Oxley came to tell me about the telephone call at six o'clock – Jan told me: "You've fucked up André's life." Just like that. Do you understand? What should I answer? Maybe. How must I know? (And maybe it is just as possible that I can *make* his life). Because everything is uncertain and how can we know what only the wind knows, child? Melancholy, child, melancholy, I tell you. Just come and hide away here in my little flat, and let the world carry on talking, and if the flat becomes too oppressive, we'll walk up the mountain hand in hand, and if that could happen, can anything still be so dreadful?

Simone and Heloïse and all the secrets are asleep – I am alone here and it is quiet. Even the old leaking tap that kept me company is quiet, now that the children have fixed it. But do you know what? Darling, on the 28th we're going to have a hell of a party for you with wine and cigarettes and friends, and us in the morning with a soundless dawn! I have always thought that the best line W.E.G. Louw ever managed is, "die wrede dag breek buite deur die vensters aan" and this takes me back immediately to the Friday morning, when you tried to wake me at around 5:30, and I didn't want to wake up, but just sleep in the abundant twilight of you – of which I was indeed, and so *thoroughly*, aware! And all our tender honeymoon days in Franschhoek. To the citizenry: This you cannot give me, but This you can so easily take away …

Thank you for your beautiful red autumn leaf, and will you wear your autumn jersey when you come? What colour is it, exactly? Don't you know I'm visually attuned? I meant to ask you over the telephone. And I look forward to your tape recording – do you want to make me go completely crazy when I hear you say you're going to do this now?

Darling, my dearest, my André, there are so many ways that we can make contact, through and over and above and near the Sahara! You must believe in me. Do you know that *no one* ever has? You must love me. Do you know that no one has ever loved me? That's why I feel so unworthy, and that's why I am sometimes so quiet.

And before I write even one more revealing word, I'm going to stop, and phone Lena, and phone Chris to bring my radio, and make contact with the lovely harbour here outside my door: "herinnering, o pragtige skip …"

Your Ingrid.

ps: Do you still remember little chick?
Your Ingrid
Or Ingrid Jon. Jo. Citadel Press.

And I do love you, my André, be a good child now and happy – and be a big strong man and stern: "Jy is rein, jy is nog reiner as ekself."

Monday, 3 June 1963

HAD TO LEAVE URGENTLY 1:30 SORRY AND UPSET DARLING GOOD LUCK TONIGHT LOVE = INGRID

Monday, 3 June 1963

My overwhelming Darling,

Do you realise that I've just – about 1½ hours ago, listened to your tape, shall I now begin at the beginning? After your telephone call at around 2:30, was it? I carried on working, far calmer, and then, at five o'clock, went to the display where I immediately looked around for your book – congratulations, dearest! – and riffled through it, turned it over, took the dust cover off and bent it and folded it and held it until I could feel the curious-amused eyes of the whole gathering on me, I welcomed them and poured myself a hell of a tot of sherry and drank to it – felt Jack [Cope] standing beside me (oh he'd organised everything for my own appearance and spoken to all the newspapers), I just looked up into those broad plains of his eyes and without a word (perhaps dramatic!) left just before the opening.

The first and the best bus would take me to Claude and Erik – *Erik*, my liefsteling, to play your tape. I fetched Simone, then the tape, then went off to them, but they received me a little *unsympathetically* – after which I – with Simonetta in hand – took a bus to Clifton – other friends with a machine – they were out, but their twelve-year-old son put the tape on and gave me these headphones – and then I listened to you. Beloved precious man – must I admit that I – after the day's tension and suddenly so much love – simply and unavoidably began to cry, so that I played the second part five times, moved by the [?] and everything and your wonderful threat: and now I'm going to sleep with you ... And best of all you really don't belong to me, but to everyone (I'll never be allowed to keep you for myself, child!). And now, at home, Simone asleep – and tomorrow I must immediately investigate a machine like this – I've arranged to record a tape for you on Saturday morning – and if I have a thing like this here then of course it will never again be quiet and alone!

I'm thinking (of course) about you so much this evening and wondering how things are going there, with all the heavy solemnity. I know so well how it is and I wish I could hold your hand: "Hande wat mekaar vasvat het geen gewig nie / Tussen oë wat na mekaar kyk loop die lig oor." "Lord I am not worthy, / Lord I am not worthy, / but speak the Word only." That's how you sometimes make me feel, darling, great generous human – I am a humble little instrument in the vast complex of your poetic truth, but at least I am there! And I will stay here, for all your beautiful feeling – oh, child! Let me rather "answer" your letters from today.

Of course I know Louise Conradie – quite well, actually – and her taciturn husband – what did your friend say, and did she comfort you? I'm glad you could speak to her – Chris confused me last night – he is very kind and honest, but maybe, still, a vote of no confidence in me, or maybe just in man. Oh my André, will it ever come right? Or are we just dreaming now again of Heloïse and Deirdre? I don't want fairy tales any more, I want to recognise the "light and life" in one go!

The Hansel and Gretel lines are from Elisabeth Eybers – *Neerslag*, darling. Do you not know it? I'm writing so ugly and untidily because I'm in a great hurry because I'm completely overflowing emotionally and now I can't say quickly enough and correctly enough everything I want to say and then what about all the impressions and dawnings and detours and hesitations of human intuition too?

Do you really think secrets aren't "washed out" that easily? I wonder! And now you're the one who's wrong again – you collect so many secrets every day that I'll never be able to keep up! You know that!

No, I don't have *Tristia* – but now I'm going to tick you off – you mustn't spend so much of your precious time-money on me – except for the tapes! And a tape-thing like this you just have to buy for me – I'll send you the bill! Now, with *so much* unsaid, I'm going to sleep – if I can sleep, I ecstatic, with you.

Ingrid.

So, what all happened last night? Just have faith, do you hear, my dearest André. I must hurry to post this letter.

———————

Grahamstown
Wednesday morning, 5 June 1963

Ingrid-my-own-girl,

I've been wanting to write since yesterday morning, but every time something gets in the way; and when I do sit down to write, words fail me. You surely know the gripping lines from *Tristia*:

ons dor papiere kom en vra woorde:
daar sal geen woorde gegee word, nooit,
behalwe die ongevraagdes …

But you will surely also want to know how things went on Monday evening (and the whole of yesterday, and this morning); and what my "motives" were for this morning's long telegram.

The last first: amid all the bitter, heavy things here, I simply knew that I had to find a way to see you next week, just so that everything can be settled ("The soul weighs up in the dark against a feather …"!) There's no sense in postponing, in prevaricating any longer, in waiting. It's not right for any of us.

Luckily, classes end on Saturday for the exams and Rob immediately – so nice of him – agreed that I could go away and stay for as long as I need to, provided I return on Monday the 17th. I'm departing from here on Saturday afternoon and will hopefully arrive at your place on Sunday at about lunchtime. It would be lovely if you could get leave, as we'll of course have the car again to make a getaway, if necessary.

Given that I'll be with you again so soon, it's actually unnecessary for me to say too much about what's going on here, behind the scenes. Just briefly, so you know how everything started and then developed, and so you don't feel unnecessarily agitated:

When I told Estelle on Monday night, she said: "I know. I suspected it from the very first time you got back." She was very calm – although she had tears in her eyes. At one stage she simply said: "Don't think that because I'm talking matter-of-factly this is easy for me." Eventually she lay her hand on my knee and said: "Despite all of this, I love you no less."

Yesterday we concentrated on practical implications – everything that would have to be considered if it came to divorce. Especially regarding Anton. I know how badly a boy, a *child*, needs his father. (Is this not the single biggest absence in your own life?)

Oh God, darling, it's so awful to hurt those who are defenceless. I can hardly tell you how much your quiet, understanding love – and your lack of *haste* – has helped me at this time.

And by loving me you have also made yourself so vulnerable. Is it not in fact an ironic commentary on human limitations that we may not love two people equally? In a cynical moment, Estelle said: "Be a good businessman. Make sure you profit from this transaction." But with human unpredictability, things don't work that way.

Despite all this, there was at least some consolation yesterday: Bartho sent me a provisional copy of *Sempre*. (I'll bring it along for you to see.) It looks good, I think – do you? That's apart from the fact that the dust cover's inside flaps would have looked better in white; and, typographically, the epigraph's been placed very poorly. Also, some mysterious printing errors crept in. But overall it's quite neat. I can't wait to see *Rook en Oker*! Did it at least arrive in time for the exhibition? I spent the whole of Monday afternoon worrying about it.

I've somehow still got to translate 60 pages from the archaeology book this week, and finish off the *Huisgenoot* article on Rome. But if this doesn't work I'll bring some of the work with me so I can do it at your place; that's if you don't get time off.

The prints of our photographs arrived. I include one that I think is lovely (it was cut from a full-length nude study – those are being printed by Hilda Brinkman, who took photos of me a while ago); the others don't look too great but I'll bring them with me. I'm holding thumbs that the colour prints will arrive this week. I'm expecting *nice* ones, too.

I don't want to sit and write any longer. I *long* for you – "Oh my honeyed and holy / skin and hair and down"! Just four days, then we can resume the glorious dialogue, be *happy*. Whatever else happens in the big wide world: we have *this*.

And yet – even though I don't want to sit and write one-dimensionally – I also don't want to say goodbye and *stop* talking to you! But my thoughts and my memories, longing and bright love, will continue talking long after this page and this letter. In the meantime, just read the Song of Songs.

With all my love,
Your André.

My dearest little house,

I almost said "outhouse", but that would be open to misinterpretation. I feel so crazy and happy today. It's for that reason you're getting another little note, despite the fact that I posted you a separate letter earlier – which you must please read first in case you were going to start with this one.

Actually, I have only a few minutes before taking my car to the garage for a service prior to this weekend's long, lovely trip; I also have to prepare for an honours class in about an hour's time. But first, darling, let me just say thank you for the most beautiful letter I have ever received. Everything in this grey day suddenly began to radiate with light, certainty and love.

In addition, the colour pictures have just arrived – and they're gorgeous; *you're* gorgeous. I'll bring my projector so you can view them in the proper manner.

And so Jan said: "You've gone and fucked up André's life"? You should've replied: "But fucking is so nice!"

Your little house – because it's really not a "flat" – sounds like such a happy place. And next week we're going to break it in properly, make it feel nice and friendly.

Have you had a chance to listen to my tape yet? I hope you can do so without interruption. (Maybe it was disappointing anyway – a real Transvaal microphone voice?)

I received your letter during teatime, which is why I'm still walking around doing nothing (I haven't had a class since then). I sat and read it in my office, with its high bright window and small panes, revealing an occasional autumn leaf whirling around. Everything is so immeasurably and deceptively *beautiful*.

And in case I haven't yet said it: did you know – I *love* you? "Ik heb u lief, als dromen in den nacht … Als alles, wat héél ver is en héél schoon." When I think of you (all the time), it is with a great sense of certainty, because I can believe so completely in you, because you are so honest and open in your love, giving as well as taking, because together we can become so much more than just you and me alone (and I'm not talking about olive branches here!). Nothing quite as precious as you has ever occurred in my life.

Little child, generous person, lovable you: only a few more days.

With love (which "makes radiant all unbeautiful things" – a kind of Mass all on its own),
Your André.

––––––––––

Friday, 7 June 1963

HOLDING BACK TAPE RECORDING AND LETTER STOP WAITING FOR YOU SUN-DAY STOP HAVE LEAVE STOP ANSWER LOVE = INGRID

––––––––––

Grahamstown,
Monday night, 17 June 1963

Darling little thing,

I'm sitting here in the literal and figurative cold, trying through writing to heal myself of my loneliness and longing. It's best to think about *now*, about what's going on here on the page and inside of me – and I should also think about our week – because if I try looking ahead, into the darkness, courage forsakes me, and all else besides.

Ever since I watched your small, still, red-and-brown figure disappear behind me so sadly (thinking at first the windscreen was unclear, until I realised my eyes were shedding tears!), much has occurred. The first stretch of road was hell – all the beach traffic on its way home after the blissful day's sea and sun; it was so bad I had to crawl along at 25 m.p.h. After that it went better, except I discovered one of the headlights was more or less dead after our first (!) bump on Saturday night's memorable venture. I wanted to stay over at Great Brak River, on the other side of Mossel Bay, but the hotel was dark and shut up (perhaps for the winter). So I pushed through to Plettenberg Bay, arriving there at 11 pm. I didn't sleep all that well – too much longing, too much wishing you could break in the lovely bed with me, drank too much, too tired, the works. Left again at seven this morning (while you were still sleeping next to your little girl?), arriving back here at eleven-thirty.

When I got to the university, I was met by a telegram that had only just been delivered. From? The good gentleman W.A. de Klerk. Its contents: "I see no good in it. Reconsider. All the best." Goodness me! If the post office could only have known what I wanted to telegraph back to him, the sanctimonious old sourpuss.

This afternoon from two to five I had to invigilate an exam: the most boring, sterile job on earth. After a while I went and sat at a table against the wall at the back of the room and semi-slept.

"In general"? Reception: neutral, cool, matter-of-fact. As I said to you: I think there's a *possibility* things could be set right again. But I don't know any more.

Oh, my love, I am so tired of tension and waiting and weakening embankments.

Luckily I received my copies of *Sempre* today and enjoyed the pleasurable task of composing inscriptions for people. It's a consolation, at least. And then a pleasant piece of news: my little one-act play, *Die Koffer*, is going to be broadcast by the SABC's English service on their Radio Theatre (only in Nov. – but still).

Above all else there's *you*, and everything that happened this past week. Even the tears, for which I deserve no forgiveness – especially from myself – and which are yet so unutterably precious ("die sout van trane, sweet en nog / die allerlaaste liefdesvog"). The hidden secrets. Shadow and light on your tummy. The childlike challenge of your breasts. Your happy, sorrowful eyes. Ingrid, Ingrid, you are everything, always.

Please write and tell me all the news about Jan and company. Uys too, and Jack. Little thing, I have rendered you vulnerable with love, but I must also credit you with the grace and strength of love ("believes all things, hopes all things, endures all things"). I don't know what lies ahead for me or you or both of us. Hoe zouden wij weten ...? All I know is: God (and this time, I think I mean this word), I am in love. Everything has mass. Everything is endlessly enmeshed. Everything is sore. And yet: everything is *joyous*, because it's all so irradiated with light that I wouldn't want it any other way for a single moment, ever.

When I really get sad, then I just think:

The black amphibians will never again
return to the waters of this pit

or something equally immortal, or about our tent-making, or about my sleepy little girl with a big appetite – all the silly and precious things about which we laughed so much and were so happy about.

And for that, little child, *thank you*. Thank you "for everything". Thank you for *you*.

With all my love,
Your André.

Castella
22 Wessels Street
Green Point
Monday, 17 June 1963

Hello, my treasure,

What a joy it would be if you came home tonight, because today I transformed the little castle into a palace – it was one of those wonderful mild days – Simonetta, chicken pox and all – because she's got it, of course – was playing around here outside, helped me wash and dust and scrub, now I've dressed her in snow white and put cream on all her blisters and bundled her into bed – why are you and I never this domestic? Now I'm having a nice drink here in my clean little palace, and one may do so, instead of all the hotels we're forever rushing to. No, child, next time (and then I'll hopefully be better equipped – even discovered a bread knife today) we'll just stay here and the friends must come round. Shall I tell you how wonderful it was to have you here for a whole week (in spite of all the tears and the necessary *have-to* things we *had to* go through) and how wretched it was last night (and when Chris came Mrs Oxley was here and later he left without us having a chance for a nice chat), and I went to sleep; terribly lonely, with this sense of loss, but today everything was right and warm and good: received your telegram around four o'clock when I was knee-deep in washing and soap-soup and scorching taps, thank you, I'm glad you're "safe" – why such a *short* telegram? Where did you sleep in the end and how was the driving? *Tell all.*

This first letter will of necessity have to be a kind of "diary" – because there is still too much that isn't necessary to say – this evening, soon, Lena is coming for a meal here, I made Spanish rice – do you know it, and do you think I really can? Didn't see Jan and them because of Simone's pox – can't go out – have even read five chapters of that awful piece of journalism *Optimists in Africa* – he was probably thoroughly remunerated by the government – that doesn't excuse his language

– and didn't glance again at Aunt Grietjie's little poem because of fear of longing. But believe me, my André, I have more than one reason to think constantly of Van Wyk Louw:

> Nou het die môre my
> oor die rand van sy glas gemors
> op die stoep waar die waterkraan *drup*
> in die uur van die donkere dors.

Mrs Oxley is sending a man on Saturday to come and sort things out. And forgetful, you (thank you!) left all your colour slides here (where is your evidence now?) clothes, books, Mikro, among others. Sorry about *Tristia,* but that one I haven't detected here yet. Mrs Oxley very much likes "your André" and seems to approve wholeheartedly of everything (of course it's not much). In any case, she doesn't mind at all that you stay here. Oh, darling, I wonder how you are this evening and whether perhaps you're also writing to me (I'm still feeling far too emotional for the little tape, but am just writing all the rot (as my ouma would say) that comes into my head). Do I disappoint you in saying that our quadruplets aren't on their way yet? (About an hour after you left.) Good heavens, André, why am I writing everything in brackets this evening? Is it an expression of longing or timidity or casualness, or a whispering, an intimate conversation, like how we also speak quietly afterwards?

Ag child, tonight I feel like I'm an onion. Maybe it's the silky night-dress (because I've already bathed, all clean and dressed for a long long sleep after Lena's visit), in any case as round and smooth and untouched as if I've just come up out of the ground (do onions come out of the ground or do you pull them out?).

I still haven't found out whether my book has arrived – I don't give a hell, know more or less what it looks like now – could perhaps have called but I didn't think of it – will send you a final copy – and now, darling, good night, I'll write a little more tomorrow, because the road to Thursday is a long one, or are you still phoning on Wednesday evening?

You must remember to love me, and in any case you mustn't *chronically* upset yourself.

To be nosey: where exactly did you put my little thing? You don't have to answer, but I haven't come across it yet!

Until tomorrow, my lovely person. Will I still have to say goodbye or goodnight if you are always here?

Your Ingrid.

ps: Cast your bread upon the waters and after many days you will find it – thank you for all the typing paper) Love you. That *bracket* should have been an exclamation mark, seems that I'm becoming unhinged, I'm so happy!

Ingrid Jonker I.J.

"Ons moet nog óns kompartement gaan soek". It's not just this that made me put down your beautiful new *Sempre Diritto*. It's the solitariness of each individual. Lena still hasn't arrived.
I.

Tuesday morning: Simone and I (no wait, good morning! Good morning, the way *you* do!) carried out the little table with much effort and groaning – little diamonds of sun out here on the stoep. You're probably all already on your way to Potchefstroom – when I woke this morning I lay and thought about all the possible things Christie and Retha [Roode] could say to you. Whatever other people say can be nothing more, nothing less than "batallions of lies". Oh, my treasure! Koos [Human], from what I hear, said, "I am glad." But I really just wanted to say hello so I can go and post this little letter, so that at least you'll have a letter on your arrival, although it's not much to speak of. Die Here het gaskommel die dice, hy't vakeerd geval vir ons, daais ma' al. [The Lord shook the dice, they fell wrong for us, that's all there is to it.] Depressing, hey? But you should be here these golden days – "daar kom in my 'n stil vermoede / dat alle lewe só sy volheid kry". I am well. I hope that you are confident, and free. I support you with all my strength.

Ingrid.

———————

Castella
22 Wessels Street
Green Point
Sunday, 23 June 1963

Lord I am not worthy,
Lord I am not worthy,
But speak the word only

My wonderful darling, beautiful abundant tender man, mine! Do you know Paul Rodenko's "Het Beeld"?

Uit het hout van de morgen
uit morgenrozenhout
    sneed ik een beeld
heel licht en smaller dan een lijsterstem
een beeld van morgenrozenhout

Het was zo schuw zo ongeschoold
dat ek het zelf niet kende
met elke windvlaag was het weg
    maar een kind
    een bloesemtak
    een onbekende
bracht het mij voorzichtig weer terug

Er waren er die het herkenden
    en luide namen gaven
Confecta Sexgiraffe Tafel mit Citroenen
Clown Tederheidsbeginsel Bloedgewricht
Naakt met Napoleon Een Huis My Country
My Ka My Lah My Lullalongsome Baby
...
Een heel small haast doorzichtig beeld
van morgenrozenhout

And difficult as it is for me to give you a name, my beautiful generous man, it is harder even to think of all the things of last week, things that go deeper and deeper, become more intangible, more unsayable. How many times now have I written to you, made tapes, and then just wiped them again – the tape I made for you a moment ago protested all on its own – how on earth it happened I don't know, but when I played it back, another voice came out, speaking backwards! Absurd. And now I will have to do it all over again, and after a repeat like this nothing ever comes right.

Thank you for your phone call, darling, it's a pity they cut us off so quickly – the telephone and telegram people perhaps find us terribly boring? The meal with Jack afterwards was pleasant after all – he shows such gentleness and understanding, sometimes he is rebellious, and then again truly loving with such a longing for the lost body – oh my little treasure! Everyone has become so vulnerable, and thus lovelier, better. I understand everything you say on the tape so well, it reminds me of Van Wyk [Louw] "noudat die bitter trots gaan skuil in deernis" ... But you mustn't worry about me – Uys doesn't want to have much to do with me, only spoke to me once, the other day, quite sharply – but it doesn't matter. As Eric Venter – remember the little guy who wanted to know whether there were sweeties in my bag – always says: Let them go ... I haven't seen Jan and Marjorie again. I've only seen Chris twice, he's scared of the chicken pox. We had tea together at Suikerbossie – I was almost poisoned by the sour milk – he says I am so "changed" and dearly wants one of our little boys! Dear Chris, I am always so amazed at the beautiful, beautiful things in people; they always seem new to me again. Also, my treasure, I've received two more armchairs and a pile of plates, am getting a carpet tomorrow, the snails ate my daisies, my bookshelf's been built, I'm reading *Sempre* and am amazed at you and everything you've done and experienced and I long more than anything to also be able to travel the world with you – now I must go and buy cigarettes in the sun, the harbour lies splendid here before me: "herinnering, o pragtige skip …"

Back. A quick walk up the big hill, it's such a Table Mountain day and I wish we were over there in the little cable car with our arms around each other and the fat American women's ridiculous remarks somewhere in the background. And yet everything here is also bright, and when you come in July we'll walk around the harbour on a day just like today – this time last week you dropped me off at my sister's, magtig, André, is no one just a tiny bit sorry for us? Yet I suppose we mustn't go round in circles … but even [J.] Slauerhoff can't get away from the "benoude self". Thank you for all your lovely remarks about my collection – which still hasn't arrived here – but you mustn't overestimate me, liefsteling – *Rook en Oker* is a tiny harvest! Rather wait for Europe. On Monday I have to – this is horrible, actually – read from my own work at the cultural association – should I take the tape recorder along? I actually forgot to listen to the bikini affair the other day – it was in any case so unremarkable.

Did I tell you that Lena stayed over here the other night? – I slept on the bed with Simone and in the middle of the night almost squeezed her to death and said, "André! André!" Lena laughed at me about it (naturally). Ag, child! Precious, pure André! Everything will be all right. As that arrogant Sally Disner (sculptor) wrote in someone's little book in big letters right across the page: "I have complete confidence in the future Sally Disner." André. André Brink. How strange your name sounds sometimes – as if a miracle is happening. But you'll forgive my silliness, won't you? I can say anything to you, can't I, my André? Now you must just be happy and come back soon, my sensitive treasure, I am waiting for you, patient and restless – who wants to save you with your hands and feet forever safe on bridges without danger.

Love, darling,
Your Ingrid.

———————

Sunday night, 23 June 1963, 10:45

I still want to say good night to you. Like this. Night. As if you're lying here next to me. Please warm your darling cold paw before putting it on me. Good night darling! After posting your letter this afternoon I walked to Mouille Point and heard Chris's little red car hooting behind me. So we went for a long walk on the beach, and had some milky porridge – the way the old people make it – at his flat. He dropped me off here around nine and then quickly left again because I'd lent him a little book about sex, which he is probably lying reading right now. He sends his regards, but to me: "Ag no, look, Ingrid, there's nothing to say to someone who's in love." I probably bored him with my babble – about you! My poor Simone is sickish again, it's just one thing after the other now, and we still had to go to the doctor first. Luckily it's nothing bad, but a sick little child is so pathetic.

Darling, don't lose hope about your tape, you hear? I'll send one – Wednesday. Tomorrow evening I have to go to that culture group – haven't prepared anything yet – so will only be able to record it on Tuesday evening – and this time I'll send it – even if you've got to listen to me talking backwards or crosswise – all I say in any case is, I miss you, I want to be, be, be, with you. Stay quiet, darling. Stay *calm*. Stay happy. I am so endlessly grateful for you: and I will always be, and will always love you.

Good night my André. Go to sleep now,
I.

Potchefstroom
Monday, 24 June 1963

Ingrid, my darling,

Little-girl-with-a-big-appetite (hell!), it's with a kind of helpless longing that I sit and write today, in these few minutes of quiet and solitude
before lunch, followed by unavoidable rounds of visits to acquaintances
(with whom I have ever-diminishing contact).

Every day I hurry to my office to look for post; and every day I
return letterless. After I arrived here on Friday, your first letter, an
all-over-the-show delight, lay waiting for me; but since then there has
been nothing. After our telephone conversation on Wednesday night
especially, I can hardly wait to hear how everything went. I want to
know, too, if you at least had a bit of a holiday before resuming the
misery at the crack of dawn today; and if you had any success with
HAUM (I'm holding thumbs); also whether you've – finally! – read *Die
Ambassadeur*; and if you've posted the colour slides yet (please). And
everything else, you neglectful little thing!

Meanwhile I am muddling along – "living and partly living" (mainly
the latter), with a kind of deep weariness that has seeped into blood
and bone and which I cannot shake off. "In this shipwreck of all certainty …", i.e. all certainty except that of longing and love.

Last evening you were with me again all night; and the night before
that I was quarrelling with you all through the small hours! Meanwhile,
my longing has already become so fierce that I had to "sleep" with you
again on Saturday night.

This afternoon I want to make time to visit [Gerrit] Dekker,
although I doubt I'll get much out of him; he's such a closed book. But
with this new storm brewing around *Lobola*, I'd very much like to know
how he feels about things. Have you seen? – the Cultural Association
["Kultuurraad"] (sic!) of Pretoria has issued a press statement saying they will definitely be lodging a complaint against *Lobola* at the

Publications Control Board. And it looks as though *Die Ambassadeur* has also been "marked" in advance for trouble. But all to the good. As soon as all hell breaks loose here, and I can rely on an overseas income, we can make a move, "take it easy" on a Greek island and concentrate on our own home industry: the production of beautiful little babies.

This morning I bought a recent Penguin anthology: *The New Poetry* (American and English) and found much that is worthwhile in it. You probably have it already? For the rest, the Italian anthology and your brown book are always with me. And your own beautiful little volume. (I'm getting really keen to see a second printing!)

Here, by the way, are a few lovely lines by Salvatore Quasimodo:

Perduto ho ogni cosa innocente,
anche in questa voce, superstite
a imitare la gioia

[I have lost every innocent thing,
even in this voice, which remains
to imitate joy]

Did Jan and his lot turn up again? And ...? I do hope you see Chris and Lena often enough. It would be better if Chris didn't go away for the holidays.

Don't be lonely, darling! –

Sometimes just being alone seems the bad thing.
Solitude can swell until it blocks the sun,
It hurts so much, even fear, even worrying
Over past and future, get stifled ...

Although the opposite is perhaps more true: solitude is in fact purifying. Even: it can create an unrivalled kind of togetherness. (We are, are we not, "one flesh"!) Or is that just me consoling myself? Because how does one hold out until September (and July is beginning to look very unlikely)? I suppose one finds the strength somewhere. If I could only *know* that you, despite all the necessary struggles and quarrelling, are *happy*. And for that I want to be with you, always. I *am*.

Be good, little child, be restful, be lovely; be *you*.

With love,
Your tentmaker.

PS: Your "thingy" should be lying on your windowsill for all to see! Have you found it?
PPS: I'm sending *Tristia* "under separate cover".
PPPS: Love.

―――――――――

Potchefstroom
Wednesday, 26 June 1963

Lovely little sunrise child,

It's neither morning nor night, so I can neither say "good morning" nor "good evening". But I do want to say "good day": to your soft hair in the sun, your pert little nose, and your coy ears with their ticklish lobes; your fragrant, laughing mouth, and your delicious eyes; your speckled, soft shoulders, lovely little arms, and gorgeous hands with the ring; those soft, firm, naughty little breasts with their stand-to-attention nipples; the light and shadow on your tummy, and your deep belly-button; the poor little chick that must sleep all alone now, and next to it the furrows made by your thighs, just to the side of it; your little hips and your round white buttocks; your lovely legs and your feet. In fact: good day to you! Good daayyy Fish! Daaag visselijn mijn!

Thank you also for today's two dear letters – you must please never again upset me so with such a long silence.

Just after I got your letters, I phoned Bartho. He's now expecting *Rook en Oker* – at last! – by the end of the week. And he apparently spotted a printing error ("werwarm") in "Herfsoggend" and changed it (but not the error "herrinner"). The red page numbers have been set a little deeper into the page, I believe; and the colophon now appears in the right place; that's about it, I think. Meanwhile the bookshop here has, on my recommendation, promptly doubled their original order (a dozen or so), and they're thinking of making a special window display.

Further: I've come to hear about a Dutch anthology, *Vandaag*, that appears annually and wants to include Afrikaans work, but doesn't quite know where to find it. I'll send you their address.

How did things go on Monday with the reading for the ACVV-SAVE Cultural Association?! I don't envy you this task. (Or perhaps I envy you your wonderful "perversity"!)

Angel child, your letters have made me quite *light*; I want to fly off with every little breeze to the sea, to you. When will we ever be together again as we were during "our" week? New memories keep coming back to me all the time; and the known memories change, acquiring new nuances and meaning, and achieving fresh dimensions.

So it *must* be. Because these days I have little else to feed on, or do. My article on Rome is *finally* done. The translations lie in wait, accusingly. Otherwise, my sinus problems have become so unbearable (only in the Cape do I escape this condition!) that I have begun – with some scepticism – to go for electrical treatment that doesn't actually help at all. And Anton is fretful; last night's getting up for him has landed me with a lovely cold. Now I'm as rickety as an old bedstead. Grim and bad-tempered. Except for the small while when I can shake everything off and be with you.

I posted *Tristia* off to you on Monday. Wrote a letter to go with it and then misplaced the thing – but afterwards it struck me the letter might have ended up inside the book. Let me know!

My dear mother came upon your volume yesterday and read the

inscription with great interest – but made no comment, and seemed unsurprised. I'm beginning to suspect she knows, after all – but *how*? And I'm beginning to wonder how much the whole thing had to do with my father's thrombosis attack. If only it would just *come out*. This kind of uncertain silence makes everything harder; and I dare not break the ice myself.

Further: Christie is still trying to "diagnose" me; I just laugh him off – and now he says I would drive any psychologist mad. But in the course of this process he did get one thing right: that his "help" doesn't "help"! He went on to say I'm a "tragic case"; and I said *he*'s not tragic, but I feel sorry for him. And that's that! Oh the comfort of "explaining" everything, of cataloguing things into traumas and neuroses and fixations and complexes – the eternal need to *name* things? With one big difference between them and us: with a name they want to say everything, and with a code they want to sum everything up, explain it; us? – the names we use are simply to say we *cannot* say; that we dare not ever have the presumption to say and to think that it's all said and done. ("I can't sum up; not a life, a conversation, / a period or a century"!) And after my sobering confrontation with this kind of cataloguing attitude (which might, *negatively*, still have some value!), I find I have no choice but to return to you:

> agteruit roei waar dit stroom
> en straal en droom nog is,
> dwars teen die breek-van-damme in:
> 'n goue klein goud-vis.

Back to the grotesque: Maish (Mouse/Rat) Levin tracked me down last night, apparently using your directions. For once I don't mind him making a "splash" with his bit of news. But I forgot to give him all the relevant information last night: which explains today's telegram. (I hope it's clear? I just want him to emphasise that even if the book is banned here, it will get recognition overseas.) If he doesn't return the photo of me, I'll send you another. Just say the word.

And when will you send me the slides?! (I'm hoping our most recent film – Hout Bay – will arrive next week.) And the MS? I need it. I want to know what you think – be honest, even if you have to show no mercy.

Lovely precious darling: I *miss* you. Tomorrow or the next day I'll make another tape (ironic: on Christie's recording machine!). Meanwhile, I'm with you always – on the mountain, on your little mound, and on the "holy mountain" (where only those with pure hearts and clean hands are allowed).

With a love that is growing ever-larger and more wonderful,
André.

PS: A kiss for our little girl. And a nice sleepie-sleepie for my little chick.

Castella
22 Wessels Street
Green Point
Thursday, 27 June 1963

Darling my André,

They were here – Jan and Marjorie – left about ten minutes ago – "just to show we're not cross with you". But to all their dear nosey questions I had only one answer: a happy laugh. Marjorie said she asked Ina [Ena de Klerk] at the party whether she does it on purpose: to which she answered: "Naturally. It's scandalous" – or something just as scandalous. After which I simply had to say to Jan it reminds of only one thing:

En die kwajongens het dit bestook
Val, val, ballon,
In Seepsopstraat

Hulle het hom bestook
Met klippers
Skeldwoorde
Val, val ballon
In Seepsopstraat
Maar hy het nie in Seepsopstraat geval nie
Hy het ver, baie ver, geval,
In die oop skone waters van die silwer see …

Or something like that.

Can't remember the poem precisely, but you know it, don't you, darling, about the beautiful tender child who made a balloon and let it go and everyone warned him that flying a balloon was against municipal regulations … It's forbidden … and then the *naughty boys …* who hated anything beautiful "because beauty is *truth …*" Fall, fall, balloon, in Soapsoup Street …

Darling, very tired. Working myself to death, but *first* I must *speak* to you, apart from saying thank you for *Tristia* – beautiful book – and for the lovely letter: always be so full of trust, as I know you are. Thank you for everything, my love. 10:15 says the radio. Did you get my tape? I was so excited about this new adventure.

My little treasure, firstly, I *love* you so much.

Secondly – Levin (how do you spell his first name: Meisch?) was here to fetch your photo – for the *Sunday Times*. Then told me everything you told him over the phone. These simple, beautiful, ecstatic little contacts!

I spent last evening with Jack – he came for a meal – and later left in the rain, cross, despondent and so *terribly* hurt. Oh *my* André, everything is so complicated! WHAT MUST WE DO?? May I perhaps catch a plane to Grahamstown in two weeks' time?? Wonderful, lovely, life! Wonderful, hellish separation! I will eat you up when I am with you again – be warned!

Love love love,
Your Ingrid.

{Goodnight, dearest. 'Night, my André. 'Night, my lovely declared treasure. 11:30. I.}

———————

Potchefstroom
Friday night, 28 June 1963

Darling,

It's *cold* here; and here in my little circle of light in the bedroom – all the others are sitting around the fireplace – it's lonely, too. This, however, is no pure, austere kind of cold that clarifies things, down to the bone: it's miserable and muddy; and my heart feels much the same. Nothing can crystallise here – at the most, things petrify. Is it any wonder then that my hankering after you is becoming ever more desperate? Because you are the real thing: light and warmth, autumn leaves, fresh air, blue sea, youth, and woman.

And tonight I sit, moreover, with the frustration and longing caused by your tape! I spent the entire morning trying to decipher your mysterious, back-to-front talking. How did you get it right?! All I can think is that the left-hand spool wasn't properly pushed into its pin, but was sitting too high, so that track three recorded onto track one and vice versa. I'll try again tomorrow to see if I can work something out. And on Monday or so I'll send you another tape – along with a blank one so you can make a new recording. Meanwhile, please write me what you said!

By the way: I shall in all likelihood be here until 7 July. You can thus post me letters until Wednesday the 3rd. After that? I don't yet know. Perhaps Johannesburg if there's enough space at Naas Steenkamp's place, and if Anton's over his cold by then. Thereafter, I *may* travel down to the Cape; but it doesn't look likely – though I'm going to *try*, because God knows, child, I miss you. I'm so depressed tonight.

This afternoon I was with Dekker, but he's a hard nut to crack. He did, however, indicate he's not unsympathetic to *Lobola*. Meanwhile, other people's reactions are typical of Potchefstroom: the *head* of the Afrikaans department (Prof. [Hertzog] Venter) said straight out he had read the book up to page 42 and then thrown it away. Immoral. Confused. And (isn't this strange!) uncalvinistic. These are the people who guide our students. One of the theology professors got as far as page 16 and then burnt the book in his fireplace. (I must send him "Sinte Brandaan"!) All of it of course ironically interesting; *and* amusing. It's just that one feels so oppressed by the thought that if the light has turned to darkness, how big might the darkness actually be?

More pleasant: I found an interesting, though often naive *The Psychology of Sex* (Oswald Schwarz) – thus not the one you showed me at [Desmond] Windell's place. He offers the following insights, among others, that seem more philosophical than psychological (and are therefore perhaps true?): "Sex love means insatiable participation in the existence of the beloved. Love is not a state which can be reached and in which our longing comes to rest: love is perpetual striving, unending uncertainty and insecurity, an everlasting act of creation." I'm actually quoting this because of the beautiful Indian myth he cites to illustrate his argument: at first the God of Love – Anangarange – tried to interfere in an argument between Siva and his wife, whereupon Siva burnt him to death. He was allowed to live again, but without a material body. From that day on he could gain form only via, and during, the embrace of two lovers. (Thus his name, Anangarange, which apparently means: "Form of the formless".) Another case of: "the third who lay in our embrace"! Lovely, isn't it, my little woman-girl-child?

He has a rather interesting belief about morality: the complete fulfilment of "sleeping together" cannot occur unless there is full surrender on both sides, and therefore full sincerity (it's pretty obvious!); therefore: "sexual enjoyment means ultimate truthfulness; thus the body becomes the guardian of the essential morality of sex" – an angle people (or I) don't normally consider. In the end it confirms what we've known for a long time: how delightfully important, how indispensable, the body is. For me, one of the most grotesque things about

Christianity has always been the way it misjudges the central role of the "flesh".

I bought myself an anthology of *Beat Poetry*, but I'm not overly impressed. I return time and time again to the Brown Bible. And your little volume.

Little girl-person, Godly-good thing, tonight my longing is insuppressible. I want to be with you. To be quiet, just be with you. But eventually also *in* you, not just a small bit, but a big bit; and deep, in the absolute happiness of this being-one together. And I want to see you, your coy, fearless little body, one-and-all affirmation, saying yes, with your happy eyes, the challenge of your breasts, and the invitation of your provocative little mound.

Enumeration doesn't do it. Neither do words – on paper, or spoken, or thought. I am now going to do the only thing I can: "sleep" with you; *now*. And I'll send a little drop on the page along with this letter.

With love,
Your André.

Saturday evening, 29 June 1963

Dear Treasure-child who writes so beautifully and who was so catty
about the MS,

I am already on page 127 where you write about Sylvia's obscenely
naked white arms and just then I loved you so much that I first had to
come and chat a few more lines. You'll get your MS back next week, I
can't help it if I've been so horribly busy; I've specially pushed aside my
home[work] proofs to read a bit of *Die Ambassadeur* and if I don't then
post you a letter tomorrow I'll never hear the end of my desertion. As
if I am not *always* thinking of you *my lamb*. The ambassador himself
is not quite human for me yet, perhaps because I am looking for you
in him and I can't find you; Nicolette is lovely now in the second part.
Just don't be self-pitying about her getting cold. Sharper. She's *good*.

I'm sorry I was so horrible over the phone in not asking how it's
going with your sinus and other ailments. I don't like the idea of electrical treatment, sounds too much like Christie to me! What do they
do, exactly?

I also don't like "psychological treatment" – Fall, fall, balloon, in
Soapsoup Street ...! Let me know whether you know that *beautiful*
poem, if not, I'll try to get you a copy; Uys is so angry with me that I
don't really want to phone him for it, and on top of it all I might get
Jack's voice on the other end too. The only honourable thing I can do
now is to stay far out of Jack's way.

His letter yesterday was so terrible and gloomy. "Oh I've made so
many mistakes," he says, and that I mustn't answer him, that he will
always love me, "and I love Simone too". Thank God and you for your
letter, which arrived at the same time, and the naughty telegram that
made me cross and within five minutes made me laugh non-stop for ten
minutes right in front of Simonetta's surprised eyes. Tried to telegraph
you this morning but the bladdy old post office officials are so dense,
they didn't even know where Potchefstroom is and honestly expected
me to tell them. So, after much struggling I got hold of your number and

prayed that your parents would just think it was the newspaper again.

Still want to tell you that Babel [Abel] Coetzee sent my money – thank you. And also thank you for the "permission" for the "little sleep" in yesterday's delightful letter. I haven't made use of it yet – was too shocked last night – you know the association with Jack lasted so long – six years, as friends and otherwise. Life is a brackish moat … Hence my date-address: because the old Castella is suddenly so quiet and strange without

you
Without Chris
Without Jack.

But tonight I'm completely cheerful, and am enjoying *Die Ambassadeur* so much; although I wish you'd given me a clearer copy. Get yourself new carbon paper.

Liefsteling, you must see our little flat. It's even got carpets now – and a [?], so middle-class-comfort and eight plates and a shiny little table for inside.

Simone is naughty – healthy now – and has developed a new thing that makes me react immediately, a thing I can't *stand* in anyone: the sulk. I have no weapon against it and it drives me *mad*. And tomorrow we're going to fetch the *Sunday Slimes* to see your lovely portrait in it – I have been photo-less for two days now – except for the colour one, and the *Pot-Pourri* in my diary and the "know-it-all" one. And we're going to look at your beautiful name that'll be there so unreal, and read all your lies.

By the way, saw Mrs [Juliana] Bouws and Freda [Linde], HAUM "has no objection against" us recording together, so, that'll happen. I must go and record again soon, and this time I'm including "Towenaar" ["Magician"], and I'll say: *For André*.

You must find out what your mom knows, it's horrible to think that this may have contributed to your dad's illness, try to find out somehow. But I don't think so, André. In the meantime, the "stasis" of your other life is – a little – sometimes – frustrating. So badly want to come to you. There is still such a long-distance loneliness ahead. But at least you look after me so well with your absolute encircling abundant love. My darling, my strong man who can *do*, and who *is*, so astonishingly many things. 'Night to you. I'm going to sleep now – guess with what? – *Optimists in Africa* – which I'm still editing, too terrible, *a disgusting book* though just one of my many *musts*.

I love you, my André. Look after yourself well, you are a very precious person.

Love darling,
Your Ingrid.

PS: Come in July. I miss you. IJ.
PPS: Still haven't seen *Rook en Oker*. Thank you for your missionary work in this direction. IJJ?

First two parts finished (*Sunday five o'clock*). Captivated. Go further. To hell with other work. Bravo!

{Your letter was inside *Tristia* with its lovely inscription. I'm not going to say thank you again. I was happy. Babs.}

———————

Potchefstroom
Sunday afternoon, 30 June 1963

Dearest child,

In the background I can hear scintillating Beethoven – but the rest of the family's gathered there and I have therefore withdrawn to the bedroom; I had to dig out a space for myself among the nappies and books and baby bottles and all the other essential mess that accumulates around one. Also had to switch the light on, even though it's just four o'clock – it's cold and miserable outside. The kind of day I'd like to spend lying with you on "our" bumpy little bed with the buttons that keep digging into my back; with a volume of poetry in hand and a bottle of red wine next to the bed; also: a pack of cigarettes (ash on the chair and floor); tangled clothes on the bed opposite; a bit of sun peeping through the gaudy curtain – and every now and again my big cold foot on your tummy.

One simply has to escape sometimes – more so in these sterile circumstances, aggravated by a flu-like cold. And Anton's just ill. Last night I went and slept in a different room with him, the poor little thing. "Sleep" turned out to be more of a wish than a reality. (To sleep, to sleep, perchance to dream ...!)

Thank you, darling, for your unexpected phone call yesterday. It's a mercy I wasn't home at twelve-thirty, otherwise the call would have been within earshot of everyone and you wouldn't have understood why I was being so businesslike! But as it turned out, it was a ray of sunlight. Most precious you, I would so love to be with you to help you fight off the tristesse. What I don't understand is why Jack had to *write* – or is he temporarily away from the Cape?

There is so little I can do, from a distance, to help and comfort you effectively. But maybe it'll lift your spirits to hear I've decided *definitely* to come to the Cape – in about two weeks' time. Probably for no more than five days; and it looks like the rest of the family will be coming, too – but they'll be staying with friends. Let's rather not upset ourselves at this stage about problems. What matters is that I'm *coming*; that I'm going to be with you in your homely little castle – and that it's all just around the corner. I think we'll be leaving for Johannesburg this coming Saturday to spend the weekend there; then, by about Tuesday (the 9th) we'll be back in Grahamstown. And hopefully Friday (the 12th) I'll be knocking on your door, and coming in, and *in*.

That bladdy old Mouse/Rat [Maish Levin] went and dragged out a whole bottom-drawer of lies for all the world to see – the nonsense that APB declined *Lobola*, and that I supposedly said: "They want to make an example of me." I've now finally decided: from now on I say nothing but "No comment" to this bugger. And I sent a strong letter of protest to the [*Sunday*] *Times* itself. I'm really sick and tired of this kind of lying. And he's incapable of using your name without tacking on the tail of your father. The only small bit of satisfaction in the whole business was that we got to be quite close to each other in print! (Next time, let's hope, both our photos will be there, below a big black headline about who's going to be whose future son-in-law!)

I spend a lot of time looking at the Hout Bay pictures. I'll be sending them soon – if you promise to send me the others! A few *beautiful* ones. Otherwise, always, *Rook en Oker* –

Thus, from page to page,
I find you many times in many terms.

Hopefully I'll be in Johannesburg on Tuesday and Wednesday as well – mainly to visit Bartho and company, and to discuss *Die Ambassadeur* with Van Wyk Louw (did I tell you? – he said he wanted to "work through" the whole MS with me). Maybe I'll pick up some inspiration there; the last few days have been full of that old doubt and near-despair, all over again: will I ever get anything written that can stand wonderfully free out in the sun and be *good* without any reservations? Am I able to write something that's worth the effort? Everything I commit to paper looks so worthless, so ephemeral. And I'm so *tired*, my girl, so sick and tired of the idea of "scandal success" that's begun to cleave to everything I do. That damn Chris [Barnard] went and soiled even *Sempre* with the smell of a pit-latrine.

Everything keeps coming back to the same yearning: to get *away*, somewhere (but away from *what*?) – everything's so vague! – just a place where I can be with you in complete honesty and purity and vulnerability. But each time some vile "drel" gets dragged along, as one of the *Tristia* poems puts it. Everywhere, disillusionment, limitation, the Sartrean hell ("other people") that stands in one's way and taints one.

Child, darling, now you can see everything I seek from you! Luckily I have the certainty (with "proof"!) that such light and grace does in fact reside in you.

Don't concern yourself too much with my reams of self-accusation. One sometimes needs this kind of "dark time" and much of the time – as now – the cause is merely physical: a thick head and a sore throat!

I follow you (during these idle days) continuously on your neat little daily round: go to work, eat, work, fetch Simone, go home. I try looking over your shoulder as you proofread, and if no one's looking, I kiss you softly on one of your ear lobes, or lightly touch one of your lovely little breasts. At night I help you feed Simone and put her to bed; I eat asparagus (and boiled eggs) with you; finally I put *you* to bed. And when you sleep … oh, the moment you fall asleep, *then* …! You wouldn't know, my sweet-faced cherub.

Wait for me; lovely, smooth little animal, with eyes like a long journey from silence and wild regions:

> My girl I appoint you with an appointment …
> And I charge you that you be patient and
>   perfect till I come
> Till then I salute you with a significant look
>   that you do not forget me.

With love, and love, and love,
André.

Monday morning.

My angel-devil girl,

This is just to say thank you for the letter I've just received, before going off to post yours. I'm so happy to hear about Jan and company's "decent" attitude; especially now that Chris is away, you'll need them. That bladdywell Bill and Ena [W.A. de Klerk and his wife Ena] ("we" are allowed a little gossip). I must write to the man now in any case about the Judas-gift he gave me that memorable evening (his pretentious little drama). I wish I could get hold of the book for review – one

118

could "go to town" on it: it's been a long time since I've read such a putrid piece of work. In fact: naively childlike. Anyway, concerning the matter he wants to hear more about, I won't say a single word. Not even to berate him. He can do his own guessing from now on.

Dearest, please go to Koos and have a look at our photos. And let me know how they came out. I must still send you Windell's book. In fact, I must post everyone's books: the parcels have already been made up, but I keep forgetting to buy string so I can secure them.

Take care of yourself, little child, my lazy leopard. Keep yourself tightly shut – until I say "Open, Sesame!" again.

Yesterday's dark mood has gone; the sun's shining weakly; and later I'll be making you a tape.

With all my love,
Once more (and always) yours.

———————

Castella
Tuesday, 2 July 1963

Dearest little treasure,

Opperman probably knew what he was talking about all those years ago when he said, "Met die jare word die kamer / Daagliks onher-bergsamer". Heavens, how one's associations jump around, it's absurd, writing this down I'm thinking of Aunt Gertie's "volume of poetry" – why? "Buite agter 'n miershoop lê / die maer lyk van Eugène Marais" and I remember that I left *this* green monster behind somewhere – took it out of the Press this afternoon, determined to get it to Maskew Miller – then bumped into a friend and had a bite with him – so it's probably still lying around in a café somewhere. If her immortal work were lost …!

But I started off with the room that's becoming so inhospitable. I'll go through hell until something happens. In the past five days I haven't *actually* spoken to a single person – acquaintances and such perhaps, hurried, somewhere or other, for, at most, half an hour or so. Because even when I called you on Saturday, friends had just arrived – I was using their open house, when they came in I went to the bathroom and lay down to chat, and then left them a bit of money after the usual unavoidable this, that and the other. And with a friend today also just skated on the surface – he asked me straight out whether he could come and sleep with me tonight – not that he's ever managed this – but I enjoyed leading him up the garden path by telling him I've been promised to the divine De Lima – wonderful poet "who is currently in SA" …!!!

Darling, thank you for your despondent letter – with the secrets! – God, child, what are we going to do? I am in the same mood this evening – I just don't feel up to this abandonment … naturally, and most importantly, not abandoned by you, but this longing for *direct human contact* – and I don't mean sexual again, do you hear! And the long weekend lies ahead – one idea, one word.

Posted off your MS – (so far) made a few notes, which I will send along with the rest – have already said, utterly gripped, in parts a sluggish pace through Paris – WATCH AND PRAY. As a whole, *impressive* in the true sense of the word. Nicolette – lovely now – I've completely absorbed into myself, and eagerly look forward to the revelation of *herself*, which *must be* the big revelation, so far, from the outside, she is beautifully and meaningfully perceived. I find I'm in a *hurry* now to get to *her*. And in a way also to the ambassador, but there's still a fair bit about him in the pages ahead. My criticism will *not* of course be literary, but rather human. What I am looking for is development (nice in *Die Ambassadeur*), unfolding, and, finally, revelation. With Erika I don't fully chime (see your marriage); feel she must write in a far more *motivated* way from Italy, *like this* – maybe knows about Nicolette, female *intuition* perhaps more than knowledge; Nicolette also *her* ideal or something like that … connection. So far, she is right and is necessarily at her core an isolated lonely figure but must eventually join the whole: to write is to lie, in poetry more so than in prose. Your *lie* of *God* I don't understand. Man has, after all, inherited mortality. But I am so bladdy proud of you. In the APB window they've made a bit of a change – you're now right in the middle, with your ugly photo, and a whole lot of books around you. See they cut us horribly in the *Sunday Times*. I said a *lot* more, about your *translations* too, of course, about which I *phoned three times*. Probably keeping it for next Sunday. Darling, darling, I can't write to you tonight: just want to say hello to you because you said Wednesday is the last day I should post anything. Hope you got the tape sorted out, glad you're leaving Potch ... phone to let me know where you are, and André, come TO CAPE TOWN. I need you.

Love and love,
Ingrid.

PS: Last night finally made use of the "permission" and longed even *more*. I.
PPS: Also cried. IJJ.

Cape Cultural Circle: Please answer this immediately, should have asked ages ago – they want to know whether you will be here on Monday 23 September and whether you would kindly address them in English. Topic: *Novel and Taboo* or any topic you prefer. Pretty please, darling – let me have dates for your visit in September in any case, for other programmes too. As usual, I forgot to ask you three weeks ago. The secretary of the group is here now – they really are very nice.

Love – be good – keep well: permission – that's for Friday night.
Your Ingrid.

Potchefstroom
Thursday, 4 July 1963

Oh my lovely little girl,

Just to isolate myself for a few minutes with you is a mercy in itself; it's become all but impossible to have any time alone. Anton is so ill he spends most of the time niggling, and there're a hundred and one little trifles that keep one busy. I've also got a good old flu-cold myself that's made my voice disappear almost completely. Etcetera, ad nauseam.

But despite all this I don't feel depressed this morning. How could I? For two days now I've been looking forward to the chance to write again. Not that I have all that much to say – it's just the *fact* of conversing on paper.

Meanwhile – and this, naturally, is why I didn't write yesterday or the day before – I've been to Johannesburg, twice. Had wonderful conversations with my old friend Naas (Steenkamp), who will strike you as a fascinating person and has in fact given me the sharpest commentary yet on *Die Ambassadeur*. (And guess what, by the way? You win, I think: the title's going to be *Die Ongedurige Kind*!) I gave Naas just the slightest sense of what's going on between me and you. He sighed – because he knows from his own parents how hellish this kind of thing can be – and said nothing. He would never offer an opinion "out of turn". It's precisely for this reason that one can talk openly wih him. I hope to get a chance to do that this weekend.

Otherwise I spent quite a bit of time chatting to Chris Barnard and Bartho. Bill of course wrote to Bartho immediately after the party to pass on his gossip – bladdy old shrew! *But*: to my surprise I find these people a lot more discreet, more kindly disposed than the Cape Clique. Their point of departure is: "that's your business". Chris especially spoke with an open heart – because, I think (among other reasons), things between him and Annette aren't going all that well (or am I gossiping, now, too?!); and this time we really "found" each other. For the first time, Bartho and I also managed to reach out to one other (we were helped, maybe, by a few brandies!) – and that was an experience to be thankful for. He's a lovely person.

By the way: *Rook en Oker* was delayed yet again when the works manager at the printers died of a sudden heart attack. But they're swearing high and low they'll have the book ready by the end of the week; with delivery *hopefully* before the end of next week, my poor lovely little girl. (I have already ordered five copies to give to friends!)

Yesterday I finally met Van Wyk Louw: a soft, lovable, shortish person with sharp, teasing eyes. We spent an hour and a half talking about *Die Ambassadeur*. I think I know quite well now what I want to change in the MS. The big issue, however, is whether I can get it all done in time for publication this year. I don't want to work in an overhasty manner – I've done enough of that in the past! – but I do still want to have it out this year. (I'm naturally also awaiting *your* opinion!)

And that's about all the "news" I have; life here remains frustratingly monotonous. The path that you know so well, and so bitterly: more and more arguments between me and Estelle; and, even worse: more and more silences, concentrating increasingly on the unavoidable bits of dialogue only, and sleeping separately – even separate bedrooms most of the time (the "reason" being so we can take turns with Anton at night) …

I went and chatted to an advocate friend about the whole process of divorce (told him I needed the information for a novella! – and then suddenly realised that I might indeed, at a later stage, take something from this information. Or is it terrible and heartless that one can be so objective about one's own life and suffering that one always remains aware of "literary possibilities"? Perhaps. And yet it's also a kind of mercy, because it helps you orientate yourself continuously in relation to what's going on, so that you're always trying to look and live more deeply than merely on the surface. If you were to allow yourself simply to get lost in the daily chaos, you would lose your greatest claim to being human. Even if you experienced everything *under* the surface as meaningless, that experience too would necessarily be meaningful. Paradox! But unavoidable).

To return to the matter at hand: he explained that there doesn't have to be any physical "leaving" of one another for a divorce to be granted. Also, that everything can be completed within three months after the first summons; and that it costs about RI10 to RI20, which is not too bad.

My darling, my *indispensable* thing, thank you for your beautiful letter yesterday. You must try and be patient with our little girl's "sulking"! I know, it drives me mad, too. But apprently it's best simply to ignore them. And she's a lovable child, after all. (It's not just Jack who loves her!)

And –! Monday I finally succeeded in getting your tape to play. What happened was that you recorded it on tracks three and four instead of one and two, and all the machines we managed to find here play only on one and two. But then we tracked down a good one – and I sat listening to your voice with great delight. (It was *not* a radio voice.) Actually it gave me much clarity and new insight: especially what you said about finding the balance between that which is transient (about which I'm so sensitive) and that which is lasting (which is an irrational thing); and in the midst of everything here looking so gloomy, it was "just right"; so true ("singular and old") that everything in the mosaic began to take shape again.

I'll try to make a tape for you tomorrow. And send you some money for another one – and for the phone call last Saturday. I don't want you to have to spend your precious pennies on these things, too.

The wind is blowing outside – such a tedious, nagging, August wind, blowing the dry leaves up and down; the air is grey; the dead tips of the palm-tree fronds are shivering disconsolately, and an old newspaper is fluttering on the lawn. But around the corner, somewhere, a bird continues to sing (whence would he have lost his way in this cold weather?). So, sing your serenity into me – that will make everything worth the effort. A few poems are rumbling inside me. It could still take quite a while – this kind of thing is so unpredictable. But I know they're on their way, at least. Also, is "Towenaar" finished yet, since you say you're going to include it for HAUM? I want to *see* it – and *hear* it on tape. In the course of a letter, in the midst of other things, I'm not able to say thank you or even tell you how I feel about it. It has to be said with more than words – when I come to you. I can no longer *wait*. This will now probably be a little later than I'd last thought: from about the 17th until, probably, the Monday after that. (It will at least make the shift after September a little shorter!)

Until then: I *miss* you. Ezra Pound will have to help me say what I feel:

> For my surrounding air has a new lightness;
> Slight are her arms, yet they have bound me straitly
> And left me cloaked as with a gauze of ether,
> As with sweet leaves; as with subtle clearness.
> Oh, I have picked up magic in her nearness
> To sheathe me half in half the things that sheathe her.

And now our ritual to keep the "little pentecostal flame" going, a radiant greeting to all your parts – the abundant, honest desire of your small body; the quiet in your eyes, breasts and legs; the kiss of your hands and hair; and the smile of your mouth and your "fugitive little footpath". I want to conjure everything into a new whole, as all the colours of the spectrum together become radiant and white with transparent light.

With love,
Your André.

Potchefstroom
Saturday, 6 July 1963

My one and only,

Today is not a writing day. Not for want of desire, because then I'd never do anything but write to you. But today is one of those days when everything is simultaneously so very subtle and so unutterably confused, that words fail to achieve any form. Still, here I am, writing, from a kind of heart's necessity; this is because I hope, at least, that the the mere process of conversing with you – as in the past, on similar occasions – will make things peaceable again.

Don't read anything ominous into this! All I'm trying to say is that my longing, and my need to see you, are now so acute that I'm no longer *satisfied* with anything else.

I received your lovely, depressed letter this morning. Perhaps it's precisely the awareness of *your* desperate loneliness that's making me so restless. That, and the frustration of my two-hour attempt this morning to make you a tape. But the machine – an enormous stereo apparatus in the psychology laboratory – simply refused to produce anything decent; my voice sounds so soft and faint on the tape that I have no choice but to wait until next week Wednesday, when I get back home. (Meanwhile, please write to me there – in Grahamstown – okay?)

About your – *our* – agony, or "distress" in recent times, one should perhaps seek consolation in [Søren] Kierkegaard: "Despair is one of the maladies of which it can be said that it is the greatest misfortune not to have known it ... because the awareness of the spirit can never be achieved but through despair." And *this* experience is impossible on a purely theoretical plane. Schwarz (he of *The Psychology of Sex*) says at the start of his book: "One must *suffer* the laws of things, not only observe them."

This is so precious and enriching in its own right that one doesn't want – or dare – to be without it. To quote Schwarz one last time: "Essential problems of life permit of no solution." I think this is

126

humanity's great blind spot, its error: why do people *want* ready-made solutions? They're not *necessary*; they deny the irrational core of life. Indeed, life is not a calculation that one devises in order to arrive at an answer, where you can write Q.E.D.! (Even Francois in *Lobola* very nearly did this – in the book's first impression, anyway!) Life is simply there to be lived (and *felt*). Once one accepts this certainty, then one has made good progress en route to the vague place called "happiness". (Moreover, people seek "happiness" too abstractly, too distantly, and also too far in the future. It actually lies *here*: here in the yearning and the never-never fulfilment of love; it lies in your tired, happy smile when you, filled with secrets, fall asleep next to me; it lies even in this great longing of ours now that our little flame burns alone between us without its being *physically* renewed every day – like the eternal flame under the Arc de Triomphe. It's in any case bright enough to keep burning between us in our away-from-each-other state.)

Thank you for your provisional comments on the MS. I think your objections to Erika will fall away when you see her "in action" in relation to the ambassador. And Nicolette? I'm going to rewrite quite a lot – and I look forward to discussing this with you in ten days' time (do you realise, just ten days!).

By the way, I could hardly conceal my laughter (and embarrassment) on Wednesday at Van Wyk Louw's when he said: "Tell me, what is the sign that Nicolette sometimes makes? I didn't quite get it."

"The fica sign – against the Evil Eye, or just a challenge to the Unknown."

"But what does it look like?"

And so I had no choice but to make the sign in his direction. (You know: when you stick your thumb through your middle and index finger!) I don't think anyone else has ever made this gesture in the face of the illustrious Louw!

Man … and, by the way: can you feel how the tristesse of this letter's beginning has just *vanished*? I feel radiantly happy, so much that I almost can't write fast enough … yesterday I bumped into Prof. T.T. Cloete, who has just returned from overseas. He lectures Afrikaans and

Dutch literature here and is one of our finest critics. Only Rob is more or less his equal. (You might have read some of his work in *Standpunte*?) Anyway, in the course of our conversation, *Die Blomblaar Is Requiem* [The Petal Is a Requiem by Pieter Venter] came up – and naturally he also thinks it's rubbish (although his judgement of certain writers is not as harsh as mine). I told him, just by the way, that he [Pieter Venter] used to be married to you.

"Goodness," he said, "now one can more easily understand why they got divorced! *Ingrid Jonker's work is so lucid and polished*." Nice, isn't it? And he said this purely on the basis of *Ontvlugting*. I then informed him about *Rook en Oker* – and I wouldn't be surprised if he doesn't prescribe the book here, at a later stage. In any case, he ordered a copy immediately.

Child, girl, little woman: I feel so *proud* when people say such lovely things about you. I'm so hell-bent in love with you. And be warned: when I get there, you're going to say "Hell!" whether you like it or not.

On the beautiful tape you made, you said: "Why are people so afraid of passion? Why do they treat us like children?"

It's *true*. I believe that the masses fear passion because it exposes them to the *freedom* and *honesty* of love. The masses feel safe only on *well-trodden* terrain, and love is terra incognita – "Ultima Thule". And: children? Perhaps this is actually a compliment. Doesn't the Bible say one must have the heart of a child to pass through the eye of a needle?

Against my will and best intentions, I must start saying goodbye, because the house is beginning to wake up from its afternoon nap and my short period of merciful solitude with you is over. But now I feel satisfied and happy and fulfilled, because all this time I've been – and am – so clearly aware of you. I hope the long weekend won't be too dismal, my little angel. Make a few tapes (I'll send a small cheque). And I'll phone you soon. We might leave Jhb on Monday – but "everything is uncertain": I'll first have to see whether I can find a discreetly positioned telephone.

The Cape Cultural Circle: Okay, for your sake, then. I think I'll be with you from 21–30 Sept. Alas too late for your birthday, but we can postpone the celebration just a little (you will in any case have your second birthday on the 23rd!).

I'm going to see if I can't siphon off some of the money from the *Huisgenoot* articles to pay for your things at the Bantry Bay hotel. I find it just too awful that you should have to live without your stuff.

Out of curiosity: who's the presumptuous (and mysterious!) "friend" who wanted to sleep with you and who had to make way for De Lima?! ("I appoint you with an appointment …"!)

Darling, dearest, smallest, loveliest: be sweet and light; I'm coming, and I miss you. I "sleep" with you far more than you might imagine!

With all my love,
André.

Are the little chick's tail-feathers starting to grow again?

––––––––––

Castella
Monday, 8 July 1963

Darling of the letter and the phone call and Hout Bay and darling of Franschhoek, Castella and at Koos's and lots more at Bill's,

Thank you for your letter, which arrived out of the blue on that god-forsaken family day, and the phone call that was such a struggle – we've had beautiful days here (as far as nature is concerned), and I've had to get out with Simone. Just after the phone call, went to Marjorie and them for a meal – she can be pretty venomous – sometimes. Jack says they're jealous of me – now I think maybe they are! He told me about the house he would build me – my god! André! I almost cried.

Meanwhile, this quadrangle still provides a lot of entertainment. One remark by a well-meaning *artist friend* is as follows: "You cannot break up André and Estelle's home and then go back to Jack, who is carrying on with a nineteen-year-old but maybe only for a screw." Child, if this remark wasn't good enough for the theatre one might lock oneself up in one's flat and never dare come out again. My sense of humour wasn't immediately accessible, and I was annoyed. But almost as funny was one of Ouma's letters to an auntie (years ago): "A wool farmer, angered, called on my daughter ..."

And then there's Bill's outrageous letter and of course one wants to laugh at it before rage and the sense of the dramatic gain the upper hand ... If you need any further information about the Cilliers-Jonker family, you can go and find out about my mother at Valkenberg any time. "Mad from loneliness" and driven by the "small murderous world" ...! But now I'm probably just bitter and every person probably just gets what they deserve, or so the Old Testament teaches us. The "item" concerning the letter to Bartho I've mentioned to M., so that Cape Town can get it properly wrought and welded and embellished tomorrow, after that I spake not a word, and went off to read a mysterious book. Darling André, do I sound bitter? But you will probably understand. Until you arrive, I'm going to stay here in my flat and be good. You say that my last letter was "despondent" but I'm sure there's at least one you didn't receive ... probably only arrived after you left. I'm still reading *Sempre.*

All that bothers me of course is *us*. But I find *Pot* better. Admit that I've already been spoilt by the lovely *Pot-Pourri*! Wrote you something about *Die Ongedurige Kind* (bravo!) in the letter you didn't get. As for *Rook en Oker*, well that heart attack was of course amusing to me at the time. A thing like that would of course happen to *my* book. Glad you found comfort in the little tape. Sometimes I chat to you on our "home tape" because "between stone and stone, and between human and human / how terrible, God, the silence and the reticence".

Do you know, darling (my handwriting really *does* look just like yours now!), sometimes (today) I think like Van Wyk that "die dood is mooi". As in the past, one beauty, familiarity – know, forgive, accept. But that's when I get SCARED, let's get a drink and talk, people, have courage, evil will change into good ... (!!!) And for me those (people) are so lekker-Afrikaans. Also don't want to *think* any more. When you hear from me again, it will be my *own body*.

Ingrid.

ps: Which suddenly makes me think of these rather good lines from [Pieter] Venter (and inspired by the paranoia that every good artist must have and which you and I, darling person, can now develop beautifully!):

> My lords, drink of me, no spoon is necessary.
> The trial will continue
> and end
> like a scorpion tail
> There will be further evidence later.

And so to bed. As you say in your letter, one always thinks (it's such a covert, guilty thought, always, in every experience, almost immediately, in "literary" terms). I know this, of course. The corpse isn't even cold yet, then … It *would be* disgusting, should we write a poem: Poetry, the Vulture …? The desolate, lonely walking away of a person, the genuine grief about it, and at the same time THE THING. How I laughed, my André, when you quote Van Wyk Louw: "die drel trek oral saam …" Went and read the poem … But it's probably not something to feel guilty about, just part of an inevitable self-awareness.

Till Wednesday, then.
God bless, God bless.
I.

Tuesday: Better this morning! This dew-ripe innocent grey dawn!
IJ.

pps: Tomorrow back in the deafening machinery.

{Simone has neatly sealed all my airmail envelopes. Perhaps just as effective, without anything inside.}

———————

Grahamstown
Tuesday, 23 July 1963

My little darling,

Just two days – and already I'm caught up in the unavoidable daily business of living, the river that like the proverbial "show" simply must go on (To where? Until when? And why? Ours is not to reason why). When our little paragraph gets written one day, our three months might well look like no more than a sentence in parenthesis – but it'll be one of the most meaningful sentences of all, bringing with it a new dimension and changing the course and meaning of that paragraph forever.

Ironic: the ambassador also only had three months! Or is it actually true that three is a kind of holy number? And holiness, say the exegetes, means something like "seclusion". Or, perhaps: exception. In which case our three months were precisely that: a small piece that splits off from predictable time ("Render us immortal for a single hour"!).

As to what lies ahead, I know nothing and I dare not hope or predict anything. One has to become quite humble in one's predictions! Still, I don't want to think about the future as empty – that would be too defeatist, in advance. Rather, then, welcome the kind of tristesse upon which Françoise Sagan based her novel. By the way, do you know the Éluard poem from which the title *Bonjour Tristesse* is taken? It reads – translated very poorly – like this:

Vaarwel tristesse
Gegroet tristesse
Jy is geskryf in die lyne van die uitspansel
Jy is geskryf in die oë wat ek liefhet

Jy is nie geheel-en-al misère nie
Want die armste lippe verraai jou
Met 'n glimlag
Gegroet tristesse
Liefde van die geliefde liggame
Mag van die liefde
Wie se beminlikheid orentkom
Soos 'n monster sonder liggaam
Ontnugterde hoof
Tristesse skone aangesig.

[Farewell tristesse
Hello tristesse
You are written in the lines of the heavens
You are written in the eyes I love
You are not poverty absolutely
The poorest lips betray you
With a smile
Greetings tristesse
Love of beloved bodies
Power of love
Whose lovableness arises
Like a bodiless monster
Disillusioned head
Sadness beautiful face.]

At the moment everything remains static; anything is possible – but nothing is an accomplished fact, and nothing, above all, is certain. There is a mass of work to be done (sometimes it's a mercy to be busy), increasing financial worries, and the daily to-do with this, that and the other. But in between, actually a quiet background to all of this, are the things that mean so incalculably much: your voice, your eyes and hands, your restfulness in the white nightdress – ready for anything, timid, certain, undiscovered earth, suspected little paradise, unconditionally full of love; there is, also, Simone's imperturbably false voice singing in the background; early daylight through a crack in the bright yellow curtains; the abstracted gaze in your eyes when you look out over the sea from a hotel room; even the manner in which you say "God" –! The tears, and the stirring of your body against mine, your breath, the swish of your hair against my face.

Little child, my own little child, it's *true*: "two who once have lain together / are forever almost one". I wander forth and carry you with me in my blood. And I worry about your loneliness in that empty little castle at night, not to mention your grey working day. I know well, very well, that everything I have inflicted upon you in this process, and in everything, will always remain with me as an immediate sense of distress and an inescapable destiny.

But you, *you*: that's not something one can say thank you for, little Cocoon; it's something for which one must *be* thankful: a lasting condition. But not passively – positive, creative, even though it's never without a little nostalgia. (Like [Édith] Piaf's "Milord" song in El Picador –! Such a neverending "good morning fiiiiish" to light and life, which in future I will "recognise at first sight".) A sort of sustained birth-rebirth because we loved each other and were together – and, because we *were: are*.

Therefore: in the uncertainty of the future, in light as well as dark, in the daily trifles and the few joys, in doubt and in the moments of recognition in between – in everything you are mine, and always, and in everything, I love you. The epigraph I wrote at the front of *Sempre* must now become true: "Allow me to experience love even though I may not possess it."

Unlike your ouma, I cannot pray for you. But I can try to live so that life itself is a kind of prayer, a reflection, a kind of thankfulness, love.

Protect yourself, precious, remain pure, stay radiant, keep on being yourself – girl, child, and woman, shamelessly one and the same.

Let me know immediately if we're going to have a baby.

Look after your little chick.

Give Simone a kiss from me.

134

Love me. And try to forgive me for what I've had to inflict upon you without ever wanting to do anything but make you happy. I love you.

Still,
Your André.

Friday, 26 July 1963

WRITERS PRAYER LORD MAKE US BREAD FROM THE STONES LOVE = COCOON

{Answer. 27/7: Writer's prayer or poet's? Remember the invisible umbilical cord that can never be severed. Love. André.}

Castella
Sunday night, 28 July 1963

André darling,

A week of a thousand different emotions – or different facets of the same emotion, a week of "herinnering, o pragtige skip ..." A morning at 7:30 in the Gardens, still misty, darling child, fresh, lovely, a pool of naked water before the Gallery, and a rebellious belief that "everything will be all right" whatever happens, and a stubborn belief in goodness and in the "benevolence" of your body. Really only began on Wednesday morning to heave a sigh after the knockout blow – Uys once said: "Oh well, now anything can happen, M. gave me the death blow." Simple memories, the handling of a book, or your woollen jersey (the hairy one) by my head when I go to sleep and wake up, like that second day. And all those crazy small things will probably be nothing more than an accent on a letter in our little sentence, won't they?

Thank you for Friday's beautiful letter – simultaneously hurts and

135

heals, actually. Thank you for your telegram, and thank you for your pills and your sponge. This time you forgot fewer things, but you left far more behind. As long as there is hope there is love, and while it's there I unlearn nothing, love is, as you know, too precious.

Thank you for *Bonjour Tristesse*. You mustn't worry about me. Like you, I say that (see *Bonjour Tristesse*) to myself, and I live like that. But I didn't, for instance, take dreams into account:

> Ik heb vannacht met u gewandeld
> in de dove lanen van de slaap
> en nu het morgen is geworden
> is er niets veranderd
> dan dat die twee, die in de nacht tesaam
> volkomen bij elkander waren
> mij weer alleen gelaten hebben in de morgen
> en samen verder zijn gegaan.

Last night, e.g., Jack and I went to see some people in Llandudno: I couldn't get far enough away from the city and the daily doing and talking. We slept in the same room – the usual test of my *refusal* – but this was accepted. When, half-asleep, I heard something moving and asked, "Darling, what is it, my André?" the door slammed shut; but when he came back in the early hours, he was calm and friendly, we walked ten miles in the foul weather, next to sand dunes and mountain paths, swam twice in the ice-cold water and had a lovely peaceful supper, without anything being mentioned again regarding my enquiry. Now I am liberatingly physically tired, and want to fall into bed, and I am not unhappy. And before I carry on writing, because it is already twelve o'clock – I want to make some tea and take a bath. With your lovely sponge. So you see, God is a God of grace. Love keeps waiting, darling.

12.30 am. Beautiful blue pyjamas with the memory of your secrets and the colour of absence. And outside it's raining a grey hell. I suppose I should also tell you some news – such as it is. Chris sends many regards and thank yous for the book. He and Jannie [Gildenhuys] apparently "enjoyed" us "terribly" that intimate Saturday afternoon. He brought me a milk tart and listened to your lovely recording of "Groet in Bruin" ["Salute in Brown"] and oh, the restless child. Uys beginning to talk again, though somewhat businesslike: apparently has been meaning to talk to me. Wrote you a note the other day – lying here in my desk with all the evidence – that sombre Thursday: "Lord, you have hedged me behind and before." The whole thing sounds far too light-hearted now: will show it to you one day. My telegram: surely it can be poet or writer (prose)!

I've started to write poems – about the "stones". The form isn't good enough yet.

And I'm looking after my little chick.

And I gave Simone a little kiss from you.

And I love you. Very much.

And "hierdie las van reën wil ek nie sien nie

Op die water van jou voorkop

Op die water sonder bodem van ons eenheid."

And I'll let you *know*, on the eighth.

Be happy, and patient, tender love, good man.

Your Ingrid and Cocoon.

ps: Why do you write to me *ordinary* mail?
Funny!

Love, my little treasure,
I Jonker.

Grahamstown
Thursday, 1 August 1963

God, thank you, most precious little cocoon,

For yesterday's letter. The last few days, especially since the weekend, I've not known which way to turn. I try to work just to keep everything under control – mind over matter – but I feel overwhelmed all the time by the finality of everything (and the impossibility of finality). The night before last I wanted to phone you (Estelle now works three nights a week in the library, and the awareness of an empty house becomes too much for me; then I'm also *physically* aware of my loneliness). But in the end I didn't, mainly because I feared the futility of this inadequate way of communicating. And then, yesterday, your letter arrived. I was already on my way to class and could read only a phrase or two here and there. I can't remember at all what I said to my students after that!

Because, darling: *I love you.*

What you wrote about the Llandudno episode first touched me, then made me rudely, horribly jealous; and finally so amused me that I had to go sit in my study and laugh out aloud. I can just see it happening. Actually it's strange that the same thing hasn't yet happened here, because I wake up with you almost every night, and try to touch you, or talk to you – and then lie awake for hours afterwards just longing.

All in all, our three months are actually a poem. As Robert Frost (who has suddenly "opened up" for me) says in an essay on poetry: "Poetry is a momentary stay against confusion" – and that's so *exactly* what our little island of togetherness is. (He also says: "It begins with delight and ends with wisdom –")

Yesterday I received a lovely little Penguin book, *Modern Poetry from Africa*. And in it I found this piece – "Love Apart" – which was an immediate "fit" (even though it's probably a little sentimental):

138

The moon has ascended between us,
Between two pines
That bow to each other;

Love with the moon has ascended
Has fed on our solitary stems;

And we are now shadows
That cling to each other
But kiss the air only.

Thank you for the clipping about your "The Child". That's the kind of naive, *sincere* commentary that has far more value in the long run – it's more human – than a long literary analysis. And you are a very precious person.

Talking about "The Child": may I send it to a friend in Sweden so he can try to have it published there – in Swedish?

I finally found some time to start revising *Die Ambassadeur*. I've been reworking it quite radically – and enjoying every moment; in fact, working myself half to death. But now I must get those last few pages back U R G E N T L Y !!!!!, you hear? Try to finish reading it this weekend, please, bigbladdyplease.

"News"?

In a certain sense everything's quite neutral here. There's no active resistance from my side, or from hers. It's a kind of "working arrangement"; a surface equability – which can actually be far more exhausting, more sterile than conflict. But it has to be like this. I don't always know just how to pull it all off. So often I feel like throwing in the towel and letting everything just "go to hell" so I can come to you. But one must learn to live with blinkers on, to adapt, prune, and prune even more. Being human does not mean being great or good.

There have been no moves toward physical conciliation yet, not even a single attempt. I don't see my way clear to doing it. You are too full, and fully-fledged, inside of me.

And I've had so many secrets that I wanted to give you, again –!

Maybe the previous ones did in fact reach some "destination"? As I worked things out, there's a *possibility* that Friday's and Saturday's could've made a little baby. We'll know between the 6th and the 8th!

I want to know immediately if you find other – more human – work. I want to know *everything*, even if it hurts me. That also means: everything about Jack.

Silly, silly letter. It's a result of all this deprivation: one is crammed so full with everything that it all becomes incoherent on paper, even fatuous, because one's in a hurry to get everything said.

I am certain of one thing only: after all the straying, and the restlessness, I now feel *happy*, sitting here and conversing with you. Clarity has returned. Because there is always "hope, faith and love". And the greatest always comes last. Has the little chick grown new feathers yet?

Is Simone well behaved?

Are you?

Are you *happy*?

Write everything, everything, child, girl, woman. *My* cocoon.

Your André.

PS: I want to make another tape for you, but I've been looking in vain for the one I gave up on in Potch; and I'm too broke to buy another. (But maybe I can get by for a few days without chocolate and buy a tape after all!) Meanwhile I'll have to project onto my miserable old yellow sponge and at least take a bath with you!

PPS: I include a copy of what I wrote about Uys for the Penguin thing. Give it to him: maybe it'll protect your precious little head from his wrath.

PPPS: I love you.

PPPPS: André.

PPPPPS: Have you realised that your signature, under your letter's PS (IJonker) actually looks like this: Tjanker!? [Cry-baby] (If that's the case: don't, be happy, be light, be free, be *you*.)

PPPPPPS: I have handed out all five *Rook en Oker*s already. They were all received with great *delight*.

A.

―――――――――

Grahamstown
Sunday night, 4 August 1963

My little angel, my loveliest,

A sense of satisfaction tonight, because I have completed a big, intensive shift of revision on *Die Ongedurige Kind*; in the process, I did some drastic rewriting, too.

Since your letter arrived last week, my "emotional curve" has slowly begun to head upwards – mainly as a result of your letter. (The preceding days had been hellishly uncertain.) And now there is, even in our separateness, a certain something that cannot be taken away; I have taken everything up inside me, and it's so much a *part* of me now that I could never lose it. And I'm taking care, even while revising the book, to add little pictures of you: your speckled shoulders, the little freckle high up on your left thigh, the lovable habit you have of twirling a curl around your finger whenever you're sad or upset –

Girlie, I'm so *angry* and sorry about *Rook en Oker*! Bartho has written to say – as he no doubt told you too – that the second run was also pulped because the print was smudged and the upper lines uneven. And now it will apparently take at least another month … But I went and wrote to him immediately (a little presumptuous of me?) and said he should try, now that there's been even more negligence, to make a slight change to the order of poems; for the sake of costs, it will have to be limited to a minimum – and so I proposed only the following: "Liedjie van die Troebadoer" ["Song of the Troubadour"] and "Ramkiekieliedjie" ["Ramkiekie Tune"] should be shifted to part

5 (the "Coloured Songs"); "Die Kind" should be placed in part 3 (together with a group of poems with greater reach and intention); and "L'Art Poétique" must go in part 1, where it should fit well. Do you agree?

And then I unexpectedly received a cheque from the insurance people for the stuff that got stolen during the holiday – see, the police do sometimes help! – and I was able to go and buy planks and bricks to extend my bookshelf along another wall; in the last while my study has begun to look rather miserable with piles of books all over the floor; now one can walk freely again.

God, my love, I shouldn't even write such things, because then I realise anew how much I want to share it all with *you*. Do you know the poem – "Lonely" – by the SA "African" [William] Bloke Modisane?:

it gets awfully lonely,
lonely;
like screaming,
screaming lonely;
screaming down dream alley,
screaming of blues, like none can hear;
but you hear me clear and loud:
echoing loud,
like it's for you I scream.

Especially these days, now that it's getting warmer, the days longer, and the twilight evenings so abundant and full of far-off sounds, I want to go walking hand in hand with you for miles and miles along my pine-tree path; get tired with you; and then lie down on the soft carpet of pine needles, under the trees, to become one with you and the trees and the heavens.

That early morning before Jan and them arrived: I think that was still one of our richest "sharing of secrets". But it's almost impossible to single any one out. The Sunday morning when you started crying when I was still inside you – remember? – was also very intense and irreplaceable; and the afternoon at Chris's – so many moods, so many notes on such a wide range. When I look back I always find myself wondering: is it possible that one can live so much, and so *deeply*, in just three months?

I wish – to the point of bursting, actually – that I could once again come up with a poem. But "my words are too few", I am not a poet, delightful, free, deep, radiant person. *You* are.

I love you so much, so very much. In my thoughts I want to touch you softly again and say goodbye to all of you – salut d'amour!

To your little tummy.

And your soft thighs.

And your tiptopnippletitties.

And your eyes.

And your ears.

And your little chick.

My regards to all that is mine. (Thus also to the poor old leucodendron!)

And, even though we don't belong to each other, let us be each other's. *More*: let us be each other. *Now*. And therefore – always.

I am now – you must please forgive me – going to sleep with you.

With love,
André.

––––––––––

Tuesday, 6 August 1963

My dearest Treasure,

Wrote to you last night but once again it was one of those letters for the desk; and now here in this grey pit I hurriedly try to establish communication ["kommunikatie tref"]. Enclosed the small poem – our moesie-child isn't there, as you will see in the little poem. Sorry. Had begun writing to you to save money for me to slip over the border to Swaziland had things gone differently. Another reason why Swaziland looks so alluring is because I am now truly cornered – should have considered a long time ago that Piet Venter has been lying low and lurking in Johannesburg. He has just sent me an ultimatum: hand Simone over to me, sign the documents … or else! So I went to the lawyer immediately yesterday to let him know that I will defend any case he attempts to bring against me. It'll be horrible if it comes to that, but what does one pay for one's child? Also, thank [Bill] de Klerk for spreading "news" in Johannesburg! But back to our "island".

Thank you, liefsteling, for your letter of Saturday. And so, why were you so jealous? I made my refusal quite clear! I am still Cocoon! In your letter my eyes dwelt on this *yet*: "There have been no moves toward physical conciliation yet". "What a miserable thing man is." For another half an hour this word kept flashing before me, I looked at it as, years ago in our beautiful Hout Bay room, you had looked at "eventide" in Aunt Gertie's poems, and repeated this repulsive word again, once, softly: "eventide". And so on Saturday in the godly golden sun on my way to a swim I said yet yet yet!

You want to know everything about Jack. It would take a book to explain everything, but let us trust each other in some essentials. Jack is dear and friendly and I see him often: unfortunately there are times (like Sunday night from nine to one o'clock) when we have words, he says he doesn't understand and apparently thinks that *we* have an "arrangement" and "you're marking time".

I don't know what to say to him. And now there are still the things in the poem. Our moesie-child! But please tear up my letter rather than your clothes!

I wish clarity would come again – everything of the last three days is so muddled. I wanted to make a little tape for you too and didn't have any money. I wanted to read "Us" to you – it sounds nice on the tape and Mrs Bouws says it's beautiful, but sad. Probably. My book (ridiculous!) has been postponed for another month or two. Bartho said they didn't use "nice Finnish paper" and hadn't cleaned the lead type. Now it has to be reprinted. My six and your six were sent down before he had seen the book.

So! Your *Ambassadeur* is on its way. This last part is brilliant: did you also want to work on that? Why?

Bladdy Barend Toerien was here on Friday night, he has a new volume at the press, said to Jack: "You're too good for her." And that's all the news. Chris [Lombard] got your letter and told me about it, he doesn't really know how to answer! He said I am slightly "disturbed". Almost went MAD the night he was there.

You mustn't be cross with me about this disappointing piece of writing: one can hardly think in this grey little cage. Make me a tape and tell all – you're alone three nights a week now, aren't you, and it's so awful!

And how are things with the papie? And are you generally happy, resigned, or are you rebellious? No, you in fact wrote that there's no resistance there … Stay well and write to me.

Love darling,
Cocoon.

————————

Castella
Wednesday, 7 August 1963

My darling André,

Thank you for your greeting this morning just when I was feeling so grey – like my last letter to you with the poem. You have to use it for *Sestiger*, okay? (The poem.) But is the dedication too personal? If it's still in time for the unlucky *Rook en Oker* you may – since you are now acting as my "business manager"! – send it on to Bartho. But maybe the title should be changed to "So" and the dedication omitted. There are others I can dedicate to you more openly. Yes, liefsteling, I agree with your rearrangement of the verses, although of course in the one case I think that "L'Art

Poétique" should be the last poem – but it doesn't make much difference to me. A friend of mine, Marcelle du Toit, whose judgement I rate highly, thinks some of the love poems are "too sensitive". Writing is just such a delicate affair. Bartho's letter about the reprint actually amused me at this stage. He should just have sent each of the critics a proof copy so that they'd have something by publication date. Wonder whether he thought of that. Hell but it's nice to be able to chat to you for a change! It's not unlikely that you're sitting inside there on the couch reading *Tristia* and getting hungry! And perhaps you'll phone later – it is Wednesday, after all – but you'll be disappointed about the moesie-child. I'd love to hear your voice again – although I play the little recording of Van Wyk's poems so often that I can imitate you perfectly!

Why do you say in your letter you're going to do *this* and then – "forgive me" – just do it! A little red spot of wine has fallen onto my letter, I'm sheltering from the thunder with the heavy red glass and the little castle is clean and tidy, and you're right. Simone's "imperturbably false voice" is singing in the background.

Oh, child! I miss you. Last night I had another one of those relentless evenings with Jack, it was my fault – I was upset about the "court case" – don't let anyone know about it, I don't want Piet to hear that I'm upset, according to Jack that's precisely what he's trying to do. "Terrorise."

André, one can look back and relive, and do you know what I think the biggest secret was? That dark early Sunday morning, when you took me like that and left, do you know that in your letter you spoke about the secrets of Saturday, and forgot about Sunday! Does Nicolette also say secrets? I know "Lonely", he's good. And [M.] Vasalis, or something like that, forgive my Dutch.

Soms als gij zwijgt en door de venster schouwt
grijpt mij uw schoonheid als een wanhoop aan
een wanhoop door geen troost te blussen
niet door te spreken, niet door te kussen
even groot als mijn bestaan en even oud.

146

And later: "Dat gij daar zit, zo buiten mij geboren …" When you talk about "belonging to each other", as if that's different from being one another's, I don't know from a logical point of view what you mean, even less do I now understand your inscription in *Sempre*. Loving is actually the *only* way of owning. Do you know this Walt Whitman? (Beautiful old Walt Whitman, with your beard full of butterflies …)

> I mind how once we lay such a transparent summer morning,
> How you settled your head athwart my hips and gently turn'd over
> > upon me,
> And parted the shirt from my bosom-bare,
> and plunged your tongue to my bare-stript heart,
> And reached till you felt my beard, and reached till you held my feet.

Liefsteling, there is so much that I would like to do with you without looking back, but one also has to live with reality. Still, it is nice to dream about the [?] mountains and the sluggish old Limpopo at night and we would lie there so *lost* in that beautiful old world.

It's going well with the leucodendron. It doesn't get much attention. Little chick is lonely. It's going well with me, I greet you with love with tenderness with longing,

Cocoon.

You don't phone. Mrs Oxley is out. Lay for two hours thinking of you and missing you and wondering …

The loss of the moesie-child happened after exactly one day: Strange! Perhaps disappeared temporarily because of the upset. Man, I miss you so terribly much; hope you aren't horribly frustrated over there because of the phone call: I am! Night, beautiful man, night, and just sleep with me tonight.

Your Ingrid.

I've got Walt Whitman's *Complete Works.* (Or as Breytie [Breyten Breytenbach] would say, I have a golden moon!)

{What's happened to those black-and-white photos? And when are the copies coming? THE WORD LAST!}

—————

Grahamstown
Friday morning, 9 August 1963

Darling, you, cocoon,

It's still early, with watery sun and an agitated wind that blows and comes after one, shredding your insides like an old newspaper that's blown against a bush.

I made a tape for you yesterday afternoon but it was just too late for the post; this means you'll receive this letter and the tape at the same time (the latter at "Castella" when you get home). It's not meant to be excessive. God, what I do give you or *can* give is already so little. I just want to talk with you a little so I can compose myself. Yesterday was another of those upsetting days. First there was the fact that I had to look after Anton the whole afternoon, from two to six, while I already had more work on my plate than I could deal with. (And if I resist then I'm apparently "not prepared to do my fair share".) I'm always happy to look after him; he and I love each other *so* much. But when it gets forced on me and I *have to* work, it leaves me feeling disheartened.

And then yesterday evening it was "story night" at the drama club – which (despite my sarcastic conjuring of spectres on the tape) actually went *very* well. I went alone. Estelle didn't really "care" to go, whether or not I was one of the people reading. In itself this was of course a mere trifle, but it just made me think again: God, we have almost nothing to bind us, never did, although this was easier to camouflage in the past.

148

Not any more. She shows no interest in anything I do; I, in my turn, show no interest at all when she comes home and tells me what the librarian said or what Mrs X said in reply. When I – ecstatically tired – told her the novel was finally done (now, after nine months), she said: "Oh. Nice." I want no "fuss". That would be even more loathsome than neutrality. It's just that there's a total, complete inability to *share* anything! And this must now go on and on. Ingrid, Ingrid, I don't know what to think any more. I can hardly think at all, in fact. I'm so tired of everything. I just want to rest somewhere, find some quiet, where I can love, and work. How does one just "carry on" – "from day to day / till the last syllable of recorded time"?

Oh God, child, I love you so much. I came back to Grahamstown and thought it might not be too presumptuous to expect happiness; the love has burnt itself out – but maybe we could at least continue with a kind of "agreement", especially since I can take refuge in my work. But now even my work has to cave in under the pressure of something as banal as child-minding? It's *ridiculous*. Humanity is not exactly something God can be proud of.

Is it really so *wrong* to ask for just a little pure love, some heart and understanding, a little sharing of things with someone, the trust of eyes and hands, the assurance of a hungry young body?

I shouldn't actually post this letter. I shouldn't upset you too. You already have so much to bear. What right on God's earth do I have first to bring you some happiness and then to break it down – and then to come complaining to you about how unhappy *I* am? Forgive me, darling. It's just that – in this morning's mad wind – I arrived at a place where I no longer know what to do.

Thank you for your beautiful poem. Did it just arise spontaneously – or did you start working on it, almost as a premonition, some time ago? It's so *well-finished*; with its contrast between "late / April" (which tells us more than it does the "reader", who's looking in from the outside; because it was late in April, that time) with its autumn, its dying leaves – and the blossoms of "tomorrow"; the double meaning of that beautiful, sorrowful "blood"; the phrase "your seed spilt on the ground" that becomes "*our* un / refined seed". Very lovely. And ter-ri-bly sad. But above all, beautiful.

In these few weeks I myself have been thinking a lot about our child, our little girl, Heloïse or Deirdre.

By the way, on the tape I expressed some doubt about your title "Us"; but I've increasingly come to realise how perfectly it does in fact work. Precisely because the "you" dominates at first and the "I" is detectable only through her voice, until the third stanza says it outright: "us" – and it breaks up immediately afterwards into "you" and "I".

Child, my whistle, my song, my own: with everything that's going on, and everything being so unpredictable, *we* still remain, now, *us*, and I love you, and it's only the knowledge of your being there that still makes everything possible. "We are fellow actors in this comedy" – but we are not exactly blindfolded. And love remains full of light, caressing light.

Write soon, my dearest cocoon. I would love to be able to crawl inside you and hide away there, and enable you to take shelter inside of me at the same time ("fade far away, dissolve, and quite forget").

> soos 'n seeblom uit die water t'rugvou
> en sy eie moer word en sy eie
> donkerte, en louer, die kou buitewater
> weerstand bied, en twee-twee (binne toe)
> ritssluitend ín-paar.

With all my love,
Your André.

Grahamstown
Monday afternoon, 12 August 1963

Little cocoon, little delicous, little *you*,

Thank you for your dearest, higgledy-piggledy letter of this morning, written from all four corners of the earth, so to speak (last Wednesday night before I phoned). I want to say thank you, just for the hell of it.

I feel so guilty about my mad, bad-tempered, downhearted letter; I should never have posted it. It's not *right* for me to make you unhappy, or make you even more unhappy. In the meantime my carousel has at least turned a little. I'm feeling more restful and quiet again, and glad about the things we do at least have. Something like Han Suyin says in *The Mountain is Young* (Do you know her? At times nicely poetic, but also often sentimental; a bit of a crescent moon) –

> I had the feeling from the first day I met you, that we were setting out on a journey together. I didn't ask whether it would be long or short, and certainly I did not know how far together we would go. But dreary it would never be, and no one else did I want for a companion. And that it would last till death is far too much to ask. It was enough that I had found you, to walk with, a little moment or a long time. And all my life I would love you for this being together a while.

This, every word, is what I want to say, myself.

I have been going around all weekend humming bits of that feeble little tune Simone loved singing so much, the one the two of you sang together that time. Oh, God, it's the little things that claw at one most deeply!

You ask so many questions in your letter! – what I mean by "belong to each other" and "be each other's". Difficult to paraphrase but there *is* a difference. "Belong" is possessive, smotheringly proprietary, *material* – like a book that belongs to me (the physical book); the book's content can *be* mine. "A state of *being*" – as against "a state of *having*". "Be each other's" is more pure, fuller, more complete, and *lasting*. See?

And you say loving is indeed having. *No!* Loving is: wanting to have: *want* to have, the always-reaching, always-exploring of the land that is yours but which can never lie before you, mapped and complete. It's a quest, a journey of discovery. That's what I meant in *Sempre* when I said I want to love you; have you, or *possess*, I can't. You're free, ungraspable – and invaluable. But now it easily becomes a play with words ("the stench of burnt offering"!).

The other things in your letter:

I'm sending your beautiful poem to Bartho for *60* (he is in charge of No 2 as well); I will keep the title as "Us" (it's better than "So"). I shall leave the dedication out, as per your request: *we* know, after all. (*Who* doesn't know?!)

The photo-prints – I have been too broke to have them done. But I'll send them away promptly.

The virginal white photos – I have added nothing further to the film and therefore can't yet do the prints.

Nicolette's "secrets". Naturally. (When will I get her back?!!!!!)

What your friend says, about your love poems that are too sensitive: not so. They are delicate, like gossamer, a few of them far more tender than anything in Eybers. But never overly so. That's precisely what makes them so meaningful for me: that the words remain so finely *balanced*.

Unfortunately Bartho has written to say it's too late to change the order of poems, as the reprint has already been done. (They moved very fast, it seems to me.) I will immediately ask him about copies for critics. Rob has received a copy (he's one of the prize judges).

Thank you for the nostalgic drop of red wine. For me, red wine will always, always be *you*. From the very first night, remember? (I still remember how I spent almost half the night leaning against the wall with a heavy head, down-in-the-mouth and full of longing, hearing you go to the bathroom every so often –)

I'm glad to hear our leucodendron's doing well. And the poor lonely little chick! But the papie is also lonely and longs "for cosmos and coherence", and I so badly want to make a moesie-girl who won't again be naughty and choose the drain over your tiny inner chamber.

One of these days I want to start a novella, which begins with the arts ball where you were the deer and came home wearing only your little horns. And then connect that with the old Sumerian ritual at their fertility feast: beautiful young people play the roles of gods and then take poison afterwards – because anyone who has once been incarnated a god, may not continue to live as a human. And then connect that to the Eastern myth about the god of love who assumes material form only when two lovers embrace. It must be a vortex of movement, the whole story – start off almost incomprehensibly like the chaos of Genesis, and then become more luminous and clear, and it must *all* be *us*, eventually becoming very chaste and still, in a holy way. It's still just an idea, a rhythmically sensory idea; perhaps it will take a long while before it becomes word or flesh. But it will come. I feel it rumbling.

Please make me a tape in which you only read poems. Éluard, [N.P. Van Wyk] Louw, your own, Van Schagen, Whitman, anything. Will you? I'll send you some money.

(I received royalties for *Sempre*! – sold almost 700 in the first two weeks.)

Lovely, gorgeous child – I say goodbye with the glowing respect that runs in me like an attuned current, with everything I have in love ("we haven't got anything in asparagus" refers!) "all I have done is yours, all I have to do is yours, being part in all I have, devoted yours".

Your André. {so at-one are you & I that I tried to write "André" with a J!}

Tuesday, 13 August 1963

Darling my André,

Thank you for your wild letter of yesterday and your urgent little tape – I wrote to you last night and again this morning on the way to work, soaked through in the rain, it rained into my bag and onto my letter too, and now I am writing again, here in a café close to the Press, having coffee, smoking a cigarette, and trying to be reflective and considered – today's reading is Lord, search my heart. Because while I love you, André, and would accept you with joy if you managed to come back to me, it would be a fiasco if I came to Grahamstown, it would mean the end of your marriage, because then Estelle would definitely not stay with you, and what about your father? Also, it would encourage Piet to go ahead with his plan, which might then also have the same consequences if it becomes public. The bald facts, which we both know so well, but which we try to skirt around; why not first go and speak to your mother – maybe she already knows?

Oh, child, I so badly want to comfort you, and I wish I had an answer, but what? And I believe that you love me, and that does make me happy. You say (naturally) that you don't actually want to hope that "everything between me and Jack" will "come right". Whatever that might mean – I don't know. Of course, I am still attached to Jack, but in a destructive way – on Saturday night I had such a fight with him again that I had to take some pills and fell asleep with a burning cigarette in my hand – irresponsible! As you say, it's caving in. So I doubt far more than before whether it will ever "come right". Now that, on top of everything, in the midst of our "work and play", I am able to run away and sit on a rock for hours and imagine that you are there, and imagine, like last night after I heard your tape, a house in which we share a "natural life". It's all so difficult and complicated, and one must of course do the right thing and choose correctly in order to live in peace with oneself and others? Not that it looks to me as if there is much of a choice, and then, then it just gets more difficult. "Irascible": plaything of your own vacillating emotions. I would that we could just have a CHANCE, just six months or a year, to live together, even if it's just to get to know one another better, but on the other hand no one could know you better than I know you.

My lovely good André, there is so much I want to pack into this letter, but there's always a rush: in half an hour I have to go to the Press

154

again. It's so difficult even just to *begin* to say something, never mind having the courage to write down just one true thing; there are so many facets. And I miss you so much, I am so grateful for you; and even though I forgot the cheque (thank you very much!) today, I'll bring it tomorrow and buy a tape, it is after all better than a letter. And thank you for your phone call, I just don't want you to be unhappy, or restless, although the tension has made even me so touchy this past week that I am constantly fighting with or wanting to fight with someone.

You mustn't blame old Bill de Klerk alone for "stories" – maybe it wasn't actually his fault.

And congratulations on *Die Ambassadeur*; I'll be sending your MS tomorrow; I'd very much like more of Nicolette; congratulations creative, generous, tender man with your amazing enormous understanding and knowledge and insight and energy and organisational ability. I am reading (one comfort) your translation at the moment. Meticulously and systematically I am reading it, every word that you typed. Anne says it's a pleasure having a copy like this. (Ten minutes, heavens, then I must leave for work.)

Was delighted to hear your naughty little baby's voice: I miss you both! Thank you, impractical, beloved as earth which always wishes to grow and gives strength for growth, for your suggestion to testify in court that we plan to marry. Won't they perhaps think it a little irresponsible? "You must lie low." We'll see what happens. I don't think it'll reach that point. You can mention it to Bartho, I'll also write to him because he requested "Die Bok" ["The Buck"] for an anthology. And now I must have my coffee and stop: but I carry you with me to the Press and wherever I go; and let me know immediately please exactly how many moesies you have! *This* uncertainty is terrible, when I try to count until I fall asleep; slept with the teddy last night. Send me the revised MS. I promise to return it soon.

And do not forget me.

I am glad you like "Us". Chris says it's "loaded". It came fairly spontaneously; from an instinctive feeling, a day or two before the "little death".

My generous-hearted love, somewhere within myself I do believe and hope and wait for you, it's probably something one cannot, praise God, argue away.

As always,
Cocoon.

—————

Grahamstown

Friday night, 16 August 1963

My serene little thing,

Thank you – *thank you* – for yesterday's dear, austere letter in reply to my emotional outburst of the other day! All the more because it must be just as hard for you in these times to think so soberly, and so neatly. Your letter was therefore actually the seal on a gradual coming-to-rest that had been occurring in me since my earlier letter. Strange how one lives through everything in a rhythmic, cyclical manner. I know very well that disquiet and resistance will take over again one of these days. But I'm grateful for the few days of quiet in which our "little pentecostal flame" can burn without too much flickering or smoke. Everything's glowing, like autumn leaves that burn from the inside out. And it's a strange time, this restless month: blossoms appearing everywhere like little girls in communion clothes; the empty wind rattling loose panes, and branches scratching the rooftops; dust blowing in one's eyes. (And here, not even an ocean!)

I posted a copy of *Caesar* to you today. More for the gesture than the content – although I think the content is quite neat.

Got an *abhorrent* review of *Sempre* in yesterday's *Vaderland*. By one Mrs R. [Roswitha] Schutte who was first R. Geggus (she wrote *Die Wit in die Poësie* [The White Space in Poetry]). Commissioned by A.P. Grové. It was so bad that Chris Barnard drove to Pretoria to confront Grové about it. But Grové replied that the review was "wholly substantiated" and therefore it had to be published as is. The kind of review that takes shots at me about my use of language because I use a word like "swabbish" – and in the same paragraph she uses the word "digress-ies" [Anglicised solecism for "digression"]!!! But you see, the Schuttes [Roswitha and H.J. Schutte] are angry because *Lobola* is uncalvinis-tic … Oh God, the little cliques and circles and gears – and *nuts*. I sat down and wrote a nasty letter to Grové; but then tore it up and threw it away, deciding, quite serenely: if one writes, this is the risk one takes upon oneself, after all. Why start a campaign now? Let this text be our morning vigil today: lift up your eyes to the hills. So why worry?

Thank you for the ms, which I will probably receive soon. I wish I were there so that I could position you neatly across my lap and slap that lovely bikini-white backside of yours into a fiery red. But then, while doing so, I would, like the man in the joke, have no choice but to say: "Fuck the rugby –" and turn my attention to more delicious things.

Over here, nothing *happens*. Except for my own impulsivity which, a few days ago, made me feel incredibly *low*. In a moment of rebellion and raging resistance – it was still during my "black period" – I asked Rob: "Has anyone been appointed as secretary for next year yet?"

"No," he said. "Do you have someone in mind?"

I should have pretended innocence. But I said – as soberly as pos-sible: "Apparently Ingrid Jonker's interested."

God, girlie. I knew immediately that he *knew* – with a painful kind of knowing; that he feels disappointed and hurt, and totally at a loss. He just let his head drop, remained quiet for a while, and then said, with his dear, vulnerable, embarrassed little smile: "Well …" And then again: "Well …" And eventually: "No, we haven't appointed anyone yet."

And after this he seems to have mentioned the matter to Johan Smuts (senior lecturer; language studies) – because now *he* refuses to greet me, walking away whenever I approach. It's so *unpleasant* when one has to work together this closely. Rob would never reproach anyone. Or say anything. It's just that I was stupid enough to ask the unnecessary thing. But, my darling, I was becoming so *desperate*; I no longer know what to do or which way to turn.

And so one learns quietly to seal oneself, tighten the bolts wherever the wind's coming in, make oneself impenetrable, like Moses in his basket of rushes, or Noah in his ark … and when will the dove fly off again and return with a leaf, when will a spirit hover over the waters once more, when will everything be new again, virginal, pure? Will we ever find serenity, little child …?

Just for a year? Six months? Darling, *my* Cocoon, *my* Ingrid: only a day, a night. Only an hour. Only *now*.

No, little flame: burn meekly, burn quietly; we deserve, God knows, but little – we human beings – and yet we've *had* a lot, and still have much. "No, candle, don't cry, candle … Candle, you've burnt down. But I – I still am."

Something that allows me to end on a lighter note (how acrobatic the human spirit is!): somebody phoned me yesterday to ask where a certain quotation comes from ("I call out to you like the crested guinea-fowl in the long grass calls his mate …" or something like that). It sounded familiar to me, but I unfortunately I couldn't help, and said goodbye. Today she comes and tells me – with quite a big smile on her face – that she tracked it down.

"So?" I asked. "Where?"

"*Lobola vir die Lewe*," she said.

Write again, love-lovelier-loveliest. Make a tape. Send me Simone's little voice, too. (Do you have *any* idea how much I miss *her*? And our little castle. And *you*. Ach du … du … God, NO! No: I am very well behaved. Quiet and tranquil. Believe me. Maybe then I'll believe it myself, along with you.)

Crazy. And yet also happy. And so in love with you, so taken up with you, so spent inside you. I hope you learn something from this letter. Five pages to say: I-love-you.

A kiss for the little chick (you'll first have to give your hand the kiss and convey it further from there). And one for the leucodendron,

Your André.

Castella
Monday, 19 August 1963

My dearest moesie-man,

Congratulations on *Caesar*! And now of course I'll have to read it again
to know what my moesie-man wrote and be half in wonderment at his
words! Thanks, darling, it looks beautiful – significant that they are
publishing you this winter in the colours of mourning, these diabolical
publishers! To tell you the truth, I completely forgot about *Caesar*,
and when I got the letter this morning, I thought you were referring
to the play that I would receive *now* (why?). And of course by that I
don't mean I still haven't forgiven you the "sins of your youth" – but I
just found it strange! Thank you, darling, who writes so many strange
things, it fascinates me greatly – my eyes must have looked enormous
to Anne when this new book arrived this afternoon; it lay there on my
"desk", to be handled, it lay in a workman's hands and everyone joined
in the conversation and looked inquisitively at the print and the binding, and probably also peeped at the inscription. As long as they don't
utter the word "Cocoon", I am at peace with it, as my ouma would say.

Glad you are so relieved (!) that I am *not* coming to Grahamstown or
at least have no plans in the meantime to take that post with Rob that is
still vacant. Very decent of him to say that they don't have anyone yet.
He is civilised. And probably often wants to die in stifling South Africa.
This image of him and his commentary stayed with me all day: why do
you think he was *disappointed*? Or was he just sad because he doesn't
want you to be unhappy and alone (which means without *me*) …?

You said my letter was sober. Rebellion? My mom once wrote to
me when she was very ill (I was about seven): "Mommy is no longer
human, just one great longing." I really think there is more longing in
me than anything else: but what does our Elizabeth Eiers [Elisabeth
Eybers] say: "verlange word aanvaarding, langsaamaan." But no, God! I
suppose I've learnt this to some degree, but not completely yet; hopefully I won't ever, it's fatal. In this case. Darling André.

Tonight a man, a Peter Deval-Smith [Duval Smith] of the BBC, is coming to meet me and to do a recording. Pity you aren't here; you'd probably mean more to him than I do! The programme's name is "Living under Pressure" and he got his insights from David Lytton's programme "Portrait of an Afrikaner". So now I am already mutinous and don't actually know what to say to him. I am a workman, I eat my bread and drink my wine and keep my heart clean of sin.

And yes, the *work*. Because a workman is what I am, and fortunately that doesn't yet include the masses; but still, I do this workman's work, and the longer I do it the more it contributes to a feeling of waste and sterility, the more I become conscious of my "calling" as a woman and a poet, the more it becomes "like a lamb to the slaughter ..." But perhaps, in this whole futile circular process, I'll become a human. Which is to say *then* I will be able to write.

But now bath and dress and entertain the BBC. Wouldn't it be lovely to lie here drunk when they arrive? To frighten a notary with a cut lily. Lovely man, thank you for your being near and your letter and book and messages. The ones you send wordlessly. {And I don't mean that it is "wonderfully quiet".}

And tell that student who asked you about the line in *Lobola* to leave you alone! This sad heart still has the ability to flicker up in a passion of jealousy and/or protection. And still, that you are mine, I do not comprehend ...!

Do you know what Anne's fiancé said to a "pushy" girl: "Are you made from *my* rib? No? Then fuck off now!" I do so love the religious values of "our coloureds". (My ouma also always draws the comparison in her letters. What I wanted to say is, I am *of* you.)

Till later,
Cocoon Cocoon Cocoon Cocoon.

I just thought that I am not in hell going to take a bath, or get dressed, or get ready for the BBC: and to think I worried this afternoon that I don't have any brandy for them! In any case, I have to give Peter

Oxley's pen back to him; he gave it to me and I'm sure he'll soon want to do homework.

Goodnight, my beautiful man: *man*, it's nice! I miss you. I have an uncontrollable urge to come and sleep with you, my purified person: by the way, how does one do without it? It's soo loong! I mean this BREAK. What on earth is going on? Or are you really being good? I believe you. But what's happening?

Treasure, my treasure! How far is Johannesburg from Grahamstown? Or is it in fact just as far as you are from me? I have a desire to go and live there, because here – I hardly see my old friends, and Uys is cross with me – your (lovely) piece about him gave him occasion to rail at Jack – but later said he was wrong. Apparently.

You've got a cheek though to always tell me that I am speckled:

toe kies my broer
die spikkelkoei vir hom
…
O waar sal ek skuil
teen die stippels wat pik?

"Ballade [Sprokie] van die Spikkelkoei". ["Ballad of the Speckled Cow"]. Opperman. Look it up. And why haven't you told me how many moesies you have?

Darling person. I love you so much. Dearest my André my P. Brink.

And on Sunday I told Jack I never never want to go to Sea Girt again because I no longer want to be a half-guest in a half-house … and now?

Went and lay in the Gardens today and smoked a long cigarette under the surprised eyes of my brothers-in-suffering. Went for a meal at the Charcoal Inn on Saturday evening. Dreamt of you. Very lovely child, together we will go and meet a new memory / Together we will speak a tender language.

Darling old André. Write soon, and come to me,
Cocoon.

PS: And now: I almost forgot the most important thing. I want to come to PE for a weekend. It won't be so terribly expensive. I will tell *no one* except the trusted person with whom I will leave Simone. And then you must send me travel money. You've got lots now from *Sempre*, haven't you!

Love,
Ingrid.

Sometimes I feel so scared that I'll forget, like in Hans Anderson's [?] poem, I have to see you complete and whole again, and when you're with me, darling my André, I don't want to look at you, do you still remember?

For a weekend like that I could simply stay away on the Monday. There's a long weekend in Sept.; but WORKERS don't have that day free; I'll take it. Do you think we can RISK it? I actually think we can. Tell me if it's not "serene" enough. And tell me quickly. Neat and tidy. Oh, woe.

The BBC is now literally on my doorstep.

BYE. Goodbye my mine.

I.J.

My André, people gone now, it's twelve o'clock. Also gave them your address; but so far no interview – am still a little suspicious of their motives – they also want to try and see Opperman and Van Wyk – all the "ondergetekendes". Spoke to Uys on the phone. His "rant" came down to this: 1. He likes the piece you wrote about him very much. 2. Must say more about the translation, the quality. 3. He was the first one in Afrikaans who used free verse. 4. Talk about his English work.

He actually sounds sweet again.

My little treasure, still wanted to say sorry about [Johan] Smuts. Don't take too much notice of it. Probably just jealous or worse. You'll just have to ignore him. And stay, stay loving me.

Your Cocoon.

162

Grahamstown
Wednesday, 21 August 1963

My dearest little playmate,

Thank you for this morning's tape after the long silence that had filled
me with such doubt and uncertainty. For me, the weekend especially,
Sunday in particular, was full of premonition and suspicion. An almost
uncanny feeling of commitment coming under threat. Was I right?

Meanwhile, you ask me for advice from within your own uncertainty:

What could I give to *you*,
I who am so poor?
Must I give of my sorrow
And of my darkness?

What you say about the tape that never got sent: the sense of doubt
about whether there's any point in continuing with "acts of communication" ["communicatie te treffen"]. I don't know. There are so many possible angles from which to view the matter. My own considered feeling,
and my only point of clarity, is this: we made our decision – it was bitter,
but responsible. At this stage, it doesn't look as if there can be any more
for us, together, than yearning and hope. Bodily, we will perhaps be able
to love each other, on occasion, if I can steal an hour or a day and come
to you, two or three times a year – *if* we're lucky. We therefore can't
count on fulfilment – or, at least: *continuous* fulfilment – in that area, no
matter how much we need it. (And I for one have a *terrible* need for such
physical fulfilment, for expression and discharge, especially now.) *But*:
is there not *very much* that we can still give each other, in the face of, and
despite, these meagre little facts – in our love, fully, *as people*? Must one,
because living together is impossible, also withhold all possibility of rich
and precious contact? I don't believe so. It might be the case that, in the
long run, it won't be as strong a need as it is now. But we decide on this

163

every day, and with each letter: *now, for* now. And right *now* I *need* you very much. All of you; but while I cannot or may not have everything, I at least want that which is in fact possible.

I must be reasonable and acknowledge that, in maintaining this attitude, I am being selfish: that such contact is likely, more than anything, to harm you? (And yet I don't believe it – or don't *want* to, or *can't*.) Therefore: speaking for myself, if I had to decide, believe, then the contact – along with the necessary hurt in every letter about what "could have been" or "should be" – is a fulfilment and a mercy, time and time again, and something to be thankful for. *I* would therefore like to continue, because it does not, in the final instance, seem futile. But *you* also have to decide. And I would have to abide by whatever you decide, because I love you in a way no person has ever before loved.

I cannot visit in September, because I dare not come alone again – and Estelle is working. I was on the point of coming down next weekend! Koos Human phoned to say they're now enthusiastic about the revised *Ambassadeur*. However, he apparently deems it necessary to have an interview about certain things, and the question arose whether he should fly up here to see me, or I to see him in the Cape, urgently. I tried to figure out a way, but if I do come I'd only be able to be there on Sunday and Monday morning, and I'd have to sleep over at friends, too, with their entire family around my ears. We'd therefore have just Sunday from about ten to about five in the afternoon. It's not impossible that I might still suddenly decide to come, after all, but it's not looking very practicable. If only you knew how I *yearn* for you these days!

You ask so insistently how things are going here at home. It's very hard to diagnose. In my last letter I said things had become more tranquil. Things are fairly neutral on the surface, with exceptions like yesterday, which was one of those mad days. Even friendly and polite. There is no prospect of any deeper contact. Estelle is being quite obliging at the moment; seeking conciliation. But not so long ago – as I told you at the time – she said: "It gives me the creeps when you touch me." And that's what *I* now feel.

164

If I were to calculate the prospects, I would say this: we will continue, like Jan and Marjorie, to live without any sex-life. Some days I can accept this. Frequently, I feel dejected and have no idea *what* might yet happen. Why must one be prudish? I have a very deep – and enormous! – need for sex. I work and write at such a prodigious pace that it completely exhausts me spiritually and then creates a physical *need* that can only be allayed by a complete sexual experience. Must – and can – one "unlearn" this, too? I don't know. I don't know anything any more. I simply long for you, with everything, and for everything.

By the way, you shouldn't get the idea from my last tape that I feel resentful towards Anton! If it weren't for him, I'd have done away with myself a long time ago. I am *devoted* to my son. The only thing that sometimes gets me fuming is the fact that he is forced upon me for half the day when I *have to* work. At least now the servant stays on in the afternoons and I have to babysit only three nights a week. (Tuesday, Wednesday, Thursday, from 7:30 to 10:00, if you ever want to phone! Number 905. But I'll be calling you tonight in any event …)

I have written already to tell you how much I long for Simone, too. I even began devising a way to get her to visit here for a week. She would enjoy Anton and I'd look after her nicely. But this is probably just another silly dream. Piet, I assume, would have a stroke. God, the complications of "other people". And we are more likely than not the "spirits that roam".

    en wie, wat die droom in ons oë
    gelees het,
    sal rus of ooit wéér wees
    soos hy gewees het?

    [and who, after reading the dream
    in our eyes,
    will ever rest or become again
    what he once was?]

Darling, PLEASE, you *must* send the manuscript back now. I have to make the changes that are on it, otherwise I won't have any record of them. The moment I've done that and Chris Barnard's finished reading it, I will in any case send it back to you to *keep*. Please, my naughty little girl.

I'll be sending the photos off for printing today. I promise!

You want to go to Joburg, you say ... which is "closer" to Grahamstown? It's 150 miles *further*. My great geographer. I must make you the gift of an atlas. Or a globe, perhaps.

Must I send some money to help pay for the tape recorder? I can help a little here and there, thanks to the new translations.

(Beware of [?]!)

It's autumn-spring here. *So* beautiful. God, God, one dream I've had for us is to drive out to a deserted, empty beach, and swim together, stark naked, and then, on that lovely warm sand under a wide open sky, lie with and in each other, on the beach; "'t zal nimmermeer ghebeuren ...".

I'll make you another tape one of these days.

Write. Darling, my cocoon: I'm beginning to hope that the one-day duration of your last period means there's a little moesie-girl growing inside you –?

I love you very much.
André.

1. Should I dedicate *Die Ambassadeur* to "Ingrid" or to "Cocoon"? And should I add, next to it: "Donna m'apparve" ("A woman appeared to me") as Dante said of Beatrice? Or just unadorned, without any added text?
2. Should I still write to Bartho about Simone? Or wait until P[iet] moves one of his pawns again?

I will count my moesies, as you asked! Except I can't see them all!

Grahamstown
Friday, 23 August 1963

Oh darling,

It's terrible. They should rather not allow people to hope than to arouse ecstasy and then destroy it. I had everything sorted out. Estelle couldn't get leave and I would thus have come on my own; I bought wine for us, quite a *lot*; and toothpaste, and even a new pair of red-checked underpants ... and then the call came through from Koos to say everything was already arranged by the time my telegram arrived yesterday. Now I have to spend the whole weekend thinking that I could have been with you.

But, darling, the moment the proofs are ready – and I'm going to chase Koos to have it done during the September vacation – I want to make sure I come down for that. I must get *something* done –!

I've thoroughly considered your PE plan, but it's simply not possible, Cocoon, because what reason would I have suddenly to go to PE? And I wouldn't be able to go on my own – Estelle has been saying for a while now we should go there to do some shopping.

Zoo moeten wij door bittre jaren zwerven;
Het is altijd een strijd en een verlangen.

Thank you for your precious, beautiful voice last night. I will phone again, next week: hopefully Wednesday night. Why was last weekend so "dismal"? I want to know everything.

And thank you, again, for yesterday's wonderful, adorable letter full of love and longing. It was funny, too. That comment by Anne's boyfriend ("Are you made from my rib" – etc.) – classic. I want to put it in a book somewhere.

I also want to know everything about Piet's most recent idiocy. And I want to help, *promptly*, if I can.

Sorry this is such a mixed-up letter. I can't think properly. I just wanted to write as soon as I could after Koos's call to tell you in greater detail what's going on. Suddenly everything's so changed. Yesterday was so dazzling: first your letter, and then a review of *Sempre* by Louise Behrens that says: "It's a rich, lovely book ... The kind from which one wants to continue quoting and retelling stories ... Something of the richness of the young writer's spirit (sic!) gets passed down when we read the account of his travels." Lovely, isn't it?

Nice, hey? God. I've heard us say these words so much this weekend. In roman, italics, everything. Each on his own, then?

Everyone on two legs: lonely. So you're actually quite ordinary.

The path just *is*, and it's solitary ...

Cocoon, most beloved mine, where do those exquisite words come from in your letter:

"Together we will go and meet a new memory"?

If it's your own, then it's one of your most beautiful. Finish it ...

We must just be positive. Reading for a sermon: Faith, hope, love ...

We have very little, little, *little*. But we also have a lot, as long as we have hope. I *will* be with you again. I *will* sleep with you again.

With love, always,
Your André.

MANUSCRIPT S'IL TE PLAÎT

Saturday, 24 August 1963

FIRST WORST DISAPPOINTMENT OVER ENJOY KOOS ALL LOVE ALL TRUST =
COCOON

––––––––––––

Grahamstown
Sunday morning, 25 August 1963

My Cocoon, *my* darling,

For three months I believed in heaven; now I also believe in hell, with
fire and all, because in the last few days it's as if things have reached a
point of frenzy. I feel I should do a variation of Descartes's saying: "I
hurt, therefore I am." And amid the great emptiness and confusion,
your call came through – in circumstances that nearly drove me mad
because I wanted so badly to express myself, and console you, be with
you – but instead I had to sound "non-commital", businesslike, while
everything in me shouted out at you:

> Laat mij nog éénmaal, in gedachten, kussen
> Die warme lippen, door mijn kus ontbloeid;
> Laat mij nog éénmaal aan dien boezem sussen
> Mijn arme hoofd, waarin de koorts-pijn gloeit.
>
> Laat mij nog eens, klein kindje, rusten tusschen
> Die armen, waar mijn hart aan was geboeid …

The whole time yesterday, from about midday, I kept calculating: by
this time I'd have been as far as Humansdorp … Plettenberg Bay …
George … Mossel Bay … Swellendam … Riviersonderend … Caledon –
just an hour to go.

And then last night Anton had one of his crazy nights, while I wanted to *sleep*, be gone; know nothing of the world. When he started crying at two and I went to him, I thought: now we'd have been sit-lying together on the little knobbly bed, naked, with cigarettes, fatigued but happy, knowing that the day was still a few hours away. And at four – by now we'd be lying exhausted against each other, divinely, deeply happy, without desiring anything other than just this being together, this utter fulfilment. At six – by now I'd have half woken up and begun to wake you up, softly and slowly – because maybe you'd have felt a little sore.

And now, at eleven –? The sun, outside (or windy and rainy and miserable, as it is here?), the bright yellow curtains, and us, again, *us*.

Oh, Lord God, no.

Friday night, when you received the letter and telegram, I went and curled up foetally on a corner of the divan in the front room and shut myself off from everything, in unbearable loneliness. I heard Estelle eating – heard the food crunching between her teeth, listened to her swallowing her tea and paging through her *Sarie* or *Woman's Own*; all she did was talk, on and on, about the trifles of her working day – not even once realising I was lying there and crying. Later I got up and walked out into the dark. Just *longing*, as you once described your mother saying in a letter.

My darling, I just don't know any more. And it has to go on like this, and on, and on – "To-morrow, and to-morrow and to-morrow."

God, I simply can't. Shouldn't one rather just end it all? How can one continue living in such absolute emptiness? I don't really *want* to die. Does one have no right at all to even a small piece of lasting happiness? Must everything groan to an end, as in Eliot's "Hollow Men", with a "whimper"? It's not just heartless and unfair – it's *unworthy*. It denies the very meaning of being. Because there *is* meaning. It's degrading "that everything that is godly" must "look backwards" in this way.

We must just hope the proofs will be ready soon; I'll ask Koos to see if he can have them done by the September holiday (20 to 30 Sept.) so that I can come down for a few days. It's better not to hope too much, but without hope I don't know what I'd do.

Darling, darling, this is the heaviest time of all for us. It's demanding more of us than anything else. We'll have to find something or we'll

170

both fall to pieces from negative yearning and loneliness. We must take something positive from all of this. We have a physical need for each other, but in the meantime we'll have to learn to give, and be precious to each other, in other areas. I'm struggling to bear the burden of guilt because of what I've broken down in you, and therefore I want, must, try to *give* also – even though it's so often just "grief and darkness".

I want to start working on *our* novella. I want you to know how much I love you. And that I *trust* you completely, absolutely. Please, please don't let my love become a poison that paralyses you. Let us *be*, let us *be human*, let us *become*. Let us *distil* something out of this – even out of this; and not become murky.

Maybe we'll make another moesie-girl, my Ingrid. But we mustn't pin our hopes to anything *specific*. Let us rather take what there is from each moment of *love* and clarity. There is so much we *can* share. You are the loveliest, purest and most precious thing that has ever happened to me. And the heartfelt nature of your giving, both your virginal *and* your mature love – without that I cannot continue.

I will write again soon, my very dear, very honest, luminous little woman. You *are* that, because [D.H.] Lawrence wrote in an essay:

Two rivers of blood, are man and wife, two distinct eternal streams that have the power of touching and communing and so renewing, making new one another, without any breaking of the subtle confines, any confusing or commingling ... We know that the one-ness of the bloodstream of man and woman completes the universe, as far as humanity is concerned completes the streaming of the sun and the flowing of the stars.

That is how I love you, and that is how I am yours, always. "And so I shall dwell in your house for ever" (my own Psalm 23).

Your André.

My darling André,

Wrote to you yesterday morning and yesterday evening but simply couldn't get into my stride; was too upset and too mutinous. Also sorry about the untimely phone call, and then I was forced to realise that I can't speak to you personally for even six minutes … was I horrible to you and did that upset you even more? Child, it's going to be impossible to go "underground" because how on earth does one live above ground? And surely Estelle realises from your attitude – also the physical "conciliation" – that everything's not "all right" any more? I realise you must now be in an extremely difficult position.

First I'll tell you everything I've done since your devastating telegram arrived. Read your letter. The facts in it were also so naked, although it was actually a nice letter, just a bit more businesslike than usual. Then had to go and have a drink with Mrs Oxley for her birthday: came back, had another drink, bawled, went to sleep. Saturday morning bought Simone a red raincoat, and a red bikini for myself; sent your telegram; met Lena, with her I can complain and it's safe, helped with the reception for her beloved and his spouse, phoned you and went to sleep early again. "Talked things out" with Uys on Sunday morning – he, and many others, apparently, think that *I* left *you*, and went back to Jack. Do you remember the lines I wrote to you the very first time: "Before the serried batallions of lies / and the organizations of hate / Entirely encompass us, / Lie one night in my arms and give me peace."

Well, now. I just wanted to say that I am not leaving you, and that I am not in a sexual relationship, and as for the rest there's nothing more to say. That afternoon (because Jack invited me for a meal) Uys was very friendly towards me, and went over your report on him again: apparently you still have to mention the verses that come closer to colloquial language, and the "Ballade van die Groot Begeer" ["Ballad of Great Desire"] contains SOCIAL CRITICISM, and say something about "The Sniper" too. Even though I'm still fond of Uys and the rest of them, this quickness to criticise and the gossiping and meddling has shocked me. "Niemand mag mos óóp loop …"

You ask why last weekend was so awful. Jack and I ate out on Saturday evening and went back to Sea Girt together. It was okay. I slept at Lena's. But on the Sunday afternoon he made me so *angry* again. God, André, I don't know where I get this quick temper, and I *can't* learn to control it; two minutes later I am always sorry about it. I hope I never get that angry with you. It's so totally unnecessary and destructive; why react like that towards your friends? In general company I am always described as "cheerful". A friend of mine, Marcelle, says, "People should be happy, then one can't see their faults."

You also asked about Piet. He says: "The *details* of your newest romance are, of course, widely known." (!) Otherwise just a whole lot of rubbish about his "model" house, his "responsible" and "mature" wife and that Simone will be smartly dressed. I ignored the letter.

Glad to hear about the "richness of your spirit", my love! Please feel free to send me some of the reviews. I can't keep up with everything. Also, you're so full-time. I've still got to get to *Caesar*!

And thank you for the compliment, but the "sensitive language" and the "new memory" comes from Éluard. I know the collection inside-out.

Woe, I lost my temper (!) God, again! With the BBC. The man is so vulgar. "One of my son's mothers had a black bottom …" he said. Then they acted as if they don't have any inborn race hatred – I decided there and then that he will not get a word out of me!

Sorry this is such a "newsletter".

Tuesday, 27 August 1963

THANK YOU LETTER AND TELEGRAM ALL CLEAR ALL LOVE DARLING = COCOON

If you loved him you would leave him …!

That's what some people apparently believe, my André. I am so *aston-ished* at the things people throw at me … as though they are living in another time, that's another thing, by the way, that I don't entirely comprehend, Calvinism – you know yourself how much training I've had in "philosophy" (!) … But Annie Retief, my ouma (that's her maiden name of course, Retief!) was broad-minded and well-bred and refined, that inner refinement that no Apostolic Church could rob her of, that refinement that allows one to say: It's "wonderfully quiet" – when she doesn't receive a letter! And then, look at the Sermon on the Mount … Christ himself said that divorce was permissible if there'd been adultery … Thus it is written, but I say unto you … Did you ever read the fascinating but naïve little story *The Man Nobody Knows* …? Oh, yes, Annie Retief … I can really get sidetracked when I start writing about her, and regretful, I wish she was alive today … she'd have understood in spite of all her training, because she had little to do with dogma and so much more to do with humans. She had eight children, six of whom died before she did. And her sympathetic attitude towards Abel (Pa). I wish you could've met her … "Poor old Van As doesn't look well, I think she has too many friends …" Indeed (!), perhaps one should say that of me now!

To get back to the first sentence: If you loved him you would leave him. Maybe something like this:

The voice of my education said to me
He must be killed,
…
But must I confess how I liked him,
How glad I was he had come like a guest in quiet, to drink at my water-
    trough
And depart peaceful, pacified, and thankless,
Into the burning bowels of this earth?

174

Was it cowardice, that I dared not kill him?
Was it perversity, that I longed to talk to him?
Was it humility, to feel so honoured?
I felt so honoured.

Oh my dearest child, I no longer know. I am so confused and, I simply have to admit it, afraid. *Security police*, subpoenas, threatening letters from Piet, and that work. God! I can't even be properly pleased about T.T. Cloete's review!

But listen carefully: I don't want you to be so unhappy, and also not so rebellious. I know you sometimes also feel rebellious towards Estelle, and it's not *her* fault, and I am really not noble. I'm thinking of *you*.

I am terribly tired and confused … or is "confused" not the right word for when you can't sit dead-still for two hours? I want to hide somewhere like an injured bird, not even an injured person! And as soon as the book arrives I'm going to apply for a bursary, a few bursaries: Molteno Trust and at the Dutch Consulate. "I'm going wandering, I'm going away …"! Because I know I'll be able to get one.

And now, my André, be good and sleep sweetly and don't get so cross – while you *can* and *must* write me everything, your letter did sadden me …! "Maybe it is better to make an end of everything", and you're MAD to say that, at least for you. Do you know what I was thinking about when I was sitting so quietly? The way in which you took the pen out of my hand, wrote CONSOMMÈ (???) in my diary …! Funny, the "feeling of a simple memory"! Unquote Jonker.

SLEEP SLEEP. You didn't promise you'd phone, but I'll leave the light on so that Peter [Oxley] can still call me. This was just saying hello, dearest mine; and here [Peter] has just said you'll now be phoning at nine o'clock. Thanks, darling! See you later.

Love Dearest,
Cocoon.

Thank you lovely phone call.

Lovely chat last night about your ice-cream and my red bikini – hello! *Child*. And then did you go off and have an erudite conversation with the other man in the sitting room? What do you think of my "application", which has not yet taken shape – though I have been enquiring all over – to get a bursary to go overseas? Today I no longer feel like going. But some time or other I will have to. I have never had a single opportunity, even took Afrikaans Lower for matric because back then my father was a SAP: just work, work, work my whole god-given life away, for little pay and even less thanks. It's so abominably unnatural, and even if it carried on like this for another hundred years, I would never be able to adapt to it. Am I really made to read that rubbish, to waste my precious eyes on it until I am blind, I am so visually attuned! I can't TAKE it any more. I only want a few months or a year to go, and to do or think or see something worthwhile, to feed this impoverishment with good art, a more natural life.

And if there is NOTHING that I MUST have and can't get, I see no point in going on. I reckon I've tried long enough now, André, without love, without an education, without any form of emotional security, even if this was just the kind of financial security that enables one to buy certain things, a measure of serenity. I'm not self-pitying, also not bitter, just TIRED. They are ongoing, these things, threatening to take away the little light (talent!) that was granted to me. Because it can indeed be taken away.

Every grey day is deadening. And after this tirade I want to show you how your love carries me through these things. Do you know how I show it?

Perhaps just the fact I'm still alive.

Love, beautiful moesie-naked-man.
Cocoon.

Darling-Cocoon,

Thank you very much for your letter, for last night's conversation, and for your soft little laugh that made me want to devour you alive. Thank you for being happy again. And yet: a certain despair seemed to lurk in the conversation, not to mention your letter. You say Jack thinks my love is destructive because if I come back to you I won't be taking your distress into consideration; and you write: "Even if you come for a few hours that are 'stolen' or 'underground', there will be consequences. And we'll have to decide one way or the other quite clearly."

I must try to reach a point of clarity – it's a process that's taken place almost mercilessly in all our recent letters. I don't want to rationalise things, I want to try to be level-headed – with the thought that Mrs Bouws's "don't force anything" is actually the truest attitude of all. I want to explain that there is *not* a contradiction in my last two letters.

For me, there are two important aspects: first, that we decided, in full responsibility, that we cannot *now*, in *our* circumstances, continue with a relationship that is aimed at marriage.

The second is that we must now decide whether we should continue keeping in touch with each other, or not at all. I have already written to you about my own conviction: it strikes me as pointless, and it would cause unnecessary suffering, to break everything down while we still have the opportunity to mean so much to each other, and give so much, within the limited little circle that remains for us. However: if futility dominates everything, if our frustrated love becomes mutually poisonous to each other ("You were so much poison in me / as I was poison in you") – as Jack thinks things stand – then we *may not* carry on as we are.

And out of this situation a conviction has arisen in me: from the little that we have, we can cultivate much that is very precious and that can become indispensable. But then we *must* concentrate on positives.

The question is: how does the possible September visit fit in? It's not a "return" in the sense of a resumption of everything – *that* would be destructive; it's thus no "cancelling" of our decision (in the way that Jack came back within a week after his "irrevocable" decision!). For me it's simply the use of a wonderful and fortuitous opportunity to see each other again, to *be*, in the way we need each other – without tying it to the future.

Or is that an illusion? Are the "consequences" that you talk about, *for you especially*, so threatening that it would be unwise and even wrong for me to come? This is something only you can decide. On my side, I see my way clear to dealing with the consequences in my own life. But it would be unforgivably selfish of me if I allowed my love for you to make your position even more tricky.

Darling, darling, I know you will say, as you did before, that it all sounds so terribly calculating. But we *have to* work with basic givens. The real question is actually very simple: do you see your way clear to us carrying on, is it sufficiently precious and necessary, even though we have no assurance about a future together? My own answer is *yes*; for me, it's a critical necessity. It's the only precious thing that has remained in my life – everything outside of it has broken down.

But all this will mean nothing to me if I know it brings you little more than confusion and darkness. How could I possibly be happy if it made your position even more untenable?

I want so much to come down for the proofs. But then I need to know it's not just going to lead to a new break with Jack and Uys and everyone else. For that reason, Jack will have to know what the actual nature of our separation is, that it was never meant to be us "giving up" on each other, but rather that what we mean to each other is precisely remaining in contact, and wanting to enjoy such precious moments together as might be granted us.

Write to me about developments with the damn security police detective, should he ever return.

I'm sending you a little money; let me know if you need more.

With all my love,
André.

178

Castella
Saturday, 31 August 1963
{Found out Aug. has 31 days.}
~~1 September Spring Day~~

My darling André,

Thank you for your letter that was tucked so dearly into my door when I arrived home laden with parcels, it's very sunny in the street, perfect for a day in the veld or on the dunes. If the white Volksie was here we could drive out to Stellenbosch or Paarl, or Hout Bay?

Did you get Thursday's *despondent* letter? Your letter this morning is very clear and I fully understand how you feel, my dearest little treasure. And yet … Abraham [H.] de Vries, for example, was here last night, phoned me at the office to meet him for a drink; I waited for him until 5:30 and then I left because I was expecting Marjorie and Jan at home. But he kept waiting for me (in the wrong place!), until seven o'clock. And came here afterwards. He was supposed to go to Bill de Klerk, but cancelled his appointment; naturally we spoke about you too; he says he hears about us everywhere and interrogated me: "I hear you've parted ways?" But your photos are hanging here large as life and I couldn't help talking about you a little bit! And this is *consequence*.

I told you on the phone and in my letter about Jack's visit, and what I'd said to him, that he wants to come and see me, and his reaction. Since then I haven't seen him again and when I placed a friendly call to him yesterday, he asked me: "How are the matrimonial plans going?" That, too, is *consequence*. And the consequences are growing, and the consequences *in* us, so that perhaps later you won't be able to save *anything* over there in Grahamstown. If it was *only* an adventure for both of us (because it is *also* an adventure) everything would of course be less complicated. But I will stay with you. Because I must and because I will and because it can't be otherwise and because you are my precious discovered treasure and because you love me. "The moment you are influenced you are corrupted." That's what [Leo] Tolstoy says, and for that reason, I guard you and me like a lioness guards her cubs. And perhaps for that reason Jan was making fun of me last night, "Good heavens, Ingrid, when I mention André's name, your expression changes!"

Dear treasure, we really must *laugh* more, about this *chaos* too that we've started in literary circles, because it's actually funny in certain respects. Why did Abraham *have* to see me, wait for me for two hours, cancel his appointment with Bill, and come here?? Of course, I invited him to stay over here (what would people have made of *that*?) as my house is open to any "brother or sister in suffering", the homeless and the displaced, the artists. But he went and stayed over at Ivor Pols, "because I don't want André to be cross with me". As if André can't trust me … but, that was a joke.

Come in September. Maybe your suggestion is in fact just a way of living, an art, then we'll go away, without anyone knowing, and come back with secret secrets. And perhaps it's a challenge. My whole nature (and yours too) flies in the face of secret-keeping, because we must share and because we are wilful – but maybe we can if we must.

I want to *see* you. I dreamt about you all night long, and about L. We were somewhere on a wonderful beach together, and wanted to try and get to one another, but we were almost hostile towards one another. It was terrible! And in reality I haven't *once* felt: You were so much poison in me, etc. For me you have only ever been light and love, in spite of everything. I don't *want* you to misunderstand me in this respect. You actually "gave me back to life" (do you remember that first weekend?). Do you remember that brandy afternoon in Clifton? Ag, do you remember everything? I love you so much. And I need you so terribly, too much. Now I'm going to make myself pretty and get tanned for September.

Darling.

Many thanks for cheque for castle and for telegram this afternoon.

Cocoon.

ps: Again today, my André, the slender possibility of our moesie-child is out of the question –

Temporarily.
IJonker.

Grahamstown
Tuesday, 3 September 1963

Little darling, little you,

Many thanks for the letter you wrote last Wednesday night; it made its appearance here this morning only. Oh little darling woman, your desperation makes me terribly unhappy. I wish I could *do* something for you; give you the protection and security I had intended to; I wish things hadn't jammed and stalled in this way. You have my love, all of it – but from a distance such as this, as I well know, that's little more than consolation and not the assurance, the reality you actually need. Your plan to go overseas –? It's so far away! And we made such plans to go together! It'll be *painful*; but still I want you to *do it*. God only knows, you deserve at least this relative freedom. It's a ridiculous irony that you, who in your *heart* are so free, should be so trapped by mere "circumstance". And that annihilating job – the thought that you, of all people, should do that kind of work: you with your wide open spaces and stillness and wildness, like the freedom of a little antelope; you with your absolute demand that one should *live*. If I could even just give you the *external* security of having enough money to keep banal worries at bay.

And here? The weekend once again witnessed several crises. On Saturday night we had a raging fight in which Estelle said: "Why don't you just say straight out that you hate me. You can't stand my guts!" And Sunday, again: she wants to spend Christmas alone with her mother.

The worst is that I can't blame her for any of it. I was dismayed to discover that I'm hard, cold-blooded and cruel; this is an awakening that makes me feel dirty and small. I've also begun to doubt myself: do I simply have a deficit in the capacity to *feel* anything at all? Why can't I be more charitable, even if I *don't* love her, even if there's no longer a single point of connection between the two of us? Must one, as a human being, be so bitter, so mean?

And still, my Cocoon, the weekend also had a positive side. I'm working hard on the preparation for "our" novella. The title (I think):

Orgie [Orgy]. I want to allow everything to dissolve in this work: your ouma and your childhood in a world of sand and sea, your swallow's nest – and, of course, the two of us, all of it pulled together in one night of New Year's celebration, a fertility feast. Sadness, too, is the bass note throughout, including the ending – how could it not be so – but it should be a glittering kind of sadness rather than pessimistic.

I want to start with a short "afterword". Something like:

So
let me say, was she found:
with some blood on her well-known thighs
and her mouth
still
among the first spring shrubs, the pointed deer horns untouched
    above her beautiful, now-always-shut eyes.

And then the "story" itself begins, with bits of Genesis and bits from the Gilgamesh epoch. Yesterday I took eight books out from the library and this morning another five: mostly mythological works and books on magic, etc.; now I'm reading and making notes, working terribly hard – and loving it. So it must continue, because as long as I'm busy, I can feel unconscious, free thoughts ferment and brew in me (like a spirit over the waters); disparate images and pieces of meaning; sensory – especially visual – impressions; rhythms … What I actually *have* at the moment, apart from the vaguest amoeba of an "idea", is just a form: an inexplicable idea of pages with white surfaces, italics and roman, prose and "verse" (I'm going to work my "poems" into the text and not make a collection out of them: they're too thin for that).

Throughout all of this I have to translate, translate: another five books. After that, no more, because next year I'm going to be dutiful and academic and write my thesis so I can become a "doctor". It's actually all a bit silly and banal, but it's about the work itself and not – God forbid! – any sense of "status"! My father tactfully let me know that "he would so like to see that day …"

I received another letter from Frank Ward. You know, the man who illustrated *Pot-Pourri* and *Sempre* and is now fucking in Stockholm and painting (in that order). He's illustrated your "The Child" and sent a translation of it to a Swedish paper to see if they might want to print it. If so, he'll send me a clipping to pass on to you. This Frank! He writes: "My latest sexual coup is an experience reserved for the privileged few" – two girls at the same time. I grant him that. He's not yet encountered a Cocoon. God, my love, I cannot imagine any other girl who has as much to give as you, or *can*. Actually: give and take; it takes a very big and precious person to *receive* without selfishness.

My thorny little rose in her castle: I want to remove the thornbushes that surround you and then I want to enter your world ("enter" in the Biblical sense) so we can inhabit our "island of repose" together.

I love you.

geen onoorbrugbaarheid skei twee
wat sterker konsentrate bind:
die sout van trane, sweet en nog
die allerlaaste liefdesvog.

I dream of a little moesie-girl … Today your period would have started again, unless the last short one was a phantom and there might yet be something …? Let me know.

My love to your beloved brown eyes;
and to your hair with its flick of a curl;
and your ears that listen so nicely;
your pert, pointed nose;
your soft girl-lips that like saying "Hell!";
your curved, speckled shoulders;
your lovely smooth back;
your white breasts with their pert nipples;
your little tummy with its tiny hole;
your bum that sits so softly;

your smooth thighs and calves that stretch so beautifully;
your feet that walk the world;
and the leucodendron;
and your arm that slumbers on me;
your hands, the dear hands with their messy red nails;
and your little hill and hair and the deep, steeply delicious, lovely
   cocoon.

You will know:

   Ik heb je nodig
   ik draag je handen
   en je voeten
   en je ogen
   in mij.

With love, with everything,
And may I *now* – quiet, satisfied and full of yearning – sleep with you?

Your André.

Grahamstown
Wednesday, 4 September 1963

Ingrid-mine,

Thank you for your voice last night and this morning's bright letter.
Thank you for your understanding and your hope. Thank you for *you*.

Last night I found myself thinking, dejectedly: must I henceforth be
no more than a "visitor" at Castella if I don't come and *live* there and *be*
with you? But then I thought: well, we always manage to get away ...
and in your letter you also talk in this way. I'll ensure that my trip for
the proofs includes at least a weekend, so we can drive to Hout Bay
on the Friday evening – or to Gordon's Bay or any other bay, far away
and white and full of summer – and then stay there until Monday. On
the other days, when I'll most likely be staying with Koos, we can still
eat together in the afternoons, and drive to Clifton in the evenings and
come back for supper-and-bath-and-bed.

This Abraham! A spy for Bill (they're *old* friends), and maybe also for
Piet? (He stayed for some time in Johannesburg at Chris B.'s house –
and he's about to start working at APB.) Did he also get married, in that
period? What kind of impression does he make? He looks a bit "smug"
in that recent photo.

I lay awake dreaming about you so much in the small hours of last
night (at first it was all sadness and separation, then gradually less con-
stricted, dearer memories – I have never before had such an *acute* memory!) that I woke up with a start at eight this morning and had to miss
my first lecture. Too bad.

Dreams? I'm only now reading [Graham] Greene's *Our Man in
Havana*. There, the worldly-wise old doctor says: "You should dream
more, Mr Wormold. Reality in our century is not something to be faced."

This weekend I read Greene's *A Sense of Reality*: his newest book,
consisting of four stories. The first and last are magnificent: they use
a childhood world to create their own mythology. In the final story
a group of children (all of them semi-stunted because of inbreeding

185

in their village) go on a search for blackberries or something like that and discover a ruined castle. The young girl has tied her skirt in a knot to gather up the blackberries and she's walking around with the bottom half of her body exposed. They discover a skeleton. At the end she goes and sits on the skeleton's thigh bones and starts rocking to and fro: "He's so beautiful; so beautiful. Why can't we be beautiful too?" With something akin to a primitive tristesse and anxiety running through it all, along with humankind's insatiable hunger for a "lost paradise". It's a library book but I've ordered a copy: if it arrives in time, I'll bring it along.

And, by the way, do you have *Stroomgebied*, the Dutch anthology? Large beautiful book with just about all the "moderns" in it.

I'm still working, translating, translating, translating. By Friday, Deo volente, I should finish off the Egypt book's successor (Mesopotamia); John Malherbe always pays very promptly. Then I hope to be able to send you something. It's so *little*, my darling; I feel almost bad sending little dribs and drabs. But I try to siphon off whatever I can.

Poor little Simone, who is so ill. I hope things take a turn for the better *soon*. I've become very fond of this child of light. If you make another tape, ask her to sing her little song as well! My heart yearns for a daughter of my own; but it doesn't look as if it's going to happen within the current marriage "bond". I've kept hoping, the whole month, that you'd suddenly phone and say: "Guess what …?" Crazy. Surely it's unrealistic? But the heart doesn't allow itself to be prescribed to.

… dit hart, zoo zwak,
Dat al zóó moe is, altijd luider slaat,
Altijd maar luider, en niet rusten wil.

I sent the slides away ten days ago for printing (only the best ones), but the process apparently takes three weeks. You'll therefore have to be more patient. If we get a chance to spend some time together – I can already see it's going to be almost impossible! – then we must take a few more, but this time with more attention and concentration!

186

I take it the little chick's not getting so cold any more. It's not from forgetfulness that I didn't strip her bare last time; I first wanted to say hello like the first time before putting her through the motions again. That very first moment remains completely unique in its intensity and wonder and anticipation and its yearning-in-the-face-of the-unknown. Remember?: When we lay together quietly in the little bed, and you took my hand and lay it down right *there*.

I can't even think about it without losing all self-control!

With love, and love, and love,
André.

Castella
Wednesday, 4 September 1963

My darling André,

As your so very sympathetic letter of Saturday said – there's a hidden despondency – in our telephone conversation last night too, for which you lacerated yourself … don't! I think it has something to do with the wrecked weekend, not as such, though, but because we had to actually *feel*, "physically", the consequences of our "responsible" decision. And then there are the different realities, practical real physical life versus this separation – a separation that will, eventually, make us unreal to each other. And so on. God! The abysses of the heart. I'm sending you a poem "Jou Naam Het 'n Kinderkarretjie" ["Your Name Has a Dinky Car"], which perhaps also contains this despair, though a wonderfully (I hope) poetic, liberating, harmonised laughter too.

And I bless you with love and tenderness.

Cocoon.

A beautiful Lucebert – "Nazomer"

Love darling come again soon.

    ik heb in het gras mijn wapens gelegd
    en mijn wapens gaan geuren als gras
    ik heb in het gras mijn lichaam gelegd
    mijn liggaan is geurig als hout bitter en zoet

    dit liggen dit nietige luchtige liggen
    als een gele foto liggend in het water
    glimmend gekruld op de golven
    of bij het bos stoffig van lichaam en schaduw

    oh grote adem laat de stenen nog niet opstaan
    maak nog niet zwaar hun wangen hun ogen
    kleiner gebrilden en grijzer

    laat ook de minnaars nog liggen en stilte
    zwart tussen hun zilveren oren en ach
    laat de meisjes hun veertjes nog schikken en glimlachen

———

Castella
September 1963

My darling darling André,

Thank you for your lovely letter of today – the little Mrs in the office came in and said, "I'm just quickly bringing you the *Cape Times*." And I'm sending Miss Padayachee's wonderful letter back. And this lovely note: PS: "So sorry, I couldn't type this letter!" And – "I wonder if I could keep in touch with you? Perhaps by correspondence??" You mustn't be too critical of her essays – and I hope you get a fat MS out of it! Greetings, my gentleman!

Silly thing. But I feel a little silly myself today. Was just as absent-minded at work today, so that Anne (who still can't manage to call me by my name) was eventually forced to ask: "But are you completely fucked in your head today?" And little innuendos about the "Cape Times" I received this morning. Dear child! Yesterday evening Chris was here for a while, and he read my little verse "Jou Naam Het 'n Kinderkarretjie" and almost laughed himself to death. He says it's "Dutch". Thank you, by the way, for your permission to go overseas – posted my letter to Coert Starck at the Embassy this morning, with favourable excerpts from Cloete's review. And one to Bartho to ask him to send a copy of the collection to Starck. Do you remember, he said: "I like you and your poems." And I sent you the *beautiful* Lucebert, which was again last night a revelation of the tenderness of those 50s writers – rare today!

You speak in your letter about your arguments this weekend and that you blame yourself – you should have seen how furious I was on Monday night – in the first place dead tired, it was over at Jack's, when I went to "fetch" Simone after work – because when I saw her I could immediately see that it wasn't flu, but scarlet fever or – measles. The doctor, who I had to wait for in the *goddamn* cold Cape wind (Anne says one shouldn't use "goddamn" in connection with the weather), arrived and confirmed measles, and serious – "severe" – said he. Dr Katz. And off he went with his Marx moustache and I stayed behind – quickly trying to calculate what I should do about work, etc. etc. The poor little thing just lies in a dark room and hardly wees because she doesn't want to eat or drink; and Jack and his family have a maid – and so he said she could stay there till Tuesday afternoon. I got up and looked out at the sea through the closed windows and heard him speak: "You'll only have to be away from work for a few days, Pie." Maybe he really didn't think further, but does he honestly still not know that I will lose money and maybe even my job? And then I said I'd come and fetch her early the next morning, and he could see I was angry. The next morning, when I arrived with the Press's car, he wasn't there. Since then no news whatsoever. Luckily I found someone who came in yesterday and today and can come tomorrow. After that, I'll have to see what happens. Simone is a little better, but the cough goes right through me; I've never been able to bear a cough; "eentonig die hoes van die kind aan my sy". One is so powerless against it, and I hate being powerless! She doesn't even want to play the harmonica, she says, "No, Mammie, because then my cough comes." And last night she sat up straight in her dark little bed "looking at" the book that I (dimwit) had brought her – she's not allowed to be anywhere near a light – and says: "This is a lovely book, Mammie." Monday night – when I caught the bus and left Simone behind, I couldn't help stating the obvious to Jack: "I'm sorry, I'll *have* to depend on you tonight." So you see, as Ouma would say, perhaps people are pigs in their innermost beings, and I don't want you to blame yourself too much about the apparent heartlessness, and a writer's foremost duty is to protect himself from RUBBISH and rubbish is everything that stands in one's way.

Try and decipher that "line of thought" if you can. I have honestly forgotten myself what I began with. In any case, you mustn't take the arguments too much to heart. After all our (terrible) arguments Jack said to me the other evening: "Of all the people I've ever known, you are probably the one I admire most." Wonderful him, or wonderful me???

So you see, you can do what you want, as long as you *"strive purely"*.

Why don't you write a drama for us – my ouma and me, and then we swop roles – do you see? – she plays the child and I play her – because we are so taken up with each other?

Thank you, my darling, my André, my own, for the beautiful greeting: and since I am so fond of ritual, I will repeat it tonight in my white nightdress.

And thank you for the poem of mine that your Ward friend translated (I'd really love to see the fuss he's made of it), I hope it is accepted. Send them our ugly portrait – no one there knows us, after all.

And I am so excited about your novella. Here, where strict order prevailed in the castle and at work – your spirited letter caused a chaos that you will have to come and quell. My darling, darling, humane human, "with all your flaws, all your shortcomings" ... and that's Éluard. And now I'm going to "veertjes schikken en glimlachen" because I am delighted and happy and completely satisfied.

Love to you,
Cocoon.

—————

Grahamstown
Sunday night, 8 September 1963

Cocoon, my dearest, most elegant girl,

Thank you for yesterday's short, pure, and distraught little letter with its *very* lovely poem. I have read little of yours that expresses as much hurt and beauty as the stanza: "Want jy word verkoop ..." ["For you are being sold ..."], especially after the light, playful beginning and the ominous transition: "Wat sal die afslaer sê van jou naam?" ["What will the auctioneer use for your name?"]. If it were me I would work a little on the lines: "Jou naam wat ek roep deur die duisternis / Wees gewaar-sku" ["Your name that I call out in the darkness / Be warned"], and perhaps also "my maagdelike woord" ["my virginal word"]. Otherwise it's so very *fine*, darling.

Actually, yesterday was a blessed day. Your letter-and-poem (and the lovely Lucebert) came my way, along with Desmond [Windell]'s photos, including the one of you. You didn't like it very much – and yet he captured so much of your intensity and tenderness. It's lying here next to me, with its gentle yet headstrong little twist of the mouth. Oh love, my love, the way I long for you!

Otherwise, a letter arrived from Chris Barnard to say that – apart from a few points of criticism – *Die Ambassadeur* is "a gift from heaven for our prose"; also, a letter from a friend – actually a friend's sister – who is a lecturer in Van Wyk Louw's department, just to say that he said to her, after my visit: "I am entirely under the impression that he is a cultured and intelligent person." And another letter, saying *Die Koffer* will be produced in Pretoria (Normal College).

It's almost a pity that all this had to arrive on the same day and wasn't more spread out over the long, grey weeks!

Your photo had such an instantaneous effect on me that I began to write a few verses again. I'm sending you two of them. Still working on a few others. They're not very "dense", but they wanted to come out; just had to. Rather call them prose pieces in lines of verse. They're in any case for *you*, of course.

Standpunte has arrived. Or at least Rob's copy has; mine always comes late. Three of my poems are in it ("Meisie" ["Girl"], "Vlug" ["Escape"] and "Selfs Heiliges" ["Even Saints"]). I'll try to get hold of a copy for you. But – that bladdy Grové! I sent him *six* poems, entitled "Six Poems / For Ingrid". In the end he took only three – and he left out the dedication. Not that anyone will have any *doubt* of course. But I wanted to see it there. And so the daily idiotic bourgeoisie-at-auction comes and takes away one's few remaining bits and pieces.

I'm working on the novella, *Orgie*. Still in "preparation". It will take a long time, yet. But it's beginning to find form.

Amid all the hubbub this morning I unpacked my drawers looking for some paper to scribble on and I came upon a bunch of rejection letters for short stories from my school and university days. One reader's report deals with a bloodthirsty novel (*The Lost City of Atlantis*) that I wrote when I was thirteen/fourteen. The reader said, inter alia: "The work is meant for the more mature stage of youth, but for these purposes the love relationships are far too erotic and the embraces too intimate. Parents will object ..." Fransie Malherbe will be happy to hear that even then I was thus inclined!

How are things with my measles girl? Please look after her nicely, lovely little thing. I would so badly like to be there to look after both of you together – because I know very well how tired and dispirited it makes you to deal with this on your own.

Child, child, my beautiful child – when I think of you, I want to say "biesie-biesie-bame", because with you it's easy to hold hands, "handjies same", and say "ame"; with you all kinds of wonders happen quite naturally.

I want, once again, to participate in the wonders of your absolutely girly life. Even a leucodendron and a navel, in your case, are little poems!

The papie, in its longing, is all too rebellious. How can I restrain it? "Als is enkeld als verlang / na heelal en na samehang".

Last night I lay awake again. Thoughts about your love, my love for you, and my longing. Oh you are "necessary, humble, precious and chaste". Mine, mine. God. You should know that, in the last few days, my yearning has not been sterile, just disheartening – there is a stillness, almost a happiness, in me, because despite the distance the *knowledge* of you is a mercy.

I want to phone Koos tomorrow and ask how the printing's going. I dare not set my expectations according to any specific date. But I'm hoping, hoping.

I love you very much; and I need you – not to bind you or make you unhappy and full of resistance, but to know you freely like wind and dunes and recklessly beautiful like your red bikini.

With love and *every* other thing,
André.

Castella
Monday evening, 9 September 1963

Hello my you,

I miss you. Was a bit sickish again this weekend; feverish – but it's probably the pace at which I live – as a Capetonian, I don't *like* busyness – Simone is still in bed but is getting better – she's really been very good! What did you do this weekend that you're so quiet? Got your post-letter on Friday. Walked to the post office to send you a telegram; re-read it there on the groaning chairs, and didn't know what to telegraph, so just folded the letter again and went off to work. MAD! What can one actually *say*? When Anne sees the letters that come and go between us, she says, slightly cattily, "Probably the same old pudding with a different syrup." Maybe our variations on love really are just a little trick?

My dearest man! Are you really coming on the 20th? How are things going with the proofs? Today, after the long, dead weekend, heard two small sounds from you; your three poems in *Standpunte*, which really look good and which were an excellent choice, my favourite is still "Selfs Heiliges" – (why is my name not with it as "promised" – you see, I even read Huck [*The Adventures of Huckleberry Finn*], and bravo! The language is delicious!) and – a short letter from Desmond telling me that you had one of his photos made for *Die Vaderland* and, together with that, the enlargement of I.J., and one (considerate) of us. Did you enjoy "Your Name", or were you a little indignant at first, liefsteling?

No more news from Piet. A letter from Bartho to say my book is appearing today (!). We're going to be together in his new anthology for young people, he says. In reality we aren't really that separated, my angel my André.

What's happening to the poor papie? It's going to shrink! Or will I have to smack those long elegant hands of yours when you get here? God, I'm becoming completely maternal (!) and then you get cross.

Uys talks the hind legs off a donkey (on the phone) and is pleased with his translation of *Twelfth Night*. He actually told me about *Standpunte* (why didn't you?) and said he finds that you are (naturally) very receptive, but that you haven't quite taken up surrealism in poetic form. "There are flashes: 'Small futile forgettable signs.'"

Otherwise static. The bladdy weather has also got stuck in winter, though the sun had to shine today of course when I had to work.

This morning when I walked into the cage, Anne had just arrived back from PE. If she or I had known they'd be going, I'd have gone with them and surprised you early on Saturday morning and invited you over for the Test. She said it was a mess at Boet Erasmus – the referee was terribly unfair towards the Australians and every time the Springboks were given a penalty kick the coloured spectators screamed MISS MISS MISS MISS MISS MISS and I killed myself laughing at all the things she described so indignantly. It's probably only in this country where people shoot at one another at a sporting event. It's as funny as it is scandalous! I wish we'd been there to join in the "chaos". Of course, the people are far more interesting to me than the rugby.

Van Wyk Louw is becoming lovely in his old age. Did you see what he wrote in *Standpunte* about censorship and *Lobola* – or did you only read your darling to-me-poems? Among other things – "God, that a people's spiritual life should depend on *this*! Not on its intelligence, but on such objects!" I read *Standpunte* right through to the Rembrandt advert and *in general* the whole thing is, as Anne says, just "the same sauce …"

And now I'm going to have a bath and then sleep, a W.E.G. Louw "geil slaap" or is only he capable of that, because he always stuffs himself with food? You'll probably say this is a jumbled letter.

I am starving on a spiritual-sexual level. And there are lots of "feathers" to "arrange" and there's much to smile about.

Phone me, maybe? You may as well again ask Bartho when, you're so close by. His letter was friendly and he's sending you a copy on fine Finnish paper. He asked me to do a translation of *Farewell to Arms* at R3 per 1 000 words. It's not much, but he is very accommodating and will pay me bit by bit. But it has to be finished before the end of the month; we can't all be André Brinks. Do you have a traditional remedy for me – when does one get time to dream? Because, as you say in your last letter, a person has to dream. It is part of one's organisational strategy against chaos.

Sleep sweetly, my dearest man. You must rest a lot, my ouma said: "You must not write so much, but rest in God." And maybe *that* is the dream.

And remain that, pure and strong, yearn beautifully, with your "shining sadness". And "Good night, sweet prince".

For the time being, love, love,
Your Cocoon.

PS: How is the thesis progressing, hm?
PPS: How is *Orgie* progressing? Send me a section.
IJonker.

——————

Grahamstown,
Monday night, 9 September 1963

Ingrid-Cocoon, my darling,

Thank you for today's delightful letter. It's so precious when you – as Anne says – are "befok in your kop". I hope the dear little sick child is much better now? I'd love to be able to sit with her and watch over her while you're at work.

Today the Volksie got her long-needed service and now she's driving more smoothly than ever before – and she's itching to hit the open road for Cape Town. I phoned Koos today, but, disappointingly, he was unable to say anything specific. Apparently Gothic Press is doing the printing – of course I was hoping your lot would do it. I impressed upon him once again that my holiday is from 20 to 30 September and

196

that I *must* have the proofs then. Now he says he'll send me a telegram the moment the printers give a date. Meanwhile, I know I *will* be coming down, even if the proofs aren't ready by then, so maybe I should request leave for early October. Just knowing I'll definitely be coming, even though the exact date's uncertain, is a mercy all on its own.

I started working on one of Bartho's translations today, a Simenon (Maigret) that translates so smoothly I might be able to finish it by next week.

I took our photos today to have them mounted; after that I'll have yours framed so I can put it up in my office. But please also send me one of the Jansje Wissema pictures. Let me know how much they cost. And if Jack still hasn't paid the account, I will.

Your idea of a play in which you and your grandmother feature, is actually full of possibilities. But I must first finish *Orgie*! Your grandmother's in there, too. I'm considering making the novella a double-decker: two novellas in one binding (subtitle, *Diptych*), both with the same title, both dealing with the same "content" – but the one straightforward and the other "experimental" (disputed term!) – each of course with different nuances according to the possibilities of the style. I'm impatient to begin, but it's so dangerous to start in an overhasty manner; it must wait out its own little nine-month period. Perhaps the biggest art of all is knowing when to start – neither too green nor too ripe, but just so.

I'm sending you a photo of Anton. There's some blurring in the picture – he *never* sits still! If he hadn't been here, I'd have gone crazy a long time ago.

I'm also sending a few poems, just for the hell of it, because I love you, and because you made today – like so many other days – radiate with light.

Your idea of "pure striving" is *right*. But I don't agree that "a writer's foremost duty is to protect himself from RUBBISH and rubbish is everything that stands in one's way". Being a writer also means being a person; it's an integral part of being a person. And it never gives one the "right" (in so far as people have "rights" to anything, or "wrongs"!) to behave unworthily *as a person* ... and this is why, in the past while, I've so often been appalled at my own behaviour.

Your letter and your love have created such a quiet sense of happiness in me that tonight, for the first time in months, I felt like playing the creative chef again; I made a "poulet basquaise" that would have stimulated even your tiny appetite.

My apologies. Me and food again! Do you know, I've never felt quite as forlorn and guilty as the – many – times when you were sad or upset and I simply had to eat. I would also be feeling very upset, and bladdy hungry, too, so I'd eat, but don't think I didn't feel bad as well ...! It's all *terribly* funny, now. Actually, there's been a great deal of generous laughter in everything we've done together; that's possibly the most precious thing about it all, because it came with full human happiness.

The "Brinkman" affair at the boarding house.

Jan Cilliers [Jan F.E. Celliers] and "Martjie" – and A.D. Keet!

The man at the Hout Bay hotel who said: "You'd better write Mr *and* Mrs in the register, else people might ask you who that woman is that lives with you ..."

And the night I made a little tent and swooped down on you like the Holy Ghost.

And everything else, too: your hair in my mouth, the sudden tickling of your elbow, or your fingers in my ribs. (When you asked so *indignantly*: "What's so funny, hey?")

And then "doing everything over again in italics ..."

Girlie, lovely you, I love, *love* you. One of these days I'll make you another tape; Rob's got my recorder at the moment. (Borrowed for his theatre production, for which he composed the music himself – or have I told you this already?)

Meanwhile, I want to say goodbye to you with all my love, which wants to keep you lovely, for a long time, alive.

And with a poem by Hans Warren:

Bij wijze van gebed

Wees, als het dan niet anders kan,
wees, als de lente dan zijn slanke
lichtblauwe hand met gouden nagels
om mijn gezwollen keel gaat sluiten,
iets als een god, iets als een lappenboom,
dat ik je in verzen bidden kan, dat ik
de flarden van mijn wanhoop aan je hang.

Honderden spiegels van honderden dagen
hebben vergeefs getracht je te vervormen.
Ik heb je lief, ik heb geen anderen goden
meer voor mijn aangezicht …
…
ik ga de liefde in zoals het water in
blind, handpalmen vooruit, mijn ingehouden
snikken zwellen jouw hart in mij en
steeds zwaarder wordt het er, steeds eeuwiger.

And a little one by Nel Noordzij:

Je ligt zo neergelegd te slapen
met twee ellebogen als wapen
en een kroontje haren aan je haar
al kijk ik er maar even naar
ik sla tot in mijn schoot alarm
en rijm een zoontje in je arm

I am always with you and always love you,
André.

Grahamstown
Thursday, 12 September 1963

My little angel,

Thank you for this morning's lively little letter, your commentary on
the Springboks and similar matters, and your confession about being
"hungry" in a spiritual-sexual way. Don't I know it! And feel it! But the
papie hasn't yet shrunk. It won't, either. Because – as they used to say
in the olden days – desire doesn't only tug at my heartstrings!

Today's a holiday: Rhodes has its own holidays, and they don't
always coincide with those of country and "volk". Today is "Founders'
Day". All members of staff are kindly requested to attend the cere-
mony. I wish you could've been there – it was like Victor Hugo's "sublime et grotesque": first the long, formal procession of academics in
their gowns and hoods, and, wherever possible, wearing medals ("each
one walks all set up in his own separateness"); then a ritual of honour-
ing the departed and a plea to Almighty God during which the assembly
answers "amen" at regular intervals – often irregularly. After a sermon
about the evils of our time (Christine Keeler, the old cow, was dug up
for this purpose), there was solemn prayer (for the umpteenth time),
a hum of Ourfatherwhoartinheaven … and a general drift towards the
War Memorial. There we formed a sacred circle around the memorial, a
stately ring-a-ring-o'roses, with more prayers, a recitation of the honour roll of the departed, syllable for syllable separately articulated (here
and there wrongly pronounced), a laying of wreaths, at least a dozen of
them, each with a bow and a salute; and then deadly silence while the
"Last Post" drawled from a trumpet somewhere – and during this stirring highlight, under the blue of our heavens and far from the depths of
our seas, two dogs made an appearance in the sacred circle, lifted their
legs and pissed over all four corners of the monument, and all over the
recently laid wreaths. *Sic transit gloria.*

In between, or meanwhile, I'm translatingtranslatingtranslating –
forunately Simenon is gripping and quick – and I'm working on the

novella, too. I started *writing* only yesterday (so far I've just been making notes, puzzling things out, etc.) and I've got as far as page seven. I decided to let go of the double-decker idea. The subtitle remains "Diptych", because each page has two columns: on the left side *he* talks; on the right, *she* has her say. Occasionally there are blank passages; sometimes left and right are versions of the same situation ... and as I said previously, a good number of my "poems" have been worked into it. I'll retype the first few pages in a minute, so I can send them along. I've suddenly begun wondering whether I mightn't be able to get it done in time for Bartho's prize [the APB Prize for 1963], but that could cause overhastiness and detract from both *Die Ambassadeur* and *Orgie*. Moreover: you're already there to represent us this year! Girlie, oh man, I so badly want you to get that prize. Thus far, I think your chances are really good. I don't yet know how good Jan's and Adam Small's stuff is, but I doubt it'll have *Rook en Oker*'s "exquisiteness". I'm holding thumbs – and all my other dangling parts – for you.

You said on the phone you're "hungry". Little person, my cocoon, this time we're going to go mad together. It's not long now. Even if the trip is shifted to the beginning of October – please, I hope not! – it's still not long, we're already halfway through September.

Next Tuesday and Wednesday night I'll be out (the movies; and Guy Butler's *Everyman*); but on Thursday I'll phone again.

Greetings to you, with love and grace, my exquisite, beautiful, virginal Ingrid: "a great deal of us is together, and we can but abide by it, and steer our courses to meet soon. John Thomas says good night to lady Jane, a little droopingly, but with a hopeful heart."

Yours, yours, darling mine, always,
André.

And a kiss for Simone.

Castella
Thursday, 12 September 1963

My dearest André,

Thank you lots for your two lovely lusty letters and the telephone call on Tuesday night. And for Simone's books, which she wants to talk to you about herself, and for the little photo of Anton, with his beautiful naked little thing, who looks just like you. It seems his mouth, which is half-hidden by his fist, looks like yours. Send me LOTS more, proof. The other evening when I was playing your tape again, I heard a child crying and later went and looked accusingly out of my door at the neighbours, when I suddenly realised it was Anton! I'd forgotten about his accompaniment on the tape. Simone, or Simnoe, as she spells it, has become very thin. I wonder whether I will ever get her fattened up again, but she's up and about all day now and will go back to school on Monday. I wish one could have them immunised against these unnecessary illnesses, and this all still lies ahead for our fat baby friend! I wish you could bring him with you when you come so that we could have our children here – and he wouldn't talk!

Darling, darling, it's about a week and a half before you'll *definitely* be here but I still want to say, it's not going to "help" anything if you go and stay with Koos and them after the weekend – because then you'll just get to bed late, and they'll know – what's more, they'll then get involved; ag, you must just come and stay here, or keep a room somewhere. I do so love new places. Shall I book a place for you at the Edgehill? Everyone will in any case, *know*. And when you go back everyone there will also *know*. You would never fool *me*!

Oh, child! The weather has turned to winter again and I long so for the sun. I want to see the sky wide open when you are here, and I want to go to [Lanzerac] with you. François [Krige] has an exhibition there, and on opening night all the guests had a meal there – but I didn't want to go because you're going to introduce me to the place, aren't you? "Straight into the jaws of death." (Uys said we should never have gone to Stellenbosch together that night.)

There's so much news in your last two letters – the little note from Van Wyk Louw is especially wonderful. Especially after you actually demonstrated what it is that Nicolette does! I am *very* proud of you.

And why do the photos have to be mounted? Send them on, I so badly want to see them again and that colour one of you laughing I want for ever (not the turkey)! that nice one taken on our honeymoon days at Franschhoek. And success with *Orgie!* Where is my MS of the revised *Ambassadeur*? You're right about the poem "Jou Naam" – I'll see if I can do something with the lines "Your name which I call" and the unavoidable "word". I'm becoming over-confident. Congratulations on *Die Koffer* – I forgot (with Simone's sickness) to listen to your "tender-beloved voice" and was so *sorry* about it. And do you know what they did at APB? They took your photo away and put mine in its place with my books around it – now the book really looks smart.

The paper is beautifully white – you've probably received yours already. I'm going to accept Bartho's offer of *A Farewell to Arms* – will keep me busy between October and December when I (maybe?) come and visit you in Grahamstown for a long weekend. If you save, because I'm not going to get out of this financial mess quickly – am also going to apply to Molteno Trust for a bursary and am going to buy, among other things, nice clothes with it, because now I want nice clothes. Apparently one easily gets £500 to live on. Or should it be saved for going overseas? Though it's far and lonely there!

You wanted to know about the BBC. They asked me about "The Child" (naturally) as if that's all I'd ever written – I read the poem and just chatted. Nothing very impressive. Will tell you when we *see* (unbelievable) each other. And until then you will just have to control your rebellious papie. And it's very clear – in "Kriptiek" I only got a fright about the "fuck" and the "Elegietjie" idea is a *good* one, but he should tremble more, and one should get a fright when he falls (falls apart?). But I'll write it myself! You'll have to be careful with your ideas anywhere around me, my darling colleague! But they are after all *our* poems!

This is such a sloppy (and actually sleepy) letter. Was up late on Monday night (with what?) and Tuesday evening with the BBC, and last night Jack and I went and had a drink at the Café Royal to toast *Rook en Oker*. (One celebrates the thing so often, do you still remember?) Afterwards he had a meal here – and do you know what, my treasure? – on Saturday I'm getting a stove *and* a table – and so we chatted; he is so timorous, it actually makes me sad, and he is so proud.

I didn't mean one should act in an undignified way when I said WHATEVER I said. The danger of there being RUBBISH in the writer's path is usually in his own mind; the rubbish he must necessarily confront every day – and there's all the news. It's actually a newsy letter, and what are you going to tell your class now? But know that I miss you, lots. Make that tape for me, then I'll do one back. And write well and lecture well and sleep well. I'll phone Koos to ask him when the proofs will be ready, or the Gothic. Sorry I'm not reading it! There's a kind of drabness here at work, and the other reader is reading your French translation.

Thank you for your beautiful glowing letter, and thank you for you. And now *I'm* going to sleep with you. I'm already in bed, dressed in white, my distant groom! My André Brink. Send me a picture of yourself. I'm already familiar with the ones I have and forget how you look when you laugh. Love dearest liefsteling ALWAYS,

Cocoon Cocoon.

Simone dictates:

André, thank you André to send me the books. When the postman bring the books I play with putty, I make a little girlie, I make my doll a little bra and a little bikini pants. Then I saw the postman standing at the door. He gave the books to Maggie. Then I looked at the books. Then I had half of the story. Maggie's boyfriend read it. The one is about a fox and one about a cat in a hat. It's a nice story. Both of them are nice stories. I'm playing with putty. A man was very kind to me because he gave me the putty. My mummy read me the stories. I'm making a stick girl with the putty. She is floppy. I'm better. There is a three chimney house by our flat. A nice dolly I got in my flat. My mummy read me a story by Mickey Mouse. I can stand up every time when Mummy goes to work. Mummy gave me a tickey. We got a nice cupboard and we got a big big stick. I got a little dolly with no arms and no legs but nice long hair. André, how are you? Are you sick? Or are you well? I got a big stick and a sun hat. We've got a little bird sitting on the tree now. My mummy is smoking. The birdies is shouting to one another: quieek! quieek! There not going home yet, the birdies. What is André eating for supper? Thats enough. And thank you. Send love. I kiss you.

SIMNOE

––––––––––

Grahamstown
Monday morning, 16 September 1963

Darling girl of mine,

Tonight or tomorrow morning early I'll try to write a longer letter, but this is just a short one so I can make the post in time – and really just an accompaniment to the parcels that I hope a) will arrive on time, and b) get there undamaged. With love and love and more love.

Last night was another of those neverending nights of longing: lots of dreams that all, sooner or later, ended up in the little room in the castle with its beloved, knobbly bed; and many hours of lying awake, hands under my head, like that first night when I met you and you said "no" as if from a dizzy height ("André! We don't even know each other!"); you even offered to bring me some milk to calm me down. Precious little devil!

I'll be able to give you a call on Wednesday night after all; and I'll see if I can phone on Thursday evening, too. Maybe you'll be eating out somewhere, then? Here on this side, I'll just have to go by the "law of simultaneity", eat the bread and pour the wine and let you become flesh and blood from that.

Luckily the weekend was not quite the desert it so often is. I worked on Saturday – work-work-worked until late on Saturday night; Sunday morning a few friends dropped in; and in the afternoon I played chef for my evening guests. Two invitees: Frieda [le Grange], about whom you already know, and a young artist, head of the art school here – slightly effeminate but very *sincere* in his thinking. At least it gave me an opportunity to have some *conversation*, something I need very badly. (For chlorophyll one has to search both earth and air, says Eybers!)

To be with you, drink wine devoutly and with love, converse, gen- uinely communicating, to take a bath, kiss your leucodendron, fuck until we're out of breath, and then finally just lie together quietly, deeply happy, chatting lazily, just being together, finding complete identification even in our sleep, van alleenzijn langzaam te genesen. Ach, du … du!

One of these days it will be like that again. Soon I'll be *with* you. We'll go stay somewhere, far from the madding crowd, just me and you, just the two of us. Drink Martinis. And laugh a lot. And be very much in love. The moment I hear from Koos I'll let you know *immediately*.

I almost found myself having to review *Rook en Oker* for 60. In fact, it's still a possibility. Bartho phoned to say I must send reviews of *Man in die Middel* [Man in the Middle] (Chris B.), *Skepsels* [Creatures] (Dolf v. N. [van Niekerk]) and *Rook en Oker* (Ingrid Jonker) "on the double". Naturally, I was especilly excited about yours. But then I thought: your work deserves a discussion that no one dares think won't be objective; you and I will know, and Bartho too, that I would never write anything about *Rook en Oker* that isn't honest. But precisely because I attach so much value to it, all those "readers" who know about us will immedi- ately think: this isn't a review, it's just a "write-up". So I asked him if there wasn't an alternative option. If not, I'll do it anyway – and to hell with suspicious readers.

The "new" edition's paper does indeed look quite beautiful; it's now almost two times thicker than before! My own copy, though, was poorly bound, with an ugly fold across the cloth – but hopefully that's an exception. And then, unbelievably, I found another two printing errors: the white space between the title and the first line on page three and page seven is quite a bit smaller than elsewhere. But it's unlikely Bartho will yet again have it re-set! "Ordinary" readers are unlikely to notice it, either. I just hope, my love, that it sells many copies, quickly. And I hope the Dutch embassy is deeply impressed with it. (You must start making moves to get an identity card with a view to a passport!)

I'm making slow progress on *Orgie*. I've got as far as page twelve. In a day or two I'll retype the part you haven't seen yet and post it off. Gradually more and more possibilities, complexities and subtleties are beginning to emerge. Precisely because it's *our* work, it *has to* be good. For that reason I'm in no hurry, and even when it's done, I'm going to let it be for a good few months before sending it to Bartho. They asked for a fragment, at this stage, to publish in *60*, but I want to keep it for just us until it comes out. The technique's in any case such that one should rather not publish it piecemeal.

I'm also sending your "Ou Perd" ["Old Horse"] to Bartho! And a few of my own new poems that I sent you last week.

This letter has become rather lengthy after all! I must go now so I can catch the post. Today there should be one from you. There *must* be. Naughty, precious little cocoon who doesn't ever write!

And for the 19th (and the 23rd!): my precious darling, I want this day and this year to be one of universal light, universal purity, a departure from drabness and tristesse.

Goodbye for now, my virginal woman, my *free* person who "pours drink like Bacchus / freely splashing the acanthus": greetings with love, tenderness and many wishes; and with much longing. Arrange your beloved feathers, and also the little chick's. And on the night of the 19th we will sleep, apart, together.

Your André.

Castella
Tuesday, 17 September 1963

My poor dearest neglected man!

It feels like an eternity since I last wrote to you – and every damned time I have a chance something happens or people arrive – it's twelve o'clock already and I am terribly tired – thank you for your letter and the first part of *Orgie* – which I don't completely understand but which I find exciting anyway – is that long dedication personal or is it going to be part of the story? Sunday morning walked to Chris and told him about it – on Saturday evening he had a performance and did the piece out of *Pot-Pourri* – you probably want to know about it – I half-expected him to come and fetch me but he must have decided against it and on Sunday morning he was very sorry, because apparently it had gone well; he says you really are a big man!

Darling André! I was so MAD when I couldn't reach you tonight; and now I have to write in a hurry again because I'm going to scream from exhaustion – you see, my sister and I decided that Simone will now go to her instead of crèche; then I pay her, and then I go and see them every evening after work, or otherwise every second night and fetch her for weekends, because she is still exhausted from measles, and needs a lot of rest. Tonight I wanted to leave early so that I could come and write; my brother-in-law walked with me, and was on the point of leaving when Jan and Marjorie arrived; and then he began chatting! And now – now it is so late again and "I want to go to sleep". But when we talk again (after the call on Thursday) we'll be talking to one another, and *seeing*.

Friday evening I told Uys about us ever so vaguely – because everything upsets him so much (seems to me he is mostly afraid that I will "take" Jack "away" from him – although he says that's rubbish!). But I had to scold him because I'd heard that he'd had an infantile conversation with Bill de Klerk about us – God! And during this conversation (between me and Uys) Jack went to sleep, with the Bible, and looked so bladdy *defenceless;* and I said to Uys, I feel *sad* about him, which he then conveyed to Jack and translated as "pity", about which there was a little quarrel on Sunday – André, André! All I want is to be pure and clean and turned inwards, to live without explanations and just bring this tiny bit of softness and closeness to the people I love, that's all that is left! And then to be left in peace!

Saturday afternoon on the bus to Clifton with the beautiful sunny sea on the side – terrible me so guilty and unpoetic, a despondent "we are all long since past grief" – "laat alles in sy donneg val" or "let God's water run over God's acre". And think "love of the beloved brown eyes" and say: God, no! no! "Above all else, guard your heart." Today's reading. In other words, I must keep and save you and myself with you. Treasures, grace, purity. Because I feel despondent and tired. Because I love Jack and I love *you*, and I can see the end of everything; and I'm going overseas (but it seems that might also be derailed, because Piet would never give permission now to take Simone out of the country, and if I leave her with him it might be a mess when I get back). Sorry, this letter probably sounds *desperate* to you again, but actually it's not – just too tired to think; to create order out of the chaos, and so, death of the poet.

But I know everything will become clear and pure again – let me count your moesies just one more time, my distant, dear stranger. Because dear you are, precious and fine and bountiful; I miss you but cannot imagine at all that you will be here *within* a week. And maybe Friday. In *three* days. No, I simply can't believe it. John Malherbe once asked with a worried scrunched-up face: *"How do you feel?"* and now I ask you, far away in your house with your garden, with your "significant love" and your amazing diligence. Dearest André! We're alive! At the moment in angst, but thank God in the midst of or at the centre of this pitiless life, so delicate and intricate, but so real. And by the time you get my letter, you'll almost be here, physical and true, and buttressed with love, with misfortune, with fear, with tenderness, with indulgence, with burdens, with joy, with purity, with dividedness. And then I'm going to count your moesies as a challenge to nothingness.

Thank you for you. Your dearest Cocoon. My dearest man, Cocoon, cocoon, con.

PS: The "police spy" was arrested this morning for sabotage. God god god! Suspicion. And again suspicion – perhaps – forgive us – a ploy on the part of the police?

You, my little treasure, must sleep well, and as you once said, stay with me tonight. I call you by name; you are mine. We who always seek meaning (our sentence?) must perhaps try not to for a while, just remain soft. "Als een gele foto liggend in het water." Glad to be alive; reality is beautiful.

Dearest man! Good night, and tomorrow, good morning, beautiful and attentive, desperately enchanted!

Your (very small),
Cocoon.

———————

Grahamstown
Tuesday, 17 September 1963

Dearest,

Today I'm really writing no more than a rushed little note, because you should at least get a letter on your 29th birthday. All this scrambling and rushing all over the place just to get through the daily routine. You, in fact, experience this far more than I do. It still astounds me that you've been able to hold out so long, epecially at Citadel.

I had a really awful afternoon yesterday. I can remember only one other day that was quite this bad – when I rode over a frog in front of the garage, and was depressed about it for a week. Yesterday I had a hell of a fight with the gardener because he told me a bunch of lies – and then he offered me his "notice". I'm fond of him and he's fond of me and the garden needs him, so what now, dammit?

Watched Guy Butler's *Everyman* last night – a very baroque, sensational version of Middle Age simplicity. I had to write a damn review for a PE newspaper, knowing that they're going on tour and that a bad review could put at risk the R1 000 they've incurred in expenses. So I ended up fine-tuning the piece until one in the morning, trying to be honest without being mean.

This afternoon at five the Englishman with the double-barrelled surname's coming around for a chat [Duval Smith] – the one who visited you. I'm looking forward to meeting him, just because – silly, I know – it's a link to you. Otherwise I'd rather be working on the novella. We should in fact be writing it together: you scripting your parts, and me mine! It's as far as page 15 now and I'm busy with your palm-reading at the Clifton Hotel and the prelude to that first night, "so safe and still …"

There was just one highlight yesterday: a gorgeous picture of Brigitte Bardot in *Paris Match*. Along with the discovery that she strikes me as beautiful because she has something of your lovely smile. In the photo at least.

I'm still waiting for the colour prints. The nightie photos came out badly – one of them almost okay, but nothing much to speak of. I'll bring them with me, one of these fine days.

And now, child of mine, I wish you a happy birthday full of joy; be assured of the serenity of my love, the whole day long and always: while you're doing your grey work; during lunch with Mrs Bouws (?); then, in the jam-packed bus; and finally in the little castle whose every little detail I can see before my eyes. When you go to sleep, *with* me, lie still and close your eyes and listen, and *feel*, knowing that – and how – I hail every part of you, with love, earnestness and play; and how, when I'm done with my greetings, I open you up softly and penetrate you very deeply, and stay there, and come, and leave you with secrets and tenderness and wonder, and a generous laugh of joy. Then I kiss your lovely eyes and you fall asleep, and the two of us are mystifyingly happy.

With love,
Your André.

I've enclosed a little cheque, as promised.

Grahamstown
Friday, 20 September 1963

Dearest lovely Cocoon,

I greet you from the splendid lazy warmth of this day, my sweet-faced cherub!

Thank you for your beautiful midnight letter.

Thank you for the joy of last night's conversation, which was a *discovery* – after the frustration of Wednesday night's call.

So, you were very tired, lazy and sleepy this morning? Did you go to bed very late last night?

And, this weekend, you're going to do some pleasant child-minding with your *two* lovely little girls?

I'm sending you a few pages of *Orgie* – many of them are in an elementary state and still need a *lot* of work: it's just to keep you more-or-less up to date with the novella's progress. I'm also sending a "guide" to the references, and a short summary of the whole "story", because you wouldn't otherwise find much unity in it, especially reading it piecemeal over a long period. After this morning's letter I'm especially eager to get back to it, but I must first complete Bartho's Simenon before getting back to you; there are also a whole lot of other little tasks to be done.

And then Friday week I'll be there! As I said last night, I should arrive by six. The two of us can either go somewhere, or stay over for the night and disappear on Saturday. Let's see how the "spirit takes us".

Meanwhile I'm sending you the colour pictures, which *finally* arrived this morning. I had only the best six printed, because they cost almost R1 a piece and the others aren't worth the price. Maybe we can take a few nice black-and-white "proofs" this time!

That damn Uys! It's a great pity, and it's *upsetting* that he – of all people – should behave in this manner. What did he actually tell Bill (and therefore: the whole world plus all of Johannesburg)? And what did *you* say to him about *us*?

Does your shirt fit? The underpants are surely much too big for your little bum. Now you've got a fly, too – not an "inessential" one like that first night in your lovely, spotless little white pyjamas.

This has been a mad week, what with going out to see *Everyman*, Alec Guinness's *Last Holiday* and also *The Bridge on the River Kwai*, plus the huge amount of time that the BBC came and wasted here. My heaps of marking have rudely stacked up, and I'll have to work like a slave during my few days of holiday. But then I'll be coming down to rest with you over the weekend before digging into the proofs (the worst work in the world … as if you don't know!).

This afternoon I'd have loved to make a leisurely tape for you, but now I've got an honours seminar from three to five, and after that I won't be alone any more, because then the servant will be gone and I'll have to take over with Anton.

I won't be able to phone next week, because it's holidays and Estelle won't be working at night. But our arrangements are all settled and of course I'll still write. You too, please! Beloved, neglectful little thing who is always forgiven for everything so easily, and so readily.

Last night I slept with you. Longing, longing and more longing. But we can start counting the days now. Strange that I've chosen my *time* in this way (if one can talk about "choosing", that is): if you follow the pattern of the past five months, then your cycle begins again on the 25th. Don't get *sick* this time! I love you, my own, my Ingrid, my *you*,

Your André.

———————

Castella
Monday, 23 September 1963

Darling my André,

To congratulate you on your success in the Netherlands, bravo! And on top of this, I am going to brag about you over there. To say thank you for your letter and the beautiful colour photos and the second part of the lovely, reckless, fateful *Orgie* – "I" just want some more *dignity*! Did I really express all that fury during our palm-reading?

And thank you for the two telegrams, my generous darling! My 2nd birthday quiet, with a mad Simone-visit and children's stories, with my brother-in-law saying, "You know why your ol' man won't come here? Because if he had to come he would come in here bleeding and on his knees …" Oh, God! And thank you, darling, darling, for your review of *Rook en Oker*; of course I *do* feel that you are prejudiced; you can take out that bit about "Anglicisms" because they're there as an indicator of the times, and are no more "inferior" than a quote from the French or whatever; in this respect we Afrikaners really have to stop feeling inferior to the English! Uys thinks it's a *kind* review (we're great pals now!); but he thinks you should rather take one or two poems and give a sober analysis of them instead of trying to give an overview within the space available to you. Maybe … maybe.

Rainy night last night; party Saturday evening; sleep Friday evening. Thursday (the first birthday) was a delight! And child, the photos, especially the one of you; transported me back to you – your darling smile and dimples. I just want to say good night. "To the sadness at the source of your valiant joy", to the moesies and the hands and the come come, hell! Goodnight, "who has said night …"

Till Friday, with pure tenderness and love,
Cocoon.

Monday night, 23 September 1963

Dearest, lovable, beloved Cocoon,

So, did you have your second birthday today? This must have been such a wonderful thing in your childhood. Childhood? Isn't one *always*

214

a child?! My own, my own guapa (before you get suspicious, that's Spanish for "cute thing").

If I could just talk like you – and I really want to – then tonight I'd have to say: I am absolutely the happiest.

Because:

Now, in just four nights' time, I won't be sleeping alone. In just four nights I'll be with the most divine, precious person I know.

And in four nights we'll also celebrate the *Lobola*-thing. I was naturally expecting this development because Koos predicted something of the kind, but then talk was just that Bezige Bij would take over a few hundred copies and also bind them. But now they're going to make it one of their Literaire Reuzenpockets, with a print run of 2 000. Financially it doesn't mean all that much, as the Pockets sell for just 20c. Commission gets deducted, and Koos and company then share the proceeds 50-50 with me. But more important things are in play here. Bezige Bij is one of the Netherlands' leading prestige publishers, and their Pockets are offered to the entire European market for translation; in addition, the assessor was Bert Schierbeek, a leading "modern" figure in experimental work in Holland.

I have some other news too. This time it's very, very *funny*. Moves are afoot to have me elected as an assessor-member of the Akademie!!! Keep this to yourself – it's a state secret. In fact it makes me rather angry, because one day I'd like to receive a Hertzog Prize just so that I can turn it down; if they make me a member now and I don't accept the nomination, I might never get a chance to refuse a Hertzog Prize. If, on the other hand, I become a member, I wouldn't be able to refuse the prize. Ridiculously complicated.

If only all our problems were of this nature.

Meanwhile I'm *working*. Yesterday I finished Bartho's first translation (I've done 20 000 words over the last two days), marked bladdy essays, read a manuscript for Bartho ... there's just no time for *Orgie*, but I'm not over-hasty. And lectures end on 20 October; then I can write until the end of February.

I saw a little something I want to bring with me on Friday. A completely ordinary, but *cute* little object. This of course does not exclude our shopping expedition, my darling. Why can't you always be with me so I can just give and give and then be in a position to f... away all our money?!

Are you happy? Are you waiting, sweet and beautiful, full of light, fire and stillness?

Divine beloved, light your little lamp, your groom is coming.

Oh we're going to celebrate, we're going to be human beings amid all the delightful, unthinkable, wonderful things that reside in being human.

I love you. Reservedly, quietly, with abandon and in wildness.

Until Friday, until I see you, with love, Ingrid, Cocoon,
Your André.

——————

Castella
Wednesday, 2 October 1963

Darling my André,

Ten-thirty and home in Castella to a radiant Simonetta – with our living bed just like that untouched and the cups and the mess in the kitchen, in the bedroom and the bathroom – and by this time you've probably arrived in Grahamstown dead tired – and I just want to say hello and goodnight and be thankful for you and go and lie down as if in a massive sickbed, split apart and *whole*.

    … Het verleden is onzeker
    de toekomst is blind

    wat men in het oog houdt als heden: levende beelden
    die van minuut tot minuut verstenen

rivieren onder onweer liefde
die uitstroomt in het laagland in de zee

wouden ben ik verdwaald in geluk of waanzin
ik slaap in en het ontwaken is bitter als stilte

steden waarin men zichzelf herhaalt en aanvult
afvalt schaduwt verliest en weervindt
…
ik geef gaan raad ik wijs geen weg
duizend sporen kruisen elkander

het lijf vergaat ons eerder dan het lachen
na de woestijn is water bovenaards.

Stay happy darling tender moesie-man; I'm going to read your *Huisgenoot* now and amuse myself with our new memory and kiss all your little laughs.

I miss you and I love you – André!

Cocoon.

ps: Later – Your article isn't in *Huisgenoot* – just a bunch of revolting muscular Springboks! Still, divine five days – though *Rook en Oker* is jumping before my eyes – it's completely irresponsible! I am a GLUTTON for talking to you – last night at the 191 was, I think, the most precious, or was it the bed, *many* times (thirteen), or on our walk when we were angry? Work today was actually "most kak" – but tomorrow I'll be eating with Mrs Bouws and meeting Lena at five.

Good night! Night, dearest, love my darling – Con. (nie?)

Darling mine,

I've been walking around for three days now feeling guilty about not writing, but it's simply a case of yielding to the final, hectic acceleration of the academic year. However, right now everything will just have to wait until I've conversed a little with you. Last week this time we were in the little castle. Or on our way there after the morning's shopping, you with your white bathing suit (have you broken it in yet on your gorgeous little body?) and me with my red pyjamas. And now? Now I'm sitting here with a few strategically located scabs and a heart full of love and quiet longing.

Here, everything has become so very ordinary, after that night's inexplicable little drama, in fact upsettingly ordinary. And who can live "ordinarily" after drinking from your fountain? "Who can live on as a person after he's played the role of God –?"

My love, my love, with a stillness and compassion and breadth, a kind of untouchable *happiness*. I've not yet had any time to sit and think about our nearly six days together, sort it all out, form a precipitate. Yet it's been there all the time, behind all my daily doings – a process of assimilation, of absorbing, of *discovery*. While there with you I was all too aware, throughout, that our sexual togetherness couldn't be as fully a surrender-filled orgy as I *wanted* it to be, all because of something as banal as an abrasion! But nonetheless we did, once again – and it remains a wonder, every time – liberate another angel from stone, gave form to a new word (and allowed a new word to become flesh); and we discovered our own island in the sea.

Your letter has still not arrived (I don't mean the long one of a while ago, or the short one you talked about on the phone); I wonder what's going on with the post. Everything's wonderfully quiet.

What will you do on Monday night at the Cultural Society or whatever? Did Jack convince you in the end? And when I phoned the other night, was there fighting and tension and frustration again?

Darling Cocoon, you who took shelter so deep in my arms, hid away underneath me, and took me so deeply into yourself – you are not allowed to be *unhappy*.

Without a certain degree of agony, we cannot exist. *May* not, perhaps, because one must always *know* life is precious, wonderful, and therefore *dangerous*; without this acute awareness (anxiety, even), we wouldn't be able to feel or experience things so deeply. However, mere unhappiness, which is really just frustration, and being trapped in a sterile and destructive way – *that* is not something you should have to endure. I'd like to protect you against it; to make a fire around you with my love to counter it, "ward off the pestilence that walks in darkness".

I'll write again, a longer and more rounded letter. This note was just to make contact so that you won't be abandoned to silence, and so you know – as if you dare doubt it! – that I love you, how much I love you, and how I carry you with me, as if I were a mother and you my little child: with confidence, tenderness, faith, hope *and* love; and with great thankfulness for everything you continue to be for me, and for what you have been for me once again in the past few days. You have become a "home" for me, and with you, always, everything is beautiful.

With much love,
Your André.

———————

Castella
Saturday night, 5 October 1963

My darling André,

It is absolutely unbelievable to think that last Saturday night we were at the Cederwood – I think we'd just started having our drinks – it's so dusky and warm – tomorrow I'm going for a swim in your beautiful white bathing suit – eventually, because tomorrow *has* to be nice weather – I have Simone here (this sad little solace has just knocked over her glass of milk): this morning we went to take measurements and have a fitting for her flower-girl dress – and do you know what? I tidied the desk and put all your hundreds of letters neatly together in their envelopes – and your documents in files and my documents in files and our newspaper clippings in files … "sorting". Even Rosa Nepgen's nasty review of *Sempre*. "He should cleanse it of the offensive little things which make one keep it from young children"! God! (In any case, a person who gorges to the extent that she is as fat as a pig is offensive to society.) Darling! I miss you. Miss you so much that I took everything away from you for myself, and last night after Jan and Marjorie – wrote you a poem, like this:

My embrace redoubled me
my breasts call to each other
the two prancing friends
and my hands enclose my secrets

in a room far away
behind the spilled autumn
your eyes gaze astounded
at the mirror of your body

Nice? Of course, they were very inquisitive last night when I went to visit them – it's so hard for me to lie about you – "a lie in the soul" – if I deny you, I deny myself. Marjorie says: "I suppose he finds it difficult to choose between you." And then I honestly have to keep quiet! And the night you called, Jack was quite chilly, and says he doesn't care about me any more. And what news from your side?

Do you want to send my little poem to *60* or do you have objections to it? How are things going with *Orgie* and please send your darling tape soon, my hello my André?

I found the poem "Prayer before Birth" (the old [Louis] MacNeice (lovely old woof) died of drink the other day).

God or whatever means the Good
Be praised that time can stop like this
That what the heart has understood
Can verify in the body's peace
God or whatever means the Good.

But I am not in the mood tonight to quote "Prayer" for you – it'll come! Heard old Louis himself read it but unfortunately he was a bit drunk, and struggled …

It's silly to say I miss you. I even miss your irritating scratching, and such a long wet sleep! Do you think that there's a moesie-chance that we will have a child?

Now I'm going to sleep in "our" bed with Simone, and on Monday I will try to find the lost letter – imagine if someone reads it? – and tomorrow I'm going for a lovely swim – and, as Abraham de Vries said that night (vulgar!) "perhaps you'll get another collection from this". I am in the mood to write again. 'Night beautiful, beloved, tender precious mine. And write soon-soon, or I'll send you a writing pad. And thank you for the phone call. Tell everything, everything. Love, my darling, and kiss the papie inside me!

Your Cocoon.

Sunday, 11.30 pm

Dearest André, had a swim, in the lovely white swimming costume; dropped Simone off and had a meal with Chris till pm, lay around at his flat and laughed and chatted about everything and more, and *loved* you, always. Come back soon.

Cocoon my André,
Cocoon.

{Your letters are now almost as numerous as our *other* total: 69.}

Grahamstown
Monday morning, 7 October 1963

My most lovely, precious Connie,

It's as if my reactions this time are slower than usual – perhaps because I fell back into work so swiftly. It's only now, and especially over the past weekend, that I've been fully able to understand, "in soul and body", just how precious was our handful of days together, how indispensable you are to me, and what a continual, inarticulable wonder you are. This long, barren and frustrating separation from each other, along with all the yearning that it caused, has also – over time – almost accustomed us to the fact that we're not together (even though this has been a rebellious acceptance). But our six days of togetherness, with their quiet time, conversations, going to bed, sleeping, eating, and *being*, have created a deep new realisation of the unutterable value of sharing things so directly. It's as if we've been driven into a bigger space, like a bubble blown from a little pipe. I need you more than I ever did before, you are more precious, and everything is more tender; *and*: it's all more secure, less likely than ever to be taken away. I live and breathe in the assurance of our love, and the days are beautiful; I long to return. You are the world outside my room – a clear summer's day that I'm always aware of, and to which my window is always open. Sometimes I climb out the window, go into the world, and become sun-drunk, happy, *complete*.

Yesterday especially was a day for sharing with you: an outing to a coastal farm (Naas Steenkamp's parents). It was a real little paradise. This is how we should be able to live one day: in an old-fashioned, sturdy little house with thick walls. It's all white, with a cellar and broad wooden floorboards, and it nestles on a mountain slope, facing a valley and a river that cuts through brushwood and palms, with open pasturage among poplars, and winding paths trodden by oxen. Anton should really tell you about it – this son of mine who yesterday, for the first time, actually did smell "like a billy-goat and flowers". This was after trampling through the cowshed with its milk buckets, playing with a large Alsatian, and rolling around in cool, green sunny grass before trailing after Muscovy ducks. "The good earth" is more than just a romantic fiction!

This morning it was back to the lesser reality of marking essays – and reading Rosa Nepgen's review of *Sempre* in *Die Burger*. Did you see it?! ("Is André Brink still seeking a doubtful martyr's crown by getting one of his books banned?" For shame!)

Thank you for your sunny, lovely letter that arrived this morning, with its beautiful poem and its tender certainty, "split apart and whole".

Now you must please look nicely after your little split, pamper it, let it rest quietly so it will be ready for the next time, for another day … my scabs have come off and I am once again "whole" – and ready, always full of love.

Have you had any more trouble with creditors? Please write to me if you need help. And you may not, must not try to "pay back" any of the rent, as you threatened, because after all I also stayed in the little castle!

I'm going to make you a tape this week. And I'll phone you on Wednesday night.

I'm saying "good morning" to you in the early morning, hailing everything, with joy and light and playfulness, and with the laughter of love,

Yours, always.

———————

Castella
Tuesday, 8 October 1963

My darling André,

This grey weekend time – six o'clock – after the newspaper is done with – luckily I still have some of your lovely gin and carnations – and asparagus. Thank you for your letter. And the telegram. How on earth do you manage to write on a Saturday (twelve o'clock) and make sure that I get the hand-delivered letter on Monday morning? If you send it to my postbox it arrives even earlier. [PO Box] 707. (I think.) And I'll send you a telegraphic address as soon as I find out what it is.

Dearest *mine*! Last Tuesday – when I was so horrible – that time – before the 191 and the long long sleep. It feels as though you are years away. Here the usual storms and floods – with a lovely Sunday in between – so I wore the white bathing suit – it's beautiful – I could run and climb and swim swim swim in it – the bikini always falls off – it is beautiful! And then, with Chris to the El P. [El Picador] in Sea Point, and a bottle and a half of white wine, we sat at our table, the one in the corner, and had the braised duck – I missed you so much!

Yesterday evening after the Cape Culture Group [Cultural Circle] – Jan (and Marjorie), who had already infuriated me at the dinner table – said they were going to Bill tomorrow evening – and carried on like this as though I've got something against him – till I said sulky bastard or something like that – and then Jan was angry – and I was angry – and then in front of everyone he said I probably don't know Afrikaans, because Jan S. Cilliers [Jan F.E. Celliers] (the darling) definitely did not mean bastard breed when he said bastard breed (I like a man who can stand his ground) but in fact meant the "Royal Dutch". Well, I had to accept this, but after the meeting he again referred to it twice (such a dear) and then I was angry again and fell asleep angered. And then I didn't want to show him your document that he has to sign; I think you must, in any case, write to him yourself, I'll sign my name; and write to Adam [Small] – I'll speak to Uys tomorrow. (Unless he went to Onrus, as he'd planned.)

One little part of your letter vaguely disturbed me – you mentioned it on Wednesday morning before you left (around 8:15 to be precise): "While there with you I was all too aware, throughout, that our sexual togetherness couldn't be as fully a surrender-filled orgy as I *wanted* it to be, all because of something as banal as an abrasion!" André, I think I've told you this before, and maybe often made you *feel* – that you are,

224

POST OFFICE TELEGRAPHS.—POSKANTOORTELEGRAAFDIENS.   T. 27.

This form and envelope should accompany any enquiry.
Hierdie vorm en koevert moet alle navrae vergesel.   No._____

G.P.-S.43461—1958-9—500.000-200. S.

RECEIVED
ONTVANG

+ ZG111 LG55 LEEUSIG 19 29 1235 =

ANDRE BRINK RHODES

UNIVERSITEIT GRAHAMSTAD =

P/N M] 41

_BRIEF BLOMME ONTVANG STOP DANKIE VIR ALLES EN VIR JOU

-ANTWOORD VOLG LIEFDE = INGRID + +

The earliest correspon-
dence from Ingrid Jonker
kept by André Brink.

Heerlike klein mens,

Ek het eintlik 'n paar neutrale "in transit"-dae nodig
gehad om tussen die Kaap en terug-wees, net om die oorgang
geleideliker te maak. Ná die week - en veral die drie dae - van
verandering, moet ek nou met heelwat renons die óu bedreiging
van die vaste, "veilige", burgerlike bestaan van vooraf belewe.
Respectability. Die voorafbepaalde reaksie op die voorafbepaalde
prikkel. Daar's mense vir wie so 'n bestaan nooit 'n bedreiging
is nie omdat hulle in hulleself te vry is om vasgekeer te kán word;
maar ek moet my voortdurend verset juis omdat dit so maklik sou
wees om maar dié opium te neem. Die Kaapse week, jý, het darem
'n teёmiddel gegee. Moet ek beleefd daarvoor "dankie" sê? Dit
sou dit alledaags maak. Veral "ons" nag. Wat Eliot gesê het -
"poetry can communicate before it is understood" - kan in sekere
sin ook vir mense geld wat só, vry, deur seks bymekaar uitkom. Dis
juis 'n kommunikasie wat goddank anderkant die woorde bly. Want
waaruit sou ek my klein inventaris (veral in dié nugter daglig)
kan bestaan?: 'n geur, herinneringe van hande, hare en borste,
stem, trane, sinisme, spel, rooiwyn; twee dubbele brandewyne;
oё: wat spot, wat nee sê, wat vloek, wat minag, wat speel; wat
ja sê, wat soet en bly is, of de-moer-in en bedonnerd...! Só kom
mens nêrens uit nie. Maar gelukkig is dié dinge net beginpunte;
is herinnerings en liggame net titels ván lang gedigte; en is
ons "bymekaar slaap" 'n soort Mis-hou waarin die transsubstan-
siasie volkome is. (Is dít dalk ons "ongelowiges" se suiwerste
religie? Waarom sou jy anders juis dán "Here-God" sê? - Giuseppe
di Lampedusa se mooiste meisiekarakter sê dan: "Gésumaria!")

Kan 'n liggaam sélf onthou? Ja. Ek dink eintlik dis 'n
beter onthou as die onbetroubare "geheue". Myne onthou joune.
En dis nie vanweё die paar strategiese pyntjies of 'n merkie
aan my skouer nie. Ook nie - hoop ek! - omdat ek maar "deel
uitmaak van jou verdriet" nie: dis meer positiéf. Die liggaam
se onthou, teenoor die brein s'n, is soos beeldspraak tussen
nugter woorde.

O.k. sê nou maar:"Twak!"   Of erger. Ek is nie besig met
'n Simone de Beauvoir-dissertasie nie. Ek is eintlik net besig
om langs 'n omweg te sê wat ek al gesê hét: dankie.

Tot tyd en wyl ek weer by jou kom, moet ek my tevrede hou
met jou manuskrip (en jy moet maar laat weet wanneer jy voel dis
tyd dat hy terugkom!) Gelukkig is daar 'n onverwagte vooruitsig
dat dié terugkeer gouer sal wees as wat ek gemeen het. Die
Studiekring-of-'n-ding op Stellenbosch wil hê ek moet nog in
dié semester drie lesings daar kom hou. Dan kom ek op hulle
onkoste eintlik vir jou kuier! Persoonlik het ek 'n skyt aan
dié soort lesinghouery. William Styron (het jy sy Lie down in
darkness gelees?) het iets gesê spos: "One thing I can't stand is
that a young writer, after having written one book, starts
lecturing and giving pompous interviews on all sorts of subjects
about which he knows nothing." Lewe Styron! Maar soms is 'n hals-
band kosbaarder as die hond wat hom dra.

O-heeere, en vanmôre kom hier toe nog 'n plegstatige
telegram om my konde te doen dat dit die S.A. Akademie vir "Kuns"
en Wetenskap behaag het om 'n "Eugène Marais Aanmoedigingsprys
vir drama" aan my toe te ken. Na die hilariteit waarmee dit
begroet is, sit ek nou eintlik in 'n debakel: eerstens weet ek
(en blykbaar niemand anders) watse ding dié prys is nie; ek
weet nie eers op grond waarvan hy toegeken is nie; ook nie wat
hy werd is nie. En nou? Moet ek terug laat weet: Deponeer
toekenning in u anus? Of moet ek dit tong-in-die-kies aanvaar
omdat ek 'n paar ekstra rand kan gebruik en tog g'n illusies
het oor my dramatiese vermoёns nie? Of sou dit "oneerlik" wees?
Sien, ek het lankal heimlik gehoop die Kakkademie ken my eendag
'n Hertzogprys toe sodat ek dié kan weier op grond van hulle
onbevoegdheid om oor enige literêre waarde te besluit. (Of is
dit verspot?)

Intussen is my grootste werk – en hoofbrekens – nou die
tik van Die ambassadeur/Die ongedurige kind. Ek wil die ding
nou klaarkry – as daar nie so baie veranderings met die oortik
gemaak moes word nie, het ek jou as professionele tikster gehuur.
Nou snork ek maar self op – en jy bars as jy moan oor foute.
Ek wil hê jy moet kennis maak met Gillian en Nicolette.
(Gelukkig weet ek jy sal nie doekies omdraai nie!) Daar kom darem
'n fragmentjie in die tweede "60". Maar wanneer kom dié?
Bartho het juis in sy jongste brief taamlik huiwerig geklink
oor die finansiële vooruitsigte. Hy kom oor 'n paar dae hier aan;
dan sal ek in elk geval eerstehands meer uitvind.

Ek het Rob vanoggend gesien, en sonder dat ek daarna
gevra het, het hy verwys na jou gedigte in "60" (wat hy blykbaar
nou eers gelees het). Hy voel "baie opgenome" daaroor. Jy't
gesê jy steur jou nie aan kritici nie, maar dalk bring dit
tog 'n kolletjie warmte. Jy het genoeg winterse dinge beleef.
Ek weet ons staan vry teenoor mekaar, bind mekaar aan niks, verbind mekaar tot niks: maar ek wens ek kon by jou wees; en help.
Nie net om 'n woonplek te kry en al die peuterighede van elke
dag te deel nie; maar – dalk – om te help "om van alleenwees
langsaam te genees".

Moenie – Here, Ingrid – in Jan se huis doen wat jy wou
doen nie. Daar is geen redelike gronde waarop ek jou kan –
of wil – oortuig nie. Dalk dring ek daarop aan uit suiwer
selfsugtige oorwegings. Maar moenie. Jy moet nog dinge maak
soos "Begin somer", "Dood van 'n maagd", "Bitterbessie dagbreek",
"Art poétique", die reeks "Intieme gesprekkies" –; en ons moet
saam weer maak wat nie in Afrikaans "gemaak" kan word nie: liefde.

Die son roep my uit (dis hier al behoorlik winter); ek wil
in die tuin gaan sit en Eluard en Jonker lees.

Skryf, Ingrid. En laat my doen net wat ek moontlik kan om te
help. Waarmee ookal.

Sê groete vir Chris, en sê vir hom weer dankie. En skryf
– vir ons – 'n gedig oor: "Die herinnering aan 'n aand is 'n
appel"; en verbind dit met Adam-en-Eva se appel; en eet die
appel aan die einde; en vra dan: En nou? Jy sal weet hoe. Ek is
nie 'n digter nie.

Met liefde,

André.

Brink's first letter to
Jonker, followed by
her response.

Citadel-pers,
Breestraat 145,
Kaapstad.
1 Mei 1963.

My liewe André,   Ek het Sondag vir jou begin skryf
maar na vyf onderbrekings maar tou opgegooi en gaan stap
teen die berg uit, daarna na 'n yskoue swem in die Clifton-
seewater, 'n warm bad en 'n drankie, en toe stuur ek maar
solank vir jou 'n telegram. Ek wil jou weer bedank vir
jou heerlike brief -- so oop en eerlik en onskuldig! Ek
sien reeds uit na die volgende!   Maar eers moet ek raas.
Waarom het jy die Eugenè Marais-prys aangeneem? Andrè,
Andrè! So maklik moet jy nie 'n kompromis tref nie en
ek gaan jou ook nie daarmee gelukwens nie.   Is jy ook
bly vir die bohaai in die koerante oor die "standpunt" van
die skrywers? Daar het nou nog 'n hele klomp name bygekom,
o.a. Ina Rousseau. F.L. Alexander het gesê dat geen
kunstenaar met enige selfrespek hom met die Raad sal laat
assosieèr nie. Het jy dit alles gesien? Ook die hoof-
artikel in The Friend?
Ek is bly jy kom een van die gou dae weer Kaapstad toe ---
jy moet my pragtige woonstel (met tuin) in Groenpunt sien;
so 'n huislike en intieme woonplekkie. Op die oomblik
bly ek (tot 15 Mei) in Jan-hulle se huis. Die twee is
vandag met vakansie weg na Hangklip.   Alles nog goed,
of soos gewoonlik.   My vriende maak my nog bitter kwaad
dan verlang ek na jou rustige beskerming. Chris is dieselfde.
Hy laat weet natuurlik baie groete vir jou -- ons het
eergisteraand saam geèet by 191; hy het my omtrent 11 uur
by die huis besorg en toe moes ek nog inpak .... Maar
vertel wanneer is die Lesings dan?
Ek skryf nou hier by die godverlate Citadel-pers wat beklem-
mend inwerk op my verbeelding ... Ek gaan vir jou verder
by die huis skryf vanaand.   Sommige van jou vrae kan ek
onthou: of 'n liggaam kan onthou? There are more things
in heaven and earth, Horatio, than are dreamed of in our
philosophy ...
Nee, Andrè, ek wil jou darem nog 'n keer sien voordat ek
skreeuend en vloekend, soos Slauerhof, die lewe laat.
Ek is jammer dat juis in die naweek wat jy daar was, sulke
goed my moes tref. Maar ek het nog altyd 'n verbasende
herstellingsvermoê besit, en helend en reinigend is ook
jou vriendskap ...
Dankie vir die nuus oor Rob. Ek is natuurlik bly hy het
van my gedigte in 60 gehou. 'n mens kan nogal afgaan op

Het nou eers gaan tee skink.   Steeds by die werk.

Net na jy weg is verneem ek uit "betroubare bronne" dat my
gewese (dit klink altyd soos oorlede) man glad nie van plan
is om Simone aan my terug te besorg nie. Ek had 'n hoogs
ontstellende brief, het dadelik aan hom geskryf -- geen antwoord
--- en net nou 'n geregistreerde brief waarin ek Simone
terug eis.   Ek hoop nou die gemors loop goed af en dat ek
en hy nie weer mekaar in die hof moet ontmoet soos gewoonlik
nie.
Het nog geen dooie woord die afgelope twee weke geskryf met
al dié dinge nie.   Hoe gaan dit met Die Ongedurige Kind ...?
Die gedig is pragtig. Jy moet tog nie die boek Die Ambassadeur
~~nog~~ noem nie. Niemand sal dit koop nie ... dis so 'n stowwerige
ou titel. Die Ongedurige Kind is poëties en lig en voort-
~~vlugtig~~ vlugtend ... Jy kan gerus al vir my die eerste hoof-
stukke stuur ... ek sal die tikfoute ook optel.'
O ja, ivm met die mense, die burgery, praat jy 'n bietjie
verward. Hulle is juis nie vry nie, dis dan hul gebondenheid
wat my so bedroef en verveel tot in die afgrond in.
Maar afgesien daarvan, ek het 'n mooi nuwe jas (Chris sê dit
lyk absoluut Frans) en ek begin myself al oppiep vir die
komende winter ... het gistraand met Simone se teddiebeer
gaan slaap, hy is so lekker warm en harig en geel soos 'n
Bantrybaai somer.
Het jy al die Drum vir Mei gesien? Ek nie. Ek hoop julle
kry darem so iets in Grahamstad. Dit moet vandag te koop wees
iewers.
Ken jy vir George Barker se News of World War lll?

'Before the battalions of lies and the organizations of hate
Entirely encompass us
Lie one night in my arms and give me peace.'

                    Skryf gou, hoor!

Jammer oor die tik –
Gedurig ook haastig!)

                                   Liefde ... alle heil ....
                                      alle dankbaarheid,

Wat ek geskryf het oor die
marais-prys is nie omdat
ek nie vertroue in jou toneel-
talent het nie hoor; het hoofde ...   *Ingrid*

To date, the only photo in which Brink and Jonker appear together. From left: Etienne Leroux, Jonker, Jan Rabie, Marjorie Wallace and Brink.

Maandagaand, 13 Mei.

Liewe klein dogtertjie,

Ek is moeg vanaand. Heeldag gesit en peuter aan die Stellenbosch-lesings — wat nog ver van klaar af is — en toe weer vanaand in sterf vertaalwerk gedoen. Dis so 'n siellose soort werk. En al is die boek Engels, het hy nou juis die soort styl wat so swaar vertaal. Ek verkies enige tyd Frans. Maar as 'n mens nie anders kan nie, help dit ook nie om te kla nie. Die kontant is eenvoudig nodig. En intussen moet ek sorg dat ek vir my tweedejaars nog in lesing vir môre voorberei kry.

Maar tussen dit alles het 'n heerlike ding vandag gebeur. Ek het in brief gekry, seune Hadsye, wat ek in die "Common room" tussen al die geleerde en kwasigeleerde here met teekoppies en togas gestaan en lees het, "an island entire of myselfe". Sommer 'n brief van 'n ligtekopmeisietjie wat ek liefhet. Haar naam is Ingrid. Dis 'n mooi naam, nè? Maar sy is nog mooier as haar naam. En al het sy aangehou met sê "Hm-hm, Chris, nee Chris," het sy my tog toegelaat om te sien hoe mooi sy is. En toe het sy een aand, een nag eintlik — maar jy sal my tog nie glo nie. Buitendien mag 'n mens nie sulke dinge skryf nie, want daar is 'n wet op Publikasies en Vermaaklikhed

GRAHAMSTOWN P.O./PK
26 VII A63
15

ZG75   CZB52 CAPETOWN 17 26 1134 =

AM 11 = = ANDRE BRINK RHODESUNIVERSITEIT

GRAHAMSTAD =

ZG

· SKRYWER SE GEBED HEER MAAK VAN DIE KLIPPE VIR ONS BROOD

LIEFDE = KOKON +

Breitral(27.7): Do dit skrywer of digter se Gebed? Onthou die onglibre
maeltynig vod die boek. Liefde - Rhoé.

Right: A message to Brink
in his signed copy of *Rook
en Oker*.

"My verwaderlike blein bakstraat
wat ek alleen in vreemde lande
en op Sand waar blein brefies sal lê
(as die see terug-trek!) nag en lan vind

o jy heerlike blein worstelaar —
worsteling in my, maar antwortel
jy: — want: fosluit. "

Anne
my liefde
van Ingrid

"I have used your red jersey to
protect myself from the world,
like I do almost every day,
isolated here in my study."

18 April 1964.

André, liefste man, my bright and morning star — ek kan jou dele nie langer onthou nie. Dankie vir jou droom brief — engel — God, Stratford upon Avon. Hier versonke in geskiedenis — ware geskiedenis — gebeurtenis van die groot man. "Stop chatting up the tourists." "Say good day to the foreigner." ... Mense in die pragtige, vermaaklike pubs van Stratford. En more gaan ons na "Sweet Shakespeare." En vannag, ons herinnering nag, lê ek hier in 'n cottage gebou in 1560. ... here, het jy die foeto gesien? Die vroumense in die gewestes sê ... "I told myself I'll be done to 140 pounds by April 23rd ... Dit is so wonderlik. Almal is betrek. Die hele dorp is gewei op die groot gebeurtenis — die feesviering in die groot ryr — ek was na die teater, dragmiddag al — agter die shows waar hul nog steeds haastig in 'n 8 maker — ek is hier in die goed (hul woon hier) en neem my oral. liefste André, jy antwoord haar jy antwoord. Dis was 'n groot tyd hier — die un by, en pit jou idee van hoeveel er alreeds jeleer het hie — het royal ora. letops John Collins — leidende kunstenaar en decor — artistic, ontmoet en Julia Hastings — 84 jaar oud en 'n karakter so jyk nat ek nog glad nie aan haar durf skryf nie. Ek eet more saam met haar in The Dirty Duck of The Black Swan — soos jy verkies. God, en au loop langs die Avon — hier het Keats gelit en ook, Wordsworth ... en so baie ander ... en ek, nietjie ellendige IJ. Maar vernuk, vernuk, vernuk ... Jij had jou idee nie ... liefing, ek had jou hakeun ti so jy kom Spanje toe — Julie of Des. maar kom nou. Kom Julie. Die jaar is so kort en so baie en so vinnig en so vinnig en jy wag die verndeel ... — daar is jou vrae meer nie ... vra jou hart ... en kom en kom nou kom gou ... leve innerlik lien 'n tempo

Ingrid Jonker
c/o SA House
Trafalgar Sq.
London

André P Brink
Dept. Afr/Ned,
RHODES University,
GRAHAMSTOWN
CAPE PROVINCE
SOUTH Africa

wat hond en kat sal malmaak in die Browe
Bongerbus, furchte Suid Afrika sonder agtergrond
sonder wôôrde sonder hulfue. Dren 'n program oor
Stynwas... Laurens vd Post "The Man who Cares" David
Lytton (The goddam white man, neef van Leipold) "The Lord
of Life" en TS Eliot "International Poet" .. dover...
Sy moet kon help en kon deel. Nee God, so kan dit
nie aangaan nie. En daar, whipped across your wonded
eyes "gaarig". Luftue slaap sy prins, met
hilfue én dringende versoek vir die liestewaare
en tôg vir altyd ──────

Kokon.

Kokon.

each wonderful new time, a sexual-spiritual surprise to me – though I've been chafed and sore I've never made such an issue of it! But your image of the angel from the stone is beautiful. Angel? I don't know either why it is so "wonderfully quiet" on your side, but you should at least have received a letter from me on Saturday and again today. I'll post your letters myself now – because the express one is lying around somewhere in Cape Town it seems. And why, while I'm scolding now, the "inexplicable little drama" of Wednesday night? Dear darling CHILD, do you know they're even writing about me in the newspapers now … "Ingrid Jonker ('The Child')" – do you know that it is LOBOLO and *not Lobola?* See *Hiemstra.*

Darling my André, against whom I drowned so wonderfully just last Tuesday, I am *not* unhappy. Just rather saddled with energy. I want to go up the mountain. And all the while I am busy "skryven en skryven en skryven almaar die heilige Name van God".

And I also want a tape, dearest one of all. This Sunday Jack again said he loves me, but when I showed him the poem "My Embrace Redoubled Me", he said, "It's for André. Hurry up, will be late, you little bitch." Strange …?

Today (lunch time) I walked in the Gardens with the new blossoms. The sun was delicious. Tonight, early to bed with Teddy. I would so love to dream about you, my prince.

Blessings and love, my sensitive darling,
Cocoon.

PS: Felt really nauseous yesterday. A strange, *impossible* premonition …
Con.

Grahamstown
Wednesday, 10 October 1963

My own little Cocoon,

The fact that today was a holiday delayed the sending of the tape, so you'll only be receiving it on Monday. I'll send a telegram on Saturday, otherwise you might feel neglected!

This is not really a letter, just "directions for use": the first side of the tape was recorded at ¼, the second side on ⅔ – here's hoping you're not too distracted. And I'm sending a little cheque so you can also make one for me. (I'm posting the tape itself to Castella.)

No news. Just roaming around in the absurd joy that our moesie-girl is maybe growing into a person after all. (Even if [Guillaume] Apollinaire does say: "The children of lovers are born in sorrow.") It's a kind of turning into the self, curling up like a hedgehog – around one-self and around the little thing, or the possibility of one, with love and care and quiet ecstasy.

I was upset about Simone's near-nasty experience. She's such a pure little thing, such a wild little animal. Protect her against the evil that walks in darkness. Give her a little kiss on her tummy.

And so, are you getting afternoon tea these days because your throat's so dry and you were so bad-tempered?

Are you, along with the separation and daily drabness, still happy, still *whole*? Look after yourself; close yourself up like a little cocoon. Write verse. Swim in your all-white bathing costume that you have to worm and wiggle yourself into so delightfully. (Probably more so now, because your soft, round, lovely breasts are getting larger and fuller.)

We have a memory as multifaceted as the eye of an insect. "So we'll live, / And pray, and sing, and tell old tales, and laugh / At gilded but-terflies ..."

Work sweetly and daringly, and when you get home from the ano-nymity of buses and crowds, pour yourself a drink and sit back, and then I'll talk to you on the tape that's waiting at the little castle.

226

Love
love
love
love,
Your André.

———————

Dearest, darling little Cocoon,

Thank you for yesterday's delightfully varied, vivid letter – about the "culture" meeting, the tiff with Jan, the white-costume swim, the "strange, impossible premonition", and lobola that should be lobolo. (I too made this discovery after the book appeared; but it's okay – I don't think the "a" is used by enough people to go through as generally accepted Afrikaans!)

And, darling: Make sure you're in fine feather. Because: although there are still some "ifs", it's nonetheless beginning to look like I'll be there with you by 6 November. I phoned Koos, and he's almost certain the book will be ready by then – if it's a day or so earlier, he'll be able to hold its appearance back until I get there. If I can get everything arranged satisfactorily on this side – the exam scripts and the trip itself – then I'm *coming*. I'd started talking about this quite a while ago, and raised it again, so it doesn't look like there'll be any obstacles.

Girlie, my little girl. Reading: The Lord is merciful and gracious.

Even the date – 6 November – should suit you better than the past few times!

I shall preserve the papie, and let it get properly well again (the last time I slept with you – Heroes Day! – the little abrasion opened up again). And I'll store lots of secrets and come to you with a *full* load.

How we live, we of the past-and-present! (Alice had to listen as

227

one of the Wonderlanders – the Duchess? or the Queen of Hearts? – said: "Jam yesterday and jam tomorrow but never jam today!") We are always *in transit*. But child, with the prospect of such a destination (even though the train doesn't stop for long!), what an adventure the journey promises to be! One sits with one's nose pressed against the window without even noticing the soot in one's hair.

Did you swim again today, and get a nice tan? Here it was such a divinely sunny day (I did *no* work before this evening, and then just one chapter of the Simenon translation). Frieda and a friend were here. From eleven this morning we lay in the sun, reading newspapers, lazing around and eating; we made plans to drive to the beach this afternoon, but we drank and ate so much, and got so lazy, that nothing came of it. And all day I lay with my head in the sweet, warm, ticklish grass, or looked up into the sky through the lemon leaves, and I was with you.

What shall we do when I come down this time? It'll most likely be ± Wednesday to Monday.

One night we'll *celebrate* together.

Another night we'll celebrate with Chris.

And the weekend –?

"Everything is new, everything lies in the future."

This quotation turns my thoughts to Uys; and to a funny little thing in a third-year class yesterday (tell him about it). We were discussing *Die Goue Kring* [The Golden Circle], and one of the girls said: "It's very nice and all, but you get tired of all the oranges. Ever since reading the thing, I've never eaten another orange!"

Willem Jordaan, says Koos, is apparently wildly enthusiastic about *Die Ambassadeur* and very eager to start with his design. Hopefully he'll send it via airmail in the course of this week for my attention. I've never before – not even with *Lobola* – looked forward to a book's appearance quite this much. Because this one's *ours*. So much of it is thanks to you.

Tomorrow, I think, I can finally resume work on *Orgie*, as the worst of the marking is behind me. I'll probably spend a few days just sitting around, "getting into the spirit" of the thing, brooding and becoming foul-tempered. But I've been itching to start working on it again. It's so frustrating, all the other, unavoidable things one has to do.

Meanwhile, I've set up a kind of "Manifesto for Sixty" for the next 60 – actually just to characterise and give a closer indication of our "nieuwe lente en een nieuw geluid". I'll send it to you once it's been typed up. Meanwhile I'm sending you the Schutte parody.

Remember to find out your post office box number and telegraphic address.

Write a lot, and – even though you're no longer a "young man" – "cleanse your way". Because I love you, and miss you; I fill my days with you. On Wednesday night I'll phone you, too.

Love, mine,
André.

—————

Castella
Tuesday, 15 October 1963

My dearest lamb,

Thank you for your lovely, lovely tape which I was finally able to play yesterday evening after a pilgrimage – to the home of my old friends in Clifton, with a beautiful view over the sea: my recorder has stopped working, and Erik [Laubscher] wasn't home. It was a lovely tape – I wish I could play it again. On Friday my recorder will be fixed; so I'll "answer" you over the weekend although I chatted and laughed along heartily last night. And thank you for the cheque, I've already bought a tape and this funny thin pen, which I am not getting along with.

I miss you, and your Anton. You must try and come in November; the Cape Town circle isn't asking *as* many questions any more – it seems to me, I may be wrong – they have accepted things more or less. Oh yes, I wanted to tell you about yesterday evening. After the tape-playing, I went to Lena, and then Chris arrived and brought me home. Then we drank a huge amount of red wine – Lena and I, and I only went home after eleven, so that I couldn't then, as I'd wanted to, begin writing to you, because this morning it was court – all okay: I am so glad this horrible business is now over, hope I won't be harassed like this any more – they withdrew the "contempt of court" ... Lovely man! I behaved quietly and demurely, and when I saw his honour look at me, I realised the curl was tightly twirled – I was actually shit-scared! It's lovely to chat to you. I haven't written to you for a while – but you write so regularly and then you say: this isn't actually a letter ... then it goes all *quiet* inside me, "what a miserable thing man is". You who gives me so much, gives everything so generously, who allows me to take part *in* you, every day.

The weekend was actually nice. Saturday morning went and had tea with Chris in town, then wandered around and here and there, bought something, drank half a bottle of wine together at the Manchester while he wrote six postcards to one friend; went to eat at El P. – "braized duck with orange" – to the beach, the white swimsuit that fits so *tightly* and constantly makes me want to *run*, drink with Jack (who gave me a lecture about my dangerous relationship with you, but friendly); Sunday with Simone to the beach; lunch at Marjorie and Jan, met lovely people who brought me home at seven, and so to dream. The rest of the previous week, nothing. Static, alone.

It's now ten to nine and I've just got back from Simone, missed her terribly on Sunday; the pig who molested little girls has, praise God, been arrested, from what I hear. I suppose they'll give him psychological treatment. Still – I would have given him a thorough thrashing if I'd seen him. Sunday night was actually terrible – "angst" – the terrible separation – from you, Simone, and also Jack. This feeling that something somewhere is wrong. But now everything is "right" again. It's always like that. Then I diligently read through *Lobola.* (Oh yes, that's right too.) *Lobola* is beautiful – sometimes I feel "never a mistake, the words don't lie" (I can't manage this pen at all). Seems I'm not getting tea after all; they had a *council meeting* about it but didn't say what the conclusion was. So now I buy tomato juice at 1 pm and have it cooled and fetch it in our kitchen at 3:30. In the end it's better for one than tea! We're reading *Murder, Mystery and the How*. Helluva interesting – I have always been so morbidly interested in the law. Anne just thinks the drinking is terrible – always in "The Bar".

Darling, moesie, always-laughing moesie-man – are you wearing your red pyjamas and are you lying heavily across the bed like that night at the Cederwood, do you remember, when you came and lay athwart me in a kind of absolute surrender, satisfied, exhausted, to be caressed? I cannot put into words the sense of softening and "destiny" which in this way you released in me.

And how is it going with *Orgie* (rest if you must) – and oh yes, the student (Éluard) probably meant "poem" instead of "institution" ["'gedig' in plaas van 'gestig'"] …? It is a very mature poem, maybe it's impossible for a student to understand. Lovely, lovely tape with all the laughter, which immediately brought me so close to you, and at the same time so immediately to my own heart. This, surely, is "being together".

The little castle is clean, full of flowers, nasturtiums to stick into all my wounds, if you were here, you'd stick your nasturtiums into them – and in a way, you already do. André, we really do need one another. Need, need, need. And Sunday night I fell asleep with this otherworldly dream of us; the house looks like this:

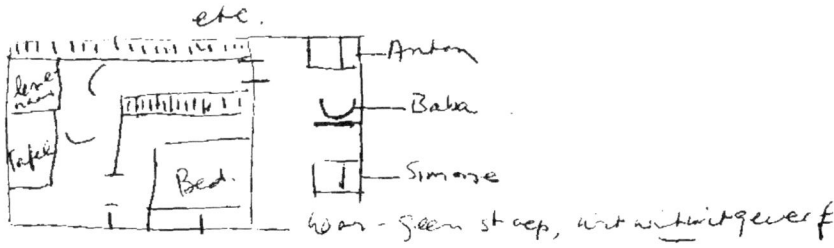

And somewhere beyond, an old-fashioned yard.

Thank you, for your really lovely little letter, which sorts and arranges – it's actually a fantastic experience, all of it. The liberating humour, the seriousness of the game, the absolute freedom from any feeling of "bitterness", the incontrovertible, lasting tenderness. My wonder man, I love you. Biblelove, Corinthianslove. I carry you cocoon-tight, and then one has to be a cocoon to be a poet. Maybe being a poet is a play-land, never really "deep seriousness", but for me, one as safe as Jesus. I completely agree with your criticism of "My Embrace Redoubled Me". That's just a provisional comment. The worst is still to come! I'm going to sleep with you now. Perhaps just sleep from knowing – we'll see how the hand leads us. But in any case, peacefully, happy, as you must also be. "Not for one moment, beautiful André Brink, will I forget thee." Love and love, liefsteling.

As always *your Cocoon*
COCOON.

Ach, du ... du!

{Thank you for the telegram on Saturday, generous child. IJ.}

Grahamstown
Thursday morning, 17 October 1963

My darling,

How did things go last night after our phone call: the "cold, distant" conversation between you and Jack? What can I possibly *do* to make sure your precious life is free of unnecessary muddying? And now you've begun to feel suspicious even of me, as you said – despite your saying it lightly. And, true to our tradition, it woke me up in the small hours last night, leaving me sleepless, disturbed and sad; and, of course, you weren't there, so I couldn't wake you up to seek assurance and some kind of solution in you and with you. Darling, *no, don't*, nothing weakens the ground beneath one's feet as much as a lack of trust. I am *yours*, everything I do and think is directed towards you; even in my least important daily activities, you are the steady five lines on which I score the notes of my life.

Especially now, with the certainty of 8 November so luminously close, everything seems to have found a direction, a kind of "resignation", and a transparent happiness. I was able to start working on *Orgie* again, though it was quite a struggle at first, as I expected, but after three days of working in fits and starts, I found my feet again last night, in fact before the phone call, writing seven pages quite quickly (I'm busy with the conversation in which "you" talk about your life in such a rebellious and passionate way, so full of resistance, that afternoon in Clifton). The telephone call's little dose of edginess and unfinished business troubled the writing somewhat, but today – because I can now sit in restful seclusion and talk to you, my dearest beloved – I'm going to write quite a bit. "Each venture is a new beginning, a raid on the inarticulate." You do of course know [T.S.] Eliot's *Four Quartets*? To my shame I must admit that I have only read them properly now – in the past, I'd read them rather spottily, here and there. (And don't you think the tone of voice of *Tristia* is rather strongly derived from the *Four Quartets*?) I've bought Eliot's new *Collected Poems*, which runs up

233

until 1962. Among the new ones there's little that is exceptional. One nice one, though, which I'll inscribe in your copy of *Die Ambassadeur*.

I've asked Koos to ensure that the very first copy is hand-delivered to you at the Citadel, immediately after the book appears. (This will be any day from about 30 Oct.) That means you'll get to see it even before I do.

I am expecting Jordaan's cover design tomorrow – actually with fear and trepidation, because if it's disappointing, people lose all interest in the book.

I phoned Bartho yesterday to ascertain whether *Orgie* might yet see publication this year, that's if I'm able to deliver it in two weeks' time, but he's apparently away from Jhb this week. Maybe it's just as well, as I shouldn't be working overhastily.

I probed Rob again about the APB books and, to my distress, he said not one of those he's read so far deserves the prize – he wants to suggest that the judges be allowed to decline awarding a prize if they feel this way. Please keep this between me and you *only*. I'm actually very upset. Naturally I'll seek an opportunity to raise the issue of *Rook en Oker* specifically with him – maybe when my review appears in *60*.

Jan's review is not just "nice" – it's thorough. A little generalising ("always lyrical even when she is sensuous" – since when can't sensuousness be lyrical, without the "even" tagged on? But I must first go and read the piece myself – I'm quoting according to what I can remember from last night's conversation). To return to what I started saying: a little generalising, although this is actually a good characteristic. (Playfully: it's quite an achievement that all your lovers are reviewing your book! Jack will surely do another one for that New Zealand journal, *Windfall* or *Landslide* or *Avalanche*? And mine in *60*.)

("I am one of your lovers, there are many" – suddenly I'm in a foul, jealous mood again!)

You neglect me with your one little letter a week, two if I'm lucky. I too am *hungry* and miss you and live in a state of continuous yearning. Love, my love, please don't be distant. Be with me, let us take shelter together under cool leaves from the vengeful gods who roam in the night winds. Let us do this in the togetherness that has become my most valuable possession. So that I can feel you in my arms, your breath against my face, your sweet, still breath; feel the taste of your soft, lovely mouth; the faraway tenderness of your eyes, half-shut behind your eyelashes; the little curl on your forehead – the one that gets twirled so much nowadays; your soft neck; the childlike touch of your nipples against my chest; the tension of your arms around my back, where your lovely sensitive fingers make their little marks; let me feel the rumbling of your tummy; the arch of your little mound; your soft, most exquisite thighs; the touch of your calves and feet – and even the pinch of the leucodendron – and then, the concentration of all that is me deep inside you, and you so soft there and so deep and with such a firm, firm clinging. And the left lip pouting, a tiny bit longer than the other …!

Just three more weeks. My own girl, mine. I miss you and I love you, in daily certainty and trust,

André.

———————

Castella
Thursday, 17 October 1963

My dearest André,

Hello! – In answer to your lovely long letter and the "prickly" phone call of last night. By that time I was probably so despondent, my treasure, about the cold emotional hell Jack and I frequently find ourselves in. I'm sorry. I didn't mean to whine. I told Jack I think it's better if we don't see each other for a while, and tomorrow evening after work I "depart" with Simone to … Bellville … that cultural town, to stay with friends for the weekend. Which means that I won't get your promised letter on Saturday; but at least I'll have it to go to sleep with on Sunday evening when I get back. It's only now that I've really had time to think back to the phone call that I've felt really sorry. In reality, I didn't "suspect" you; and – apart from that – if you had to for some reason or another – I would understand. Love is not love that changes with the tide – no, heavens –

> Love is not love
> Which alters when it alteration finds,
> Or bends with the remover to remove:
> O no! It is an ever-fixed mark,
> That looks on tempests and is never shaken.

My darling André, if there's anything I still believe in, then it is your purity and singularity. And that's actually fully sufficient. About Estelle's not-knowing – I still think the same – *I* would certainly know … because I really don't believe you're a good actor. Every writer has a little touch of it – but in general they're pretty clumsy in practice. Still – maybe – you're right. Another person's ways are a mystery to me …

Walked home quickly to come and write to you – I now walk there and back over the beautiful hill behind here – in the morning, especially, it's lovely. (Oh yes, ray of light yesterday afternoon – apart from your letter – did you see the portrait of Brigitte on the front page of *Huisgenoot*?) Evenings, mostly: reading *Stroomgebied* – about every third poem has something, an image or thought, or atmosphere, or everything. And I want to talk to you about everything. Have you for instance read this lovely little thing by Hetty van Waalwijk: "Poesje":

> Geef mij terug
> alles wat ik had
> mijn tien talenten
> mijn geluk en mijn onschuld en mijn witte poesje
> en mijn revolver en mijn groene wereld
> en vooral mijn pop
> die pop met het domme poppengezicht – en geef me dan ook mijn
>   duikelaartje

236

en mijn witte poesje
en mijn schommel tussen die perebomen
perebomen waar appels aan kwamen en kersen
en aardbeien
bomen vol aardbeien
en al mijn boeken en mijn kleren
en al die mensen waar ik van hield
en mijn grootmoeders die liedjies met me zangen
liedjies over kleine witte poesjes
met witte pootjes
en witte nageltjes
maar die kan je nooit zien … en mijn hockeystick en mijn raket
en mijn witte poesje
heel klein en heel wit
het mag bij me in bed slapen
en ik zal het elke dag borselen
en verszorgen en eten en drinken geven
het mag drinken aan mijn eijen borst
het kleine witte poesje dat ik nooit gehab heb

This Dutch tenderness, or maybe fifties-generation tenderness?

My dearest André, I would so much love to read and experience everything with you; and I have so much to learn from you. Why can't you just come and live here always, in the little house I drew – I am so often there with you! And that gives me a brilliant idea. Tomorrow I'll place an advert in the newspaper – then we'll go and stay in a place like that for the time that you are here. Somewhere in the Malay Quarter … or I'll ask Chris to take me there, and find out whether there isn't a pretty, clean little place like that which is currently vacant …? It would be wonderful! If we have to find a place like the Cederwood again, I'm not staying. Although, the Sunday evening there – and especially the walk – stays with me as something absolutely unique. Especially a "belonging" to you – which has nothing to do with our husbanded and wifed – why? This here, my darling, is going to be our best being here.

I know you now. And I know you as: loving, lavish, friendly, tender, impatient, passionate, teasing, precious, refined. All I want in addition to that is a pretty pretty dress, and I'll wait till you are here so that we can choose one together. This time it's going to be summer, summer, summer, and you must remember to bring your new bathing suit and especially the red pyjamas, and also the striped pyjamas – and then of course there'll be *Die Ambassadeur* with the most beautiful dedication – and your photos – shall I lend my big one to Nasionale Boekhandel? – in the windows. By then I'll be suntanned and my hair will be nicely cut. On condition that you won't have had yours cut or cut it yourself for two weeks. I know it's a helluva sacrifice, but I want it to be long. And then the other "visitor" won't be here in my house of love. Because I *love* you and if you carry on talking, because I can hear your beloved voice and your little laugh, I'm going to phone you right away.

Your darling, darling,
Cocoon.

ps: It's too early to phone (seven o'clock). From when till when may I do so? Probably not before eight. Wanted to include a nice poem, but my eye's been caught by a Lucebert, which for my sensibilities is a little obscene: "In de diepte en onder zwijgzaamheid / trekken toekomstige handen naar / het werk aan waters en aan de *wortel*."

Better, darling: "Hoor dan uw handen, haast dan uw hartslag / Ik ben een donkere droom in de zon."

Ingrid Jonker.

Andrew: L. Andreas, Fr. André, It. Andrea, Sp. Andres, Ger. D. Andreas, Rus. Andrei, Gr. Ανδρέας, from ανδρεπής "manly". The name of the first disciple called by Jesus, the brother of Simon Peter, and patron saint of Scotland and Russia.

Nicola, Nicolette: – from Nicolas – "the people", St Nicholas, Bishop of Myra c. 300, is regarded as the patron saint of children, sailors and wolves, and was much venerated in both Eastern and Western Churches.

Deirdre (f), the name of the heroine of *The Sons of Usnach*, one of the *Three Sorrowful Tales of Erin*, the subject of many plays and poems by modern Fr. poets.

Ingrid (f), an O Norse name of which the first element is from the hero-name Ingri and the second rida "ride"(!). Ingirith is found in England in the 13th c. "blonde, clean".

{ps: And then I forgot to tell you how much I enjoyed your satirical piece! Bravo! And for that arrangement with the Swedish newspaper and your Ward – thank you.}

Grahamstown
Friday, 18 October 1963

My delicious, always-new Cocoon,

Ever since receiving your tender, enchanting letter this morning, I've been wanting to write, but I first had to make notes about "the novel in the twentieth century", and then go through this afternoon's lecture on *Tristia*. After that, Anton came running into my study, chasing a blowfly, and we started playing together. He has a smell all of his own: a mixture of earth, warm grass, strawberries, Marmite and pee.

Thank you for the superb letter. If the result is a letter of this quality, it's almost worth the long wait. Divine little fire of my loins, whose glow reaches the furthest corners. "Ik heb u lief als droomen in de nacht." And I want to weave myself permanently into your dream cocoon. Thank you also for the dream house, with its three small beds

239

in a row, the table and desks arranged so prettily next to each other, and the seclusion of our *huge* bed. You've forgotten just two practical things: the *big* bath, and the toilet. Especially you, who runs barefoot into the rain every 2½ minutes to empty your minuscule little bladder!

Last night's chat was lovely, you with your beloved, sleepy voice that woke up ever so slowly; then I could hop back with you to your castle – sleeping beauty – and get into the rumpled bed with you, languid and warm and full of the fragrance of your mystical girl-ness. And sleep *in* you, and then sleep *with* you, with your warm little bum against my tummy, and everything pleasantly moist.

Child, child I am *happy* about you, happy to be at your side, happy to be with you. I'm working so wonderfully on our *Orgie*. In yesterday's piece I wrote a litany for the lost child. It goes like this:

li
ta
nie
kyrie eleison
lam
tie
tie
dam
tie
tie
doe
doe
my
lief
ste
tjie

It's wonderful to go mad (but responsibly mad!) with typography. All the more reason why I shouldn't be overhasty ... even though it could mean R2 000! But you're right, my darling, of course, it must get finished now and then go and incubate in a dark drawer; and ripen; and then be revised mercilessly – but with love. I'm now on page 33. Today I'm resting a little (thus: resting from this project, doing other things instead) so that I can get everything set for the next episode (the first evening and the first night).

I've been steeping myself in Eliot and reading Cees Nooteboom (young Romantic poet from Holland). And perhaps after that, *finally*, I'll read *Anna Karenina*.

Is your tape recorder working again?

I'm happy the court case is over. But I want to hear the truth, the whole truth and nothing but the truth about the "contempt" business. Surely you know by now how inquisitive I am?

This afternoon you're all going to Bellville together. I hope you enjoy the weekend, my child of light. Give Simone a kiss from me. I'm glad that perverted bastard has been caught. Has *she* shaken the whole business off? I was so upset, so *angry* and disturbed.

It seems Jan's book [*Mens-alleen*] appeared yesterday; I'm likely to get my copy from Bartho on Monday. I'm looking foward to it.

Koos sent a telegram to say he'll be sending the dust cover on Tuesday's flight. Hold thumbs!

My own mine, just in case you want to punish me once more with silence: this one *is* a letter!

Never mind, I'm not angry. I have seen your frantic life at close quarters and I understand if you're too tired or busy. Meanwhile, I love you continuously –

Not till the sun excludes you do I exclude you
Not till the waters refuse to glisten for you
and the leaves to rustle for you, do my
words refuse to glisten and rustle for you.

With love, my Kontjie, my always-mine,
Your André.

PS: 1. Send my regards to Maggie, and tell her the white sheets will soon be laid down on the honeymoon bed (three weeks today the white Volksie will be whizzing along the open road –!).
2. Thank you for the picture of Anne and her "shock" about the "Bar". With everything else, your grey job has at least some splashes of sun!
3. Love.
4. Love.
5. LOVE.

—————

Grahamstown
Sunday night, 20 October 1963

Beloved as the earth,

This evening, actually after midnight six months ago, you became mine for the first time; we explored, discovered and came to know each other's bodies in your little room, in the half-light falling through the window, from twelve-thirty to two and from four to five-thirty. Then, momentarily, there was no past, no history, no future – "the still point of the turning world".

> … Except for the point, the still point,
> There would be no dance, and there is only the dance.
> I can only say, *there* we have been: but I cannot say where.
> And I cannot say, how long, for that is to place it in time.

And now? Now the little centre in the dam has become a circle that includes everything, getting larger, more lovely, more precious, inescapable.

Child, mine, my gorgeous, my lovely. This weekend has been one of singularly acute longing, love, yearning and awareness. It was almost like walking into a magic circle where all wonders are possible, where the ground has been consecrated, where a Bush burns and burns and burns.

242

I dealt with the yearning by working on *Orgie*; I'm on page 44 now, just finished the "first night". It's occupying all my senses and intuition. (Do you realise that "sintuie" and "intuïsie" are made up of precisely the same letters? I've just disovered this now, for the first time. Material for a poem with subtle development from the outside in … right into the heart of the cocoon!)

Had supper with Frieda last night. There were some other very dear people there as well – and stimulating, satisfying conversation. However, throughout the evening I was also – in the midst of all the talk – in a world of my own that was sweet rather than unpleasant: a "smile in my calm heaven still", as if I wanted to say, all the while: I know something that you don't; I am in love with someone, a woman, a child whose feet make gentle contact with the earth, "and where you are, there must always be joy". It was a kind of thumbing the nose at "ordinary" life, as if I were sitting in an ordinary room though looking out of a window onto a landscape of dazzling light and water. The host, a woman, a young artist (married, so don't worry!) was wearing the same fragrance as you. (There, however, the similarity ended – it was just a little stimulus for my imagination and memory. That unique scent of yours, of smoke and sun and sea, of melancholy and happiness – *that* remains unrepeatable.)

Cocoon: I have never loved you as much as I do now. And it's multiplying the way germs do! I have to count the days – 19 – the way I did when I was small: three weeks before my birthday, I'd put 21 stones in my wardrobe, tossing one out every day. (Some days, out of pure eagerness, I chucked two away – but this didn't change anything!) I think I also had Nicolette play this game. Can't quite remember.

I'm sending you another little cheque, since I got R9 from Bartho for a manuscript assessment. It's just to help keep you alive! I have to get a move on with translating the second Simenon, so we can have some money to fuck around with when I come on the 8th!

Did your weekend turn out to be pleasant? Are you perhaps also sitting and writing to me right now? Or are you too tired and lazy – or maybe still with Simone?

I'm feeling a little anxious about a report that *Dagbreek* was supposed to run today about the interviews with Duval Smith. They got wind of it and phoned me yesterday, so I gave them the entire statement, just as I'd given it to him. They must just not go and give it a sensational twist as if I, and we, meant it in a traitorous manner. I still believe in *"loyal resistance"* (although, God knows, there's almost nothing one dares be loyal to in this country!).

My tender, open, anemone darling: stay lovely, good and beautiful, and wait with patience and impatience, because I'm coming. Verse for today: Behold, the bridegroom cometh.

With all my love,
André.

––––––––––

Castella
Monday, 21 October 1963

Darling my André,

About two hours after the telephone call which couldn't really go smoothly because old Muis [Levin] was in and out of the office, and the *Dagbreek*-slant. But thank you for your darling voice and laugh and for Anton's in the background. At first I thought the phone call would also come to grief because it rang and rang and Muis doesn't know how to manage the switchboard. These newspapermen – big human rats.

I so badly want to hear your tape (BBC) again, and I wonder what they'll make of my conversation. And I wonder who went and informed about the programme – surely one has the right to speak intelligently about censorship …? But what the hell! I am so sick of the incessant intimidation, the whole situation in the country; and the newspapers, which are no platform for anyone because they always twist everything to fit in with their party politics; the recruitment to get someone into

244

whatever kraal – sick, sick and tired and gatvol now … what does Jan say again, liefsteling?

I've loaned *Lobolo* out. I miss it. It is so you; but then, thank God, I still have *Die Ambassadeur* and all the others, but especially *Die Ambassadeur* of course. Our *Ambassadeur,* which will be ready at the end of the month – I really *live* to see it. (Afterword: Jack, oh God, is dedicating his latest book – as far as I last heard – to me.) I also find that touching – Saturday on the beach (my friend and Simone and I went to 3rd beach) and I, despite my intentions, walked over to 2nd – curious too – but Jack's godchild, who is or was in love with him, was there – no, my André, I don't think this friendship can erode any more – I will of course miss him terribly – in my loneliness he was, in his way, and in spite of everything, a pillar of strength – it'll be uphill and a challenge, but here or *there*, the bright light of you and your love waits – and then always the reunion – that wonder in which everything is rediscovered. And I am not far away.

We will remain lovely and free, this time even more than usual, because now the slight feeling of guilt towards Jack and the fear, I am no longer "responsible" for him – he's allowed me to cut myself off from him. Oh, it probably sounds terribly complicated, but you'll understand. Words on paper. Telephone. Really rather inadequate, moesie-man?

And thank you for your lovely letter from Saturday and today's which *is* a letter. But I *know know know* how despondent or helpless one can feel before such a white (paper).

My friend is here; asks whether I've not finished writing yet – there's still so much to say, the court case – I'll tell you when you get here, it's such a long story; haven't seen Jan's book yet; the tape recorder not fixed yet – magtig! it's one of my main "contacts".

Oh, so Rob doesn't think that *Rook en Oker* deserves the prize? He is of course quite correct; but what does he think of *Mens-alleen?* Or of Small's? And I hope your cover design is okay. (Dust cover Willie Jordaan.) Chris and I will be eating out on Wednesday evening; but if you're going to phone then we'll go afterwards. He's terribly busy with exam papers, that hell lies ahead for you now too.

My friend told me an inexplicable story about an African preacher on the Parade; he spits so much on everyone when he preaches that they stand around him in a wide circle and he shouts: "'He who sitteth, shall be damned!' says the Lord. Oh yes! 'You can LIE, you can STAND, but if you SIT, you will go to hell,' says GOD!" (What on earth …?) A lame old African then went and sat in the middle of the circle, took his shoes off, spat on his feet; the preacher says to him, dead normal: "Listen, man, you mustn't sit here, this is a preaching place this," and then, "He who sitteth, shall be DAMNED!" God, child, we must go and listen on Saturday the 9th. Maybe our love-madness sounds like this to the Bill de Klerks …

I miss you and I am completely dependent on you. And you are the most won-der-ful thing that has ever happened to me. I will make you feel good … joke. Be good, always mine. The reading for today: Keep your heart with all diligence, for out of it spring the issues of life.

MINE. André Brink, love love,
Your Con.

PS: This is a *letter*, this. C. –
Don't forget the photo album.

————————

Grahamstown,
Wednesday, 23 October 1963

Darling, little white poesje,

Strange – or actually not strange at all, but obvious! – that you wrote out the lovely Van Waalwijk poem for me, because I remember once wanting to send it to you but then I forgot all about it. (Whatever the case, you're not getting your little white "poesje" back – or does it have a brown coat again, shining in the light? – it's mine, and you're just keeping it in "safe custody" for me.)

246

I've been thinking so much in the past few days about our little moesie-girl. Has she joined her brothers and sisters down the drain? Or is she *coming*?

Darling, dammit, I feel such frustration today! First the call that didn't go through last night, probably because Mrs Oxley was out. (And the frustration doubled because I knew you'd be out, too!) And then today's frustration because I can't phone tonight. You see, Estelle was going to swop her shift tonight with someone else – that's why I wanted to phone yesterday; but then the whole thing fell through and so I let it be known I'd phone tonight rather, but guess what: the two of them agreed to swop after all, so once again I had to send a telegram! I hope you were able to keep up with all the conflicting reports. (The swop, by the way, is only for this week.)

I wanted to *talk* with you – especially about the moesie-girl, and about the *Dagbreek* matter. I've been through a few highly upsetting days because the wrong twist they gave this "sensation" has buggered everything up. I heard from Chris [Barnard] in Jhb that a good number of subscribers to *60* have withdrawn their subscriptions because they don't want a journal in which a "national traitor" is one of the associates, and Bartho might have to resign from the editorial team as a result of pressure from APB. Etc. etc. etc. Oh this lunatic country of ours!

But I've just sent *Dagbreek* an urgent statement – to set the distortion right, and to motivate my position that I'm attacking a *law* and a *situation*, not South Africa itself ("loyal resistance"); that the truth remains the truth, "singular and old", whether it's inside or outside the country. Now, as far as I'm concerned, the whole row is a thing of the past. Over to the readers.

I will say NOTHING to the *Sunday Times*. When they quoted me incorrectly, I didn't rush off to *Dagbreek*. The ST has got nothing, fuck-all, to do with this matter. It simply adds sensation to the whole thing, and that messes everything up. We've had more than enough sensation. *You* too. You must also say nothing to Muis [Levin], my little thing. The ST doesn't exist to present points of view. They want circulation, via sensation. Finis.

Our lectures came to an end today. Finally. All this reaction has tired me out, though. And the Simenon translation still awaits me – from Monday I'll be working at a rate of 10 000 words a day; I want to finish so that I can work unhindered on *Orgie*. Perhaps it'll be completed by the time I come to you.

The cover still hasn't arrived, but I phoned Koos today and it's apparently arriving on Friday's flight. I hope it's good. Going by what Koos says, my fear is it'll be too "realistic".

Koos is apparently driving through Grahamstown on his way to Natal on 3 or 4 Nov. and is likely to drop in. I'll have to play my cards carefully – because I'd been thinking I would say I'll be staying with Koos! I'll think of something. Thin ice. But I'm *coming*, hell or high water.

I love you. I *need* you. The past few days, and all this work, have exhausted me. I want to be there and rest with you, and feel happy, without tension and longing, just you and me, my shining person of light with your soft hands and little curl, having a Martini. Will we be enjoying some drinks again? And we'll buy you a beautiful dress. Swim, play and live recklessly, fully; and then we'll come to rest, exhausted, but oh so delicious in the marriage bed that Maggie prepared with such "awe" and scorn?

My Ingrid – my "clean", "blonde", beautiful, lovely bride, in quiet enchantment all my muddiness dissolves in you – "a last spot of quiet among the reeds".

I hail you with love and longing and impatience and yearning and grace, André.

Wednesday, 23 October 1963

TELEPHONE BROKEN YESTERDAY NO LITTLE ONE MUCH LOVE = YOUR COCOON

248

Castella
Wednesday night, 23 October 1963, 9:30

My lovely little sparring partner of the disarming letter and the lovely cheque with which I bought something that is going to be such a surprise to you – against my nature, I'm not going to tell you what it is; you'll just have to come and see on the 8th.

The dead telephone calls – Lord! Waited in a sort of sickness for it last night; and had to find out that the Oxleys' phone is not working – received two telegrams at once; one sent at three o'clock and one at four o'clock – with the same message – are you mad? Thought the tidings were at the very least disastrous. So I postponed the visit to Simone – till tonight – from there to Chris at seven – cancelled our dinner; and had a drink; he brought me back here at 8:30 where this telegram was waiting: "Impossible after all …" Ag, I know it's not your fault. You mustn't be sad about it; I understand and I love you. Did you then not receive *my* telegram? I sent it myself from the main post office at 1:30 and said, among other things: There is no little one … Yesterday already, but I felt it coming about two days earlier and was expecting it. Wonder what became of the telegram; you should have received it by at least three o'clock.

Chris and I just had tea together and, laughing, read the terrible "poem" by Susann Kotzé: there's a blatant dedication: To Ralph Palmer (poor thing).

> Beminde man, ek vra, o laat my nou reeds gaan
> voor hierdie hunkering in my siel steeds hoër gloei
> en voor my bloed ontstuimig deur my are vloei
> en ek ontblote van my weerstand voor jou staan.
>
> Want môrenag, as jou liefde deur my diepte roer
> sal ek miskien jou lippe op my voel verstyf
> en ek, aan jou gebind deur bande van die lyf
> sal blindelings uitdryf in die nag, deur pyn ontroer.

This book will accompany me to Gordon's Bay, because I've decided *that's* the place for us; sea and mountain, and (apparently) lovely accommodation.

I'm no longer far away; today I was very near to you; sometimes even closer than when we are together; "your supreme *reality*." But I am sleepy and tired; this is not a letter; it's a goodnight, much more than a letter: 'Night to your moesies and your beautiful teeth, and your papie, upon which my hand may rest.

Your Cocoon.

Grahamstown
Saturday morning, 26 October 1963

My Kontjie, darling,

I'm sitting here, waiting for eleven-thirty, because one of those affairs that are the cross of academic life will then begin – the inauguration of a new chancellor, where we all have to make our august appearance in togas and stuff. Hideous. I'll be bunking this afternoon's "garden party"; one has to draw the line *somewhere*.

The worst of the upheaval around the cover is finally over; I've only just dropped it at the station and phoned Koos to let him know. It doesn't look like there'll be enough time to change much. It doesn't really matter, either. I'm sick to death of covers.

Thank you for last night's wonderful, peaceable conversation. Today in two weeks' time we'll be lying on the beach or walking somewhere on a mountain; the air and sea and the stillness will be ours.

I wanted to send you another tape, but the last few days have just been too hectic. Monday I'll have the whole afternoon to myself, and I'll do it then.

I'm feeling a little frustrated because, with all the bustling about this week, I've not been able to get back to *Orgie*. It's such an insult when one is unable to do one's *work*. It's only when I'm with you, and when I write, that I live fully; the rest is just marking time, "spying out the options". I want to be done with it by the time I come to you. Maybe I can start again this afternoon, or tomorrow – it's a slightly difficult section, because "his" life must now emerge, especially his married life … and I'm not neutral in this regard, I can't just separate myself from it; it's an oppression. But maybe it'll come out right. After this section the "search for the deceased god" begins – and that should go well.

Oh you, you: I love you. And I *need* you, urgently. I am terribly tired; after this year's work, the rush with the recent translation, and this week's disruptions around *Dagbreek* and the cover, I feel rather trapped; not free; far away from the sun. And for that reason I want to be with you, come to rest, be touched by life again, be moved towards the light; you do all of this, and for that reason you are so good, so precious.

I dreamt that I earned R2 000 somehow in prize money, and the two of us went away, far, untraceably far away, to small Greek islands with those old white pillars from the time of Homer; and a blue sea, a world full of myths, a sky full of gods, a forest full of satyrs, a little village with old brown fishermen, nets, superstition, piety and the scent of sea and seaweed. We roamed through it all, happy, hand in hand, swimming, playing, lying under the trees talking, and sleeping together in rapture. One must always take into account that "beautiful dreams never return to life". But our dream is *coming*. In just two weeks we'll be in it, and it's going to be our loveliest and fullest and most happy time of all. Fill your little lamp with oil. Make sure you're in fine feather. I'm coming – with love that "conquers all things" (verse for today). Now I'm going to have to sprint to be on time.

With love and love and love and softness and passion,
Your André.

Length shirt – armpit: 16"
Length arm (armpit – wrist): 24"!

It's going to be lovely, my beautiful!

———————

Castella

Monday night, 28 October 1963

My darling,

I wanted to come and say goodnight to you calmly tonight, without shadows, but now the night still stretches far ahead, with *Dagbreek* here next to me. I was astonished to read Chris Barnard's attack on you; he is after all a *friend* of yours and apparently that involves "loyalty" – or is that just towards the press? Abraham de Vries, well. Did they read your statements to the BBC … did you send it to *Dagbreek* – if so, why don't they quote from that – for or against …? No, my André, I get the impression that there's a lot more jealousy at play than anything else. Don't take any notice of it – envy has a nobler twin – admiration.

My first reaction was that you should resign from the editorship of *60*, is this now an ultimatum … you or Bartho? God! Why must Bartho and his precious APB-bladdy-work always be protected? Of that, I've now also had enough. I *like* Bartho. Everyone likes Bartho. And we know it's better that he rather than anyone else is head of APB … but Bartho came and asked me, against his principles and convictions, to leave "Die Kind" out of *Rook en Oker* – Bartho's play, *Die Verminktes* [The Maimed] – which is a sharp attack on the South African situation, has been performed in *England* – do they call *him* a "traitor", and my God – if Chris Barnard can publish his miserable *Houtbeeld* [Wooden Carving] or whatever abroad – would he refuse … (Just one ray of light: Preller's stupid letter!) (That's just by the way.) And now: your explanation to *Dagbreek* … why does poor old Uys get dragged in by his balding head and is then left aside? "Creative resistance must always be loyal." To whom? Yourself – the truth – fine, then. But I think more consideration needs to be given – (Lord!) to the meaning of loyalty. I can only be loyal towards something I believe in, admire, something I can identify with. "My people." I do *not* believe in the Nazi's policies; I couldn't be loyal to them, even if I were a hundred times a German. I cannot defend them. Therefore loyalty is out of the question.

Anti-South African (the *Sunday Times*). God! What is South African and what's anti it? Anti-government, ah! So, my precious, "to the country I remain wholeheartedly loyal". But South Africa or "the country" is not the Nats, thank God! At some point or other we'll all have to start thinking, a search, relentless, along the lines of "Liberal Nationalism", but much, much further than this. What a task! "Loyalty alone to the highest I know, more than to a friend or brother …" and maybe Chris Barnard found it …! His *ambiguous*, rather "clever" declaration to *Dagbreek* concerning *60* makes me weep out loud. Unless you remain editor, I'll withdraw my subscription and my hitherto meagre contributions, expose this skulduggery in *Contrast* etc. etc. etc. (But I am busy with a song of lamentation, my first long poem – which I naturally wanted to give to *60* and for which I've already been approached by *Contrast*.)

Dear child! I love you. The *Sunday Times*. You've probably also seen that mess. I was sitting reading it perfectly calmly on the train to Bellville when my eye caught that tasteless photograph of me … I can assure you I'd given Muis as little of a statement or whatever for publication as you'd done – and so did Jack – I phoned him (Muis) today and when he said that Jack had given one, I said: "That's a lie!" God, André, I can't bear it when someone *uses* or *abuses* me. I don't *want* cheap publicity in this slimy (probably like all Sunday newspapers) – why not rather a ban on their filthy sensationalism than on a Sunday swim? No, I gave this Muis a good telling off. I once gave him his miserable job back after he'd almost lost it because of his unfounded reports about me – because he's got a whole bunch of kids. But today I told him that in future I'll simply be greeting him – "and that goes for

André too …" And that's probably all there is about this dirty business. And then one confronts the shocking fact – there is no longer a platform for the serious person – everything just gets used – in whatever way. The *Sunday Times* and similar newspapers "play into the hands of the enemy". And the enemy is stupidity and callousness and bondage and fear, and dishonesty and recklessness, all of which probably *is* stupidity and the celebration of stupidity, the greatest POWER on earth.

My André, my heart, defend yourself against the "battalions of lies and organizations of hate". Because I'm going to "entirely encompass" you again (in just eleven days). Thank you for your letter; and your telephone call on Friday – and you are right, this time is going to be the most wonderful, in the Van Riebeeck Hotel – thank you for your measurements – I'll see to it – and stay CALM till then – with the longing and passion and love that you know so well by now. As always for always,

COCOON.

Today's reading:
Father, forgive them, for they know not what they do!

Dearest my mine,

I have *just* missed your phone call – when I opened the gate, I heard Mrs Oxley put the telephone down – I was with Simone and came back early precisely because I thought you might phone – sorry, my heart – the stupid bus drove past and then I had to walk across the sports grounds – all the way home. And now you're probably wondering where I'm roaming around? And I still wanted to ask you whether I should dye my hair white – it's been cut short. Last night, when I wrote to you, I was too angry about the BBC affair to even tell you properly about the weekend. Went to the beach on Saturday – I ended up not being in the mood for a whole weekend in Bellville – and had a lovely swim with Simone, and Saturday evening had a peaceful braai on the beach with Jack and Simone – Uys and his teacher-girlfriend joined us at the house. Only went to my friends in Bellville on Sunday – home at twelve o'clock. Yesterday nothing – today supper with Mrs Bouws – and that's all the news! (And this is, in any case, far more than your usual "news", my emotional darling!) And, oh yes, did I really forget to tell you – I'm now getting tea. They decided against tea in the board meeting and so I went to see the Brigadier.

After these meagre offerings it probably seems that I'm not very busy, but my heart, I hardly have time to read the beautiful *Stroomgebied* and by this stage I am ravenously hungry for poems – intellectually-sexually-poetry-hungry. Now you'll probably read something into *that*. The jersey is coming along – thank you for your measurements – maybe it's a bit big – because your measurements were late, but that's just how it will have to be. I'm looking forward enormously to *Die Ambassadeur*. Koos says the first copy won't be ready before the 6th. What plan have you now devised with regard to your "accommodation"?

You'd have a heart attack if you had to walk into the castle now – newspaper clippings and cut-out newspapers EVERYWHERE – but Maggie is coming tomorrow. I'm going to have a bath and sleep immediately now so that I don't have to look at the mess. With you – because I actually haven't for a long time – you are very close these days – are you calm and happy? I would so much like to speak to you – *now*. Now I will just have to rely on "the silence (that) becomes the dancing". I'm looking forward to the tape and I'm so sorry I haven't been able to make one for you yet – yours will probably have to be played at my good friends in Clifton again.

Love my precious my André my own. There are ten little pebbles left then the Volksie is red and you dead tired and bathed and *happy beside me*.

Love also for little Anton from little Simone,

Cocoon.

Grahamstown
Wednesday morning, 30 October 1963

Sunchild, moonchild, starchild,

I miss you!

I hoped there might be a letter from you this morning, but no such luck, and last night I wanted to go to the movies (Brigitte …!) but stayed home precisely to phone you, except "Miss Jonker is not in this evening". Never mind, I know, it's my fault; I was the one who said I'd phone tonight.

But I wanted to talk to you so badly, because I finished *Orgie* yesterday at six o'clock. 88 pages – not quite double-spacing, which means it'll run to just over 100 pages in print. I'm very pleased with it. I think it's gained an increasingly musical form, in which the emotional, irrational, "non-significatory" impression of the words become more important than the text's logical import; and in which symbols, words, and bits of sentences all recur, like musical themes. I am not, as in ordinary prose, dealing with one line or one row of notes at a time, but trying to work in chords. One of the pages is entirely black! (The walk into night – which is not merely a real night.) And as I've already said: I'm going to base the cover on an enchanting, dynamic red rooster by [Marc] Chagall. (I've suddenly developed an obsessive adoration for Chagall. When I'm in the Cape – just *ten* days, darling! – I want to buy some beautiful art books, and shut my eyes to the cost.) I'm so broke. But I'm going to start working on John Malherbe's new book today – not too long, the same as the Pharoahs' one – and see if I can't finish it before I come down. Not sure, because piles of exam scripts will be arriving on Friday – awful work.

Dagbreek went and made a vulgar little sensation out of my state-ment. Abraham de Vries's commentary strikes me as especially acrimo-nious and unnecessary. I'm going to have a falling out with him, soon. The trouble is he's going to take over Chris B.'s post if Chris goes overseas – and then he'll be in a position of power sufficient to squeeze the rest of us to death. Making the most of their talents!

I phoned Koos again yesterday about the cover – they've apparently not changed it very much at all – and he said Uys may be coming with him on Sunday on the trip to Natal and then they'll be sleeping over here with us. In that case he'll no doubt have a lot to say to you when he gets back. But I'm still looking forward to having him here.

The charge against *Lobola* has been withdrawn. I'm sorry it didn't go ahead. I so badly wanted to remove the taint from the book – and have a lovely little fight. (*Not* for the sake of pleasing Rosa Nepgen!)

Ag, all this news. What does it matter, in the end? I love you, most lovely one, I want to be with you again, be enraptured with you, unquestioning, happy, serene and stormy. We'll enjoy the sun and the sea, be boisterous and reckless. The sun's shining brightly here again after a few miserable, sad little days of drizzle that made my sinus condition unbearable.

To be with you – "to sleep, to sleep, perchance to dream"! My delightful, still one, my busy little bee, my constant, inconstant little whirlwind. Come blow through me again, blow away the dust, blow it all clean and bright.

Love, my love: clothe yourself in light and wait for me, sweet and exuberant and happy. We'll be celebrating Mass with the bread and wine of our bodies and our blood; we're going to live beautifully and perilously, like poetry, and we will be unstoppably happy.

With a heart full of love, shamelessly romantic,
André.

———————

Grahamstown
Thursday, 31 October 1963

My ravishing, absolute woman,

Thank you for this morning's heartfelt letter about the *Dagbreek* matter – De Vries and Barnard. Bright, bright child, you are so wonderfully pure in your loyalty. I still think Chris's intention was good (or am I very naive?) but Abraham's motives grieve me – the self-satisfied fool. I made my statement for *Dagbreek* because I believed that they – like the BBC? like the *Sunday Times*? like any print media, mass-media – "used" me; and I wanted to make sure people understood what my loyalty actually meant. As I said in the statement, "honesty about the truth that doesn't change its character depending on whether one is inside or outside the country". Naturally, I also wanted to get across that I'm not just a convenient, hysterical slanderer, an "enemy". (An enemy of that which is half-hearted and false and wrong, but not of the idea of SA – that's bigger than people or governments.) It would be just as impure to see *blindly*. The problem, I now know, is that one must never try to make subtle distinctions for the masses. They function only in black and white. And, as my mother wrote yesterday in a dear letter: "Never try to *explain*, because your friends understand you in any case, while your enemies never will."

But darling, I am upset by what you say about the *Sunday Times*: my edition has nothing in it of that nature, and I know Chris Barnard's also didn't – I phoned him to ask. This means that only certain editions carried this news (about the BBC matter). Keep yours, please. I'm *angry* with them. (The *Dagbreek* statement, which appeared the week before last, also didn't appear in every edition – they all had the front-page story, but not my statement on page 6.)

Ag, it's a load of crap, all of it.

Pure: let us remain pure. ("Even beauty endures in the dirt".) And live high and handsome and humanely: I don't mean we should be "chilly" and "elevated", but live at full throttle: high, and biotic, warm, earthy. We are a mixture of "a little water, clay, and prophetic breath", remember!

Thank you for our lovely conversation last night. And for the deliciousness afterwards – a little forestaste of what's coming in a week's time, lovely, lovely; hell, man!

I'm working like a madman on Malherbe's *Peoples of Africa* – started yesterday afternoon and I'm already halfway; I'll be done by Sunday. Then I'll see if I can re-type *Orgie* for you. I feel good in my heart about this novella. I think it carries both light and darkness, the abyss and the coming of clarity; it has the subdued sadness that I wanted. It was born of the two of us, except that the roles have been reversed: you the father and I the mother! (Like the silly joke about the innocent girl who didn't want her boyfriend to lie on top of her – after he'd taken off her clothes – because her mother said she should not allow it: if she did, she said, "my mother would end up dealing with the matter"; but she was quite willing to come and lie on top of *him* – because then *his* mother would end up having to deal with it!)

I'm reading [Arthur] Rimbaud – *Une Saison en Enfer* (A Season in Hell) – and am very taken with the work. And Gerhart Hauptmann's *Heretic of Soana*, which is less striking, perhaps because it's a translation.

It's as hot as hell here. During the day I chase a naked Anton all over the lawn with a hosepipe. I should try to get a bit of a tan before I come down, otherwise I'll look far too much like a country bumpkin when we get to Gordon's Bay. Not so, my brown girlie? And I must say farewell again, though now in hues of brown. Bring your red bikini along, too. I want to see you with your nice short hair (but not dyed!) and your lovely slovenly red nails, and your leucodendron, your laugh and your shy, naughty eyes, your provocative full breasts, and your little high mound into which I can disappear so deeply, so completely. Oh delicious, lovely one, always mine, pure and happy and lovely; clothe your loneliness in my love and wait in delight.

Love love,
André.

———————

Castella
Thursday night, 31 October 1963

My dearest man,

A clean castle – Maggie mercifully came in – and the groceries – two dresses I altered at my sister's for the wonderful summer that is close at hand – because it is indeed close at hand – where I always feel everything first; and a summer that I will carry in my hands – precious warm-time after the long winter; another two pretty dresses back from the dry cleaners; the shiny (pretty satiny) yellow one you haven't seen me in yet – so you see for yourself how the Lord guides! Thank you for your telephone conversation last night; these conversations are terribly funny; we immediately tell all the news that we've already written or are about (even worse) to write; at a feverish pace so that the – I almost said the announcer – because there is something so public about these conversations – the Oxleys – although they understand little Afrikaans – are hanging around – and I am sure that the exchange is also listening in, bored stiff; and everything one says sounds so "boring" (Preller) and not at all like you feel – God! – then we get cut off and feel vaguely alarmed – still – I need our telephone and wonder of wonders, am again laughing because I can hear the pomegranates laughing!

Liefsteling, only a week, because today is done – then I can break open the pomegranates in my hands – take, eat, this is my flesh and blood! Haven't received confirmation from the Van Riebeeck [Hotel] yet (that vile filth piles up everywhere, (V.R.)); probably tomorrow. The manager there sounds highly civilised. Don't think there'll be the same mess there was at Cederwood. Jan and Marjorie invited me for a meal there tonight; they're having an evening about [Edward Albee's *Who's Afraid of*] *Virginia Woolf* – apparently Chris [?] sent the script – but I preferred to go see a little child-face. I'm afraid of Virginia Woolf … Jan's book hasn't appeared here yet; did you receive a copy? But at my sister's all the little faces were disobedient and she was upset; thank God I can rest now for a while here with you! Did I tell you that after our week I'll be taking Simone back; my little anchor is "worried" about me and I am also not whole without her.

Wonder what you're doing now; probably writing to me too; because you "neglected" me on Sunday, Monday and Tuesday of course – that wasn't serious; or no, you're busy with exam papers, my poor lecturer-doctor-man! What's your thesis about? I am really jealous of Koos and Uys who are moving to your little town – excuse me immediately, horrible suspicious: *He will influence you against me* – only protection really: shock about the attitude of all those months and now he will see you with your house and everything … "Oh! We have to trust each other again in some essentials!"

I am looking forward so much to our few days, so:

overhandig mij brekend
je peilloze bloem, je kus

als een dar dolzinnig dijf ik
op het aquarel van de dorst
…
hoor dan met uw handen haast dan uw hartslag
ik ben een donkere droom in de zon
(Lucebert)

And dearest mine, you'll just have to wear the jersey, hot or cold … and you'll be surprised at how the wind can blow in Gordon's Bay – I'll go and show you my old school – the place has many walks – I lay so low this week that "no one will miss me at the dance or the dish".

I'm burning to see *Orgie.* You must immediately send whatever's finished; it's lying in pieces here in a special file; and I even began a scrapbook for you – mad! – but my own lamentation isn't really progressing; maybe just that terrible five o'clock in the afternoon when you leave …

Why did you ask so half-anxiously how things are going at work? Or was that part of the rush of the phone conversation – it's all terribly dead normal; news there: I'm getting holiday money in February – your money dream and the island – I dreamt I was in England; landscape and climate enchanting; you weren't there, just old English gentlemen with walking sticks and umbrellas; but the dream had such atmosphere of reality … You must in any case not worry about my work; I fit in well and "everyone likes me very much", as Jannie Gildenhuys would say – Chris says he'll also be here during our time – then we'll go and have a meal together; this work actually takes up little time because I don't have to work on Saturdays, and after five working days I don't have to think of it again! And it's lovely to see the clean little castle with all the food and soap and to know: I worked and paid for it …! Small, essential vanities …!

Dearest my André. This is really not a letter; it's the last week and I am waiting for you, my precious groom: "The only thing that matters is being together." Bring me some nice books to read, because I'll die if I have to steal all the hotel's *Feminas* and things again. And there's only one joy bigger (MUCH bigger) than lying in bed with you reading.

'Night, my angel.

Love and love,
Only yours,
Cocoon.

{PS: My hair really and truly *is* still the same colour! Okay!}

Grahamstown
Saturday, 2 November 1963

Precious poetry-hungry, poesy-hungry child,

Nine in the morning: are you still asleep there in your enchantingly untidy little castle, my Sleeping Beauty, or are you up already and fiddling around; or maybe lying on the beach, with your tan and white bathing costume, freckled shoulders and short hair? Next week this time we'll be lying together – in bed or on the beach? Delicous, delicous. "I miss you and I love you: therefore I am."

There is some bad news, too: Koos sent a telegram to say *Die Ambassadeur* will be delivered a week later than expected – the 14th at the latest. But I decided I can't change my plans yet again, so I'll be coming down as arranged on the 8th. And if necessary I'll stay a day or two longer – until Thursday or, at the latest, until Friday. Happy?

Thank you for yesterday's lovely letter. You are forbidden ever again to walk alone across the sportsfields in the dark. That's an order.

Your consternation on the phone about the fact that Uys might come and stay here amused me (he's no longer coming). Darling, strange child: why would you think anything Uys or whoever might say could influence me, hmm? You'll start me thinking that your "quiet braai on the beach with Jack" was more than just enjoyable! I'm just teasing, so don't worry. My dearest love, I believe all your lies …

We're going to play delectably this time. Play seriously, play playfully. And the sun's going to be ours. You are eternally mine.

The marking has begun. So far it's not all that bad. In one essay yesterday I found this gem: "The poet stands head and toes above his contemporaries." (Some toes they must be! Worse than Ampie's!) Otherwise I'm translating myself into the ground. I'll be finishing John Malherbe's book today, and I'll ask him to post the cheque to your address so we can have money to f… around with. I translated the book in *three days*! Now I just have to type out an article for *60*, continue typing up *Orgie* for you, mark scripts … and come, come, come (hell!).

Cocoony-kontjie o' mine: this is not a *note*. It's a little *letter*. And it comes to you with exuberant love and laughter and longing, with a kiss upon your earlobe, and a soft touch on your little, big round breasts that announce your arrival to the world so fully and provocatively.

Love; and a command (verse for today): Be of good cheer with me, Your André.

———————

Grahamstown
Sunday night, 3 November 1963

Child, most beloved, most delightful,

It's the kind of night – cool and still, after last night's passionately wild thunderstorm – I'd like to be with you, swollen and satisfied, inside your little cocoon, physically and spiritually taken up in the poetry of being together, aware of the mercy of it all –

... om van Hom

die skaduwee net van Sy genade
oor ons te laat passeer, om te verkry dat
(het Hy nie gesê ons moet bid, geloof,
soos in 'n mosterdsaad nie?) dat Hy

wat as allenige die Beskouing kan gee,
daardie opperste mededeelsaamheid
van Hom ook aan ons enkelde siele
in Sy genade gaan bewaarheid.

It was a quiet day today. All day I wanted to write, but I was lazy this morning, reading newspapers; and this afternoon I slept. Tonight Frieda

264

was here. Estelle kept bringing the conversation round to curtains and clothes and the library – work stuff – while I wanted to be liberated precisely from the fuss of the everyday; so I stretched myself out on the divan, shut myself off despite the conversation, and pleasantly took residence in you. It was the same all last night, when I dreamt about you and our coming week – unserious, satisfied dreams about small things, restfulness and fulfilment. Cocoon, my own, you are near to me and I live in nearness to you. On some days I worry that I – that we – are looking forward too much to the 8th and the days after that; I'm afraid something might come up on the cusp of the visit and prevent it from happening. But surely no such thing is possible? Also, Koos did not arrive here today, and so there was no discussion (something I was worried about!) where it might've emerged that he knows about my accommodation in the Cape. (By the way, I am now – officially – going to be staying with John [J.C.] Kannemeyer! Inter alia because he doesn't have a telephone.)

I finished off John's translation yesterday; today I typed out the article for *60* – I'm sending you a copy – and tomorrow I'll begin typing up *Orgie* for you.

To my surprise, Grové – in a chilly little letter! – accepted my parody of R. Schutte for *Standpunte*. You will be glad, too, now that you have also suffered her inefficiency and up-her-own-arse attitude.

Darling love, have you seen in the most recent *Sarie Marais* how wonderfully enthusiastic Audrey Blignault is about *Sempre*? (With that old photo of me from my matric year next to her piece.) I've suddenly shed my suspicions about her. Maybe *Die Ambassadeur* does have a small chance of getting the prize after all …!

Monday
Tuesday
Wednesday
Thursday
And then Friday!
(Uys would say: "Oh Ingrid, oh name, oh longing.")
What might today's *Times* and *Dagbreek* have to say, this time

around …? I don't give a damn. It's water under the bridge now. I love you – what else matters?

My sweet little cherub, my pretty flea – tonight I want to sit and come up with crazily lovely names for you, and be happy with you. I'm feeling a little mad. And very happy.

I'm living chastely and saving up my secrets.

I love you,
André.

———————————

Castella
Tuesday evening, 5 November 1963

My dearest André darling,

You really kept your word – to write to me before you come down – opened my path into the wilderness! Thank you for your letters; I'm now alone for the first time since Friday, except of course for sleep! – and still had to go to Simone last evening. This week I must see her as often as possible otherwise she's going to feel terribly neglected this coming weekend. She grumbles about wanting to come home – I am so glad I'll be able to discuss her with you when you're here – next year of course it's school, and I don't know if I should put her into a boarding school – poor little thing – etc. etc. By the way, I haven't heard another word from Piet. Dear man, I phoned Human & Rousseau myself and asked after *Die Ambassadeur* – and they told me there's a delay with the dust cover and that they'll make sure in any case that you can leave here with a couple of copies.

Evidence? So how did it go on Sunday, and did the thin ice crack? One can make out nothing from your beautiful letters. All I know is that the Van Riebeeck Hotel and Gordon's Bay are going to be lovely, they wrote me a letter, I was so proud of it; they look forward to our arrival; they don't know us yet! It's summer in Cape Town; Friday night's helluva storm is over; was dead scared all night long; we're not used to such lightning and thunder. I have noted that I must not give my (uncompleted) lamentation to *Contrast*, but on the other hand I'm not much in the mood for that cowardly *60* – God, I was angry! You can help me with two reviews for *The New African – Modern Poetry from Africa –* and *Poems from Black Africa.*

Glad, of course, that you're staying till Friday! Booked for us at Van Riebeeck Hotel from Saturday till Monday and warned Anne that I'll be sick on Monday; the rest of the time we can just stay in the castle. I have again forgotten how you look and how you laugh, my unfamiliar darling. In two days I will know everything again, because Friday isn't a day; and then I'll in any case be busy arranging my little feathers! For a week we can again forget everything, oh happy, huge fire of my loins … am I neglecting you with these shortish letters? … but your lovely letters I cannot mimic! Yet you are already a part of me, I call you by the name André Brink with love and tenderness and trust, till Friday.

Your Cocoon.

{PS: Thank you so much for your cheque, my treasure, which rescued Simonina for a week! Where do you get the money from? IJonker.}

Grahamstown
Monday, 18 November 1963

My darling, my Cocoon,

I should've written already, I *wanted* to, and yet everything was still so unsayable, too tender to touch with words. Especially because the return here was such a tumbling back into banal realities like marking exam scripts, making my way through piled-up work, and – so difficult – learning to adapt to a life without communication.

Darling, all that remains of our last, almost surreal night is a strange, unbelievable and vaguely terrifying vortex. Were *we* involved in that? Did we say all *that*? From where – and why – did everything come down on us like that?

And yet if I look at the week as a *whole*, then it remains one of revelation; we succeeded in seeing each other more deeply than ever before, despite – and through – all the surging passions. And I now feel more *attached* to you and more wholeheartedly in love with you than ever seemed possible before. "What a piece of work is a man ..."

I remember Gordon's Bay especially, our crystal ball of wonder and happiness and fulfilment. It *was* in fact what we believed it would be before the time: unalloyed togetherness such as we've never known before.

And the other things, darling, about which I can hardly speak, perhaps they were also necessary, in an irrational, cruel way, because it made us face up to each other in all our forlornness and importunity. About the unforgivable hurt that I inflicted upon you, I can say nothing and ask nothing that would be adequate. Only that it will remain a matter of acute conscience for me, always. Because I love you, and I'm devoted to you in my need, and cannot bear the thought of you being hurt.

The trip back was a nightmare of guilt and longing and yearning. And I was *tired* – still am, now. As if this wasn't enough, I was involved in a collision outside Knysna. Absurd, actually, and thank God only a slight mishap: I'd just begun accelerating from 35 m.p.h. when a scooter on the far left of the road swerved in front of me to turn right. I swung the car round and the one mudguard knocked him over. I thought the man was stone dead. But when I stopped to get out, the old bugger was standing upright next to his (almost undamaged) scooter. He was through-and-through Afrikaans, but in his shock he spoke English. Just wanted to know, in broken English: "Joer not gouing toe meik trabbel fôr mie hei?" And when it appeared that he and his scooter were unscathed, and that only my car had suffered a dent, I got back inside to drive away. At that point he let out a shout and came running up to me, his hands stretched pathetically out before him, uttering the classic complaint: "Maai paaip ies brouken, mên."

About that I laughed for the next 50 miles.

I arrived home at eleven, completely exhausted. Had exams on Saturday and went to Port Alfred to see Naas, who was there for the day, so I could give him his copy of *Die Ambassadeur*. Yesterday I lay around in a swoon all day. Today I'm working like mad.

Your lovely, dear letter had arrived in the meantime; it lay open, with all the details about our week there for all to see. Estelle said nothing specifically. Just let it be known that it had come as a "shock" to her. Presumably she did in fact read it. When will the embankment collapse? "Blow, wind! Come, wrack!" I am *tired*. I don't know what lies ahead. All I know is that I am impossibly in love with you, and that I've so foolishly hurt you.

Your parcel ended up at this address – ridiculous! I got it today (the slip arrived last week). The black-and-white set looks especially nice. The rest are more ordinary. I'll send them on to you. I would so love to see you in them, especially in the little bikini with the ribbons.

January?

"Lord, I am not worthy."
The spirit is dark across the darkening water.
The stag calls out in the desert.
Creation is unborn and waits, yearning.

I say your name, Ingrid. Your tender, lovely, virginal name. I say it with love and painful tenderness. And I hail you with need and yearning.

Your short hair with sun, sea, smoke, and with hair's own fragrance,
and the little curl on your forehead;
your lovable ears that don't always listen,
that are so very sore, especially after car accidents;
and your brown eyes, happy or sore,
laughing and crying, quiet or cursing;
and your soft mouth, kissing and talking;
and your chin that teases and provokes;
and your fragrant, smooth, speckled shoulders;
your back, brown from the sun;
your white, round breasts, full and with milk,
with those lovable nipples – breasts that calmly move as you breathe
    and read;
and your soft, labile little tummy;
your little arms with their beautiful hands,
the messy nails and the notch in your back;
and your legs, enticing twist of calf-muscles when you wear black
    shoes;
and your loveliest feet with the leucodendron, walking across moun-
    tains, refusing to take rides with strange men;
your white backside that turns sitting into an enchantment;
and your small, high hill, nestling confidentially under my hand
and deep and warm and soft the cocoon
my cocoon, eager and hungry, tender and passionate.
Everything. You. You.
Mine and also not mine.
Mine.
My darling I love you.

Appallingly yours,
André.

270

Castella
Monday, 18 November 1963

My dearest André,

What exactly I'm drinking this Martini to, I don't know; your dust cover didn't arrive; and you are not here. Then "to the sadness at the source of your valiant joy". On Friday night the castle was so clean and bare with all your stuff gone that I decided to go with Chris after all – but the performance was terribly bad; you probably saw in the newspaper that Pietro [Nolte] disappeared on Saturday – they found him in the bushes that same night "battered" and without a shirt or jacket, in a state of shock. Poor thing! Phoned today, his mom says he's playing again this evening, at least. He gets these "slumps"; apparently he had an argument with Laurie van der Merwe. We "artists" are probably quite a miserable lot? I missed you so much, especially on Friday night when there was a man in the audience who looked just like you. Thank you very much for *Die Ambassadeur* with its impressive cover (binding) and the BRINK on it. It looks LOVELY. I've lent the sewn one to Chris in the meantime. He can't wait to start. And thank you again for everything last week, my dear treasure. There's always so much that I'm grateful to you for that I feel completely embarrassed. I received your telegram on Saturday. Glad that you are at least physically safe. ("I who wanted to rescue you / with hands and feet forever safe / On bridges without danger.")

And on Saturday Marcelle du Toit (Varney) and I went to fetch the old know-it-all's daughter and her little girls for Simone (with her beautiful "Cinderella") – and went to the beach; on Saturday evening Jack had supper here; Sunday, dejectedly, I went to sleep at my sister's flat from two to eight; no moesie-mine. I wonder what you're thinking and doing and whether everything there also tumbles and plunges like here with me and at Van Wyk's. Probably, how can it be otherwise? I am so sorry about my part in the tumult of inner tension that developed in you and which probably caused that sudden "crash" (be warned!). I wrote or tried to write to you so many times over the weekend; but at this stage we can probably just say, as you did in your little letter: just love. "Perhaps the heart will remain for us, perhaps the heart ..." And: "Wij gaat dood, en wij leven ..."

Amusing: Anne was shocked at my bare hands: "Ag, Ingrid, and he was your last hope!"

I *don't* think we should deliberately break off or "decide". God, not again! Also, not that our "row" isn't important in its own right, but that the *circumstances* are dangerous. Will all this thinking actually matter when you're standing in front of me again one day? Probably not. But form and direction we'll always seek, because we are born to *give* form and direction. My beautiful and precious André, I still love you and you love me, I am still your friend and I am still here.

Love for your red hair;
Love for your beautiful tooth;
Love for your moesies and your navel
And your long hands and the papie;
For your singularity, and your purity,
Love for your love,
Cocoon.

———————

Tuesday, 19 November 1963

NO MOESIE-GIRL JUST LOVE ALWAYS = COCOON

Castella
Wednesday night, 20 November 1963

My dearest André *darling*,

Thank you for your heavy letter this morning at 9:15. My God! Child!
And in a while you'll call; the Oxleys have just come back, and I from
Simonetta – I have finally decided – the child must come back to me,
she feels "cut off" without me – I'll simply have to make a plan to get
her here, whatever it costs.

Dear man – so *the* car accident happened after all – thank God you
were only driving at 35 m.p.h.; you probably got quite a big fright
though, my dear lost darling.

Last night when I was preparing the meal, strangely calm – chicken
– sacrifices – for Jack – you were wandering around the kitchen with
me – I was so acutely aware of you and your need – "how sensitive to
the details is pain". You mustn't feel so guilty – I must have needed
punishment. *Try* not to worry about it. Thank you, treasure-mine, for
the call earlier. Had to have tea after that with the Oxleys. There's in
fact little time for oneself. It's 9:30 again and then I still have to sleep to
be prepared for the MADHOUSE tomorrow. It was lovely chatting to you
earlier; if you were here now, you'd be lying sleeping on that little bed
and tomorrow I'd have written a beautiful poem and you your engross-
ing *Orgie* – I hope you're chatting nicely with Frieda and sleep sweetly
and serenely, thank you for your voice and laugh and impossible analy-
ses, and for the parcel that's on its way and for the love that endures and
compensates for everything. And thank you for the letter.

On Friday I'll celebrate *Die Ambassadeur* again. Tomorrow I'm having a meal with Mrs Bouws. Saturday I'm going to go and thrash the
lawyer about my money for Simone. On Sunday I'm going for a swim,
longing but comforted. One wants, after all, to live "quietly". I bless
you with love and tenderness. My André.

'Night my beautiful,
Cocoon.

Cocoon, darling,

This is happiness. It's ephemeral and quite soon everything might – probably will – be quite different again. But as I sit here, now, I'm happy; suddenly whole again, and completely and entirely yours. In spite of a sleepless night (because I lay there all the time thinking: last week this time, on this night ...) I woke up feeling well-rested. It's as hot as Hades outside. Here in my study it's a little cooler. When I look up, I see the picture of you on the bookshelf on the other side of the room – so tender, so intensely vital. The fine raindrops of a Mozart composition playing on the turntable are nothing short of scintillating. Below my left elbow lies *Tristia*, on my typewriter, to my right, are the first rough notes on *Die Ambassadeur*, which I've just finished sorting out. This afternoon my first copy of *Die Ambassadeur* will be arriving by plane (the rest have been delayed and will be arriving in Port Elizabeth; Koos arranged – guiltily – for a taxi to bring them here. It's 84 miles, but I think I'll fetch them myself). Koos read W.E.G. Louw's review over the phone to me yesterday (he received a proof).

All that is urgently lacking is you: your beloved, fiery, soft *presence*. I very nearly took to the road this morning with Rob – he left for the Cape to do examining work. But two members of the department are not allowed to be away at the same time. This of course did not prevent me from *wanting* very rebelliously to go along – I still do – and to arrive at your doorstep; this time we'd celebrate properly, in full knowledge of each other.

I know I should've written yesterday already, but it was one of those tasselled days when one sits and picks at all manner of disparate things that don't form any meaningful pattern, until you yourself just unravel.

I want to walk through town with Simone again, feed the squirrels and watch her offer Koos a single peanut from a warm, clammy hand; I want to lie with you on the warm sand, in the beaming blue sun, or in a cool little cove under a rocky overhang, and let my secrets disappear deep inside you while the light and dark make patterns on our half-closed eyes. I want to walk again with you in the dark, fragrant evening, through avenues of blossoms, laugh and be irresistably happy; I want to sit on the settee's red cushions in the little castle and think and listen as you busy yourself companionably somewhere or get fed-up and say 'God!' I want to see you in your black-and-white bra and panties. I want to bath with you and kiss the leucodendron.

And I never again want to fight with you.

I love you, delightful person, indispensable person, woman, girl, child.

This afternoon I have to deal with the second section of *Tristia* in my honours class – "Groet in Bruin" ["Salute in Brown"] and all the other divine stuff he wrote for you, on my behalf.

These days offer summer sun, but they don't offer your presence. Little bride, little Ohola, little virgin, I wander about in terrible – but *cathartic* – longing for you; it's a kind of penitence, my purgatory; I drift like Dante's figure of the lover, yearning, on the dark wind. But on the other side of this purgatory awaits the holy wound, paradise, heaven, *you*.

I don't want to bind you. I just want to love you, always, always, always.

I want you to be happy. Little swift lost in the sky: *sing*.

Forgive my unforgivableness. Love me the way I love you.

Man and woman: so the Lord God of the hosts created us and nothing can separate us. Let me always love you.

And this small human happiness,

Let it last, oh Lord, let it last long.

I'm sending you a small cheque because I know you need it, with Simone's birthday just around the corner.

Always with yearning love,
André.

Friday, 22 November 1963

BRAVO CITIZEN BRILLIANT AMBASSADEUR BRILLIANT CAREER ALL LOVE ALL
CONFIDENCE CONFIRMED = COCOON

———————

Castella
Saturday night, 23 November 1963

My dearest André,

A mad day yesterday, mad today, sand sun sea, and Simone and I wonderfully burnt; I have just fallen into her little bed. Dearest man, firstly,
congratulations and once again congratulations on *Die Ambassadeur*,
which only appeared today; and for which you had to drive all the
way to PE; and now you're having a party; who's there? Since Guy
[Butler] is in Cape Town, not him of course, but Rob and company and
Frieda … I hope you got my telegram yesterday; the dust cover I have
not yet seen – definitely Monday; when our lost parcel will probably
also arrive. W.E.G Louw's review is of course very favourable; but as
a *review* it is not clear and not good enough; I read *Die Ambassadeur*
again; quick this time, hey? and once again found it revelatory in every
respect; my only objection remains that if the ambassador was in reality
confronted with our situation, it would contribute to his fall. W.E.G.'s
objection, therefore. But the human relations are fine, true, good, and
the characters grow on one – even this Stephen; though not yet Gillian;
but maybe personal – because this "conflict with God" is for me, personally, such an unthinkable situation.

It is exactly the objection that I have against Jack's new book, from
the first page; the actual MS is lying here in front of me: Ag, child!
I miss you – Antje, a Dutch woman who read the cutting about *Die
Ambassadeur* with Uys today – says you look like me. For some stupid
reason, this touched me. Are your shoulders better again and where did

276

you swim? The Caligenic is still on the window sill behind the yellow curtain. Mercilessly cruel words. Can anyone *hate* them more than a writer? Words instead of *your* hands, instead of your beautiful red head against my breast. I wish we could be together just once without feeling that we're buggering up other people and ourselves in the process, free and peaceful and responsible and *whole*.

I received the three Vasalis books from Mrs Bouws on Friday: *Parken en Woestijnen*, *De Vogel Phoenix* and *Vergezichten en Gezichten*. Do you know her? Apparently she was awarded the Reina Prinsen Geerligs Prize in 1957. Everyone loves me so much, as Jannie Gildenhuys says.

André, you must please not have an "acute conscience" about our clash or whatever. I see you as a *whole* person, and I love you as such. And don't be afraid. Fear is evil. I read your heartsore letter of Monday over and over again. I was damn insensitive as far as your distress is concerned. And about that I am *sorry*; but the pangs of conscience I feel about all that are positively subsumed in love, which heals everything. I want to exist in reality, and not be deadened by a dream. Lovely man, reddish longish hair, precious mouth, hands, lovely white moesie-body and cute little cock, protective force "that looks like me, that looks like everything I love" –

Yours in passion and longing and happiness and acceptance,
Your Cocoon.

ps: I'm meeting (hopefully) with Johan [Cilliers] on Monday and with Koos about *Die Ambassadeur*.

And come again soon, and tell me everything.
Your Ingrid Jonker.

pps: You do belong with me after all. Love *and* darling. IJ.

And more: Write, man! "Stage fright?" Had it too, but it's nonsense. Read [Adam] Small: good, hey? I.

Grahamstown
Tuesday, 26 November 1963

Beloved, faraway darling,

Day after day I am errant, wandering, aware of "all that fall", of an ever-increasing need to communicate, to break through to you, to exorcise you (like [Gerrit] Achterberg's dead lovers), to utter the "Sesame" that will make everything open up. "But wherefore could not I pronounce 'Amen'? I had most need of blessing."

How many times haven't I come and sat here, and then all I have to show for it is a blank sheet. And my heart. "Forse il cuore ci reste, forse il cuore ..."

Paper – pen – letter. But how do I capture everything in this futile little snare? Over and over again, the shimmering bulbul slips away, teasing me from the nearest branch – "parrot-gaudy echo". And I know, all the time, that the same desire afflicts you, because you're also not writing. The silence is wondrous. ("Die woord is daar om die stilte reg te stel. Maar die stilte is on-her-stel-baar." Karel Jonckheere.)

This has now become a week in which I have done nothing and cannot do anything, trapped in the daily round, on purpose, because it keeps my hands busy. (But the heart – "dat altijd luider slaat, altijd maar luider"?)

De profundis clamavi. Out of the depths have I cried unto thee, oh Lord. Verse for today.

What happened has done nothing to change the preciousness and the irremovability of that which existed before; but it has placed before us this mountain (not even a "holy" one) which we're going to have to climb, as in the days of myths and legends, when obstacles had to be conquered before the hero could take the young virgin away from her castle.

You in *your* little castle?

Oh my love, my cocoon, oh mine. We will get beyond this, too. We will be spared nothing, neither pain nor darkness, because we're only human.

278

But *you*: you didn't *deserve* this. I, who was supposed to be your guide through these "three days of darkness", I sit here upon the waters, forsaken, not knowing on which distant shore I will find the light again.

Everything here has tensed into habit – a mimicry without sense, a complete lack of communication. I feel written-out sick-and-tired – not even *this* little harbour is a refuge. So I'm translating, mechanically, day in and day out. Suspend "life" and learn to exist like a Pavlov-dog?

We've no longer even got the *telephone* to reach out to each other.

But perhaps – I want to *believe* this (I *must*) – this is the deep darkness before daybreak (without the bitter berry). The guard on the wall …?

"News"? *Die Ambassadeur* has *finally* arrived; I had to drive to PE twice, on Saturday and Sunday (170 miles each time), to fetch the parcel. Friday night's little celebration with Frieda and Jack Meyer went off without the book, again (he says he met you last December? You're not likely to remember: that was a time of great confusion for you). I received W.E.G. Louw's review. Rubbish. Ignorant. Even his praise has a hollow ring to it. Iritating sloppiness and overhastiness. What does it matter, anyway? *Die Ambassadeur* actually *exists*; and – for me – it's now in the past. Forward march. *Orgie*. Always the horizon that one never reaches. Will-o'-the-wisp. Why does one do this? *Vanitas vanitatum*. And each time, Sisyphus again begins to roll his rock to the top. Uncrucify us, Lord. And yet: what would we *do* without this? It's the only bit of "being" that we have. (For the rest, we're orphans!)

Should I send this misery-on-paper? It's unfair, and yet: if I throw it away again, when will you *ever* receive a letter from me? You will know well enough to see through the darkness to the love behind it that always remains, and *remains*.

… die klein, skuilende

verontregte, verontwaardigde
ding: wat in die looggat
afkyk: homself gaan bewapen.

And I think about a morning, naked in the sun, at a river mouth: our last dazzling morning before the "battalions of lies" and the "organizations of hate" made their approach. Our small little Paradise. Sometimes the angel with the sword has to fall into a slumber at the gate. Then, we go back, we become whole again, me me, you you, us us, little dual-unit in the flesh, and the God of love born from us, short-lived, but *there*.

Love: with everything that I have in me, your holy name: Ingrid, from André.

―――――――――

Tuesday, 26 November 1963

My André,

Your lovely letter that touches the earth nowhere arrived yesterday. The one you wrote in the study; was that in your house or at the university? The one after your sleepless night. Was it awful to mull over everything like that, and why do you do it? Did you get a letter from me on Friday or Saturday, though? Or on Thursday already?

And what notes are you making now for *Die Ambassadeur*, my treasure? I only saw the dust cover today. Koos hasn't sent me mine yet; he would have on Monday already, and then we would have gone and had a drink to celebrate. Today I went to Nasionale Boekhandel and looked at it there. Initially I didn't like the cover AT ALL, except of course for the lovely heavy paper and the production, but later actually more comforted – and now that I think back on it, it works. The ornate little section with the mirror just *maybe* a bit jarring in terms of tone – or not? It's all over the Boekhandel, and then I asked Kosie (Nasionale Boekhandel-drudge) if they weren't going to put it in the window, and he said no, they only put their own publications in the window, especially at this time of the year. The TASTE of the boere!

Then Kosie said caustically: I see you have a whole page for yourself. So then I went to Juta's and told Mr Herbst that he should exhibit it well, I'm taking him a review tomorrow as well as one of your photos. He was happy.

Hello, darling! Oh yes I saw Rob on the beach on Sunday, he came to visit Uys. We were all busy reading bits of the Sunday Slimes, and Uys put a sheet down for him to sit on. Rob said, "Oh, I'm sitting on Uhuru." "What?" shouts Uys, "You're sitting on a whore?" Rob then shyly explained "the news about Uhuru". Etcetera. It was a divine day. Rob arrived still warm from you. But he didn't say the post was still available in Grahamstown. That evening, Jack and Manfred Hirsch (advertising manager for *Contrast*) and I went to a party, and last night I'd have gone to Beckett with Manfred (*dead dead* innocent), but Jack phoned him, and then me too, about my "pitiful behaviour"! Was completely astonished. I find Manfred not in the least attractive – that's the first thing – and secondly, I am still unfortunately boss-less. Further news: saw Freda Linde. I sent her a book and we went to have tea together, and everything there is right again.

Liefsteling, thank you *very very* much for the cheque from yesterday, but you mustn't! I know you work very hard and you can't also support me and Simone! Still, I bought her the most beautiful white-and-gold sandals today. But I have lots left for the birthday cake, among other things. And I actually don't know what I would have done without the cheque. Asked Bartho to send me my honorarium, but haven't heard anything yet. Thank you, my generous angel, and don't work yourself to death and lie awake all night, like you do.

Your parcel STILL hasn't arrived! I think you must enquire at the post office; maybe they sent it via goods train, and then it will only get here by the time you come again, January?

"Forgive my unforgivableness."

My André – you are not unforgivable, you are pure and precious and generous, with moesies and little laughs, and you make me happy.

As soon as my tape recorder is fixed I will tell you about Éluard. And the unsayable, all of it.

Love darling,
Cocoon.

PS: The unsayable? Sat quietly for a long while now and looked at your name on the envelope. André P. Brink: "Zo buiten mij geboren …" and then read a few of your letters again. Lord! Last night I dreamt you were a girl, we had a meal somewhere together; you ordered so much food they had to bring it in a big bag, and then I wanted to kiss you, but I wasn't allowed to. Public opinion, etc. But in a hotel we had a little island. Then you weren't a girl any more! My God, my André, is it all possible? And here we live in such an ordinary way, and why, "I don't understand …" But love you, I do, in my way. André, the unsayable. You alone know what that includes and means. "I was born to know you, to name you …" Kiss, kiss the papie. *My* papie, which is waiting to get little wings.

And with love, love,
Ingrid.

{Thank you for review *Sestiger*; I'm going to read all the other stuff this evening too, but especially *yours*, of course. *Where is our lost moesie?*}

Grahamstown
Thursday, 28 November 1963

Most dear, lovely darling,

I feel guilty about my sombre letter of the day before yesterday, which is likely to make you miserable, too. But the scales are tilting; I see light again. "Stage fright?" you ask in your letter of yesterday. *Yes*. But let us join hands and rise *together*, beyond the lights, *in* the light, and stay there. The actual turning point in my pessimism was yesterday when I phoned Chris Barnard and he told me, without any prompting, about *Rook en Oker*'s selling almost 700 copies. That's really fantastic. I mean, not even *Tristia* sold that quickly. This means you're being *read*, that people are eager to read what you're writing, and your work is being anticipated. I'm glad about this, and *happy* to hear it.

I have now – at last! – retyped *Orgie* for you. I'm sending it with this letter. I think parts of the 4th and 5th cantos are some of the best writing in the whole work. Some dull spots remain (too much "realistic story-telling", occasionally?), but they'll be reworked. I want to refine it for Bartho though only in February; it need not appear before September.

Last night I did a sample translation from *Die Ambassadeur* – the start of the third section ("How can I talk about her chronologically …"); the handful of people I showed it to say it's even better than the Afrikaans. I hope the rest goes smoothly, too. It's hellishly difficult work, but also a challenge, and a very good exercise. First, however, I must do Colette for Bartho – 250 pages in fine print – and it doesn't translate easily!

Rob returned from the Cape last night. He would have "heard" a fair amount from [Ernst] Lindenberg and company. I would very much like to talk to him. Why can't a person just be completely open? You are the most precious thing in my life, I love you, and whatever happens at times that seems to muddy the waters, please just know *that*, keep *believing* it. If I hadn't possessed the conviction of your love, I would've taken the (melodramatic) "final step" just a day or two ago. I got up on Tuesday night, almost physically *ill* with longing for you, and from deprivation arising from a life here that has to continue without any form of communication at all; I came and sat here in my study for hours. Drove out the next morning to the bluegums overlooking the town and just sat there. It was as if everything was finished, as if all that remained was for me to perform the deed with my litte black Beretta, or with a length of hosepipe attached to the car's exhaust.

Everything was so incredibly desolate. And there was only *one* thing that I knew for sure, and know now, still: that I love you, and you me, and that I should at least remain worthy of you.

Child, my darling, I want to come lie against your bosom like an infant, comforting you, and being comforted. I am unsettled; but I love you. If Anton hadn't been here, along with the huge responsibility I have for his entire life, I would come to you without a second's hesitation, and stay, and never again drive away on a Sunday afternoon or a Monday or Friday morning. I would even accept the risk to my father's condition. That much I know, now.

Let us continue to live in reality, *and* continue to dream.

And *you*, darling, Cocoon, my own? What's going on with you? Did Jack go off to the farm? Was he sorry to leave? Were *you* sad? What's his book like? How is he towards you?

On Sunday it's your blonde little girl's birthday. My best wishes; give her a kiss from me, because I like very much to think of her as mine, too. Will I never have a daughter of my own? Or might the next time I come down be more "opportune"? Because the thought of *you* bearing my child and giving birth to her – it's begun to mean so very much to me.

The future's lying in wait, slumbering in a crystal ball. ("En wéér het kristal. / Nu vóór nie.") Anything is possible, the creation is yet to be brought into being, God continues to wander through his garden in the nightwind, everything is still untouched, virginal, beautiful. Tomorrow a new day begins. Tomorrow *we* begin.

I charge you in your beauty and splendour: sleep like a little lamb, like a brief sigh, until my words awaken you.

I will sleep with you. Now. In everlasting love,
André.

{Postscript to last night's letter, which has already been sealed inside a large envelope:}

Dearest mine,

Thank you for this morning's adorable letter that almost brought me to tears, so very happy was I that it was there – because when I checked the first time, there was nothing in my postbox.

Just to answer the few questions you asked: When I write "study", it means here at the house; "office" means I'm at the university. I always write to you *here* – my office is too impersonal.

I meant the first rough notes for *Die Ambassadeur*, which I sorted – dating from Nov. last year to Jan. this year. Not new ones!

Personally, I'm quite impressed with the cover. Are you satisfied with it? And did you and Koos have your little drink together?

I'm concerned about the parcel. They wrapped it up in such a flimsy sheet of paper, and then I put the whole thing into a big white envelope and posted it, just like that. If it doesn't arrive within the next week, I'll order another one. The parcel wasn't registered or anything and so they won't be able to track it down.

Have you spoken to Johan Cilliers yet – and found a new job? I'd be so happy if you could get out of that grey pit. But wouldn't you lose all the bonus money you'd get in February?

I'm glad things are okay with Freda Linde. Despite that unfortunate episode a long time ago, I think she could still mean a lot to you.

Oh love, my darling, I long for you hopelessly, despondently. Thank you for your restful, glittering recent letters.

Thank you for your strange dream about me as the eating girl!
BUT I CAN'T KISS THE PAPIE!

You kiss *your* hand with those gorgeously messy nails, and then use them to greet the little cocoon, and the electric switch inside there. (As I say this, I can feel the papie growing!)

I love you. And I am no longer "unbalanced", either. In love I become whole for you.

Always,
André.

———————

Castella
Thursday evening, 28 November 1963

No, God! Child! This is *not* a letter, this is a note. Letters I *did* write, and listen well, redhead, here are the dates they were posted:

19 November: Telegram: No moesie.
20 November: Letter.
21 November: Letter.
22 November: Telegram: Bravo citizen brilliant Ambassadeur brilliant career all love all confidence confirmed.
25 November: Letter.
27 November: Letter.

So you see, I committed acts of communication with you almost every day in spite of your drawn-out silences! Like you, I of course also feel hopeless about the words-words-words-on-paper, but I would not be so *heartless* as not to write you at all; especially now. Notes, evidence: even dates posted. You'll make a methodical person of me yet. I'll keep waging a campaign for you with statistics and love. Funny that you, before your word-despair (I refer to your letter which considerately arrived today at Castella), also thought of a bird: so often in the last week-and-a-half I have thought of Elisabeth [Eybers]'s "klein koggelvoël wat roep in my".

1. Why do you speak in the past tense: didn't change anything about the preciousness and irremoveability of what was.
2. I don't understand French.
3. Who is Koos Meyer and what does he say about me?
4. This evening I'm writing to the good Sir J.B. Braaksma, Council for Press and Cultural Affairs.
5. Molteno Trust kindly disposed towards me (I.D. du Plessis and that joke).
6. Going to the Brits with Anthony Delius. (For another bursary.)
7. Heard nothing from Johan Cilliers. Mainly I've got to take a walk because I can no longer bear to be dehumanised at the Press. God! I was almost hysterical there today.

> … Oh fill me
> with strength against those who would freeze my
> humanity, would dragoon me into a lethal automation,
> would make me a cog in a machine, a thing with
> one face, a thing …
> …
> Let them not make me a stone and let them not spill me.
> Otherwise kill me.

8. Juta's made a lovely window for you with the review and the photo. I wrote to you about it a while ago.
9. Be still, my dear heart. I haven't changed. And "hierdie las van reën wil ek nie sien nie / Op die water van jou voorkop / Op die water sonder bodem van ons eenheid". Write soon – any bladdy thing – but write! Go and enquire about my letters. I wouldn't like it if those tender things were lying around at Rhodes University. I also don't want anyone to know that we fought. They'll say it's my fault (!).

If anyone had to read how sorry I am, how much I love you, they'll think I'm chasing after you.

10. Come here just one more time and run to the kitchen to tell me: "Do you know what? I had a John Collins today!" Let me again put the radio on to provide a banal background to our unseemly squabble. And then let me sleep with you, allow me to forgive and be forgiven. André.

Cocoon.

Grahamstown
Monday morning, 2 December 1963

Dearest little devil,

This morning I received a surprising letter from one Mr Prinsloo who addresses me as "darling" and signs his name as "Cocoon". He asked me a whole lot of silly questions, but as he didn't supply a full address, I'll send my answers to you – then you can pass them on the next time he spends a night there:

1. Why do I say, in the past tense, that nothing has changed about the preciousness of what "existed before" –
   a) Because the preciousness of what exists *now* cannot be taken away by something that happened in the past (our "evening").
   b) Because it might have seemed, that night, as if we were "breaking down" everything that existed before – but now it's quite obvious that it didn't change anything – it just made everything more intense and profound. (Often a whole past is changed by its future; but our past – like our present – can be disavowed by nothing.)
2. You don't understand French. But what I wrote wasn't in French, it was Italian, from Quasimodo, a poem that I read to you in Italian. It

288

means: "Misschien blijft het hart ons over …" Don't mind me while you blush a deep pink of embarrassment.

3. Who is Koos Meyer?
   I don't know. I wrote about Jack Meyer, head of the Centre for Arts here, Frieda's friend; 34 years old, very dear and kind, slightly effeminate; when he saw the picture of you, he said he remembers you with longer hair, last December at the sea.

4. That's it with the questions.

5. Dear-dear-darling, little goddess, it's fucked-up amazing how much I love you this morning. If only we could be back at Steenbras River Mouth right now …

Your voice last night was a mercy, yet again, a blessing that made me wonderfully positive again and full of happiness about you. Today I just want to do crazy things. I'm so ecstatically happy about the probability of your prize. But *please* keep it a secret! ("A woman's idea of keeping a secret is refusing to reveal who told it to her"!) You must get a bursary, too, and go overseas; and if *Die Ambassadeur* perhaps wins the CNA Prize, then I'll see if I can come over for a holiday and *show* you Paris; we'd walk around where no one knows us and the nights belong only to us. Rob says he and Opperman and Ernst [van Heerden] all said *Die Ambassadeur* would have won the prize if APB had published it. But I'm glad the book's with Koos – because I've been wanting *you* to get the prize all this time, not out of charity but on *merit*. Yours is not an insignificant little voice. Rob says some of the poems in *Rook en Oker* are "great".

I'm holding thumbs for a job with Cilliers. You've had enough of your current hell. Oh, be happy, and *free*. In February you must come and visit here.

Bartho says he's not in a hurry for the Colette, so now I can finish translating *Die Ambassadeur* first. The first 30 pages have been completed and checked; I handed them over to a well-attuned English friend for critical revision. I'll have it typed up bit by bit, as it emerges. I'd like to have a completed manuscript by the end of January. Koos will act as my agent overseas; he's already entered into agreements with publishers in England and America. (I mean: *general* agreements, not specifically for *Die Ambassadeur*.) He also had my contract worded in such a way that I get 75% of the translation income and not just the usual 50%.

The fact that Colette has to wait is a bit disastrous financially because I'm so terribly broke I don't even know how I'm going to get to Potch. But I've sold a plot there and should get something from that – not a lot, because I still have to pay a R500 debt I owe my mother.

But now I have new hope for the future. I feel I'm *living* again. I felt extremely close to you all day yesterday; then, last night I was able to *talk* to you – make *contact* with you so enjoyably – and sleep with you afterwards. (Did you ... with me ...?)

Congratulations, again, on *Rook en Oker*'s *deserved* – and, hopeful – success. Let me smother you with kisses: your happy eyes and your little curl; your naughty ears; your enchanting mouth and the playful tip of your tongue; your soft throat and your speckled brown shoulders; your full, gorgeous breasts and those provocative nipples; your long soft back; your little buttocks and your tummy; your unbelievable thighs; your dearest calves; your hands and feet; and your beloved leucodendron. Then, let me kiss your little mound and that deep, living love-stamp until I hear your breath, feel your stomach moving – and I continue kissing until you say "hell!", clamping your legs in ecstasy such that I can no longer gain entry.

That's how much I love you. And even more, every day more.

Always, jubilantly yours,
André.

Castella
Tuesday night, 3 December 1963

Dearest my André,

Thank you for yesterday's two letters and the really dynamic 2nd part of *Orgie*. Review yes, but later. It's too late now; 11:30. Thank you for your telegram for Simonetta, her big wish for her birthday was for a BACKPACK, which I found at Garlicks. And thank you for your call on Sunday with the unbelievable news: alas! so all was not in vain! But I must say that was the last thing I expected. God is a god of surprises.

News here: Lots. Saw Johan Cilliers this evening at 7:30 at the Café Royal, but he was befuddled and I am aware that I'll just have to stay at the Press for the time being … at least it's not so long any more … Will write you later in more detail about the interview; now just saying good night, little treasure, every night it's so late with people and appointments and Manet [Simone] and obligations. Also saw Dudley [D'Ewes] (Molteno Trust) this evening; bought a *beautiful* expensive dress; yellow; sunlightdress, sweet. I am half asleep; you ask so many questions in yesterday's letter; but I'll answer comprehensively tomorrow evening. One thing I am more than upset about is your pessimism on Tuesday and the gun and all that. No, my darling – you must never think that way, things always get better sooner than one expects; and you don't *know me* yet, my spirit is just in-des-truct-ible.

Rob. Rob. Rob knows.

Liefsteling; I am so terribly tired. Just know that I think of you constantly – and you are with me more than ever before.

'Night to your precious red head,
And to your beautiful tooth,
And to your long hands,
And to all the moesies,
And to your beautiful papie,
And to your tenderness,

And to your protection,
And to your loneliness,
And to your purity,
And to your humaneness,
And to all your little laughs.

Love is what I feel for you; your sleepy girl and your
Cocoon.

———————

Grahamstown,
Wednesday, 4 December 1963

Most beloved Cocoon,

I don't know what the red number at the top of this page means; it's the first sheet from a new ream of paper.

I have a few minutes before my honours class begins, so I'm writing to say hello and send my love. And I'm sending you a funny piece of "evidence" with this letter.

Here it is:

That, my little pixie, is a thorn, a Gordon's Bay thorn that came out of my big toe last night. Now you can see a) that I wasn't complaining for no reason, and b) that Gordon's Bay wasn't just a dream!

Here on this side, things are somewhere between Scylla and Charybdis. Fortunately I'm feeling positive and happy about you; and for that reason, all the more disillusioned about the emptiness here. It's starting to look as if I'll be moving to the study soon, bedding and all. I've been so terribly negative; can't do anything and don't want to, either; I feel as if I have no energy, quite vegetative in fact. I want to *live* in the way I learnt to live with you. Things are coming to a head. I have no idea what might still happen in this holiday period. You'll have to keep carrying me with your love, and keep trusting me; and be *good*.

The translation of *Die Ambassadeur* has now reached page 50 or thereabouts. Heavy work, but also enjoyable. And now at least I'm catching all the printing errors (god, there're a lot of them!).

I'm reading *Offerland* [Land of Sacrifice] [F.A. Venter]!!!

Enjoy the wedding this weekend and send me a photo of our little Simone-flowergirl as soon as you can.

I miss and love you; I believe and I trust, and I'm happy, in full certainty about you in this uncertain world.

With everything,
André.

Castella
Wednesday night, 4 December 1963

My dearest André,

When I got home from Simone a moment ago (it's ten o'clock) your letter was lying here; the one in reply to Mr Prinsloo; had to rush up quickly to borrow Mrs Oxley's pen, and since I did some gardening on Saturday and gave her some roses yesterday, she is very friendly again. But all my little plants are dying in the heat; will definitely have to wake up at seven o'clock tomorrow to water them – heavens, the responsibilities. My whole life is taken up with fulfilling obligations.

Dearest *treasure*, I still can't believe that about the APB; but why do you say "probability" in one spot. The other two books that are due will surely not be something? I'll *die* if I don't get them *now*. Only Chris and Jack know – those two will definitely say NOTHING, or even imply in the slightest way – of that I can assure you. You still speak about visiting there in February. Where, exactly? At your home? And will I still be in SA then? Because I leave as soon as I get it. I hope you get the CNA, which you ought to get, there is surely a possibility that the committee won't just automatically give it to Opperman. God is a god of surprises. Chris and Jack received the news with much excitement and emotion. And one of my first thoughts was: so then it wasn't all for nothing … and the Pastor is just lying. And I will have to go to Johannesburg? I've got a lovely yellow-and-white dress with a pleated skirt, which I'll wear. It's an expensive dress, too.

News, news. Met Johan Cilliers at half past seven yesterday evening; he had a few fantastic stories that I'd rather not write down; the work – SA Litho, is apparently "giving" him an office, he "may" use their typists – those would be my duties too if I go and work there – Hey, hey. Sandberg "resigned". The rest of the staff "can't come to Cape Town". I think the company's had it. And so – the grey – in the meantime – Paris – Holland – London – Rome. And that's that.

Saw Molteno Trust's Dudley Dewes [D'Ewes] yesterday evening at nine. He says it would help a lot if I had another bursary too or something like that – the Molteno is a "rounding up" bursary. And so I had to just keep quiet. But he was kind, even though like a priest. Wrote to Braaksma and also to the Brits. And now wait wait wait. When will the APB thing be made public? At work of course I now constantly feel the need to say "Fuck you, sir" or to stay away.

Thank you for your beautiful lovely letters. You ask some questions.

1. Jack's going to the farm tomorrow.
2. No, I am not sad. I bought him some biltong.
3. Don't think he is sad either.
4. He is kind towards me, just wants to be with me, walks quietly around in the garden, is a bit of a pig if you phone or when I talk about you, treats me like a million Rand.

On Friday night I have to accompany Simone to Upington (Oh god!) and next Friday again; the wedding is on the 14th. Two weekends. Joys of motherhood.

André, André, *do* speak to Rob. He is sympathetically disposed towards you. I think he'd like it if you spoke to him. I *know* it.

And BE CAREFUL of women.

I can't bear it that you have to be away. This letter writing. "De daad is proza, maar de klacht, de traan is poëzie." And the writer? Piet Paaltjens. Letter-writing. It *embarrasses* me. God! You should have been here this evening – the castle is wonderfully homely, but so *empty*. My mother had a cricket for company at night. I'll have to get myself something like that too.

Saw Lena today. She says W. says it's "unbearable" at home, but she says she is often there and it's not unbearable at all.

Beloved red pyjamas with horns. What will you do when I am overseas? The last part of *Orgie,* I *think* (very tentatively) is better than the first – affecting, but where is the greeting, "hail tristesse", at the end? I was giving it a quick read-through on Monday evening, when I was again held up by guests. Now I am (like [Louis] Hiemstra) going through the whole thing carefully and systematically, with notes. I'm thinking and half feeling my way around everything. Thank you for your thoughtful notes. I'm not so stupid!

I'm glad you are now happy again. Sunday (at the beach) I went through everything so carefully, details, also the horrible ones, but there was an intense "atmosphere" of presence – as W.E.G. Louw would say.

Uys was SICK. He told everyone (in detail) how many times and also how he threw up. But he's better again now. Jan and Marjorie have gone on holiday. Chris sends loving regards; he's writing to you – the lazy thing! Hiemstra says you're a "fantastic person". He says it so inquisitively and then looks at me, so sweet.

And you, read Éluard page 184. (Revelations …). And you, lovely and preciously fierce you, my André Phillipus Brink (did you see your review of *Caesar* in *Die Burger*?).

André Brink, I carefully draw a cross on your forehead, André Brink, I call you by your name, you I love with a love broader than the Limpopo (or does that sound funny??).

Good night, sweet prince.

In happy love,
Your Cocoon.

{PS: My ear is sore. IJ}

Grahamstown
Saturday morning, 7 December 1963

My Cocoon,

My rebellious but compliant, restful but passionate, laughing but despondent, unemployed but hardworking collection of paradoxes; my angel and succubus, virgin and bitch: hello!

Salutations from the morning, with its fragrance of soft rain and gleam of a pale sun.

"The ups and downs of love"! – after our phone conversation the night before last I felt depressed and dispirited. It was one of those hide-and-seek routines ("Oh, where are you, where are you?"). Mischievous little thing, with all your accusations, grudges, and provocations. And the damned intrusive exchange operators at the end.

But yesterday morning your dear, sleepy letter arrived here, and I could hear your drowsy voice and guess at the lazy movements of your hands and your body as you surrendered to rest, to the little bed at the window.

(Are there still so many flies early in the morning?

Are you still so beautiful?

Are you still as wonderful as ever, *girlie*?
Is the castle still a little refuge?)

I'm glad that you're finally free – or will be in a day or two – of the monotonous job. But I'm concerned about your itinerant condition, my splendidly rich, dirt-poor little wanderer. Let me know if you need material help, whether a lot or a little.

I'm feeling calm and whole this morning. I've been lurching from pillar to post in the last while. And I'm no longer enjoying translating *Die Ambassadeur*. I need to find something else to whet my appetite. I have a *huge* amount of work to do during the holidays, not least preparing for two honours courses (literary theory, and modern Dutch prose); these are courses I didn't ever take myself. The prose especially is taxing – these people all produced such long novels, and wrote so much!

My plan is to leave here for Potch on the 19th. You can therefore send letters to me at this address until Monday morning the 16th.

Tonight there's a dinner at Frieda's place; a whole bunch of people getting together for one last time before we all go our different ways. Should I give her your address? She's leaving for the Cape on Monday and she'll be there for a month. I wish I could also come to you that soon, for Christmas.

Will you be at Anne's wedding tonight? And how will you get there? Oh, damn! I've just realised it's next Saturday. (Why did they have their wedding invitations printed in *English*?)

I'm looking forward to Bartho and company tomorrow night; I want to show him *Orgie*. The "salutation" at the end will be there. And please send me a complete list of your objections, because it's *our* story, and it mustn't be half-baked.

Hopefully I'll write again this weekend. Just *know* that I love you. I know you're feeling restless about not having work right now, but I'm very much with you, a *huge* bit; and I love you and everything that's in you, for your name – Ingrid, pure, beautiful; Cocoon, deep, penetrable, safe, of the future –

Your André.

Sunday night, 8 December 1963

My dearest treasure, dear god, have I had *people*!

It seems everyone likes Castella very much – yesterday one of Uys's cousins was here from two till ten and I couldn't get to anything. Don't worry, jealous, he doesn't appeal to me at all! At least he helped me move my stuff from the hotel; unfortunately the clothes are just GONE, but I could at least save some of my books. Thank you for your Thursday evening surprise – I told you, didn't I, it was a mess at work, I sent them ten complaints and didn't go to work on Friday. So maybe things will be better tomorrow. It is truly fantastic that they really think they'll succeed in making a THING of me. I haven't yet been able to get hold of Johan [Cilliers] (who called) – maybe I should accept his proposal; for the time being ... because everything here is becoming more uncertain and temporary for me now, since the big possibility of going overseas has sunk in. Marking time. It'd really be a great experience. And I want to make it all worthwhile – it's a responsibility. I may not disappoint anyone – and must simply read and write a lot – with the grace of God.

Child, do you know what? That bladdy Maggie threw the sponge away. I was quite upset about it. She probably thinks I'm mad to go on about something like that. And you know what else? My tape recorder is working again – and this week I'm going to make you a recording of Éluard poems. Thank you for you, darling! So, have you been walking around with this dagger of memory the whole time? And are you in the study now and how did it all work out? Write to me about it. And when are you going to Potch? Can I send you some money?

It's cool here, was a beautiful weekend for going up the mountain, but my pals are all so lazy, and I can't go alone. So Simone has gone; and next Friday I follow her.

Bambi said she saw you at the Sea Point Pavilion – having tea. She said you were wearing your rust-brown shirt – remember, you wore it often last time, my beautiful thing. She says you were sitting looking at the sea. But she wasn't certain it was you. Was it?

I've only now read Eric van Dyk's stupid little piece about *Die Ambassadeur* in the *Argus* – I'm including it in case you haven't seen it. He is the stupidest I have ever come across in a daily – and he's been writing for them for years. Everything on the same six-year-old intellectual level.

Listened to your last tape again. Listened again to your "Groet in Bruin". Perhaps in a forlorn effort to bring you into the flat. Everything looks so uncertain and vague – like the harbour in the thick mist outside – and here – the silence. "I no longer want to sleep alone." And this:

Ek het die mag om te bestaan sonder noodlot
Tussen ryp en dou tussen vergetelheid en teenwoordigheid
...
Koelte warmte hulle raak my nie
Ek sal die beeld van myself wat jy my bied
Laat voortreis deur jou begeertes heen
My gelaat het net een ster

...

Ek bly in my eie blare
Ek bly my eie spieël
Ek meng sneeu met vuur
My klippers het my soetheid
En my seisoen is ewig.

Dear, beloved lonely André. It must be terrible to live there like that without communication. Patience! I think of you constantly "like a lamb looking for me". (That's from my "drama", do you still remember?) (How dare Eric van Dyk use your beautiful sensitive face next to his piece of banality ...!) This "thinking" of someone – it's actually funny, because "think" isn't the right word, it's mostly just a vague presence. You say you're doing nothing, I'm glad you're doing nothing, but then you must REST and relax, and go and play tennis or something. You MUSTN'T work so much – I know the translation – and it is indeed a big job – must use up a lot of energy – but apart from that you must do nothing, can't you understand that you are tired?

Apart from your work and translations and writing – there's all the other emotional stuff – here as well as there. And it's been like that all year. "Now you must sleep, my tender, beloved child ..."

With tenderness, with longing,
With love,
Cocoon.

———

Castella (untidy)
Wessels Street (windy)
Cape Town (empty)
Tuesday, 9 December 1963 (sick)

Dearest little-old heart,

Thank you for your letter of a moment ago – if you hadn't annoyed me in it, I probably wouldn't have written again tonight! Horrible child with an ugly jersey! In the telephone call I didn't "accuse" you at all – all I said (that I can remember) is that it is out of a feeling of loveless-ness that one commits suicide. And that you must have felt that way that Tuesday. I know, after all. And I often feel that way, you or no you, Simone or no Simone. But it passes again. I didn't mean that you were feeling specifically loveless towards me, and this you surely feel at times, otherwise you wouldn't be human! And of course I also wanted to scold you about that, because that letter upset me so much more than all that other "misery" in the previous one which was torment-ing you so! Because you are PRECIOUS. What else did I say, André? I'm sorry about it in any case, but didn't actually mean anything, other-wise I would have remembered it exactly. (And on top of that maybe THOUGHT UP.) But Thursday was a TERRIBLE day at the grey pit, and then Bambi came for a drink and I was too tired to eat. See? So I told the old lot that I'll stay on a while, in case I don't get that money. That in itself would make me jobless for a week. Everything went fairly well today and we were given (as a favour) a fictional work to read about a decomposing body.

What makes me despondent at the moment is purely and simply physical. Everything infected, sore-ish: the sensitive membranes: eyes, mouth, bladder, ears, the canal. God knows why. Headache. Fever. Nothing too bad. Just there. This started creeping up on me yesterday. I just wish it would get a little worse, then I won't have to go to work tomorrow.

You people in the North really dawdle.

Child! Darling! What's going to happen? How are things with your precious little soul? (Read S.)

I was lying on the beach yesterday and I said to Uys: "I have a secret."

His eyes swivelled away from the sea in a wide arc – I wish you could have seen the display then! Later on he even threatened me. "André?" "No." "Jack?" "No." "Jan?" "No." "Then why do you look so happy if it has nothing to do with you?" Etc. Etc. But I didn't tell him. Mean! (Commentary on my feeling for others, hey?) But it was absolutely worthwhile. Oh yes, and he wants to know which five Afrikaans books you regard as best. Prose. And except for your own.

Dearest darling, I am not accusing you of anything. You are human. Just with MORE of everything. And like me.

Love, darling,
Cocoon.

ps: I am afraid of Frieda. I.
pps: Your medicine – "The Mixture – One tablespoon every four hours. sp. 30. 55c. Brink 91 – 95 High St Grahamstown" – it says here. It makes me miss you desperately. I.

{ps: Why do you now always write to Castella? IJ.
Finale: I've just re-read my letter with great delight. We should have gone to the 191 tonight. But right now my eyes are really red!}

Grahamstown
Wednesday, 11 December 1963

My darling,

I just hope this letter gets to you before you go off to Upington. (Are you going by train?) You're likely to feel very neglected this week; especially now, when you'll be experiencing the inevitable reaction to giving up your job, I should have been more attentive, instead of curling up into my own ball of misery. (Do you know where the word "ellende" ["misery"] comes from? *Ali landi*, cf. "alien land" in English; thus a kind of outcast-in-strange-lands ...)

It was, and is, "most kak" here. Daily strife, growing distance, stiffness, desolation, guilt, responsibility for Anton, and my longing for you, my need for you. This morning it led to a long, honest conversation without any euphemisms, emotion or evasion. The question, on both sides, was whether there was any sense in staying together simply for the sake of keeping things the way they are. And the inevitable answer, also mutual, was *No*. At the moment the sticking point is whether Anton's future should weigh most heavily; also: what will, and can, that future be? But, believe me, my darling, I know this holiday – terrible as it's going to be – will result in a crystallisation. Please just trust me in the fullness of love, and stay true *yourself*. In you my entire happiness rests.

What a year this has been. I don't know if I've ever been this exhausted. It brought the greatest, most complete happiness and enchantment I have ever known, but also the worst hell; it was my most creative year ever, and also the most sterile. Still, I wouldn't want it any other way. "Misschien zullen wij nu beter kunnen leven en volkomener." One grows sadder and wiser.

Bartho and company were here on Sunday night, dog-tired but in high spirits, and the conversation was wonderful. He is excited about *Orgie*, and it seems they're going to enjoy the experimentation with typography.

The Paul Kruger biography has appeared. To my surprise, Bartho said it's brilliant. Rob hasn't received his copy yet, but I'll check with him regularly and let you know the moment I hear anything. I'll be holding thumbs hard for *Rook en Oker*. Apparently there's no second publication on its way, it's just the biography. Bartho says he'd be happier if a prose work or poetry got the prize rather than something like biography. When I saw him, he hadn't yet seen Rob and therefore didn't know about *Rook en Oker.*

The prize, by the way, will be awarded only in March, although the winner will of course know what's what before the time. The award will apparently be made just after the CNA Prize. If a miracle occurs and the two of us make the "grand slam", we might be able to arrange things so we're both in Jhb for the prizes at the same time. Dream, dream … But I don't hold out much hope with the current prize committee, even though I'm convinced *Dolosse* is nowhere near Opperman's best work. We shall see. It's just such a long time to wait.

Everyone's left for the holidays and Grahamstown feels quite abandoned. I'm working like a mule on *Die Ambassadeur*'s translation, but it's very slow going. The result, though, will hopefully be good. If it ever became a bestseller overseas, we could emigrate to a place like France or Spain or Italy and buy ourselves a little fisherman's cottage (or a small Medieval castle, like Durrell?) and then *live* with our band of children, happily ever after.

What would we humans do if we couldn't dream? Where would I run away to if I didn't have *you*? [Anton] Chekhov wrote: "He who is afraid of loneliness should not marry." It's true, *now*. But "until eternity, thank God for you".

Be good, my little child, my Cocoon, be bright and whole. Wait for me in purity. I'm coming.

I love you dazzlingly,
Your André.

Grahamstown
Friday, 13 December 1963

Beloved, indispensable Cocoon,

I'm *tired*, my girl. These days I have to work non-stop until eleven at night or even later, and then, on days like today, when Anton's teething makes him fretful and he wants to get up at five, Estelle says she's "tired" (from reading *Femina*?). Then I have to jump out of bed and look after him until the servant comes in at nine.

But I don't want to complain today. I have used your red jersey to protect myself from the world, as I do nearly every day, isolated here in my study. I am complete, and I'm with you. Today I feel especially close to you. Do you have any idea how much your beautiful letters mean to me? Any notion of the extent to which I live in gratitude for you every day? Do you *understand*, my lovely, beloved one, how much I *love* you, and that my love is growing bigger, more mature, more tender and passionate by the minute?

Today you're embarking on the long journey to Upington. Try not to get too tired. Enjoy it and be happy. Are you still feeling ill? How are all the parts that were feeling sore? A kiss for each: the little nose and the cheeky ears and the sweet, naughty mouth, and the deep, enchanting little cocoon, *all* of it. I was very worried about you; it all sounds so wretched, and you need to be *healthy*.

How did you manage to get your things from the hotel? With Bartho's advance? You should have given them hell about the lost clothes. I'm happy about the books. And where is the swallow's nest picture? Will you send it to me? *Immediately*?

Thank you for the *Argus* clipping, which indeed I hadn't yet seen. Quite a shock. "Disgusting." It makes one feel so despondent when they take a thing apart like this – undoubtedly with good intentions! – reducing it to repulsive pettiness. "The secretary *flirts*, among others, with the ambassador's wife. He, in turn, *flirts* …" God! And: "The ambassador can do no better than catch him out on 'undiplomatic behaviour' ..." God Almighty, he didn't even read what's written there. Why do such things still upset one so much? It's undignified.

In the meantime, I'm translating. Finishing off the "Chronicle" section today. (Do you see how much still lies ahead? I want to have it finished before New Year's Eve, otherwise I'll be in a tight situation with my impossibly heavy workload during the so-called "vacation" (dark gallows humour).) The friend I'm giving it to, Ron Ayling (actually, his wife, Janet – she was the first "model" for Nicolette's *outer* form – without her knowing it) said yesterday: Can't I go a little faster? They can't wait to receive each day's batch of pages – so much so that they're fighting to read it first! You once observed, and with such accuracy, that our ridiculous little egos so desperately need this kind of vanity!

My own, my one, mine, unnameable, irremovably mine – how divinely happy I feel about this year, a year that grafted you onto my life, that taught what it means to be human (with growth pains and birth pains, but also with ecstasy and with heartfelt gratitude). "I can't summarise it, neither a lifetime nor a conversation ..." But my year, *our* year, nevertheless has a magic formula, an "Open Sesame" that revealed the treasure in the cave (the location of the treasure remains a secret!): and the formula consists of two sweet words: Ingrid Jonker. Strange, strange, my child. Previously this name simply represented two neutral words on the white cover of a slim little volume of poetry, and sometimes a tiny headline in the *Sunday Times*. And if I thought about it, it called up the image of a "lady" – civilised and rebellious – of about 35 or so, wearing glasses, and with longish feet.

And then: (listen, child, listen) then a young girl arrived in Jan's living room carrying with her the scent of paint and food; she was small; everything about her was small. Her hair was long, light-coloured; she was wearing a bright yellow blouse and green slacks, with beautiful feet in gold sandals. She had soft, neglected hands, one of them coolly enveloped in my own for just a second, and a nonchalant voice and questioning, lovely, slightly displeased eyes; and a very prominent little mound. We (supposedly) read a letter together at the table. And we began talking about poems (!). I was offered a glass of milk to calm me down. I lay awake all night long, just thinking. The next night, she was sleeping alongside me. One night later, she slept *with* me. God, my little thing – "I'll make the babbling gossip of the air cry out: Ingrid!" I am mad with love, and soothed. As long as you're there I can, like a daisy, "say something in reply, believe something, know something".

Remember, after receiving this letter, to write to me at c/o The Magistrate, Potchefstroom. I'll try to phone you from there, probably in the afternoon (a Saturday, possibly, if you're still working) – I'll telegraph you in good time with details. If I phone on the afternoon of Christmas day, which number should I use?

I received a long letter from Christie [Roode], terribly self-reproachful. I can't understand how, in the heat of the moment, he could have been so rash with the telegram, how he thought he might be able to assist in "solving" a human "problem" with a "diagnosis". It sounds like he understands a little more, now, about living "in irony".

What remains is faith, hope, and love – these three things. But the greatest of them all is love.

I beseech you to be happy and quiet and patient. I'm coming: a groom to a girl with a lamp that runneth over with oil.

Love and happiness,
André.

We were both born on a Wednesday. Children of woe.

─────────

Study, Grahamstown
Monday, 16 December 1963
DAY OF THE COVENANT

Little pixie, Cocoon, darling – Ingrid,

I won't keep you in a state of unnecessary tension but rather give you the main news immediately. I've just come off the phone with Rob. He says he's quickly read through the Kruger biography, "doesn't yet want to give a final judgement", but adds that it doesn't seem to him like "the kind of book that one awards a prize"; as far as he's concerned, it won't even be considered. And yes, Ernst van Heerden is overseas, so the final decision lies with Rob and Opperman. But insofar as it's humanly possible to be certain, it looks as if our "very young poet", my precious little chick, is going to be on the receiving end of R2 000.

Go to the bathroom now before you finish reading, otherwise you might wet your nice little white panties. (Or are you wearing the blue ones?)

Thank you again for Saturday night's call from so far away, which surprised me even though I had a hunch you might call. I would very much have wanted to be there to test the hotel out with you. And now – 10.45 am – you're probably lying and sleeping after the long night-drive? This afternoon it'll be the sea, and the sun on your smooth, tanned body ("as brown as the baked earth near Siena –").

Your call had certain consequences over here. Estelle apparently got wind it was you – I think she heard me calling you "my precious" – and while at first she remained distant and stiff, she later went for a walk – and then returned with a new "tactic": loving affection, "pretend nothing happened", and cooking a "stylish" meal. God, this is actually more nerve-wracking than everything else.

And now, my angel: make a booking for us at the Van Riebeeck for the weekend of Friday afternoon the 17th January till Monday morning the 20th. Do it right away, otherwise they may not have room. I'll be in the Cape a few days earlier and we'll have seen each other, but the weekend must be *ours*, alone. It should be just "right" – although with your overseas plans it might not be quite "right"?

Did your period arrive on Saturday – with all that fuss and the tears and so on?! Let me know so I can get my notes up to date.

I'm sending you another letter; this one came from an Indian. Send it back again, please! I believe that these naive, sincere little missives are, in the long run, one's greatest reward.

Did I tell you that an English woman wrote to me saying she wanted to translate *Lobola*? I don't mind, she can do it, and then I'll do the final editing myself.

The Ambassador is now at page 130. God, it's hard work! I'm sending you two sample pages to "evaluate". (You can keep these.)

I'm also sending a small cheque, mainly to cover the phone call.

What's going on with the job? Be careful of Cilliers.

But you always tread lightly, because you're a girl; a small, intense, tender, absolute being "who does not even have to think of God".

I love you. In you everything finds a form. Even the four elements: fire, water, air, earth.

I greet you in longing and secure love.

A kiss for the little chick.

Always,
André.

———————

Castella
Tuesday evening, 17 December 1963

My dearest André André,

Thank you, liefsteling, for your two letters – the one of Friday, the one we spoke about on Saturday evening from Upington – heavens, I wrote back a piece or six that night, tore it all up and phoned – and the one that was waiting here on Monday afternoon when my Transvaal friends and I got back from the beach – the beautiful one with the story – the Bethlehem story about us. Tired tired tired. Left Sunday evening at six, drove through the night; home Monday morning at nine – safe – after an almost-accident at Hex River – my girlfriends were here and we chatted till eleven – slept till one-thirty and went to the beach. And last night only got to bed at two again – so you see, I am *the* most TIRED of all. But I want to say hello, and I hope you got my telegram today and don't feel deserted because my quiet time (pray, pray) was so long. And with your driving to Potch, there's even more of a delay, of course. I hope everything goes quietly and clearly – whatever happens. You are so lovely and precious. Hello mine!

Bonnie [Davidtsz]'s little friend [Iris] is nice; she's an art student but can't continue because she doesn't have any money and first has to work for a year or two to save. For now, she's going to stay here at Castella.

What else is happening …? Heavens, what's *going to* happen? When are you planning to come? I live in your "pendulum existence". The uncertainty of everything holds a kind of horror *and* enchantment. Just to be able to rest in your arms safe and without any questions and the tangled undergrowth of words.

I telegraphed about Nico [Hagen] – god! – Wednesday evening (afternoon), he sends me a little letter: "Meet me five o'clock at the hotel where we once had a drink. I have something to say. I'll wait for you till half past five, maybe longer. Nico."

So *simple*. I had an appointment with Freda but went to meet him first, because I immediately assumed that something was wrong. But we had very little time; then I had to leave. He couldn't actually say much – inner problems, I think, and problems adjusting; wants to chat, get clarity. Made an arrangement then to talk the next evening – he didn't arrive; on the way, a car accident; skull fracture; back; still unconscious. Only family allowed. And all those bladdy rubbishes are walking around in the sun outside. While the saints have to be maimed and mown down.

Er is een boom geveld met lange groene lokken.
Hij zuchtte ruisend als een kind
terwijl hij viel, nog vol van zomerwind.
Ik heb de kar gezien, die hem heeft weggetrokken.

O, als een jonge man, als Hector aan de zegewagen,
met slepend haar en met de geur van jeugd
stromend uit zijn schone wonden,
het jonge hoofd nog ongeschonden,
de trotse romp nog onverslagen.

He's getting the gold medal for Art this year. (*Maybe now*, hey?)

Ag, my André, I don't want to sound despondent. But daily the assaults and the shocks and the whys. "Like a lamb to the slaughter." Immoral, humiliating.

And your light, lovely, loving, radiant letter of light. Your love. Your lovableness. Your surrender. Your sparkling youth. Your *you*-ness, my Other-me. André.

Sleep time. Tired time. Quiet time. Pray time.

Everything good and healthy again. Maybe just a sensitivity at certain times, maybe a lack of certain vitamins or something like that.

Why are you wearing jerseys now? It's so warm here.

Why do you write to Castella, Philippus?

Why do you love me? "Come to my heart …"

You mustn't work too hard. You *must* get rest. Please. And you must sleep with me lekker and often. I see you. And it puts me in the mood.

I miss your being-here. Far away, "begrijp ik het niet …"

Silly letter before bed. Good night, sweet prince.

Tender love from
Your lovely Cocoon,
Ingrid Jonker.

Grahamstown
(I almost wrote Green Point!)
premonition?
Wednesday, 18 December 1963

Dearest,

Very briefly, amid the bustle that precedes a holiday – and this with a pen that doesn't want to write!

I'll be posting your parcel(s) today. Please let me know if, and when, they arrive. By this time you should already have received the new bra-and-panties parcel that I re-ordered a week ago.

I need Anne's vocabulary to describe life here. One HELL of a fight again this morning. (Is this what they call the Christmas feeling?!)

I'll be on the road at the crack of dawn tomorrow – a fourteen-hour drive. And it looks like we're set for murderously hot weather. So be it.

The translation [*The Ambassador*] has reached page 164.

But I'm not writing to give you "news". I just wanted to say I love you impossibly, and I'm happy – no matter how strange this may sound in view of all the daily frustrations – because I'm living in a state of such complete certainty about you.

I'm looking forward to your letter about the Upington excursion. Where and how did Nico hurt himself? How does he fit into the picture?

Look after yourself nicely, be good, live in light and patience and grace, my lovely, lovely, indispensable person.

I'll write again soon. Please also write.

Meanwhile, I hold you with love and fullness and continuous thankfulness.

André.

Potchefstroom,
Saturday afternoon, 20 December 1963

Most lovely child, my darling,

Thank you for your beloved letter of yesterday, arriving as it did in this impossible heat. And thank you for the beautiful parcel. I didn't want to wait until Christmas, so I took a quick peek and tried it on. It fits wonderfully; it's really lovely and I can see I'll be wearing it a lot over here. (On this side – as there, too, it seems – the weather's insufferably hot, literally unbearable. Grahamstown, on the other hand, is often cool in the summer, cool enough to wear a jersey sometimes.)

I've been wanting to write to you very badly, but the first day's settling in here, and especially the lack of a much needed place to isolate myself, frustrated my efforts. Now, while the others are having a nap, I can be with you in quiet contentment. And maybe sleep with you a little later to heal me a little of my longing (although that also makes it more acute).

What a massive expedition this business of visiting the family is. One realises what a *complete* lack of connection there is. Nothing to talk about. I can't even express modest outrage about a newspaper report on police abuse of convicts without causing an uncomfortable silence, as if it's an "attack" – everyone here is of course NATIONAL, in capital letters. The same goes when it comes to the church. Even *family* bonds are nothing to write home about. My adolescent brother is an irritating little shit. My sisters wear very long, prim, calvinist dresses, and they wear their hair in frizzy little curls; my mother and her lot pick up hideous, monstrous "paintings" at bargain prices and think it's culture.

That's all there is here – just downcast Doppers who wear forced expressions of Christmas "goodwill" on their faces like OK Bazaars masks; self-righteous moral prigs who pronounce the word "Lobola" as if it means "Antichrist". *Platteland* people. So Transvaal, so Afrikaans, and with a hot-as-hell God. Not even a sea in which to cleanse one's sins, or those of one's family.

312

I haven't done any work yet. How *can* one? I first have to get into the "mood". "Our delicate and tender souls." "Sinful artists that we are."

In this place I feel like a [Moses] Kottler statue on display at a public building.

("Of course no one's allowed to be open …" and there are so many PeePee-de-thises and PeePee-de-thats, it's like the whole place is steeped in its own peepee.)

Thank the Lord we can laugh at the spectacle of humanity (oneself included!). Let us close the catechism for just a second, dear congregation, and laugh.

Let us laugh and fuck and be human.

Beloved child, I miss you. But my longing comes from purity and quietude, without the distress of a while ago.

I'm shocked about Nico's news. I hope things are going better now. It's always so perverse, this "family only" attitude. If something like that were to happen to me, family's the *last* thing I'd want around me; just you. My little sister – oh your dance is delightful, with the mountain eagle's fire-plume on your forehead, blessed are you among women.

I'm sending this to Castella, minx, because I haven't yet heard from you what eventually became of the Citadel job; and I don't want any of my letters to have to pass through those corridors (or tunnels).

Have you phoned the Van Riebeeck yet to book a room for us? If you don't, we may have to "lie low" in the little castle (or lie flat) – and you now have a chaperone!

How are things with our little blonde child?

And with *my* soft, fiery, virginal little whore?

Write – a lot.

I love you and live quietly for you and remain happy for you; soon I'll be with you again.

I hail everything, with tenderness and enthusiasm,

In fulfilment and longing,
André.

Castella
Saturday night late, 21 December 1963

My precious André,

> With your hands that have a future
> that burn like dew
> that live like weighty birds ...

A few lines for you. Heavens, child, Cape Town is alive! People. Bonnie and Iris still here. Bonnie is out; Iris was – Simone asleep – me, you, with our kind little candle, now. Liefsteling, *thank you* for the beautiful beautiful gifts you sent me – that Jean Patou Amour Amour is the most precious perfume – and the Van Ostaijen wonderful – I haven't begun my voyages of discovery with it yet; but you spoil me so. And you're naughty. You don't register your parcels. No, the little bra and things haven't arrived yet. You refuse to learn, don't you? But that'll probably come later. And thank you for the cheque. I always have to say so many thank yous, and they're so inadequate, because one lives so completely in prayerful gratitude and compassion and tenderness and concern.

News. I saw Bartho and the rest of them – he told me openly that the choice is between me and Jan – I tried to look surprised – everything very secret – the award has to be an absolute surprise – the writer will be notified confidentially about a month before and be given an airline ticket – it's going to be a real occasion in March; Jan and I made an agreement at the party last night – if he wins, he gives me R50; and vice versa. The dear old crowd were all at Stephen [Etienne Leroux] and company's place. Jack friendly and concerned; he was here when your Patou arrived; I opened it and, thrilled, showed it to him and Bonnie – he brazenly says it's rubbish (!). Organised the house thoroughly today; everything in its place – washed and combed and dressed Cinderella – everything down to the last detail. Iris can stay here; a fine, especially sensitive little person, I think we'll get on well ...

314

Booked at the Van Riebeeck; child, love-child, it's not too long any more – they have to write me a confirmation letter, Castella. Heavens, it's going to be an island with your laughter, desirable, disarming, *you*. But tell me more, are you all in Cape Town then? And how …? Sleepy, man. I'll write more tomorrow. And I can't even sleep with you, because Simone and Iris are sleeping in the same room; but still, I am with you so unutterably often – participating in your existence.

Dates: Early; period 11 December; 17 January will be about "right". Dearest my own papie, for now I'm saying Good night, sweet prince. Tomorrow, bright blue day, I'll write more – but first I urgently want you to know that you are a part of me – in love and an unbearable tenderness – and for you, ag, du … du … in my arms, in my bed, nightly, beloved …

Till tomorrow,
Your own Cocoon.

PS: Do you like your little gift? You're bound to look very impressive in it! I see you.
IJ.

───────────

Monday, 23 December 1963

THREE O'CLOCK 399363 STOP THANK YOU AMOUR STOP OUTSTANDING CHRIST-MAS JANUARY LIES AHEAD MY LITTLE ELEPHANT LOVE = COCOON

Potchefstroom
Christmas night, 1963

Beloved, beautiful, "fairly good" child,

Finally, some seclusion in which to converse with you, as I promised this afternoon. *Thank you* for your voice, your light, and your happy spirit. It brought a certain radiance to the rest of the day. I know how clichéd it sounds to say that I miss you; but it's *true*, dearest darling. Things are going *badly* here. Today we said "good morning" to each other – just perfunctorily, because there were other people around – and since then not another word has passed between us. She knows I phoned you this afternoon; and she knows about your lovely gift, which I stored, with note and all, right at the top of the drawer. Oh god, child, it's not the alienation that upsets me – I *welcome* that. It's the frustration of keeping up appearances in front of my parents, for my father's sake especially – and for the sake of the general good, given the situation. But how much longer can it go on like this? I want to break free, come to you and stay with you; and be with you *always*.

This is the reason why you should remain good, rather than just "fairly good". Entirely. Yes: I am jealous. But it would be unnatural for me not to be!

Last night I *knew* you were sleeping at Jack's (even if it *was* just sleeping over!), because I was restless and upset, and I lay awake almost the whole night.

I believe you. (All your lies –?) But if you do *sleep* with him, please don't *ever* hold it back from me just to make things "easier", or because it's too hard to explain. It would be hell to know, but necessary. This is an honesty that keeps things unsullied – I'd much rather have it this way than let it be unspoken out of "consideration", thereby creating "suspicions". PROMISE?

I'm happy to hear you've found a flatmate, but how on earth can you afford it, my generous, open-hearted little thing? Shouldn't I help you again? *Just say the word.*

I said to you my plans for the trip to the Cape hadn't been finalised. But it now looks like I'll be back in Grahamstown on 10 Jan (evening). That's a Friday, and I'll probably spend the weekend there, arriving in the Cape on Wednesday (15 Jan). Our island of quiet and rapture will thus be from the 17th to the 20th. In all likelihood I'll be gone again by the 22nd.

We can talk – must, in fact – about the possibility of you visiting Grahamstown when you get your vacation-cum-bonus (though obviously I'll cover your expenses).

Are the people at the Citadel treating you more humanely these days? Do you still get your tea? Does your boss still accompany you to the bathroom? Who's reading with you now, in Anne's place? There's nothing that's *not* important for me to know!

Chris is probably out of town, Uys busy with translation. Jan and Marjorie? And: Jack …?

Now begins that really awful wait for the prizes. If I only had your sense of certainty. But I have strong doubts. Even so: I dream about next Christmas, the two of us in a sunny Spanish fisherman's village (in spite of the winter); God, so happy.

Yesterday morning I woke up with such a strong sense of you that the papie almost got me into an embarrassing situation – with untimely secrets. And this despite the fact that I sleep with you a lot as it is. (If you want to know, that's when I say: "Darling, darling, darling – ")

I'm still carrying my little scar, proudly and happily; and I hope it stays there always.

I want you; I love you. All of you, which I hail with passion – the way I'm doing it now at the end of *Orgie*:

A vivid salutation to all your vivid parts:
your fair head
and the faraway tenderness of your half-closed eyes
the mysterious pain and happiness of your mouth
the tension in your arms
your beautiful hands

your legs
and your speckled shoulders
the shy, intimate touch of your breasts
your smooth back and stomach
and the narrow, hidden path to the anemone.

This is how much I love you.
    And I ask you to remain chaste and lovely.
    "My girl, I appoint you with an appointment."

Always, for ever,
Your André.

───────────

Castella
Boxing Day, 1963

My delightful little sparring partner,

Your voice (rather dejected) yesterday afternoon on the phone; we should've been able to go up the mountain; and you should have been an interrogator: dearest my André, it feels as if it's been years since I last wrote to you and yet it was Sunday; you have been entirely assimilated into my existence – my existence, at the moment; Christmas rounds; presents – Pa let me know that *Simone* may "come home" *if* she's at Anna's – which is why my Christmas Day was with Jack and Uys and the rest of them (the old lady hates me and the children are stiff and unfriendly). I think stiffness and (usually false) obtuseness are sins. I turn away from you (like a swinish God). And the stiffness yesterday after your phone call; that's also sinful. "For he hath made him to be sin for us, who knew no sin." Reading for today.
    Liefsteling. Iris is out; went to buy some cigarettes; we were on the beach today, burnt; hitchhiked there and back; I was quite crabby after

your phone call because one can't properly communicate that way; it's like this – everything magnified and out of context, because words are all there is, without facial expression or the touch of a hand – the rushed conversation because time is gold; etc. etc. But *our* time lies ahead. Had a letter of confirmation from Van Riebeeck Hotel addressed to you; they say they have a mountain view for us, with breakfast. I asked because we had a sea view last time – and "we would like to have you again". Civilised, at least. So, golden, valuable, precious, whole, again.

Did I tell you I read *Lobolo again*? And each time I know you better, I love you more; still a little scared to go through *Orgie* again, have a week's "holiday" – when it will happen. *Busy* on my play *'n Seun na My Hart* [A Boy after My Own Heart]. Did you ever read it? Uys says he and I should rewrite it together. I wonder if you and I …?

I miss you, far away, strange, but still, you remain strange. "The paradox" of love. As you once put it. Always amazed. "Always born outside of me …" And yet … Maybe because of that, "make love".

For always,
Cocoon.

ps: Did I write to tell you I visited Nico in hospital? God, but he's confused – recognised me only occasionally. Funny, too. He teases the man next to him – the man upsets him because he sometimes ignores him. Nico can't hold onto anything – coordination gone to hell – and speaks with difficulty even though he speaks so rudely – and laughs.

It's now early Friday morning, I want to quickly go and post this. Have already forgotten what the other news is – the bra-parcel very cute. If one had a baby you wouldn't need to take anything out. Now I'll put it away nicely till you come – just had to wear it once. And how do you look in your charcoal affair? You must bring it with you next month. Have I told you yet that Stephen [Etienne Leroux] and Renée [his wife] like *Rook en Oker* very much and Bartho does too – the party at Stephen and Renée's was lovely – wish you'd been there – it reminded me a bit of old Bill's. Morning, beautiful. Must rush off now to post. Be good, my little elephant with the little trunk.

Cocoon.

————————

Potchefstroom

Sunday night, 29 December 1963

My own darling, Cocoon, Ingrid,

A few moments of quiet before I have to bath Anton. Had a lovely swim this afternoon, and yesterday. But I'm still far too white. I'll do my best to add a bit of earth-brown before I come down so as not to embarrass you too much, divine little woman. Tonight in just three weeks' time we'll do another of those long walks along the sea, cut off from the organisations of hate, completely happy, and together. And shortly thereafter: *inside* each other. I have a very *physical* need for you, too!

Before I go on and forget to mention it: forgive me the "ignorance" of my poor memory, but who wrote "For each man kills the thing he loves"? I want to use it as an epigraph in *Orgie* and need the information URGENTLY. In between translating *Die Ambassadeur*. I'm also typing up *Orgie*. On nice stiff white sheets, with a new typewriter ribbon. Looks impressive; I've done quite a thorough revision. Want to hand it over to Bartho as early as January so I can work with [Marc] Achleitner on the typography, otherwise there'll be delays and misunderstandings. *Orgie* isn't a *major* work; but it has to be poetic, and pure. It's very important because it's so completely *ours*.

The final sentence of the dedication now reads: "All of this, conjoined, is hereby yours, with love: 'private words addressed to you in public' (T.S. Eliot)." Happy?

"News"? It's a morgue, this place. I'm working sixteen hours a day.

320

(But *The Ambassador* will be done by tomorrow; Christie's Retha is going to type it up.) I've seen Christie twice, and will see him again tonight – "they" (!) are going away the day after tomorrow – but he's very subdued, doesn't ask any questions, and refrains from offering unsolicited comment. Actually it's all rather uncomfortable.

Bill sent a Christmas card (as "subtle" as a bull in a china shop): with a picture he took in France when he visited us there. And a note: "Come over for a chat some time"!!!

Otherwise: a different kind of hell: Estelle drives me round the bend playing the "patient, long-suffering wife". As if there's nothing wrong. But I keep to myself. And, thank god, we sleep in complete separation. After New Year she and her mother are going to Pretoria for a few days.

That's about it.

Delightful child: (*good* – completely good – child?) I love you, find life in you and wish to bring you living water; thank you for sending me those precious, lovely lines; wait sweetly and quietly, with restrained passion. Before very long I'll be there. Then our new memory will begin. Then, together, we can write a new stanza for our lovely poem. We'll suspend time, in just "*one* blind deed" of love and trust that keeps us pure and human. With much love, and with everything, always,

André.

HAPPY NEW YEAR!
Castella
30 December 1963

My dearest and most jealous god of the elephants with tiny trunks – lord of my heart, prince, André,

Your two letters arrived simultaneously on Saturday – the one where you're so the hell-in with Potch and the stranger-family (but don't you know you have to make your own family, your friends? God, then you can at least use your own discretion!) and the jealous one from Christmas Day – after which I lay in a swoon for 24 hours – or I swooned, as Iris and I now say. I already feel afraid when I share a bed with another man, afraid that you'll be angry and afraid for the whole false situation in which we find ourselves. And then you still *talk* …! (I forgot to say, it was excruciating for two hours, just until I fell asleep, and then I woke up again and went and lay with Simone.)

Seems to me you think everything here is always friendly and kind, but Jack is sometimes so morose and unpleasant towards me, there's almost constant tension, and ever since your phone call, petulance and open quarrelling. You're not the only one trying to make life "liveable"! I don't want to argue with you too. I just want to say. And I say it softly, considerately, and I am holding your hand nicely, and see your mouth like that time at the 191 when you said: Your hand, which will never manage to turn me away from you. Listen, darling, I *do* love you, I am even *more* prepared to stay with you always. Do you understand? But before you can come to me like that, I am afraid of all hope, all surrender to possibilities … always possibilities … I don't want to be "killed by a dream", to quote myself. And it will be devastating for our relationship as it is now. And that's why I try, in spite of my oneness and connection with you, to simply accept things as they are. Fine, if I am not allowed to lie with other men – I understand that you will be jealous because you love me, but Estelle is after all also *someone*, and someone you once loved and with whom you *stay*; and I don't WHINE like that!

And now; another thing – the "camp", the "John Kannemeyer" – little heart, you also "keep up appearances" – which you so kick against in your letter. You must decide – as indeed you *did* once decide, whether we don't dare rescue ourselves from this entrapment – if I win the prize I can take you with me overseas – there is nothing I'd rather do. And before I dream about that – child, everyone will know that Estelle is also in Cape Town and that I am just running off with you: which puts me in a highly unpoetic light. But I am *prepared* to do it. So you mustn't get so terribly jealous. I also have to live in a reality here, such as it is. I have to take the child somewhere for Christmas, and I haven't been invited to my parents. I suppose I've preached enough now, hey? And I framed your beautiful portrait, and tomorrow I'll be eating with Koos – and I still work in the grey pit – like a big human rat – darling treasure, you must see Castella now – we've arranged it to make room for Iris – a lovely person – the bedroom is her room and "studio", mine is the "library", and Simone's little cubbyhole is the "study". She, Iris, knows about you, of course – if we want to be alone we'll simply lock her in her room! And now I have to go and eat. Oh yes, your "greeting", which is now far more literary, is less beautiful than your heartfelt greeting. You must use the original in *Orgie*.

Yours with longing and flaws and joy and love and again longing and a salute for the 15th.

Cocoon Cocoon.

Potchefstroom
31 December 1963

My darling, mine,

Thank you for this morning's lovely, desolate letter, so full of rebellion against the dourness you've had to endure there; and so desperate to make the estranged me closer and truer. I want you to know, my Cocoon, my Ingrid, that you have been especially *close* to me over the past few days. That I lay alone in the room this morning for a long time, half-sleeping, half-awake, dreaming up a long scene with you: we had a house, a Malay type of dwelling, double-storeyed, just a little box with windows top and bottom, with a little door, and it was dazzlingly *white*. I was sitting and typing; you were on your way back from work and I went to meet you, one block up, under shady trees. As we began kissing each other, our clothes fell away, right there in the street with its patches of sunlight and pools of shade – and we walked back arm-in-arm, God, so *happy*.

And so my day began, with beauty and feeling – New Year's Eve.

This year of thankfulness and truth is over. Will the year ahead be one of fulfilment? Why do I believe so strongly that we won't be apart next year this time?

This is no mere adolescent yearning. I want to marry you and be with you; be a father to our children, contented and fulfilled. I've had enough of emptiness and lack of contact and a life with no physical touch because it is devoid of spiritual content.

Stop.

Christie's just arrived, so I'll continue writing later.

Later. Once again, thank you, little child, for what you opened up and liberated inside of me this year, allowing me to remain open, from now on and always, to the winds of paradise and to you, fleet-footed child. (Leucodendron: how are things with *you*?)

I'm off to Johannesburg this afternoon, just for two days, staying with Naas Steenkamp. Anton will remain behind in Potch. Be back here on the 2nd. Please continue writing. From Monday the 6th you can send letters to Grahamstown again.

And then – and then: the two of us in our bedroom facing the mountain, to which we can raise our eyes when we need help. I'll wear my lovely sweater, and you your naughty bra-and-panties. This time I'm going to take beautiful pictures of you. With those exquisite breasts of yours, you'll be full and voluptuous. (But won't it be too late for us, yet again, to make a moesie-girl? Your last period came a little early, didn't it?)

Keep working on the play. You told me about it; but you've yet to send it to me for reading. And *yes*: let's work on it together. Not Uys!

I still want to write a new story for Bartho's anthology. Apparently pictures of all of us will be appearing on the back cover. I told them to order one of you from Desmond.

And now it's time to take my leave of you, you with your lovely,

precious parts: I hail your dreams, your words of tenderness and wonder; your sleepy, truth-laden eyes. I hail your hands so full of compassion; your shoulders with their freckles; tummy with its shadows softly
playing in the light; the small, dear, tanned back; your breathtaking
buttocks, delicious legs, fleet feet; and a parting shot, deep and long,
passionate and tender, with mouth and hands and eventually the papie
itself, for the cocoon of quietude and fire, the essence of *dance*, with its
secrets about the future, beginning tomorrow.

And a wish for the New Year: that it will indeed be *new*.

And happy.

And serene.

With love, and more love, whispers and a song,
Yours,
André.

———————

Thursday, 2 January 1964

LOVE AND BORN BUTTERFLIES FOR OUR NEW YEAR MY PRINCE = COCOON

———————

Castella
Thursday, 2 January 1964

My dearest Prince,

Prince of poets. And Prince, God, *stupidest*, "Yet each man kills the
thing he loves ...", "The Ballad of Reading Gaol" – Oscar Wilde – I'll
send you a book about it:

Yet each man kills the thing he loves,

...

Some do it with a bitter look,

...

The coward does it with a kiss,
The brave man with a sword!

...

For each man kills the thing he loves,
Yet each man does not die.

Or something like that. I'll send the complete thing. Beautiful ballad.

Darling, my own André P. Brink, I am *sorry* about my angry and ill-considered letter the other day, but "everything is necessary" and your two letters today were so amiable; don't know what I would do without them. I got up at 10:30 this morning and in my pyjamas tottered out sleep-drunk to the postbox and they aroused me; and then I felt like such a CAT about my last letter; but more than anything I was upset about your unhappiness and our separation and the *fact* that we cannot surrender completely because *always* maybe, maybe, maybe, and now your leaving and the "deceit" – "the battalions of lies and the organizations of hate"; but never mind, never mind, my papie, when we get to our island again on the 17th the doubts will *disappear* so easily and naturally and freely and mercifully.

Child, it's one o'clock; really tired and burnt to hell, I want to be *brown* when you come again, you really don't have to worry about your whiteness – and then you'll always have your lovely brown moesies and your long big papie which opens me up and hurts and heals so beautifully.

Your innocent white paper; your new typewriter ribbon – your *Orgie*. When you come, we'll go through it word for word; *Child*. Yes, the dedication is lovely. And I believe in your love and I am proud of it, that someone like you "can love ignoble me ..."

Glad Christie's behaving better; Bill's postcard message is a scream. Poor thing.

Little "martyr" woman – I do, nevertheless, feel sorry for her; and GUILTY.

Yes, *completely* well-behaved. And you are nearby and good; it's so good ... You say "thank you for the lovely lines"– does that refer to a LETTER from me? Thank you for your telegram – I froze when I thought your father might open mine because you wrote you'd be away for a few days – the "born butterflies" is our baby, out of the papie-cocoon. Dream ...?

Now your two letters are mixed up. We're still going to get that Malay house; I've already chosen it; just from the outside, beautiful, white, without a stoep. Heavy door, and cheap. Hey, I object: "I am sitting and typing and working, you were on your way back from WORK ...!" Good God.

Wait a while with *Orgie*; we'll do it together; you need to get rid of all the self-pity; remember your "glowing sadness", don't be in such a hurry, my love; just be in a hurry with me.

Leucodendron; means Silver Tree. It's nice and sore and happy. Full breasts with "the milk of human kindness" (hopefully).

Iris and I alone on New Year's Eve; waited up till twelve o'clock: slept; entertained [?] 1st; only went to the beach today.

No, time's right (according to my calculations) for the moesie-girl – ours. It's probably also not very wise ... and won't old Piet then come and take Simone away ...? But I so badly want to be pregnant with you.

I'll keep the play for us. Small parts (intimate conversations) I've reworked in *Rook en Oker* and will have to find other images. They must put our photos next to one another on the anthology's back cover ... Sentimental ...!

Thank you again, my heart, for all the beautiful things you are and which you give to *me* – and sleep sweetly and happily, I love you and would so much like to have you here always. I draw a cross on your forehead; good night, good morning, tomorrow through the little curtains, and to the moesies and your hands and your heart that beats and to your beautiful tooth, which doesn't always want to listen.

With love,
Your Cocoon. Kontjie.
Non Con.

PS: What else did you get for Christmas? IJ.

{Braaksma (cultural attaché for the Netherlands) sent me a beautiful diary for Christmas. IJ.}

Potchefstroom
Sunday night, 5 January 1964

Beloved mine,

I've isolated myself here in my brother's room to share with you, once more, my drawn-out days of longing since I last wrote. However, it's no longer a matter of dejection or simply feeling trapped. And it's *more* than just the fact that, tonight in two weeks' time, you and I will go walking far into the dark of Gordon's Bay together ... It's a very interior kind of restfulness, a belief that we have now arrived quite close to a point of acceleration.

The general atmosphere here has also changed – I mean the oppressive "family atmosphere" I fulminated about in one of my recent letters. My people and I have rediscovered a sense of connection after planing away the inevitable differences that arise following six months of total estrangement. I had a few long conversations with my mother about the two of us. It weighs heavily on her, and she still dare not raise it with my father; but she realises it's *my* life and that no one can or dare cast judgement from the outside.

And: I will never again sleep with Estelle in the double bed. (Here we sleep separately anyway.) I've therefore also removed that prickly little matter for you.

Because, delightful, essential one: I am yours, you mine, we are one flesh and one future. If I didn't have this to believe in, there wouldn't be anything left for me.

Tomorrow it's back to Johannesburg again for a few days, until Thursday morning. I'll be seeing all my friends, chatting with everyone, helping to plan *Orgie*'s typography, and talking about you *a lot*. Bartho said he wants to start the reprint of *Rook en Oker* soon – with the same setting and paper, but in a larger format – like Adam Small's. And then he'll do the revised arrangement of the poems – which we can discuss again when I'm in the Cape. (And the Dedication? Or do you want to keep it the way it is, after all?)

Child: write to the Population Registrar, Dept. of Internal Affairs, Pretoria – IMMEDIATELY – and ask for an identity card. You will need it for passports etc. and they can damn-well take their time if you don't get the process going soon enough. I must also renew my passport one of these days.

Remember to let me know at the Grahamstown address, by telegram if necessary, and *before* next Monday (the 13th), at what number I should call you before I come down. When exactly in February do you get leave and your holiday bonus?

It's only now – after completing the translation, and getting *Orgie* print-ready – that I'm actually begining to take a few days' holiday, and swimming a lot. But it's always damn-well cloudy when I go, so I'm still barely "off-white"; pinkish, like suckling pig. But with a little mercy – and some sun – from Above, the worst of my "whiteness" might yet be camouflaged before I make it to Gordon's Bay. (Oh the ecstasy of those sun-and-sea days, for us; you'll be having so many Martinis, and getting so *lazy* again, sleeping a lot, and grumbling when I want us to stay awake.) Then you'll say: "No, André", "Hm-hm", "HM-HM" as I slide in behind your smooth, brown little back and lazily begin searching for your cocoon. And, I'll be giving the leucodendron another bath. And I'll run my hands through your hair. And maybe I'll start itching and scratching at myself, as always, to your great annoyance and dearest exasperation. You'll be wearing your whitest, most see-through little nightie – just so that I can pull it off again for a big little wet-and-warm sleepie. And we'll go swimming, and talk, and read poetry, and your play, and eat asparagus, and bath, and laugh a lot, and be still, and passionate – hell! so lekker – and be consoled. *Together*, in the reaffirmation of the flesh, the new and far flight of the spirit, and all of it, entire, poetry.

Virginal child, ripe, ripe woman, blessed person: fill your little lamp, your bridegroom is coming.

Meanwhile I hold my hands over you and say an incantation against evil; I lie on you and protect you in love, and *become* with you: human, and free.

Your André.

———————————

Castella
Sunday night, 5 January 1964

Dearest beloved man,

Do you know what the time is? 2.45 am. Iris and I are sitting here with a drink of "sea, carnations" – gin – but then I have to add that I slept from eight to ten. Thank you, my dearest, for your letter – child, child, where you write that you "accept the separation", and for what you said to Bartho and Kita [Redelinghuys] in Jhb. It makes me feel so much surer. Not that I'm not sorry about the mess – but still, still, we need each other so much. Ten days. Already said I was sorry about the letter where I climbed into you again: *thank you* that you are so understanding: knew you would understand how utterly difficult things are here *most* of the time. Of course you can be as possessive as possible; when we live a reasonably natural life! Estelle's reaction is STRANGE, but you will probably have to bring it home to her; the "columns" in *Femina* say one should ... (cat).

Still. I'll send you the HEART-greeting when I can find it amidst the radiance of all your letters – or record the 17th on tape …? Haven't ever flown before, hope you'll be able to from Grahamstown – god, it would be unutterably wonderful! Did I tell you about my beautiful golden yellow "twistdress" and my white BABY-DOLL DRESS – wait a bit. I'll write everything. Now I'd like to meet Estelle, so that she can *see* I exist (and I can see that she exists?). Darling André, I'm just saying goodnight to Potch and greeting you, you must drive safely and well; I am waiting for you, IMPATIENTLY.

Apart from this, you'll just have to read *Die Wit in die Poësie* [The White Space in Poetry].

Date: Early, again; Friday. That's right. Right?

Stay with me, my treasure.

Your darling COCOON. (*Good.*) Fixed up?

(I'm getting a real kitten in two weeks' time.) Simone is flying to Jhb on Tuesday for a holiday. Otherwise, everything flourishing. And my garden is full of flowers, both inside *and* out.

{Dearest Papie
    Man mine
    André P. Brink
Bye, Potchefstroom. Welcome, Grahamstown. But not too much like last time. I accompany you with love.
    Your Ingrid.}

Thursday, 9 January 1964

My dearest André,

The wings of your "child of light" are fairly creased today – I've had a swinish letter from my father; I wrote him that I would very much like to give him *Rook en Oker* personally (a first edition, which he collects), and this was the answer.

> Dear Ingrid,
>
> After all you've done to me in interviews with the *Sunday Times* and other newspapers in the past year, I am not inclined to meet you in a café or any other public place.
> If you want to discuss anything with me, you know where I live. All that is required is to call me to enquire as to a convenient time. On weekend afternoons I usually go fishing.
>
> With love from
> Pappa (ABR. H. JONKER)

Typed. All day I've been wondering whether it's really possible – how and where and why it all began – the injury, mostly the secrecy – and does he honestly think – does he expect – that I, who may no longer meet him in public – will do so in secret – not on an equal footing, not as one person to another – never mind daughter to "father" – and WHY? Where does the pettiness and the rot and the "narrowness and small-ness and bitterness and closedness" begin – and where does it end?

> Teach us to care and not to care
> Teach us to sit still

But thank you for your preciousness and for your darling letter of today – you must come and tell me everything you said to your mother – I

332

am so glad she understands – and yes, the double bed (!) but my little treasure – does the gradual dying and uncertainly really help us all? Questions. Questions. I don't want you to have to remove this little irritation for *me* – but *only* for *yourself*, if needs be. And now I must say good night again, and that after such a "piece of misery"! But first: while I was writing, old Jan and them hammered at the door, visit – and I went for coffee and Van der Hum at theirs – it was nice – Jan quite kind and courteous and friendly, and showed me the favourable review of Rob's new *Standpunte* and *Rook en Oker*. And your Schutte satire and her humourless little sentence; and the attack on you by the journalist in J. at the back – and the little Van der Westhuizen article. Just scanned it – wasn't your satire cut? News: mostly alone with my little chaperone – reading *Sê Sjibbolet* [Adam Small]; *African Poetry*; swoon, and have (had) slight kidney infection; done with pills – just don't want to swim in Clifton cold yet. I can never get *properly* sick – everything just so latent, constitution like a (little) bull.

Ag, my André, my beautiful and rich human being and man-mine in your red-pyjama surrender, with your hands and feet safe for ever – in less than a week you're in the city – may I then have a meal at your place one evening? I want to meet Estelle and especially Anton (my little word). Arrange it. It's probably necessary that the three of us become more aware of one another's existence: Estelle, me and Anton. And we'll order a bottle of wine for Dutch courage.

It's been a while since I saw Jack – went away to the Koue Bokkeveld with his two-faced mother – and I am completely good and pure and virginal. I greet you with my body, my Royal Highness.

1. Love for the papie with the scar of light and love.
2. Love for the redhead and the green eyes without glasses
3. and the creative hands that make the world of my body blossom
4. and for his laughing tooth.

Till then till then,
Your Cocoon-est.

PS: Monet left by plane for Jhb; she looked *beautiful* and was very excited. There is our child of light. I.

{Drive safely, precious. IJ.}

———————

Potchefstroom, for one last time
Thursday, 9 January 1964

Child of light, my Cocoon,

Thank you for your *two* letters – the one on Monday, just before my trip to Jhb; and the other, today's brief missive just as we're leaving Potch. Both luminous; the first one with a kind of lucidity that I read and listen to over and over again.

I had three days of *hell* in Johannesburg. The whole idea behind my going was that Chris would be back and that I'd be able to talk to him during the day, but in the end he returned only yesterday – after mixing up the dates – and so I had to sit in Bartho's office day in and day out, talking about the same old stuff. And then last night the visit came to an appropriate end, with *Cleopatra*. Oh my good Lord! If there's one thing that makes me the hell-in (as Gert Pretorius might say?!) it's *those* two saggy tits with Elizabeth Taylor's face looming above them.

But there were some light moments, too. Bartho (*and* Abraham!) are crazy about *Orgie* – they've already sent it to the printers – with the understanding that I can still make changes on the proofs. And I *will*. I told them that you and I would be going through it all from scratch. Bartho says he doesn't think there's any self-pity in the closing poem; Chris thinks there may still be one or two passages I could clean up in this regard. Strange, they all prefer part 1 – and I think it rests far more firmly on the solid (impure) earth than the rest; not quite so lyrical, so "clean". One valid point of criticism, I feel, is that I should make more

334

of her search for herself amid all the roles she plays. But that's something we can talk about – DO YOU REALISE – in a *week's* time.

But the *expense*! The format's going to be identical to *Sê Sjibbolet*, bound with the same fine German thread as *Rook en Oker*, on that Finnish paper. Printed in roman, italics, *and* purple (the underlined parts). And, as I've already mentioned, the book reads sideways, with broad left-hand margin, and two identical page numbers:

I'm very excited. Delivery date provisionally set for my birthday, end of May; but given the layout issues there could be delays.

I've received a copy of *Rook en Oker* where we must make our changes next week (sequence etc.) for the book's reprint. Bartho wants to put the dust-cover design on the back of the book, too, so it no longer has an empty white space. Nice, isn't it? My poet, my Sappho, my Ingrid Jonker, Cocoon; *you*!

I'm reading a book on magic – or maybe I should say nibbling at it. *The Key of the Mysterious*. Beautiful things in this volume. This is specially for you:

> The least perfect act of love is worth more than the best act of piety.
> Judge not; speak hardly at all, love and act.

My only issue with this is that *every* act of love *is* an "act of piety", *is* essentially religious. That's all the religion we have, all we can be certain about, and – perhaps – all the religion we *need*.

The book also provides a magical explanation for all the different numbers in the occult. Your birth-number, 19, goes like this: "It is the number of light."

Unfortunately, the magical numbers only go up to 19! I therefore remain in outermost darkness!

My thoughts are jumping all over the place: back to Jhb and the three days among Naas's yelling children. The youngest is just four months old, a little girl, as sweet as honey. And, like a mushy sentimentalist, I walked around with this smiling little thing in my arms and looked forward to our own little girlie with all her moesies!

But your date is so *early* – the 3rd. That means it will come around again by the 28th; the best "period" – by my calculations, and conviction – is therefore between 12 and 16 Jan. But I'll be sure to come and fetch you from work *before* the 17th, take you home, and send Iris to the beach …! Hopefully I'll arrive in the Cape on Wednesday evening the 15th, probably quite late. I'll make arrangements – Thursday afternoon at lunchtime and at five or so.

This time Estelle will *know* – not by deduction, but by my telling her – that I'm going to stay with you and not Jan. I want to walk openly with you – under the sun and the moon and the stars.

I live in a state of anticipation, in peaceful ecstasy; you were such an object of *desire* for me during the dreary Jhb days.

Tomorrow, the long road back home.

And soon thereafter: you, *us*.

Live sweetly, my precious Cocoon, live happily and in love, even inside that grey cage of yours.

And let Maggie spread the chaste white sheets across our bridal bed.

Yours, impassioned and whole,
André.

Monday, 13 January 1964

SIX FIFTEEN TONIGHT OXLEY STOP WEDNESDAY THE WORD BECOMES FLESH
LOVE = COCOON

Grahamstown
Sunday night, 26 January 1964

My darling, Cocoon,

Verse for today:

> But wherefore could not I pronounce "Amen"?
> I had most *need* of blessing, and "Amen"
> Stuck in my throat
> …
> Glamis hath murdered sleep, and therefore Cawdor
> Shall sleep no more. Macbeth shall sleep no more.

Nights, nights – not of "ecstasy's duress", but of lying in burning wakefulness, lasting agony, the knowledge of love and yearning; and so mixed up, so confused. And the future: absence.

And then your voice that night: "That I asked you to lie for one hour against my bosom to be consoled, and to console *me*, and you refused – *that* I cannot forget."

And *me*? *Ever*?

And this from a sense of anxiety that seems meaningless in retrospect, but was meant from the bottom of my heart: such an hour would just hurt you all over again because you would face this inexplicable confusion for which I haven't been able to find any answer – not even for myself, nothing.

May I just say that you can be sure – even just a *little* – that I look upon myself with repugnance? And this when my only certainty is that I love you; need you.

On that first night with you, you said No – you didn't want "it" to happen all over again; you were wounded, tired, suspicious. But later you heeded my call and we learnt to love each other; and then I did to you what you'd predicted that first night.

My tender thing, my sensitive, precious child: if only I could give you some sense of what these past few days have been like (a prelude to my future?) – every little blonde girl I see becomes Simone; here, a small gesture by an unknown girl in a café reminds me of you; there, the colour of a dress; or someone wearing a white shirt with black slacks. You, you, darling, everywhere, you.

And in the wakeful nights, still, despite everything, the certain knowledge – this much at least, thank god – that our nine months together were expectation *and* fulfilment, an encounter with life, an intensity and a kind of poetry without which everything would be pointless.

"News": an urgent telegram from Bartho saying he needs *Rook en Oker* for a reprint; I'll send it off tomorrow morning, after discussing that one change with Rob.

Did you see the review (P.D. van der Walt) in *Tydskrif vir Geesteswetenskappe*? *Ignorant*. I'm sending it along "for the record".

Rob will be getting *Orgie* tomorrow. After that I'll send you the original copy, as I promised a while ago.

Tomorrow I must start working on the Colette translation for Bartho. (*How* am I going to get into working mode with such an unsettled heart – and with the practical, daily confusion of a boy for whom I must care day and night, along with an ill wife? Nerves. And, of course, the unbridgeable chasm.)

Last night, as I sat here on my own – I arrived home only late yesterday afternoon after two days of neglect, from sheer necessity, in the wake of the Great Brak River trip for Estelle's illness – a bunch of policemen arrived to arrest my "trusted" gardener, whom I had paid extra to look after the house and who, in the meantime, had been breaking into houses elsewere, also stealing some of my clothes. And I had such *absolute* faith in him.

You will say: the minor upheavals of middle-class life.

Perhaps.

But child, woman, *human being*: more urgent than anything else is *you*, along with the love I feel for you, and the great burden I must always carry with me – knowing in my own heart that I have damaged the most precious thing of all: unquestioning trust.

Misschien, misschien, blijft het hart ons over.

And in the twilight I lean wordlessly towards you and hail you.

Your hair all mussed-up on the pillow.

Your eyes half-closed, and free.

Your naked ears with their little lobes.

Your mouth that laughs, possessing poetry.

Your lovable arms and your small, still hands.

Your dark back, like the earth, and your freckled shoulders.

Your soft, playful breast, tender-tipped.

Your coy, labile tummy.

Your plumpest, most provocative mound with its deep quiet and plunging happiness.

Your narrow, smooth thighs, and the moesie.

Your calves, around which my fingers fit.

Your lovely feet, made for sand and sandals.

And your leucodendron.

All *you*.

And in the future, *also* you.

Want héel dit leven is een wond're, bange,
Ontzétbre dróom, dien eens de nacht weer vaagt –
Maar in dien droom een droom, vol licht en zangen,
Mijn droom, zoo zoet begroet, zoo zacht beklaagd.

In quiet affliction and love,
Your
André.

Castella
Wednesday, 29 January 1964

My dearest André,

Thank you for your long letter of yesterday: I have replied so often but then I put it aside again or tear it up: God, it really looks as though we are retreating along the same path as E. Eiers [Elisabeth Eybers]. Or like W.E.G.'s "Terugtog" ["Retreat"]:

Die digter worstel met sy engel
Weinig wol, baie wind:
Terugtog heet sy jongste bundel –
Juistemint

Oh, my little treasure! I've been sick-sick-sick. This long year, the ecstasy of it, and now – this rupture – as I rather romantically put it in a previous letter – I feel like a plucked flower. It is a bright sunny day outside: for the mountain and sea, quiet and open. And thank god, this morning I was down at the sea, an isolated little beach, so at least I can now sit here calmly and write to you.

It must have been terrible travelling with Estelle who was sick and Anton – greetings from the Gardens to our beautiful little boy – and, as you say: "how can I work with this agitated heart …?" Courage, André. I have not changed, though the circumstances certainly have. The invisible "battalions of lies and the organizations of hate" have finally won, it seems. I will not simply throw in the towel, because maybe you will come to me one day as a free man, and I can meet you on an equal and better footing. We're still young …

I don't know what all I said to you that last night on the telephone, which I wanted to smash into smithereens, in fact. But I know I was quite het up and so absolutely hopelessly trapped. But I am sorry about it. And what more I can say right now, I do not know –

Because I do not hope to turn again
Because I do not hope
…
Because I do not hope to know again
The infirm glory of the positive hour
Because I do not think
Because I know I shall not know
The one veritable transitory power
Because I cannot drink
There, where trees flower, and springs flow, for there is
    nothing again

Because I know that time is always time
And place is always and only place
And what is actual is actual only for one time
And only for one place
I rejoice that things are as they are and
I renounce the blessèd face
And renounce the voice
…
Pray for us sinners now and at the hour of our death
Pray for us now and at the hour of our death …

My André, will you no longer turn around for me after you have locked
the cupboard, with a smile in your hands?

Cocoon.

—————————

Thursday, 30 January 1964

REPEAT POEM US FOR ANDRÉ STOP SORRY DARLING = COCOON

Grahamstown
Saturday, 1 February 1964

Dearest – Cocoon,

Thank you for yesterday's telegram about the failure to make a moesie-girl. Given the Dutch precaution we followed, it wasn't entirely unfore-seen, and yet – "hope springs eternal"! I read "Us" again, solemnly, and with a heavy heart (as if reading was actually necessary: I know it so *well*). *My* dear, intense, sensitive thing.

I'm sending *Orgie* back to you – not the second-hand copy that you had, but the original, as I'd promised. It's messier, of course. But "straight from the heart". Rob read it in his capacity as an assessor, and he wrote a wonderful report that concludes like this: "The publication of *Orgie* might well become an event in Afrikaans literature." That's what I want so badly – not for the sake of the work itself but because it's *our* witnessing, and I wouldn't be able to endure it if something that emerged directly from *us* was anything but good.

Rob also read "Us". I'm sending you his letter, where he says it's set to become one of the loveliest poems in the new edition. And where he sug-gests that you retain "Gesien uit die Wond" ["Seen from the Wound"] and rework it a little to make it a "great poem". I'll be telegraphing Bartho today to say he should use both poems, and that you'll write to him as soon as possible about a revised text of the poem about the cross.

Rob leaves for the Cape this morning. He'll be there for a week, staying somewhere in Green Point. You'll be able to get in touch with him via Lena, Jan, Uys or Koos; maybe go through the poem with him line by line? I suspect he might also try to look you up.

I'm isolating myself and working terribly hard on timeless modern prose for one of my honours courses. I'm living ascetically, in devotion to you, feeling sad and guilty, but no longer *confused*. Because what has emerged from the distillation of my longing during this period is that I now clearly understand how my confusion did not arise from any incom-pleteness between *us*, but exclusively from the guilt of responsibility for Anton, something from which I could never distance myself. In my heart, *you* remain unalloyed, a need, a love, a great longing. And I'm not just saying this to make nice-sounding words, magic woman. It's because "my maelstrom has passed and I can now *see* clearly again".

With driving lack, continual gratitude, yet knowing that I dare not ask you to forgive me for what I broke down inside of you, with love,

André.

———————

Tuesday, 4 February 1964

WAIT FOR MY ORGIE EDIT THANK YOU BEAUTIFUL MANUSCRIPT ANSWER HEAR LOVE = COCOON

———————

Castella
22 Wessels Street
Green Point
Wednesday, 12 February 1964

My darling André,

Thank you for your letter of the other day – the one with the lots of news – and the new (?) slanted handwriting that looks much like mine. It doesn't sound as if it's going too badly with your soul – or are you just being "considerate" …? Because I'd really like to know whether you are well, and everything, and everything. Are there still fights or are you now more or less back into the "normal" routine? Or am I not allowed to ask so many questions? You say you're busy on a new work – *Bevryding* [Liberation] – what's it about and where does it come from? I'd like to read your new "Paris by Night".

I wrote to you late last night, but now I'm busy rewriting. I will in any case send you the Éluard tape this afternoon, you've wanted it so long – and which I made on Sunday evening (night). You might have to adjust the volume now and again because I was sleepy and couldn't sleep. "Nou na jou sterwe kom jy my eens nader, en soms is jy so helder en heel hier by my" ["Now after your death you come closer to me, and sometimes you are so clear and whole"]. I miss all your letters and tapes and everything – but I no longer have faith – it's as though nothing will be built between us – or are you just punch-drunk? So many questions. Frustration about the phone call – I'm standing on the other side of the glass door again – entry prohibited – it's clear that you "went back" but *really*, and different to last time. This is not a reproach, you hear. It's just so bloody sad.

I have discovered a new capacity for this sort of sadness – hail to it! It looks like an endless capacity for sorrow. And you? I wrote a little poem for you "Waterval van Mos en Son" ["Waterfall of Moss and Sun"] – that little sex metaphor I told you about – do you remember? Let me know what you think of it. And I'm busy with *Orgie* and am scrupulously making notes of the suggested amendments – and will send them next time. But I do not want me and you – our gleaming love – to die like this – with a now-and-then friendly-loving letter.

I heard from Bartho – and I'm in the mood to fly over to Grahamstown for the hell of it and to get off there, just like in our old plan, but you say nothing in your letter! I want to take you overseas with me. I have the form for the passport – probably leaving on the *Cape Town Castle* on 17 April. Simone is a problem. Everything will go very fast and quickly now and bare – quick stripping off and leaving, completely and utterly alone and screaming lonely. My darling treasure, precious creator, I can't *bear* that something so virile and positive and powerful should silt up. *You. Us.* And yet …?

Mrs Oxley is being pig-headed about Castella. I don't care. She has 101 silly little reasons – she, too – but I am leaving regardless. Your big portrait is here in front of me. Your ring I wear on my finger – my ornamental lamp – but it doesn't talk to me about Spain and Paris. It just sits there, like a sick little bird whose bloodied heart beats feebly.

I hope you don't think it's a miserable letter – as I say, the endless bottomless capacity exists. I just miss you so much. I would so much

344

like to sit opposite you and have some ice-cream and chocolate sauce and *know* ... tonight ... now. There's too much to say and to tell. *The blue in the letter*. Where are you, do you hear me, do you see me? Good night, sweet Prince. My Prince, André Prince Brink. With the unsayable and love.

COCOON.

———————

Grahamstown,
Thursday, 13 February 1964

My darling: little child, generous being,

May I *please*, just for fifteen minutes or so, come and and rest against your bosom *now*, as I experience this desperation of the heart?

I wish there was a counter somewhere where I could go and complain: "This life you people advertise is not what it's made out to be. Can I please have my money back?"

I've been feeling things so acutely in the last while: the "I", this spirit, this *body* that has experienced what it is to give and receive generously, freely – must now remain closed down until further notice, for a whole lifetime, waste itself in sterility, making a mockery of longing and yearning? It's so *undignified*.

And through it all, one must suffer the trifles that disrupt one's existence (maybe the rude awakening lies in the fact that irrelevancies can upset one so!). Like this morning's mean, piggish letter from Chris Barnard. So very "friendly". Then incidentally, in a five-page missive, this kind of thing: "Don't you guys maybe also have a post for me there with Rob? Seems it helps one a lot in getting good reviews." Or (about *Orgie*): "Have you noticed everyone's always writing about your work. The idea is old, but the form? Well, for me new ideas are a lot more important than playing little games with external form."

God, why is one so defenceless against "friends"? Against life? Everything, actually? And above all, oneself.

Always, always it is you who resides in me so light-filled, and so heavily: you embody Baudelaire's words, my "green paradise of childlike loves". A paradise from which I expelled myself and allowed myself to be expelled, now guarded over by angels with glinting swords. Most bitter of all is that I know: for the sake of my child's future it *dares* not be otherwise. But my own future? God, Cocoon, if only it wasn't so *empty*.

I am confused, terribly confused. I gave you a dream and then destroyed it. How might I have any further *claim* to happiness? I'm so snarled up in it all. I don't see light anywhere.

And how dare I come to you with all this bitterness after already wounding you? I just want you to *know*, however, that everything that's happened, that happens, and that never stops occurring, breaks my own heart, in my tiny core of humanity. One must apparently "be strong and endure". But *how* does one endure that which is unendurable?

I love you. I can't do without you. But now I *must*. And *there's* the rub. For me, too, it's a matter of "to be, or not to be", of longing for, and the struggle with "the bare bodkin" that must put an end to the futile *everything*.

You will be in Johannesburg on the 28th [to receive the APB Prize], lovely, lovely thing, woman of light. I should also have been there. We should have been able to enter the wonder-world together.

I shall have to turn the ending of *Lobola* around, and let it talk to you: "Candle, *I* am burnt out. But you – you still remain."

Still. Still. Still. Remain so, darling. Stay there, my woman. *You* live. Live without restraint, free, elevated, worthy; and *meaningful*.

I love you and kiss you gently on your mouth and breasts.

I kiss your fair-headed child and mourn the moesie-girl who never arrived.

I hail you with unembarrassed tears,

André.

Castella
Thursday, 13 February 1964

Thank you André for the doll you gave me, she's got such lovely hair. Thats why I got it, I wanted it. And thank you for the crayons that other time you gave me its such a lovely doll this. André, her name is Cindarella. You know what, there was a big fire and three houses was in danger – there was two policemans and they didnt do nothing they just watched, and you know another policeman he hided his revolver and he took off his shirt and he went to fight the others what made the fire down.

What are you doing? Are you well? And is it nice there. Isnt it raining? Cindarella sleeps with me and I wash her, I wash her hair. Are you well? Sometimes I let it hang, her hair, and sometimes I put a ribbon over it and I make a phoney-tail and sometimes I do it up. Im back from Johannesburg and Ive got new things. And my mummy is so happy. The house is very tidy and its got flowers in; Jack and Granny gave her flowers for the prize and gave my mummy a vase. Me and my mummy are well and we go to sleep so nicely.

Cindarella can do cartwheels and handstands. Wait, Im going to the toilet …

(Absolutely wanted to write to you: funny, she constantly asks how you are … I'm listening to a radio programme meanwhile – here she is again.) I musnt say I want to do no. 2. I must say my tummy wants to work (!). You see, I play very nicely and my mummy goes to work; sometimes she has to stay with me and she can't go to work. My mummy is in bed and I'm telling her what to write. I got lots of dolls and dresses, they cant even fit in a case. I have a beautiful tiny little case. My mummy is going overseas. Im going to school – to [?] Convent; I love it; sorry, Im just going to give Mummy an ash tray. And thank you for the doll. When are you coming again, and you know my mummy drink lovely

wine and smokes and she gets smaller and smaller and smaller, shes so
young (!) Cindarella's surname is Brink. Love,

S I MONE

← Cindarella.
Brink

———————

Grahamstown,
Saturday, 15 February 1964

Oh my beloved Cocoon,

Thank you for this morning's dear, sore, sore tristesse-on-blue-paper;
for the tape with its gorgeous *famous* poems – and the hypnotic conclusion with its sense of the inexorable. Time, the alarm I know so well.
Sleepy child, slumbering girl, night child, wise and heartsore little swift
– thank you also for the long narrow waterfall poem with its beautiful
ending and lovely repetitions. (To be soberly critical: take all the capital
letters out except the very first one and the "You"; maybe "heart/thief/
thief" is not entirely essential: I'd like to see a stronger whirlpool, in
just one word, penetrating the heart of that unforgettable little pool in
which I have so often, in fact always, found myself – a pool with a frisky
frog, glimmer-eyed, wet-snouted, living, trembling, tender.)
   I love you.
   Today in two weeks' time it'll be the Big Day. Darling, I'm still
searching – in this vacant Grahamstown! – for something to send you
that you can wear on the big night to go with your ravishing yellow
dress. And I want to send you a small gold cross so you can wear it
round your neck when you're overseas, cherished next to your breasts.
   17 April. To think that the heart, too, can be summarised so

348

prosaically in a mere date. But what right do I have to be selfish? (And *yet* –!)

News, you ask: "everything". But all that matters, in the world of events, is *inside* of me. My days go like this: I work from eight in the morning to midnight, taking off ten minutes or a quarter of an hour for lunch; in the evenings I go for a little walk on my own; or bump into Rob or someone when I check for post, and then spend a few minutes chatting. Play with Anton. Sleep alone. No, no fights – just neutrality. My body's healthy. (Except: my "seed spilt on the ground". I sleep with you a lot. *Plenty*. Escape.)

I'm not really "busy" with *Bevryding* yet – just thinking about it, sorting out my thoughts, because I don't know if I'll have any *time* for writing this year. It's a very old thought that's only now making *sense* to me – through us, through *you*. Even so, it's still quite vague: a stranger, an individual, "I", returns from a foreign, idyllic landscape to an anonymous Big City to deliver a message or something at an apartment somewhere high up on the thirtieth or fortieth floor, close to the moon. While he's there, it appears that a plague of sorts has broken out in the building and the whole place gets sealed off; all the doors walled up from the outside. So, there he sits, trapped with a bunch of strangers (a kind of bourgeois South African microcosm) who start committing suicide one by one till he's the only one left. All narrated very prosaically, in a no-nonsense way, with italicised passages – his longing for his home country, for *someone* there, for sense, for something beautiful – scattered here and there. Across the street, visible through a separate window, is a girl, a symbol of the past, of an unattainable beauty: *you*. They are unable to talk to each other; all they have is a wordless yearning via gestures. Until she puts on her wedding dress and they both leap out simultaneously, towards each other, into oblivion. All that is found on the hard city asphalt underneath my character is a tiny pool of blood and some seed (and perhaps a small shoot of grass emerging from a crack in the road?).

But, as you can see for yourself: it's still just a rough idea that has yet to find form – both poetry and substance.

And you, you?

How are you getting by? Where will you go and stay now? *When* are you leaving Castella – irrecoverable little dream castle with its colourful curtains, heavy with our whispered nights: we would always speak so serenely, in carefully hushed tones, afterwards …

Further, the question I have no right to ask, and yet must: Jack …?

I lie awake a lot at night with you very close to me, seeing you, feeling you – with my empty hands, and my hot, desolate loins.

Write to me, darling. I won't abandon you to silence again.

Because I want to say to you, simply, crudely, youthfully, even beseechingly: I love you, I carry you in my dreams and in my blood, you live in my eyes and my hair and my chest, my gut, my hands and my papie; in the deep, hidden seed from which the future is born every moment.

I call out to you, listen to your voice – the voice of your body; and your breath; and your heart; the voice of your virginal spirit,

Your André.

Citadel
±18 February 1964

Thank you, dearest my André,

For your beautiful golden lucky *cross*: it's not hanging between the doves. American Swiss still has to lengthen it. And for the delicate little blue-and-silver pendant. Thank you very much for the enchanting everything and for your letter.

    This is a telegram:

1. Depart from Castella this coming Saturday, probably to Mt Curtis Hotel, Main Road, Sea Point.
2. Leave Citadel 26th Feb, in a week's time.
3. Simone is flying with me to Jhb. Piet refuses to let her go overseas. God, I feel so terrible about this away-time. You'll know.
4. Jack and I tried again, but it's not working any more.
5. Therefore, overseas, naked, alone, stripped – already in that terrible train and see everything through wet windows.
6. Trying to distance myself.
7. Don't work so hard, please. You'll get sick.
8. Rather go and play tennis, otherwise you'll get FAT.
9. SLEEP enough. I am worried about you.
10. I hear you cancelled Spain.
11. I'm including a poem – also have it in Afr. It's my own translation. Beat. Bitter beat. ["I Am With Those"]
12. Letter from Simone. God, once I was also like that …!
13. *Maybe* the heart will remain for us …
14. And maybe a sense of humour.

André! André! I am overwhelmed – people, arrangements, changes. "Simply by living one does not perish."

My love,
Little Cocoon.

ps: I've always told you! (Chris Barnard.) IJ.
pps: Did the ms arrive on time? Chris Lombard promised to send it immediately. He had it. Couldn't get hold of him *immediately*. – Con.

———————

[incomplete letter]
Grahamstown
Thursday, 20 February 1964

My thinking on the novella is moving at a pace that sometimes astonishes me. I'm beginning to consider giving it a different title: *Elders Bewolk en Koel* [Elsewhere Cloudy and Cool] (referring to the "elsewhere", the lost paradise of shelter from the Sun, for which one never ceases to yearn).

It's now developing into something with blood and violence: the group of people in the closed-off flat begin to become primitive, tearing off their clothes and conducting devilish sabbaths; rape and murder occur at night … an old woman is embalmed alive and venerated … and through it all, memories of paradise, seeing the serene girl across the way, unreachable; until this small civilisation wipes itself out and humanity returns to blood and seed. I want to use it to shout out all my powerless resistance against my entrapped life; it has to be an indictment of sterility; a destruction; longing for the dream, the *one* Woman, *you*.

"Now, my love, it's time to say goodbye" – "in thy orisons / Be all my sins remember'd".

Forever loving you,
Your André.

352

Grahamstown
Saturday, 22 February 1964

God, my Cocoon,

You who become smaller and smaller and smaller as you smoke and as you drink all that lovely wine! Thank you for the agenda-like letter, and Simone's dearest chatter, and the painful, iron-hard, powerful poem. I want to see it in Afrikaans, too. I would take out "with those coloured africans depressed" – it's too obvious, not as shockingly genuine as the rest; "atom-bomb of the days" is perhaps a bit too strong given the context; the rest – oh God, it *hurt*, and it's major. Have we both changed so much in a month that I am now going to write a novella about terror and violence, and you, *this*? God, posterity will probably say it was all very good for our art – but I'm *not* the next damned generation. I am what I am – someone who loves you, sitting here, captive, experiencing ever more "the thousand natural shocks / That flesh is heir to".

Yesterday's little shock: Opperman got the CNA.

And what did I do? ... went to my room and *slept*, the whole day and right through the night ("I am with those who get drunk ..."). Even felt, with a kind of diabolical pleasure, that I was repeatedly being stabbed in the heart. Which today persists.

Well, if I must perish, then so be it. Rather that than the "petty pace from day to day till the last syllable of recorded time".

I feel I'm living in transit, waiting for something to happen, no longer bothering with anything, because what *is* there left to bother about, anyway? What do I have to *show* (your ouma would have said: "Must I go with empty hands, must I meet my Maker like this?") – all I can show is that I made you bitter and broke you down. Good – then I'll break myself down, too. And fuck the rest. To hell with the rest.

Remember life.

My child, my little child, my soft, small thing, my life: in *this* manner I do not want to write to you. I'm the one who came looking, and made a decision, and now I'm getting my just deserts. But you, but you; *you*!

353

You are still here, in the midst of my pointless days, and all I know is that if I *hadn't* known about you, then there would simply have been nothing. But in you I can believe, and know – my Namaqualand daisy, little saint, little flame.

Now, today, Castella is also just a memory. Gaudy curtains; knobbly bed with its little buttons; ash-filled orange saucers; ant-covered kitchen; white sheets; lunch in the nude at the tiny table; the always-locked wardrobe; sandals lying around; Dutch hat on the window sill; tube of ointment on the bathroom shelf; a plate of asparagus butter-sauce on the bathroom shelf; your fleet-footed movements: a naked little girl with pale buttocks and pert nipples; long, wet nights; laughing together, crying together, *being* together; kissing, touching, making love; passion; serenity; day and night; cool light and caressing darkness.

There's still another letter I sent to Castella; please go and fetch it. (I posted it yesterday, or the day before?) From now on I'll write to you c/o Bartho in Johannesburg.

I'm thinking of you, through all the current pressures and loosening of bonds; I am with you.

Will you be staying in Jhb very long? And will you be working at Citadel again, until 17 April?

I'll write again once I've emerged from this terrible depression. Just this little bit of contact with you has already helped. Because you are luminous, always have been and always will be.

With love from my ailing heart,
Your André, always.

Grahamstown
Tuesday night, 25 February 1964

My own darling,

I'm so happy we had a chance to talk yesterday, so unexpectedly, despite the upsetting news about your father's unforgiving spirit. As you say, corrrespondence is of little help. And yet, as long as that – and the heart – remain, it *is* at least something, and I must, I want to make use of it to communicate with the only person who is precious to me and who possesses human value.

And – strange, inexplicable, how subtly everything clicks in – it was precisely this little talk that lent a slightly more positive shade to the terrible misery of the past while. Now I *know*, again, that the heart is indestructible. And, in spite of your understandable resentment about going to Jhb for the prize and everything, it's a wonderful thing that's happening to you; Saturday is a *big* day. It shows that people believe in you – in the beauty you create – and the necessity, the meaning of your *being* in the world.

If only I could help with the destructive fights-fights-fights on your side. But are they *really* more destructive than a blend of neutrality and distaste? In the form of a void, a futurelessness? And maybe – says my jealous, longing heart – maybe through it all, you do in fact still sleep with Jack every now and again to get a *taste* of human contact? (On this side, the thought of "sleep with" doesn't even appear on the horizon of my sterile bed.)

The past week was just too frustrating for any kind of work (thus creating the *extra* frustration of knowing one's work is piling up!); tomorrow, and the day after, I have to do admin work, of all things: help with student registrations. On Friday, lectures begin all over again. Such a *mountain* still lies ahead of me. If only I didn't have Bartho's damned Colette translation to do as well. (After all this time – and I won't be rid of it for a while; worse than Ela Spence!)

If only I had time to *write* something. But so much work still needs to be done on *Bevryding* before its own liberation sees the light of day.

But – in connection with your Éluard quotation – people do not perish merely by living.

I spent the whole day in court today – my gardener's case. I feel *dirty* from the contact with justice. There is so little dignity in legal procedure. (In between all of this, during a break in proceedings, a jovial sergeant who'd read about *Lobola* tried to get "pally-pally" with me by stating that I must surely teach the "arts of pussy" at Rhodes. God, the *bourgeoisie*. This is how one is dismantled. This is what remains.) And you probably saw: it [*Lobola*] is likely to be dragged before the [Publications Control] BOARD after all?

The only recourse is to live small, within oneself, the "I" barricaded, armed – writing letters to you, slotting an envelope into a postbox – while *I* want to enter *you*, to be, to become, and to know about being and becoming, alone and together: a small journey in the void, but so very certain, so happy, so irreplaceable, so beautiful.

Cocoon, despite everything, in spite of it all, let us love each other, let us *be*. And let us make a small advance against oblivion and lies, with enough purity and beauty and compassion and dignity never to perish, always to remain precious.

This is how I'll be going out to meet this big weekend of yours, and the future, and everything.

I love you, and you are lovely,
Your André.

Cocoon of light, beloved,

> Ik wilde ik kon u iets geven
> tot troost diep in uw leven,
> maar ik heb woorden alleen,
> namen, en dingen geen.

Dearest beloved, I'm sending this via a carrier … just a letter, just more words, more words of love, more love, *more*.

You're very busy this weekend! You've travelled by air and felt just how precious your own little share of humanity can be, and you're happy, excited, tired, a little confused, and lost. You're wearing your yellow dress, the beautiful one, along with the tiny blue-and-silver pendant. You've just taken a bath in the bathroom of a lovely hotel.

Me, on the other hand – trying to read Giuseppe di Lampedusa and just sitting here with the book shut; it's simply too painful, too full of piety, because I started reading it during that first weekend in Gordon's Bay, in that sea-room, sun-room, bedroom, our room.

I carry with me an imaginary garland of roses with ninety-four rosary beads. With that, and with everything that continues to live on in my heart, and that's become part of my blood, my dreams, I am with you this weekend, very much with you – a big little bit. Terribly proud of you. Madly in love with you.

I don't want to use up any more words to say this. Because you *know*, after all. Just [Herman] Gorter's words:

> Gij staat zoo heel, heel stil
> met uwe handen, ik wil
> u zeggen een zoo lief wat,
> maar 'k weet niet wat.

Uw schoudertjes zijn zoo mooi,
om u is lichtgedooi,
warm, warm, warm – stil omhangen
van warmte, ik doe verlangen.

Uw oogen zijn zoo blauw
als klaar water – ik wou
dat ik eens even u kon zijn,
maar 't kan niet, ik blijf van mijn.

En ik weet niet wat 't is wat
ik u zeggen wil – 't was toch wat.

And, like the conclusion of a [Ingmar] Bergman movie, I feel myself becoming smaller and smaller and smaller, until I completely disappear in you, dissolve in your light, glow in your light.

For now, and for always: love, pride, gratitude and humble tenderness. Sister Water, you are so very needed, so modest, precious and chaste.

Smoke of dreams, ochre of the earth – that's you. And that you must remain, always.

Because I love you.

André.

———————

Saturday, 7 March 1964

AFTER CONSIDERATION I CANNOT CHIN UP DARLING LETTER TO FOLLOW FLYING TO CAPE TOWN = COCOON

358

Grahamstown,
Saturday night, 7 March 1964

Cocoon, love,

Tonight I'd like to write to Salvatore Quasimodo, and say to him: Dearest, naive old Salvatore, you were wrong, too optimistic, because the heart does *not* remain for us, after all.

Your telegram today –

So, it *was* too good to be true, after all. Everything was ready: we'd have had the whole afternoon, from two to six, to ourselves here at home; my bed in the study made with clean white sheets; my red pyjamas freshly laundered; and the hotel room booked. I'd have a "meeting" that night, and the world would have been ours from seven-thirty to eleven-thirty. You'd have strolled with me along my bush-path; my classes on Wednesday postponed so I could be with you from eight in the morning until your plane took off. God, to suddenly begin counting off days and hours in anticipation of *something*, a trace of happiness, a bit of meaning. I lived so completely for this visit.

"The heart has its own reasons –." And you'll have your own reasons for the direct flight back. "Good sense"? "Wisdom"? "Consideration"? There are so many names one can give to things that are in fact too subtle for words.

There is so much toxic, sterile, arid cynicism in me tonight.

Among other things, I looked at the calendar and discovered that your ship – "memory"? – sets sail during our term time; even for that I won't be able to come down. All the banal little realities that so often shipwreck one's dreams.

Too disturbed to write. Too wounded to live.

And yet there remains a thin little candle flame, the belief that I trust you in everything, to the fullest extent; I love you, still, still, fatally so.

– Me.

Sunday night, 8 March 1964

Sappho: "Pain penetrates / Me drop / by drop."

———————

Mt Pleasant
Victoria Road
Clifton
Tuesday, 10 March 1964

God, my André, I thought I was doing the *right* thing – on that desolate flight to Cape Town without Simone and without anyone even to meet me – I tried to write to you – Sunday, Monday, wrote to you, but things became completely unsayable.

Johannesburg and the big prize are now behind me, and now I must look ahead – I depart on 27 March. Were you very disappointed with my telegram on Saturday – ag, André, everyone would know, they always know, and how would it go with you then, and with us? I'm going away, but you'd have to stay behind with the big new changes there. On the other hand, things have already been destroyed at your home – what's to become of you? Are you still going to come to Spain? (I would so much like you to come. And I missed you so much in Johannesburg.) Nothing is accomplished here. It was all just stories. And god knows it's as hot as hell.

Here before me, the sea is making a noise. And it'll carry on making a lot of noise for me – it's a two-week boat trip. How did you go? Did Estelle go over with you? What I mean is, did you go over together? Mad! Because that's a prospect I do not relish. The going alone, the breaking off and distancing myself from everything here, and how now, with this wounded heart? Did you see your own precious poem in *Die Vaderland* with that lukewarm review? And where did you get that photo? Will we meet one another again here or there? What will the answer be, yes or no? I'm not really being silly today, I am distressed, and angry, and feel

360

ungrateful that every damn curse that has ever landed on me is thanks to my "talent" which often makes me so over-sensitive and makes me think so small. But I want to be light-hearted like God:

> Incubus. Anaesthetist with glory in a bag,
> Foreman with a sweatbox and a whip. Asphyxiator
> Of the ecstatic. Sergeant with a grudge
> Against the lost lovers in the park of creation,
> Fiend behind the fiend behind the fiend behind the
> Friend. Mastodon with mastery, monster with the ache
> At the tooth of the ego, the dead drunk judge:
> Wheresoever Thou art our agony will find Thee
> Enthroned on the darkest altar of our heartbreak
> Perfect. Beast, brute, bastard. O dog my God.

Maybe ironic, also [George] Barker. Darling, I still have to talk to you about *Orgie*. I can't write, even worse on the smooth paper with the smooth pen that slips and falls. And now I must go, to fetch my passport photos, and to get the thing signed. My travel expenses there and back were R393.30. My room here is warm and solitary and on the walls of my boredom I write your name. When I come close to you, I come close to God. Then I think of your smile and your precious hands and your big heart and all your writing and experience and thinking and your tears and your little laugh and the 89 times, and by then I have hanged myself with a rope of tears and consolation.

News: I'm sending you the *Transvaler* cutting.

And love,
Your Cocoon.

My delicate, absent, present darling,

I read your anguished, desolate letter, and the nice newspaper report you rummaged through barefooted, while playing with your stray little curl; wearing the tight slacks that drive me so mad, and the smile that makes your voice deep and full, like a pomegranate – oh, Christ Almighty I don't know what to think any more. I sat in my office and stared at your picture until I no longer minded that tears made seeing impossible. The day before yesterday, especially, was terrible, when the empty plane arrived and the bed in my study waited in vain for the weight of our bodies; when the bush-path remained untouched by the gentle steps of your feet, with the leucodendron.

And now you'll be leaving on 27 March. In which ship will you be sailing off into the future? Two weeks from today. Everything in the future tense. Will you, when you get back, give me a baby daughter? Or when I'm in Spain with you – because I'm negotiating urgently with Koos about December. There's nothing left for me here, except daily emptiness and brokenness. But darling, darling, during these two weeks I don't want to feel wounded and desolate and then not be there for you because my own heart is lost. These two weeks, *always*, I want to be with you in stillness and strength, so you can *know* I support you, carry you; I touch your breasts softly with my lips, I cast a quiet incantation over you. Because I am you, you are me, we are a true grapevine with shoots and we must bear lustrous grapes that grow from deep below the earth, up towards the sun. Your going away is not a going *away*, just a journey of discovery, an adventure. Little child, walking through an autumnal forest, stirring soft, fragrant leaves with your feet, your eyes full of wonder, and quiet, and everything gleaming, happy, and melancholic; strange and known; great and full of wonder.

You must please give me a cool, clear account of everything: is your first stop London, where I can write c/o South Africa House? Just three months in Amsterdam? (Getting to know Elisabeth Eybers –)

How long will you be drifting around? When? Where?

Did you get the other bursaries and awards?

Let me know if you need money while you're there. I want to know everything, even the most banal things. And the most beautiful, of course.

Where can I phone you in the evening? Don't be confused, Cocoon.

And write to me, despite your being so busy and on the go.

I love you. Over and above all else, *this* remains firm.

About you, Plato said: "For the poet is a light and winged and holy thing" and that is you, just as exquisite, just as pure; for that, I live, and that is why there's meaning in life.

For always and always,
Love,
Your André.

———————————

Mount Pleasant
Victoria Road
Clifton
Friday, 13 March 1964

My dearest André,

Your letter of the day before yesterday. I only read it once – but remember it always in my sad memory …

In two weeks' time my boat leaves. I've bought a few nice things, and begun to feel excited. Lay in the sun this morning, read *Tristia* – this afternoon, finally, *Swart Pelgrim* [F.A. Venter]. Phoney, with a nice turn of phrase sometimes. Already travelling, reading, untying … will I one day be able to pick up the strands again? I'm lying naked under the cool sheets now and I'm burning from the sun, your bitter letter is chafing somewhere … God,

363

Wou [Moet] ek gee
My
Goed
Wou [Moet] ek gee
My
Reg.

I conducted myself correctly. I know one doesn't feel hugely justified and puffed up about that. Do you think it was easy? Do you think I didn't want to come? And on top of it all I remembered your hesitation ... And: "the moment has actually passed ..." Hesitation because it would have been difficult for you afterwards. Unfortunately we don't only live in the present. "Want al ons dade, al ons dénke selfs, lê so ons lewensgang aan bande." You have to learn to leave me a little room as a WOMAN. I have to protect myself, and in turn protect my "precious ones", as Uys would say. *You* are precious to me. I don't want to scrutinise and speculate, but remember the Grahamstown idea was mine, right from our letter-writing time: during our last call you said: "Send a telegram about what you decide, I'll understand." And I think you do indeed understand, now. My André, I want to be reasonable towards you, not just for one night, but a reasonableness that endures, I want to give you a thoughtful, selfless, edifying love. You musn't feel "cynical": look, I am not cynical! I understand you, really I do. Do you know what? After the breaking off of our engagement I had three attacks in one day (I am ashamed of anything like that, where your breathing becomes so disturbed that you faint, struggling to breathe until you faint – and Dr Katz with his syringe). It's nothing. I come out of it and next day I walk in the sun again, in love. It doesn't disturb the inner growing and bleeding, and that's all that matters. And God knows I don't hold it *against* you. God threw the dice and it fell wrong for us, that's all. My little treasure, I would love to comfort you in some way or another, but *how*? You know I accept you as you are, and will take you into my heart as a free person and hold you there, in this situation everything looks difficult, but *not* unresolvable. (Love will find a way, so why worry!)

364

Here next to me on the bed close by, you are lying and sleeping, sunburnt, redhead, in the lovely knowledge of a Martini and a long soft night that lasts and lasts … My pure, humane human, stay faithful, in the true and broad sense, and believe in me. Don't be cross with me. Don't be *against* me, because then you are *against* yourself.

All which I took from thee I did but take,
Not for thy harms,
But just that thou might'st seek it in My arms.

I'm going to sleep now. Absent. In the wonderful womb of sleep and the childlike unconscious. Still with love and tenderness.

Cocoon Cocoon.

―――――――

Grahamstown
Wednesday, 18 March 1964

Darling darling,

I've just returned – yet again – from the postbox. And once again, nothing from you. This silence, silence, is driving me *crazy*. I know you're terribly busy, but in ten days' time you'll be gone, and then letters will become very scarce; I still don't even know which boat you're sailing on, and whether you're first disembarking in London and will be able to pick up post there.

Even if you just write a short note. Just to say "I miss you" or "I feel afraid". God, even if you have to say: "I've just slept with Jack" … *Anything*. But this sterile silence, *no*.

Did my little parcel ever arrive? It went off on Monday by airmail. It's not a gift – it's too small for that, and I'm terribly broke! – just a small something for your darling feet.

And, *ironically*: from Good Friday onwards (you're leaving on Easter day, like Nicolette!) I'll be alone here with Anton for the whole long weekend. Estelle's going to visit her mother in Pretoria. Thankfully I'll be able to phone you on Thursday night – at which number?

Oh my dear little thing, this is such an entrancing time to be in Europe: now, late winter, and then the first rush of spring, everything new, so delicate, and good.

I'm reading – Zen! And I feel inspired. Discovering with a sense of near-astonishment how much of it I've already come up with on my own, as a matter of conviction. And how much of it you and I have already experienced in sex: the full metaphysical enquiry, stripping away all that is incidental, life in the essential wonderful irrational moment – eternity. So *aware* of each other and of meaning.

Busy, buzzing little bee, retain your serenity during the superficial pressures of making preparations. Keep your passion. *Live*. And remain *human*, my little thing, my woman, for seconds, for nine months, a year, always.

Let us live
Among the white clouds and scarlet woodlands
Singing together
Songs of the Great Peace

(This is what Zen sounds like!)

Please excuse the desperate rebelliousness that my letter began with. I'm feeling calm again, because I've been talking to you, because you're so close by, and so familiar to me, so strange, holy and beautiful.

I bless you with outspread hands in the name of the lover, the loved one and the unborn child.

Love,
Yours.

Wednesday, 18 March 1964

EAST TELEPHONE STOP REACH YOU OUT OF BREATH SOMETIMES BETWEEN
SUITCASES AND SANDALS YOU HEART OF THE DAWN LOVE = COCOON

———————

Grahamstown
Wednesday/Thursday, 18–19 March 1964

Cocoon, my own darling,

It's seven-thirty, and I've worked myself into a state of exhaustion; I sit here and exist in my little spot of light, which is no more than a starting point for the eternal journey towards you, you in your unknown, warm little room somewhere that I'll probably never see, like all the rooms of your most distant past. But still, I do know it all, because it's full of you, full of your fragrance: you're freshly bathed, lustrously soft and sleepy, and sublimely untidy, like the chaos that reigns before the spirit comes and hovers above the water. With cigarettes, a bottle of wine, a pair of leather shoes, a bra strung across a chair, and you in bed, smoking or reading in your white nightie, the one that gently brushes against your breasts; your curls are tousled, with the one on your forehead ready to be twisty-twirled.

Thank you for the lovely telegram that brought me back to life with such a sense of gratitude, back from the outermost darkness; and forgive, *forgive* me my reproachful letter of this morning; it was nothing more than desperation pouring forth from a yearning heart.

Now things are quiet. Quiet? Also not. Because everything is *alive*.

"Mijn bleeke denken dwaalt tot u door diepe nachten …"

Little child of light and warmth, with dewdrops on your fingers and poetry in your laughter, and the soft butterfly in your cocoon – even if I must fall back on inadequate words: I love you.

Go far into the big, wide world, but come back, come and give me a child. I'm still urgently negotiating with Koos about Spain. I can already

367

see us lying on a pale-gold beach among fishing nets; at night we'll sit under plane trees, drinking dark-red wine and listening to the glimmering of an invisible guitar. Then we'll return to our small white room with its big golden bed and live many hours in the full, unbearable bliss, the honesty of our bodies; then we'll sleep, languid, drowsy, spent, fulfilled and sweet, your arm across me so you can hold my papie, mine folded around you, resting on the satisfied lips of your divine little sesame-cellar.

Believe, hope, continue to love. I carry you and live through and for you. The sun is still there. And the heart. And the body that will remain chaste; true to you. *Live* on the boat in the sun, and pick up an even deeper tan in your white bathing costume. Make poems, and work every day on a long letter that you'll post in London.

I'm going to sleep now, knowing that you're with me. I hail you, and say goodnight:

> 'Night to the curls of sun and smoke.
> 'Night to the ears that listen to the stars.
> To the mouth that touches the wind.
> To the speckled shoulders so lovely and smooth.
> To the back that carries the weight of love.
> Good night to the cool breasts that are always full.
> To the soft tummy that touches me as it breathes.
> To the derrière that sits so nicely, so deliciously.
> To the tanned legs that are so playful, and lazy.
> To the little feet that step over a world so lightly.
> 'Night to the inimitable leucodendron.
> And 'night, 'night, 'night, little cocoon with your one pouting lip,
>   voracious kontjie, generous kontjie, precious konnetjie.

With love and mercy and passion, and with generosity and gladness and tears, everything,

André.

Mount Pleasant is not, I hope, the same as *Mount Venus*?

Grahamstown
Thursday, 19 March 1964

My own Kontjie,

Your letter for today has already been posted. But after the call and your beautiful letter, which says: "Stay faithful, in the true and broad sense" – I want to sit quietly for a moment and talk to you, as honestly as you talked to me. My distress about your "news" has passed. And I just want to "explain", in rather woolly words, so that you can understand: I'm not jealous in the narrow, rational sense of the word. And I understand; fully understand your need, your fleeing from darkness, grabbing hold of the possibilities that present themselves to you.

What I do feel, however, is conditioned by the way I regard sex: not as a means to an end, not as escapism, not "unimportant". But: *ultimate* sincerity, *ultimate* truthfulness, *ultimate* reality. I cannot use sex to achieve this "ultimate" experience – and therefore I cannot, and I have never wanted to, sleep with Estelle after you.

This is *all* that I fear, all I'm uncertain about. Two things: first, that you do this with Jack out of need and *not* "ultimate sincerity" – and in doing so you damage your own purity. Second: if you're sleeping with him out of "ultimate sincerity" … then I fear this indicates that our own sex was not quite as essential for you; otherwise how could it take place so *soon* again?

And with that, we're back to the conversation of Saturday 18 January, and the shadow that looms behind you.

That's all. It's not jealousy. If I didn't feel this way, I wouldn't love you.

But going overseas breaks the evil cycle; out of this distance something will "gather itself into crystal". And my trust and love and faith remain pure. That's the only justification that still remains for my existence – an existence that, without you, has become extremely limited and meaningless.

"Stay faithful, in a true and broad sense."
Come to me Tuesday, please, if you can.

I love you very much,
André.

———————

Grahamstown
Monday, 23 March 1964

Love, my love,

I've already thought so much about the letter I wanted to write you for the ship, full of faith in the future, full of sea and sun. But it's me, after all, who said to you I shouldn't create pretty images of the future. God's dice doesn't fall quite like that. And now, god knows, the irony: I'm unable to send you a selection of platitudes – especially not *you*. I'm simply feeling too desperate to write today. But if I *don't* write, then my letter might not arrive in time for the boat, since it's almost Easter. Now I need your help: please believe me when I say I'm fighting my way through the bush.

> It is better that you never know
> how burdensome talk is for boys.

Virgo, virgin. Those born under the sign of Virgo are apparently practical, down-to-earth. And in that practical, sober manner you decided about the right and wrong of your coming here.

There was a time when we didn't have conversations about "right" and "wrong", when we simply loved each other.

> The conflict between right and wrong
> Is the sickness of the mind.

370

If you want to get the plain truth
Be not concerned with right and wrong.
(Seng-Ts'an)

Please: I'm just *talking*, *feeling*, not blaming, because I'm only human, and sinful.

I just want to know: if it was wrong for you to come to me, how can you ask that I come to you? What would make that "right"?

And was the very first night also "wrong", then, and afterwards? Love will not allow itself to be denied so easily.

And – it's *cruel*, but it has to be said: Why is it forbidden for me to come back to you unless I can offer you a future; but for Jack it's not forbidden to use your little body and your heart, knowing full well that he offers you no future at all?

For the sake of purity between us?

Darling, darling: we must not err on one extreme by mutually building up an ideal of purity just because we need a sense of the pure. We're just human, and impure, too; full of deceit. The little honour we discover, must arise out of our being together, must be distilled out of our turmoil.

Nothing is simple. You are virginal; you're also a little bitch. You're thoughtful; but you're also cruel. Spontaneous; but also calculating. Unemployed; and yet self-sufficient. It's because of the endlessness of what you are that I love you – and why I feel despair; why I know ecstasy, *and* agony.

This is exactly what I've been *trying* to achieve – I don't believe one ever gets it right completely, and I can only try: the fact that everything is *not* merely simple and straightforward. That you can write to me about my coming back, in complete sincerity – while you're sleeping with Jack, and *enjoying* it. The one doesn't exclude the other. And, for a while, I was wrong to see it that way.

But I'm still young in matters of love and have much to learn. I am inestimably thankful for the precious part of your life that you did in fact open up to me.

It was just, up until now, the *torture* of living chastely for the sake of someone who can't herself live for me in the same way. And *that* was my blindness – that I didn't realise you were in fact staying true to *me*, despite what was also happening in parts of your life that didn't belong to me. Nevertheless, in my limited, human way, I remembered how you'd told me you'd lived chastely for months for the sake of Jack, when he was away; for me, not even a month.

Once again, let me repeat: this *is* the way I saw things. But now I get it. I won't again make comparisons. I won't again think only on one level. I shall learn to live in irony. (I mean this seriously; I'm not being cynical!) That's why you should've been here, so that our words wouldn't fall flat, on their own, but derive meaning from voice and gesture and eyes, a whole body with a hunger, hunger, hunger, a body that's lonely, full of longing and darkness and uncertainty, flung to the dark winds.

You're going away, on a sea of light and sun.

For a while, at least, I will say, with Baudelaire: "I am embarking on a sea of darkness."

Oh Lord God, darling, now I'm sounding self-pitying again; like I don't believe in the honesty of your decision; as if I've forgotten that it all began when I left *you* in the lurch.

But oh you should've come, you should've come and talked to me, ambled with me through the bush. Since you phoned, I've wandered around there like a lost man, haven't even eaten, got soaked in the rain, lost among the tribes, lost to heaven.

But you said, and so urgently: Nothing has changed …

Everything changes, *always*.

But I believe, I *must* believe, I *know* your decision was made for the sake of love alone.

It's not just you who's going on a journey. I'm also about to go – through a very lonely region of the spirit.

"Lasciate ogni speranza, voi ch'entrate": "Abandon all hope, ye who enter here." But at some point ("on the other side of the water, bright and happy" as your ouma would say) I'll reach the light, and find you.

I hail everything about you. And I'm not embarrassed that I have tears in my eyes.

I'll write to you in London.

The heart, the heart remains.

With love,
André.

———————

Grahamstown
Tuesday morning, 24 March 1964

Dearest Cocoon,

In forty minutes' time the plane will land, empty. Today the world is all absence, all illusion:

Suffering alone exists, none who suffer;
The deed there is, but no doer thereof;
Nirvana is, but no one seeking it;
The Path there is, but none who travel it.
(the words of the Buddha)

But there's a melancholy in me as from the vine: yearning, longing, love – but clear, not murky.

Forgive me the chaos of my other letter. I don't even know if this one will arrive in time. Falling leaves …

Autumn is on its way. *Our* season. Our burning, bright April.

And Easter. I shall go to Mass on Friday.

And perhaps it had to turn out thus that you, like Nicolette, would leave. Because you, too, cannot be possessed. Ingrid, Ingrid, Ingrid: You who slept in the crook of my arm. You who, at times, were mine only. You who read poetry in that lovely voice of yours. Who, with your finger, twirled your little curl. Who could laugh so sweetly, so wickedly. You of the morning sun, of the luminous dark. The conversations of our bodies. The fulfilment, always. You, so bright, so dark. So true to me and such a little whore. You who console me, drive me crazy.

I cannot live without you.

I love you.

There is an indestructibility in our love.

Rock to and fro on your ship, and sleep; lie in the sun; play. And write poems – send them all to me.

Long for me, sometimes. Love me.

Ingrid, Cocoon, I say goodbye to you, fair child, and I believe.

André.

———————

Thursday, 26 March 1964

GOODBYE MY DARLING LONG LIVE SPAIN = COCOON

Little thing of love,

Over the past few days I've inevitably dreamt a lot about how perfect it would've been had you carried out your initial plan and departed only on 17 April – and then hidden away out here for those six days with me. For a while I was so *whole*, so sadly *happy*; the ongoing sense of longing was no emptiness, but a fulfilment – a yearning for paradise before the Evil that one *must* experience if one is to maintain spiritual equilibrium. Everything was so nicely rounded off. And I was once again able to enjoy my ritual of eating alone – nine at night, Anton in bed, the house quiet, with a can of those thin little asparagus (like little cat-peepees) that we ate at Chris's place. Remember, remember.

I listen to your voice on the tape, and every time, afterwards, I say a small prayer:

"Yesterday I was poor, but now I am wealthy."

I lie on my back in the quiet and remember and miss you; every moment is a little candle that burns in the pit of memory.

Yesterday we went to a farm, me and my little boy, who could marvel at piglets and dogs and cows; there were geese, a cat with kittens, a hen with chicks – the "wonder-filled eyes of a child"!

The only disturbance in this entire period was on Saturday when Estelle phoned to arrange for her return (tomorrow); just bare no-nonsense talk, and hearing her voice brought on such a sudden sense of unrest, such a feeling of entrapment, that it took quite a while for me to feel quiet and whole again.

Darling, Cocoon, I'm making *tremendous* progress with the novella's "conceptual work". It's now going to be called – definitely, I think: *Elders Mooiweer en Warm* [Elsewhere Fair and Warm]. I probably won't be able to start writing any time soon, but the child is starting to come alive, and it's *kicking*.

I'm sending along Maish [Levin]'s *Sunday Times* report (quite sedate, for a change!) with its characteristic jargon – and its presumptuous lie about Collins, etc.! Further than this, I know *nothing*. If they approve the book, only the complainant is notified, confidentially, and nothing further is said. Quite apart from the scandalousness of it all, it's also plainly impolite!

May I tell you how much I love you and how very much I long for you? How my days are white gulls that travel with you and, at night, come to rest with folded wings on your little breast?

Are you at rest? Are you *whole*? Being good? Living poetically? *Resting*? Writing poems? Is the sun changing you into a little fairy that dances with dainty feet across the waves? Do you dream about us at night? Do you stare at the phosphorus bouncing off the waves? At flying fish skimming across the water? Are you walking with those little feet of yours through the streets of Las Palmas; are you being conned on the streets by a thug? At night, do you drink Martinis? Twirl your little curl around your finger? Are you having a good time, hey? I'm sending a little kiss for my little chick.

Write a lot; live full of light; continue loving me.

Always yours, darling, Cocoon, with love,
André.

———

RMS Windsor Castle
Nearing the Equator

My dearest André,

Sail, sail, sail – it's late, and I was already up in my clean little bunk bed – but for a very long time I've been wanting *to communicate*; even if it can only be posted from Madeira; and then came here to the dance hall. Dear man, thank you very much for the really beautiful flowers – proteas and heather – that you sent me. Apparently there was a picture

376

in the paper. The press took some photographs on my departure from Cape Town. Ag child, there are so many new and *lovely* things – the night here, the enchanting damp blanket of the equator: the strange life at sea, the anticipation of the big adventure on the other side – and all of you, and *you*, whom I left behind. Your letters I received, your dear letters, parts of which still upset me. Of course. I thought about us a lot, and your distress, the "metaphysical anguish" about me – and, as we say here on the ship, "I do not know about life any more." All I want to say in connection with Jack is that my relationship with him is, after all, a genuine relationship. Maybe it's correct to say that the "evil cycle" will be broken overseas – I already feel so distant – I also feel lonely and cheerful – cheerful as I suppose one is on a boat – continually half-drunk from the motion of the ship and the sultry weather.

I went off to the library – where it's peaceful – alone thank god for the first time – because there are three women in my cabin and people constantly milling about. What are you doing? Do you hear me? Do you see me? What happened to the daisies? Have become wordless these days – of course you know that all too well – read Tolstoy – chat to Laurens van der Post – and try to take everything in and experience and wait for a revelation. I sometimes think – wrongly – about the return to South Africa, in a year – which in the circumstances would be a kind of suicide – and yet I have to return, to Simone. Maybe the *trip* will change everything, and perhaps you will come to me.

There is so terribly much to learn, and so much depends on the success of the trip – languages, people, works of art, and "to know about life". And the latter is the most important, and "give rest to the innocent". I don't *sometimes* miss you – I am very aware of you – and god, now what – maybe – *could* have been. Laurens's laugh, which is *just* like yours, the face or gesture of some or other young man on board. But I feel as if I am on my way somewhere – to a better insight, a bigger love (general). How do all these words sound at this late hour while all the old people are sleeping (practically the whole ship is comprised of old people). Just words, but among them a few that say I miss you, I miss your voice and your nearness – forgive and forget the other things – the only thing that matters is being together. And if *that* cannot be – then all the gods who separated us will surely find a way for us to go forwards into another life that can be precious.

My André, tender heart, I salute you and bless you, remain good and compassionate, and teach me to be like that. My study year will be genuine study – but, I already know, different to what I expected, and a lot more meaningful. Remember, like me, the "rose-garden which is ours and ours only".

Good night, dear prince – love,
Your Cocoon.

RMS Windsor Castle

My dearest Prince,

It's one o'clock, but I don't want to sleep. I want to go and walk out there in that damp blanket – but then I wouldn't be able to speak to you on paper. Listen, I don't want you ever to doubt what you meant to me – and still mean – and will mean in the future. You made me so much richer – nothing will ever be the same, praise god! And if you think you dare – give me a chance – a true chance – to love you. Here, on the ship, I can tell no one – because how would they *know* – "No you don't understand, Levi / Nobody understands / How the sight of his face moves me / The touch of his hands".

I sometimes think that faith is bigger – and you must keep believing in me – it's perhaps unrealistic to ask that – since I didn't prove that last "act of faith" to you when I was still in Cape Town. There were so many factors, darling, and one was precisely this: that I didn't believe any more. We'll have to start again, if you can, and defend, love and hold! André, I did not take the broken engagement well. We both know that, and we are afraid to say it – we are so scared of hurting one another in this way – but we both sinned against one another terribly in our lack of faith – it mustn't happen again.

And yet you are so precious in my painful memory. And I feel that I failed you with the Grahamstown thing – "if I could only see now your dear face again" – you see, I have degenerated among the English – but – and this you must believe – for you, for me, for everyone around us. My little treasure, it's a lost world this, and we two lost little people who can only seek shelter in one another. "Come to my breast …"

I'm just nattering on in a desperate attempt to bring you inside here – to this neat library – I'm so happy among the books and with writing, where I belong. But it's one-thirty and I should also be sleeping peacefully. These equator nights are far too warm and entrancing – God, a small cabin with you – Mr and Mrs André Brink – that's not a reproach – but a longing. But I'm alive, child, I'm alive – and just by living a person never perishes – tonight I truly hate the little bed I have to creep into so quietly and lie there until daybreak when raucous wonderful life breaks out around me: listen, my darling, I am not sad – but rather a "sadness at the source of (my) valiant joy". There are so many possibilities and so many Everests. Write to me, see me and remain your darling self. Let me know about Spain. Everything. And things at home. Monkey. And don't be afraid to "hurt" me. The only thing that hurts me and makes me afraid is uncertainty. Sleep with your papie, sleep with the whore.

Love, darling,
Cocoon.

PS: I *must* see the proofs of *Orgie*. It's *urgent*. And very important. I'll send them back immediately.
PPS: My body speaks to you in hope, faith and love. Till then.

Grahamstown
Friday, 10 April 1964

My bright child,

Thank you for your two equatorial letters from Los Palmas, so serene and full of the entrancing *detachment* of life at sea, an "island of repose" that came at just the right time for you, away from the world of involvements, and allowing you to see everything "from afar behind glass, as if before a god". My own heart hopes and yearns for the same, and needs it, like "a consummation / Devoutly to be wished".

I am so glad about the light that you bring (even if it turns out to be temporary?), your hope and all your radiant prospects, and the sensible thankfulness with which you formulated everything. That our faith fell short. That we must start anew. Even that "the relationship with Jack is, after all, a genuine relationship". I am learning that, too, trying to, accepting it as reality, jealous and everything but not smotheringly possessive. Just very much in love love *love* with you.

I'm living in a purer state of longing for you than ever before. When I was young, my mother kept me good by saying "Don't break dear Lord Jesus's heart". My Cocoon, please become my dear Lord Jesus. So that I must always first ask, in every little act, every day: am I being worthy of your love? Will what I'm doing light up the happiness in your lovely blue eyes – or make your lip twist into a stony expression – or make your little curl fall the wrong way?

Spain. I heard from Koos again. If we can agree about the nature of the book I must write – right now we still differ – "then you can make your arrangements on the assumption that we will give you financial assistance".

Let us dream.

And let us also be clear-headed. Going to Spain is a more drastic undertaking than going from Pinelands to Green Point, or flying from Cape Town to Grahamstown. It's not just a holiday; as you know, it's also a chance to encounter you on an "equal footing". So: I will be able to let you know at the end of May. ("Be alert and pray. Then hold firm." Do you remember this old Sunday-school maxim?)

Estelle is back. My six-day rest has been disrupted. It's upsetting because – after the silence of the past while, before she left – she's now suddenly very loving towards me. Is it my *fate* always to hurt people?

I'm working a lot. Next Saturday the university closes for a short vacation. During last year's autumn break I went to Cape Town and met a diminutive girl with petite little feet, big eyes and pert nipples, and I learnt how to *live*. This autumn I'm living like an introvert, quietly, in mature longing. And I'm going to try writing the novella. It's busy finding its *form* now.

My demonic little angel: you are always with me, like a fairy-tale that is handed down from generation to generation, a story for a long, happy evening, a tale about enchanted trees and laughing leaves, a burning bush, a man and a woman in a garden, without clothes, with an apple, a tale of pomegranates, of sadness and love and joy, of waiting and fulfilment.

Do you sometimes wear Persephone's little garnet ring?

And between your doves the little cross that protects you against Evil?

I love you.

And I send a gentle caress, with piety and longing, for the lonely, concealed little cocoon in autumn.

Your André.

South Africa House
Trafalgar Square
Saturday, 11 April 1964

My dearest André,

Lo and behold, in London. And where shall I begin? Because on the boat I couldn't really write so nicely, and to all your questions in the first boat letter I couldn't find answers – shipboard life, as you know, is indeed "living in the centre of a highly polished saucer" and lots and lots of engagements with people that you'll never see again and whose names are already forgotten, and then I landed up in the ship's hospital with a fever, a kind of English flu … did you also sail on an English ship like this …?

With the result that I couldn't get to the mainland quickly enough – the little I've seen of London so far is, of course, enchanting – but oh magtig! landed up among South Africans again, because I'm staying with a South African family (Sheddrin) – don't know how long, so write to SA House, I'll send you a telegram when I leave for Holland (where I'll be staying, I don't yet know, so you see, confused, confused, confused).

But how are you? Dearest man, I feel so guilty that I haven't written again, but it's been a continual bobbing around on the open sea, literally and figuratively and I have no ground under my feet, and here at the Sheddrins' it's a madhouse – the dogs and the people and the children and the cats have gone out for a while and the TV is quiet – but my heart is still hammering from the heart of London, the tubes I just took, and especially the National Gallery, which I visited rather tentatively today and God! that [Leonardo] Da Vinci and the giants. I no longer know whether I can say *you*, because you are so far away, and sometimes I feel rebellious towards you *because* you're so far, and should have been here now with me for a long wet walk through the misty heath. Child!

Went out for dinner last night to a madhouse where they sang old English songs – why must old people always be so ridiculous? But you,

382

my South Africa, if I could just have held your hand and squeezed it under that funny old table and laughed … What are you doing? Thank you for your last boat letter, so unexpected, my precious; and I only got to SA House on *Monday* – it was of course over the weekend – to fetch your fat letter. One lives in a kind of vacuum without news – and yet I know how you are, and sometimes feel so concerned about you out there on the godforsaken vlaktes of Grahamstown. And how are things with you and Estelle? And with the little one? And the classes? And the writing? And the soul, and the heart …

My André, often in a busy street, right in the middle of a conversation or standing before a dazzling Rembrandt [van Rijn], I fold my hands together and wonder why *this* year, this huge formative year of space and privilege all alone and how it would have been *if* and if it'd been different. I don't want to stay in England. I want my own room. And I don't see my way clear to facing the wonderful preordained time alone because I want to share it, but with my "populated heart" I meet every revelation with a memory: "The only thing that matters is being together."

Write soon about what's happening with your overseas visit, André. Time is short! I have written nothing yet – but things are already starting to happen, after visiting the gallery today even the plainest old lady on the tube looked fresh and full of meaning. But look after your precious self. Know that I'm thinking of you. And stay pure and clean and good and love me and forgive my silences and impulsiveness. Send loving regards to Rob and the rest of them and come here, my little flame in the snow.

Love and love,
Your Cocoon.

André, lovely man,

My bright and morning star – I suppose I can no longer deny you. Thank you for your dream letter – angel – God, Stratford-upon-Avon. Submerged in history here – genuine historical event of the big man. "Stop chatting up the tourists." "Say good day to the foreigner" … People in the beautiful, charming pubs of Stratford. And tomorrow we're going to "Sweet Shakespeare". And tonight, our memory night, I am lying here in a cottage built in 1500 … God, did you see that stuff? The women in these parts say … "I told myself I'll be down to 140 pounds by April 23rd …" *That* is so wonderful. Everyone is involved. The whole town is focused on the great event – the celebration of the great poet – I went to the theatre, early in the afternoon – behind the scenes where they were still diligently learning their lines – I'm here for the weekend with David Lytton and his wife and four little ones (they live here) and they take me everywhere.

Dearest André, you're being missed, do you hear, you're being missed. This is after all a big moment for me, and you have no idea how *much* I've already learnt – by the way, have met among others John Collins – leading artist and décor-artist, and Julia Hastings – 84 years old and a character so complex that I don't dare write about her yet. I'm having a meal with her tomorrow at The Dirty Duck or The Black Swan – whichever you prefer. God, and just recently we were walking along the Avon – here sat [John] Keats, and [William] Wordsworth too … and so many others … and I, insignificant, miserable IJ. But fascinated, fascinated, fascinated … I had no idea …

Darling, I got your cable saying you're coming to Spain – July or December. Rather come now. Come in July. The year is so short and so much and so new and so unique and you must come and share it … there are no questions any more … ask your heart … and come and come now and come quickly … *live* inwardly at a tempo that would

384

madden both dog and cat in grimly bourgeois, miserable South Africa without background without words without love. Do a programme about writers … Laurens van der Post ("The Man Who Cares"), David Lytton (*The Goddam White Man*, cousin of Leipoldt) ("The Lord of Life") and T.S. Eliot ("International Poet") … so far … You must come and help and come and share. No God, it can't go on like this, you *there*, whipped across your wounded *eyes*. Have a lovely sleep my prince, with love and *urgent request* for the last time and yet for always –

Cocoon. Cocoon.

————————

Ned. Zuid-Afrikaanse Vereniging
141 Keizersgracht
Amsterdam C
Monday, 27 April 1964

My dearest André P. Brink,

My God, darling, I'm here. I came by aeroplane and I have a *genuine* true-blue old-fashioned room in the attic. It is clean and nice with a double bed that takes up just about the whole room – in any case, it's better to write to the address above because I don't know how long I'll be able to stay here – it is in any case close by and the noble highly esteemed [K.E.O.] Von Bose is looking after me and is sending me to Elisabeth Eybers at eleven o'clock tomorrow morning for an … interview? Now that I'm in Amsterdam, at the Café Eijlders – I know how much I *hated* London: God, it takes everything – it was impossible for me to live and exist there … I couldn't so much as buy a stamp for your letters there … it was as if I couldn't even speak the language. The constant dinners and "entertainment" of it too.

But now I'm fine again and like the cat, I've landed on my feet. Suddenly *everything* is expansive and good. I am so glad I decided to

385

come here and to meet you here. What further plans are there and are you *furious* that I didn't write sooner? Believe me, child, England was not easy. And I was so *busy* enjoying it and "appreciating" it, I was very much like a freed lunatic. And now I'm off to buy a whole lot of food and then return to my wonderful own attic room, own room, at last! after months! I *miss* you so. And I am so excited about your faith and neverending letters ... Can't you maybe be here before June? (Tried to call B[ert] Schierbeek; sick; Simon Vinkenoog is out of jail: it was because of dagga: tomorrow I'm going to beat up De Bezige Bij!) Thank you for being so well behaved, *thank you* thank you for *everything* and that you're here. I'll write you a proper letter tomorrow. In the meantime, till then, *you – remain.*

Your
Cocoon. Cocoon.

{PS: I am horny too. IJ.}

——————

Tuesday, 28 April 1964

ARRIVED CARE OF NED ZUIDAFRIKAANSE VERENIGING KEIZERSGRACHT 141 AMSTERDAM STOP ENCHANTING [STOP] LETTER FOLLOWS LOVE = COCOON

——————

Queen's Birthday
Thursday, 30 April 1964

My darling pet,

Thank you for your little letter, which SA House sent on to me and which relieved the loneliness. Because this beautiful city is probably the loneliest in the world, and these first few days have been hard. Haven't met any writers yet – well, Elisabeth Eybers, went and had tea with her on Tuesday morning. She is an attractive person, but seems to live a completely isolated life and doesn't go around with the [?]. (I found out Simon was in prison because of dagga, but he's free again!). Tomorrow I'm going to De Bezige Bij to find out about *Lobola*. When I called, Bert Schierbeeck was ill and I hope he'll be there tomorrow. In the meantime, formal evenings here and there where you're offered the strangest food – inedible, like a bowl of peanuts and a piece of cheese – you'd starve here, man! And then of course the television replaces all conversation – I've just come from a little evening like that and saw *Romeo and Juliet* in Dutch and laughed so much at the Hollanders' guttural Ggggod! Instead of Dear God … Ag, my André.

What's the news there and what are the feelings about your Spain trip? You are so dearly devoted and I sometimes feel so unworthy – because I still lurch between my two loyalties and I wish you could come immediately and put a stop to it. Jack is so very angry with me now because I write so seldom that he sent me a resentful note about a week ago which made me feel absolutely miserable. You'll just have to bear with and tolerate me. Distance and absence are so terribly destructive unless one is constantly on guard. And this stay in Amsterdam seems so futile at the moment – and so I'll be starting at the University on Monday already (last lectures of the year).

Thank you dearest man, precious heart, that you are so patient with me in this time of little writing, almost-not-knowing, wind-blown full-well knowing. Everything will be okay once you're here – that, at least, I know. And even though I said in January that if you *do* come back you should come back *free*, I now know that we need this chance to be together – we owe it to ourselves and to life. So you must come soon to your lonely cocoon and distressed heart. As my ouma might have said: For you I would do anything … Darling, I wish I could write down and convey all the interesting and exciting strange things. Do you see me do you hear me … I have a new room in the Hotel de Maas, but only until tomorrow – then the search continues. There isn't room for a mouse in

Amsterdam, because it's the Queen's Birthday and 1 May ... something to do with tulips. People here are always celebrating something ... they celebrate their summer of now-and-again watery sunlight. But tonight the heart is more important, this pining heart without a harbour. How is *your* heart and how are you confronting your life and your leaving? Do you still know what I look like? Yes, I'm wearing *both* little rings and guess what, the blue pyjamas. And I'm lying here on a big clean white bed and I'm winding the curl around the pen.

If only you could lie here beside me my moesie-man, everything would become clear again and tenderness would like a wave spill onto the shore. But now I must wait, wait, so *long*, so *strange*, so *far* and will it really happen, my guardian angel, that I will walk out one morning and go off to greet you at Schiphol, as if we'd never been separated in this strange mystery, and will the separation, my star-crossed, deliver something that will, after all, remain strong and creative with us? How can the heart lie like this and [?] in the new life, but tonight I feel like Romeo, banished and removed from everything I love. But now you mustn't upset yourself – communication at such a distance is difficult and defective, stay serene until you can come and tell me *everything* and remain a beautiful prince in my love and longing,

Your Cocoon.

———

Grahamstown
Sunday, 3 May 1964

My own Cocoon,

It's early Sunday morning. Quiet autumn weather outside. The days are pure poetry. Are you lying fast asleep in a double bed in your little attic room, finally in an intimate space that you can call "home" again after all your "toil and wandering"?

388

Your dearest letter of yesterday made the past while's quiet longing so very poignant. Your lovable helter-skelter letters from England felt very far away, despite the enchantment. And now you're suddenly so close again.

Spain is now very much a reality, so *close by*. AND. I have been given an extra week's leave; and will therefore be leaving Madrid for home only on Friday 7 August.

HAVE YOU BOOKED YET?

My love, all of it, is beginning to feel so full of nuance, tenderness and passion that it cannot be conveyed on paper. If I say: I love you, it sounds like a proposition. If I say: I lust for you, I feel unbearable lust for you, and then it sounds blatant. What does such a statement *convey* about everything else, besides: to be with you; to lie next to each other and talk; to play with your hair, and your cheeks; to kiss your closed eyes and take your earlobe between my lips; to say hello to everything: soft mouth of rapture; smooth, speckled shoulders; narrow, dark, elongated back; arms that clutch so softly and so tighly; those hands with their lovably untidy nails; your round, tender breasts with their tiptop nipples that stand and wait pert and erect for a thirsty mouth; the vulnerability and rumbling of your tummy; your little hips that fit so well between mine; your extended legs with their shiny little hairs in the light; your fine feet, with the leucodendron; your nice cool bum. And, finally, the opening up, the ecstasy of our deep hello to each other, in your hungry, caressing little cocoon.

God, my darling, how does one wait another six weeks? But we shall light up our little flame of chastity and bathe in its glow. And then, on 20 June, we celebrate.

Please get me a room nearby. Best of all, of course, will be if they don't object to my moving in with you.

And then our play-play dream of earlier will become true as I take your little hand in mine and walk with you through the streets of Paris; we'll drink at sidewalk tables, sit in the shade of the Luxembourg Gardens, roam along the Seine and through the Notre Dame, saunter up and down narrow, crooked little lanes. And return to our room, Monsieur et Madame, and fuck ourselves half-stupid.

It's just too good, too lovely to be true. Afterwards I'll be able, like Simeon, to say: Lord, now lettest thou thy servant depart in peace …

And Spain: fishermen's villages, sea and sun, old Moorish castles, the elongated shadow of Don Quixote. I'll be the "spare, gaunt-featured" Don who charges into windmills, with my horse Rocinante. We can christen our car Sancho Panza. I'm arranging for a hired car in Barcelona so we can drive wherever we want.

"Blessed are those who love each other, because they will see Spain." (Reading for today.)

Elders Bewolk en Koel is done; finished it yesterday. 103 pages. A good deal of revision is still needed; the ending needs sharpening, too. But I feel happy. The poison has been expelled. And I think, I hope, there's something of "evil beauty" in there, something of a contrast between the lyrical and the terrifying, which the book *must* have in order to be anything.

Ag, but then there's censorship, too …

Beloved one, lovely you: write *everything*. About everyone you meet (what's Eybers like?), everything you see.

Don't go to the Vijf Vliegen: I want to take you there!

Go see the Volendam.

Let me know if I can bring along any books or other stuff for you.

Sleep with me. I'm sleeping with you, a lot. A last little kiss for the little clip between the lips of the purse. And the sign of the cross, with piety, over your forehead and your heart.

With love, always,
André.

Monday, 4 May 1964
Freedom Day Tomorrow

Dearest André, Treasure, Letterman, Redhead, Heart of the dawn,
Hello! Hello my fish! Hellooo little fiiiiish!

I am so happy – I received a letter (eventually) and this afternoon, a
room. A *beautiful* room, just below the Kommunistiese Gebou near the
Leidseplein and here is the address: 477 Prinsengracht, Amsterdam C.
But for now, write to the association until I've let you know the name
of my landlady too, I think it's Mrs Bosse or something like that. She's
old and lovely, a big doll sits in her witch-room, and she writes poems.
This is what the room looks like and look, my pet, there's a big drawer
under the bed I can squash you into. Because you're going to stay here
with me. A hotel in Amsterdam, that will not work!

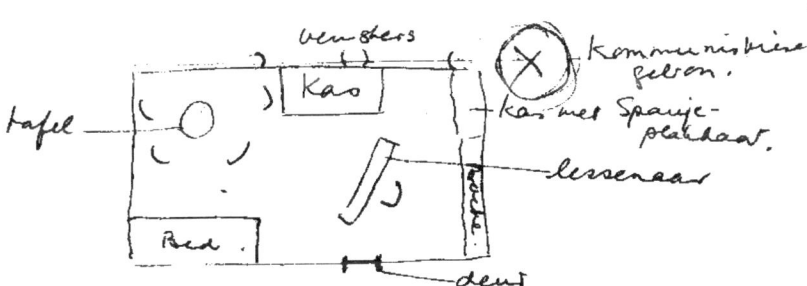

It's big. It's authentically Amsterdammish, with thousands of little
stairs, creepy corridors, but away from all the swarming, with a view
on to roofs and its own rooftop where one can apparently (in summer)
lie and tan. I was completely disheartened about the room situation
and then I got it through Dutch acquaintances: and him you know too:
the lord H. Brinkman. You had to accompany him once at Potch. Do
you remember? You were about third year, he says, and rather shy.
I've landed safely among some theology students who have healthy
self-doubt and who invited me on their bicycles and the backs of their

scooters to cosy little pubs on the Leidseplein. And do you know what? I'm probably going to perform in an Afrikaans woman's programme for Radio Wereldomproep Hilversum. In any case, I have to make them a programme about IJ whose arrival they announced. So you can see for yourself how the Lord guides.

I get homesick for London sometimes and I'm going there again for the weekend. And I'll also learn Spanish when I'm peacefully in my room again – so that we can at least see on the tape how it is in Spanish too. Bring your *Elders Bewolk en Koel* with you, remember, and also proofs of *Orgie*, which I must edit with a razor blade. And don't work yourself to death like that, because I want to brag with you and so you mustn't be so thin and you must have long hair. Think about that and in the meantime put away the scissors. Everyone here thinks you are astonishingly beautiful, from the photos.

Thank you for the motto idea. Do you think this is sufficiently dignified: "En vergeet maar / van geregtigheid dit bestaan nie / van broederskap dis bedrog / van liefde dit het geen reg nie" ["and please forget / about justice it doesn't exist / about brotherhood it's deceit / about love it has no right"]. I'll send you the whole poem. Everything's still so mixed up because of all this moving around. Sorry about "Waterfal". It was a poetic slip. You can print it anyway. One should in any case read it more than once. And don't be too placid over there. Does she know you're coming to me? Of course. But doesn't she *say* anything about it? How on earth does one live ...? And now I'm getting sad again. But I await you in all joy and cheerfulness. No, you are not completely distant, liefsteling. Because see, I am already used to you. And I'm even beginning to believe that you love me! But come *quickly* then. I'm booking everything tomorrow definitely for our pilgrimage. Come soon and surely; I miss your moesies and little laugh and papie and your beloved hands always,

Your Cocoon.

Darling André,

I am neglecting you terribly in not writing. You must please forgive me, because I still feel so horribly dislocated in this strange life here, which at the moment makes no sense to me. Thank god for you and Spain! Did I tell you that I've received another bursary – from the Ernest Oppenheimer Trust? And listen, I've booked with KLM like this:

Amsterdam – Paris: 22 June with flight KL 401 (9 am)
Paris – Barcelona: 26 June flight AF 527 (11.50 am)
Barcelona – Madrid: provisionally IB 211, as you said. Fixed up.
And then return to Amsterdam.

But André, I don't want to come back here. Do you know, I've only met one poet and that was Elisabeth Eybers and she lives completely isolated and is always busy with God-knows-what. With the other people I've met, absolutely no contact at all on whatever level. But don't be too concerned. Today the weather was nice and I went wandering around. Did you ever do that? Strange, hey? And on Friday night I went to look at the whores at the Walletjies. At the Zeedijk. Reclaimed land. But I don't really want to send you such a negative letter. Because there *are* nice moments everywhere – and there is longing and love and dedication. And I bought myself a nice light coat for the plane, and a striped dress that buttons up the front because you'll be impatient – like me. Tomorrow I'll be going to a gymnasium where one can at least take pleasure in one's body. There's no mirror in my room and everyone finds it very annoying when you take a shower (there's a mirror at the shower in the kitchen). I find it really necessary to be in touch with my own body. Otherwise it's just like a nun – precisely.

On Friday I was also at Radio Wereldomroep. They did a voice test and if it is successful they want me from August for a year – in other words until August 65. I met Abraham [H. de Vries]'s fiancée at my function in Johannesburg. Your description more or less fits, but as bad as that she cannot be. You say "if you're struggling, go and speak to the man whose name I sent you". I don't recall any such a man at all, my dearest boy. And I am STRUGGLING. Not with accommodation, but with the whole goddamn affair they call life and I have never needed you so much. To just be able to see your young familiar bright face again among all the old antique buildings they boast about! André, it's not always so serious – I mean this spiritual need – but maybe today especially because it was a nice day and I had to gather all my warmth into a bunch of red tulips that I could give my weather-beaten old landlady.

PS: Why is your writing so weirdly small these days?
PPS: Where is our little castle?
PPPS: Where is the snow of the year before last?

It's almost your birthday, my lord – 29. Tomorrow I'll buy you something nice. I love you. I wish I could write you a nice poem, but for that we will have to wait. An extremely boring teacher has just visited me here. And his name is André! I called him Klaas by mistake, magtig, what could it all mean? A crude South African wanted to kiss me the other day.

Yes, I remember last Ascension Day. That wasn't the Tent Day, was it? And you were certainly not inexperienced. You were ex-ce-llent. You're a little like the gamekeeper (I read *Lady Chatterley's Lover* in Dutch! Murder!). I can't resist reading all the vile pathological books that are available here.

Afraid the letter's jumping around ever more wildly. But for you I can write anything. I had a letter from Jack. He says he always knew what (I) would do! (In relation to you.) "But that's a dreary subject." He says he might still go to America sometime this year (Carnegie grant).

My André, I live here without any outward shape or form. For you. For Jack. For Simone. And that is probably good. It *must* be good. One has to believe in something. I know you won't disappoint me, my precious virtuous man.

We'll probably still be arguing in the days of the flood. So bring lots to read! And how's it going with the Spanish? Will you teach me? I'll try in any case to get the necessary here. It must be most kak when you don't understand the language at all. Well, my liefsteling, my-André-who-is-coming-to-me, tell all. Especially about your soul and what do other people say that you are coming? And forgive your angry Con for restlessness, shallowness and lightlessness! Come soon, and save my immortal soul!

With love,
my little boy,
Your Cocoon.

ps: I wrote a poem and was deeply disappointed at the appalling lack of talent it revealed. IJ.

<hr>

C/o South Africa House
Trafalgar Square
London.
Friday, 15 May 1964

My dearest André,

Just an sos-note to let you know that I left Amsterdam sos – don't get a fright now because it's just for two weeks. I came by night ferry last night from the Hoek van Amsterdam and arrived in Liverpool at nine this morning. My God, Child, it's a beautiful city and all, but the brutality and narrowness and mistrust: And it's just a plain waste of time if I can't get hold of a single *one* of the Dutch writers. So – I've secured my room and gone wandering. Of course, because I do everything on the spur of the moment, I arrived to find no one at home in London, but strangely enough I feel in any case more at home. It might be throwing in the towel and all that, but now I'll arrange things better with the writers from England, and I luckily still have the room until the end of June. And I asked the dull, devout NZAV to address your letters here for the first week. The esteemed mister Von Bose talks a great deal though he is not up to the job. The night ferry was lovely, and the trip very pretty through The Hague and Leiden. I'm going back with the day ship. At least I wrote a naughty poem, so, here goes:

Two Hearts

Two hearts I have
the one pumps blood
and the other really looks like
an appelliefkosie
or a paddatjie.

It's a nice day in London. And probably also in Amsterdam today. But love, I am glad to be here and I'm going to find myself a room and be serious. I am good, and open, and naturally chaste, and miss you and Spain. Don't take offence at the fact I can't take the Amsterdammers right now with their damned prejudices against everything that is South African or German or English.

The boss of the house (the people I stayed with last time I was here) just called and it looks like no one knows what possessed me – at least he sounded happy to hear my voice! But you do understand, don't you? Maybe an emotional deep sea, because I was left to my own resources so much there. Radio Hilversum hasn't reported on the position – but they know in any case that I'll be away for two weeks. Just before I decided to come, I called Elisabeth Eybers – I think I told you, to chat. But even she was too busy to meet me. Seems I have much to learn! Arrange ahead of time, think ahead of time, and adapt, always just adapt. Hopefully it will still come. I'm still a novice at the art of travel.

Have behaved primly in any case and didn't curse the murderous traffic even once. Now, my liefsteling, till tonight or tomorrow, and keep your window open to Spain, where the puzzling pattern will indeed fall into place, and maybe, if we are lucky, become meaningful.

From the heart,
and the other,
Your Cocoon.

PS: Planes booked and paid and ready. I.
PPS: To the Tate, with William (Plomer) (62). IJ.

C/o South Africa House
Trafalgar Square
London
Thursday, 21 May 1964

My liefsteling,

I received your little letter today; you know, the disconsolate one. Written on 12 May – time, distance, presence – God, my André, that Tuesday (12 May) I was probably equally disconsolate. Everything was going quite well and civilised in Amsterdam, but I'll die if I have to go back – listen, beloved man and slumbering papie, the night ferry was lovely. By nine o'clock I'd landed at Liverpool St and then off with a family to their cottage in Cambridgeshire. Yes, all the heaths and the beauty and a real village barn-dance nearby. You should see how your Cocoon can *shake* by now. Do you far-away people know the dance yet? On its way out. The kind Australian friend also went along and now I'm staying with her for a while in Highgate; but how long, I don't know. All I know is that I am definitely not returning to Amsterdam before 30 May. So, letters to SA House, because a permanent address I do not have and don't want for the time being. I'm beginning to learn little things about life that I only intuited before or maybe only came across in books; yours too; and am starting also to develop quite a sense of privacy because it is so necessary here – growing up – 21! And slowly I am learning to love the English, and *you*, even *more*, because you, my darling André, are so English. That you are, and that's final! Because the Dutch themselves say this: we Afrikaners have inherited far more from England than from The Netherlands. It's all so strange, because I had such a different expectation. But my inner war with the Netherlands is not over by a long shot. Maybe I'll carry on living there for a year, working for Radio Wereldomproep. I am now busy warding off the intimate charm of The Netherlands, as well as that of England: landscape of poets. Out there in the miserable English rain is a tree – this is Keats's world – and it says: "All things betray thee, who betrayest me."

But dear God, darling André, you: you mustn't work so much and sleep so little – in God's name look after yourself because I say so: and don't take any notice of the attacks from whoever in *Standpunte;* in any case, send me a copy via airmail; and listen – if they can change a Nicolette into a Beatrice (also my mother's name), you haven't yet strayed too far from the point! But I am worried about you. At all costs you must come away from the narrow-mindedness and the rot of those foul attacks. Don't for one minute take it personally. Because then you become hopelessly involved in it, and you are far above malice. Come and lie here against my heart, dear heart. I know all the answers concerning your related [?]. My dearest André, I want to ask you for a great favour and gift. You must *trust* me – like a soldier in a war; and like I trust you. I wish that I could comfort you with something, with a nearness as I alone can comfort you, but we have to rely on words; and words have always been my enemy, "my quiet child", Abraham Jonker always called me. That was then. And even before. And long ago. My treasure, I am so pleased your hair will be long, but you've really got too fat! Fifteen pounds! And how did you achieve that? As far as I know, I am still just the same; inspected myself well in bed (with a mirror) this evening, around 115 pounds and tanned! Mostly lay in the sun this weekend in Cambridgeshire though at least (I'll show you the photo) scrubbed a floor too. Strangely enough, I still have a cocoon, and everything –

Saw Johann van Rooyen today and Laurens van der Post – they both know you're coming – but don't worry, they're discreet (and they also rather love me).

How is Estelle "very loving"? André, if you were here I would murder and love you in a rage.

Your
Cocoon.

I asked my bank in South Africa to send you R20 for your birthday. Happy birthday, 29! Worried a small parcel would get lost and airmail and insurance and so on, you probably need money, and buy something nice.

Cocoon.

———————

Friday, 29 May 1964

HAPPY BIRTHDAY AND LOVE FOR THE YEAR AHEAD PRECIOUS = FROM COCOON

Amsterdam C
June 1964

My dearest boy,

I've really neglected you with letters, do you forgive me? Because I've
just done a quick tour of Europe – so where shall I begin? My Australian
friend Fay and I decided to go on a little tour through France and
Germany because she happened to have leave and so we did! You also
got a telegram from Berlin for your birthday. I am now sick and tired of
flying and rushing and I miss my own little child. I have rather serious
doubts about Europe, which I don't quite dare put on paper yet.

But one thing I know: I don't like Holland. Not for a whole *year*.
And now that I am back, I've also not sought anyone out. I chat to the
old lady here in the room next to mine and go to the Leidseplein with a
friend who lives on the floor above me. And read. And walk. De Bezige
Bij is busy with the translation of your book: did I already write that,
little darling? I will still go and call on them but to tell the truth, I am
so thoroughly the hell-in with Holland that I am completely withdraw-
ing to my own little world. The old lady next door just brought a little
present for Simonetta.

Thank you my darling André, for all your hundreds of letters that were
awaiting me here in Amsterdam. You are so loyal and you NEVER reproach
me for writing so seldom. And look! I don't even go searching for that
nice theology student and I don't go on Harry Brinkman's scooter any
more. And yet I have much to tell and I'll do so when we're together,
because it's actually just chatter. It's now less than two weeks and then
you land at Schiphol and then life must become good again! And why are
you AFRAID? Because we haven't seen one another for such a long time?
Six months, my treasure? And then we might fight too? God, I would so
much like to get out of this sadland and back to the sun. It's raining, and
I am getting whiter and ever "smaller and smaller" from longing.

I am busy with *Orgie.* It looks nice printed and I am following the
changes because I do still remember the MS. I have some changes for

you, which we can discuss together. In God's name, bring the proofs with you again because there are parts I still feel unhappy about. Apart from those, bravo! And bring *Elders* with you and don't worry about the price of the car and don't be so nosey about the amount I got from the Oppenheimer Trust! I have LOTS to discuss with you, god I was alone: "All those yearning looks I had bestowed on the buildings and statues, I had looked at them so hungrily, so desperately, that by now my thoughts must have become part of the very buildings and statues, they must be saturated with my anguish." And tell your government over there they should send their political prisoners out of the country for torture! *These* cities! *This* waking nightmare!

Waiting in Amsterdam

I can only say that I waited for you
through western nights
at tram stops
in lanes
by canals
and the tower of tears

You came
through the forlorn cities of Europe
I recognised you
I prepared the table
with wine with bread with grace
but unperturbed you turned your back
you took off your cock
laid it on the table
and without a word
with your own smile
forsook the world

Ingrid Jonker

No, my André P. Brink, I still don't completely believe that you are coming here – it is a dream that was never dreamt. Miracles no longer happen, do they! But I will at least go and take a peep at the airport. And don't think we'll be going directly to the Prinsengracht, because the whole of Wereldomroep and Bezige Bij are also waiting for you! God, now Hilversum is playing "Nooi nooi die rietkooi nooi". What other forms of torture do they still have in *this* impossible country?

At least I still laugh. A lot. And especially at Henry Miller. "His only ambition in life was to get a fuck every night." And boy do I sleep! In the day. Because at night I sit on Leidseplein until "Dames en heren, dit is die hoogste tijd" and read until day breaks over the Kommunistiese Hoofkwartiere. All of it probably good for the soul! Till later! Till tomorrow! Till 20 June! Love, my dear prince, 'night my André,

Your Cocoon.

PS: The auntie next door tells me she killed herself laughing over my sad poem, that "cock" is "pikkie" in everyday Amsterdam Dutch. IJ.

—————

Amsterdam C
Saturday, 13 June 1964

Dearest, my dearest child,

It's a beautiful evening with the grachte lit up and everywhere music and bright light; I've just come back from a documentary film about the Spanish Civil War, but even that cannot dampen the enchantment of the lovely evening – in ten minutes' time I'll be visiting some friends on the Heerengracht and then to the Leidseplein. But first I want to say hello, boy, and goodnight all the way to Schiphol on Saturday. You ask if I believe it. Of course I don't believe it, but am starting to believe in it a very tiny bit; bought nice things today; beautiful, and am going to book on the Leidseplein because my landlady might be difficult. Tonight it's as though I've awoken from a long winter sleep and the Amsterdam buildings are standing more sturdily on their paws. It's not even worth writing "news", because in a week we can chat the hind legs off a donkey. God, do you know how lonely and desolate I felt in this Netherland? But now everything is good again and is beginning to fall into a pattern. That's not to say that God is not a God of surprises because maybe tomorrow it'll rain again, but it won't matter. Darling, thank you for you. Bring everything that you have and what is mine with you and your beautiful rescuing hands. I call you by the name you are mine: André.

Till 20 June and afterwards.

(Chaste Cocoon) Your Most-Cocoon Cocoon.

Follow the instructions in the little book on the aeroplane. If you have to jump with a parachute, land at 477 Prinsengracht. Let your hair grow long and dress nicely. If the Wereldomroep is there, they must at least see what I have in you. Till then and till further, my unerring heart,

Cocoon.

PS: SLEEP on the plane. And EAT everything they give you. And drink a whole white John Collins to our Spain. Meanwhile, I drink to you and a horizon of joy. IJ.
PPS: I've *got* my DC. Unused, of course. Presumptuous! Hell!

Paris
Midnight, Tuesday, 30 June 1964

My dearest André – Just to say I've arrived safely in Paris; at Breyten's house things are still in disarray; today I'm in Hotel NOUVEL ORLÉANS. Sitting here on a nearby terrace and quickly writing: only arrived at Breyten's at around nine o'clock: wait for taxi and then the long trip through the city; I search everyone's faces for answers to impossible questions about the impossible: but thank god Paris is still here. I will begin to feel at home here. You're probably asleep already: in the green room without eyes. I am worried about you. Reading for today for both of us: "You have got to be good ... if you are not good your love is a mess and your courage a slaughter ..." or "vitality shows in the ability to start over".

Or anything. Or love.

Your Cocoon.

"If it *must* be" (Japanese greeting)

Paris
Thursday, 9 July 1964

My dearest André,

Although I haven't heard from you I want to let you know – at least to prevent you from hearing the "news" from others – I am going back to South Africa tomorrow. I don't want you to reproach yourself about this in any way at all and rest assured, if it is at all possible I'll come back, this time directly to Paris. In South Africa I am immediately going to start learning French, to work, and to save money from the beginning again.

I wasn't able to stay with Breyten and them after all though Breyten nevertheless helped me a lot.

What's going to happen to *Orgie* now? I'll go and see Bartho in Johannesburg immediately, also in that regard, I just hope he's home.

No one except Breyten and them and McNab and Jeremy know that I was (am) back in Paris. And I asked them to keep it quiet. Chris [Lombard] is apparently posting a book (*Windroos*) to me in Barcelona – keep it for yourself, I'll get another one from Bartho.

Paris is still beautiful.

Alas, child, that is probably all the news. I'm enclosing a poem I've just written. A bit of an Éluard-rhythm. Don't know. If you want to you can use it in *Sestiger* – if you want to you can leave off the dedication. Anyway, it's for you, with love from,

Cocoon.

ps: A little late – but no baby.

C/o Volkskas Ltd
84 Adderley Street
Cape Town
Pls also inform Cooks. Barcelona.

C/o Volkskas Adderley Street Cape Town
July 1964

Thank you for your little letter, which I at least received just before departure. In a way it feels as if I was never gone and in another way Paris is still swarming around inside me. I'm trying to get my old room back here. But god knows I won't be here long either. Jack is as one should presumably expect angry and cold and sits and reads to his children for hours, probably so that he doesn't have to have too much to do with me. What's the point! And what's the point of everything. Good remains good whether in Brakfontein or Brussels and angry remains angry {misquote evil remains evil} ... And there is one ray of light. Simone is flying back to me tomorrow until I go to Paris again. Thus the old contract will only have to be changed slightly. So you see yourself how wonderfully the Lord leads. Best just to type out for you a little section from my wonderful diary:

Paris. 10.7.64. Flying over France, soon into Spain and over Madrid. Hello André, where are you roaming? I had your little letter today (maybe too late, I'm ready to depart). I'm flying at 23 000 ft. Will have to tell Bartho and the rest that I have a lot of money over and when I've learnt French I'm coming back to Paris. Because come back I will. I never thought I'd have to go back to South Africa like this, without excitement, unsure. If Jack is cold and angry, it will just be another cross to bear. "We are dying Egypt, dying, / And not expecting pardon." The light in my glass is pretty, the sun shining through the aeroplane window through the clouds is pretty, my two hands around the glass are pretty, with the nails that I had done in Barcelona. Toledo, even though we become more lonely and more tired every day ...

Toledo, Spain. I hope you never see a brown donkey André and especially not a good bullfight. This is what you must write at the top of your bullfight: "You have got to be good ... if you are not good, your love is a mess and your courage a slaughter." [F.] Scott Fitzgerald.

LISBON. 8:45. Deeply moved by view of the harbour; little boats, man with red drums giving the all clear for the landing. Enchanting Lisbon. "Give beauty back, beauty, beauty, beauty, back to God, beauty's self and beauty's giver" ... dusk on the dying hills, watchtower with two red lights in the distance, something about this city looks so homely ... god, why are poor people always so decent – sunset a red scarf around the decorated city – why didn't we come here? Or everything just looks that way from afar, does the world perhaps always look beautiful to God?

The air stands there so quiet and red like a matador, above an unbeliev-able orange, green, blue, purple, and then the black wing of the plane.

11 July. After sleepless night with at least other wakeful passengers we landed at 6:30 at Luanda. In a while I must go and do my face, "to prepare a face to meet the faces that you meet". God, it's going to be a mess. Everyone disappointed, just the prickly Annette [Barnard] who gossiped about me to Breyten, will be crowing at the news. She's stupid. I'm going for a swim this afternoon even if it's snowing in the sea. Below me is a piece of ground God smoothed out very well. It's ghastly. Probably the Sahara. Lord, let the daisies blossom there!

Thus ends the celebrated trip around the world.

So there, child-mine, not that I think my diary notes are exactly interesting, but oh well! at least it's a little contact. I saw *Windroos*. Ugly cover. Horrible photo of me, and that biography! How does one manage to swallow it all in one go without mercifully choking? I've written a poem about Cape Town, and am sending it. But it's for *Contrast* if they want it. "Reis om die Wêreld" ["Journey Around the World"] is for *Sestiger*. If you want it. I'll write again later. I am tired now and feel dramatic. Me! Miserable human!

Love,
Cocoon.

Sunday. I now have a better address:

C/O BAYSIDE HOTEL
SEACLIFFE ROAD
BANTRY BAY

and a beautiful room, Simone sleeps here with me. It's wonderful to have her with me again; tomorrow I'm going to look for work and a school for her (it's school holidays now). André, André, tonight while

407

I was unpacking that nice photo of you where you're looking down was gone! You'll probably be interested in my reception here, well, so icy that I went to sleep at Lena's last night and I didn't even overnight in Uys's room. Jack "no longer believes in (me)," etc. *Now*. Saw Tippie this evening, do you still remember? God, "where are the snows of yesteryear?" And I could see the old flat from my bedroom window. Paris seems very far but vivid. And you there in warm Spain probably know by now that I am 6 000 mad miles away, and it does indeed matter. What did we do?

Your Cocoon.

———————

Bayside Hotel
Seacliffe Rd
Bantry Bay
Wednesday, 15 July 1964

My dearest André,

I never realised how terribly far and unreachable Spain is until yesterday when I first became aware that I am in Cape Town; and a changed Cape Town, because I see everything now with new eyes and with a terrifying calmness. Jack's intransigence surprises me more and more, and I think that the night when you lay "dreaming in my arms close by the Seine" was the death blow for that relationship. Still, it leaves one a little dismayed – this ephemeralness. And with you, boy? At hand, your *Tristia*:

Ons was so aan die gaan gewend
dat ons gemeen het: gáán is goed.
Maar elke gáng word: sterf-orent.
Die end is bitter. En dis end.

Still, still, what a joy to have Simone here. I got her into the school close by this morning: Kings Rd Primary. And went to buy her a school uniform. Brown and green. She starts tomorrow. And now I must apply for work as a translator, get enough money again, and try again. Let Paris make everything bright and strip away what was "show and ornament". I think about you constantly.

Love, your
Cocoon.

PS: I have your two white underpants here. IJ.

––––––––––––––

Bayside Hotel, Seacliffe Road
Bantry Bay, Cape Town
Wednesday, 15 July 1964

My dearest André,

Today I looked at the map of Spain and saw that you may not get my letters in Barcelona, I didn't realise Granada was down from Madrid. Therefore, a letter to the address you passed on: I don't know now on which wanderings you'll receive what. In your letter to Paris you ask *how* I live, *how* I am. On the one hand, I no longer AM. "Mommy is no longer a person just a ..." *Just an a*. Use that if you can: it sounds like *Orgie*! I've been to the Alliance Française, I'll learn quickly, man. Just a pity there are only two classes a week, Mondays and Wednesdays. When I arrived there and thought of Granada and roses and pomegranates and you, I wrote a few lines on the bus, but my mood faded when they stopped at the police station to drop off a coloured man for 5c, god! I'm sorry, but I can't take it any more, not *now*, not AFTER. I phoned Koos, who was surprised of course, but didn't phone back. I went to look up Freda Linde, fetched your photo from Juta's, and saw Louis Hiemstra

409

who asked me to call him by his first name, god, he and I laughed so about the French class! (He's also taking it.) I dropped Simone off at school and fetched her (mommy-mommy) and bathed her and bundled her into bed (just the little blonde head sticking out) and Jack remains silent like Jack. "True innocence can never be corrupted by cruelty," says F. Scott Fitzgerald, have probably written that to you already, and I'm not hinting directly at *you*! I fear I'm beginning to lose my innocence; in this respect. How are you, my little garçon? I still love you, in *my* way. That's all that matters. Heavens, how bright the memories are! Now I must rather stop. Good night, dear prince,

Your Cocoon.

———————

Bayside Hotel
Seacliffe Road
Bantry Bay
28 August *until* 10 September 1964

Dearest and dearest André,

Moe als ik mij en oud
als ik mij voor mijn tijd voel worden,
is mijn gebeente koud
van ingevroren haat tegen de horde
die 'k nu al in geen weken heb beledigd,
omdat ik niet meer kan,
omdat ik niet meer wil,
omdat ik niet meer weet,
of ik niet beter stil
wat er nog is aan ziel
laat weiden in de rust,
in wat mij hier nog lust

410

aan wat er rest aan geur
en licht en klank en kleur
en stilte.

Immediately after your letter of almost a week ago I wanted to write;
beautiful child, *you* know how hard it is. To be honest, your first letter from Grahamstown made me so angry that an (amateur) painter
here made a portrait of me entitled "Virgin with Thorns" (!). That you
are able to feel "whole" – I should probably have been happy, but I'm
human (still). I didn't know *what* you really felt – whether you didn't
rather want to forget – *obliterate* – the whole Ingrid Jonker. André, I
have lost so much self-confidence. There have been so many defeats.
And yet, sometimes "only now after your death, do you come closer /
Now I see you and possess you". Perhaps then we can sometimes still
write to one another pro amico. But it makes one so *despondent*. Why
in the name of God were we created so similar?

News here: you've probably seen the Sunday Slimes yourself where
I at least say something about *Orgie*. Who is your new mysterious publisher and may I please see the page proofs? It's *important*.

On 10 September I'll be moving to a beautiful little flat in Beach
Road, Sea Point [Three Anchor Bay]. I've bought a few pieces of second-hand furniture and a three-quarter bed – just for the illusion. I
want to make it nice and live nicely. One of these days I'll be 30 – and
probably find a certain rest and stillness. Also for Simone. Don't know
when I'll see Paris again, but I surely will, one day.

Yes, Jack is friendly, but distant. You probably know as well as I do
what that means. If you are interested, yes, I am chaste and Barcelona
was, as far as I can tell, the end of my existence as a sexual being.

I probably shouldn't leave you so long in that wonderful silence, but
I *know* so little. And write, god, write all the time, the holy name of
God. I would love to *see* you, but then, and then, and then …?

spel wat ál verder na buite toe
kringe laat uitdy; weg,
weg van die klein, skuilende

verontregte, verontwaardigde,
ding: wat in die looggat
afkyk: homself gaan bewapen.

And so, I don't see at all how wonderfully the Lord leads – as you said in your first letter from Grahamstown. And look, I don't want to write you a depressed thing. But to say "don't be worried" would be one of those false, classic lies. I am worried myself – as you can probably conclude!

News: I'd really like to hear about your *Negentig Dae* – was quite involved with "something similar" – by the way, one never speaks of "negentig dae" – it's always Ninety Days. Finished and klaar.

"Mamma" ["Mommy"]: of course you can use it for *Sestiger*. A small one – *written in a rush* – is going to *Contrast*: "Wiegelied vir die Beminde" ["Lullaby for the Beloved"].

Tula tula
your little body rolled
your little lamb sleeps
deep in his wool
tula tula

You say little about the "quiet distance". I probably have no right to know but I do sometimes wonder: about *you*.

Yes, I'm swimming already. White costume and rings and god! Mostly go to friends for the weekend. Not working at Hiemstra any more. The dictionary is finished. Hardly dare to think of Paris. The enchantment and the defeat, and also the "mixed feelings" – too much. Actually see very few friends. Sorry, love, this is a rather small sad old attempt. But I no longer live gladly. And must I really post this now? Where and when will the summer's day come about which you speak so positively. Good night, dear prince.

Your Cocoon.

My dearest André,

I wrote you another letter about a week ago that disappeared mysteriously from the peeling desk in the whitewashed hotel room. It was standing next to the portrait of you with the hand, and perhaps it conveyed some of the hesitant late-night thoughts written down when I couldn't sleep. There was a stamp on it and it's possible that one of the servants posted it and so my "news" is perhaps now superfluous.

It is September weather. "Where are the snows of yesteryear?" … in the Cape the mountains are in any case white and an icy wind is blowing from the north. I work in an office the size of two Castellas with a red carpet, trays of tea and little excursions to Rondevlei and Seekoegat where we (that's the Cape Divisional Council) build towers and generally try to clear up some of the ridiculous troubles with the neighbours. The dictionary has been supplemented and completed and is being printed and neatly published.

It's now lunch time and I have to go to an appointment – don't know when I'll be able to finish this letter – really don't know where to begin. Europe is slowly returning and I have a terrible nostalgia for Paris or one of your mysterious Spanish islands. Everything is just cape again and small, afrikaans. The little circle of friends has shrunk and I live in absolute nunishness. It follows of course that Jack is aloof and that I am perhaps still defeated and "I no longer live gladly". Of course you may use "Mamma" for *Sestiger*. *Contrast* has three. "Reis om die Wêreld" and the cut-off cock lies in my desk. But I must leave now. I hope I'll have a chance later …

Further news. I am leaving the hateful hotel on 10 September for a little flat, 204 Bonne Esperance, Beach Road, Sea Point. Bit too smart for my taste, but the bloody immigrants make it impossible for one to find a home. Go to exhibitions nice art of rocks and marrow bones and sometimes visit Freda Linde. You. Your first letter from Grahamstown made me angry. The "whole" feels like those emotionally damaging slaughter houses of Barcelona. Will we ever get it bright again, child? Who is your mysterious publisher of *Orgie*? Please remember I MUST see page proofs. God, I should have been able to speak to you. What does a quiet distance mean and how are things really between the two of you and with your soul? Do you still sometimes think of me? Let it be beautiful then, because here there is mostly criticism and spite. And tell me more about the summer's day.

Love,
Your Cocoon.

2:00. André, there's nothing to do here now and maybe my hurried ending wasn't entirely fair. After the European defeat there was naturally a lot of criticism and now I avoid people as far as possible. Unfortunately, in a little hotel like that, there are also various groups of gossipers fiercely opposed to the young woman with her face buried in the newspaper. But soon I will also make myself a study like you have where I can hide away. And only a few people are permitted there and only by appointment. An artist MUST do that at some stage or other in order to think and to find a tiny bit of human peace or rest where so little of it exists. What are you up to in Grahamstown, you probably don't have many [lectures] left. The tension and intimidation in Cape Town is also running high and the p. [police] even treated me rather roughly on one occasion too. It probably sounds mysterious but there wasn't much to it. At the hotel of course it set "the battalions of lies and the organizations of hate" in motion and St James was called to add the charge that a strange man (Jack) had stolen my child. But smile … You probably saw my little piece about *Orgie* in, among others, the Sunday Slimes with the pop-eyed photo that also appears on *Windroos*. W.E.G. treated you horribly in *Die Burger* about "Paris by Night" and I came off best from all the stupid old criticisms. Did you see? What do you see? What are you reading? What are you doing? And especially what are you thinking? I am of course interested in *Negentig Dae* – it's Ninety Days. Like the English use apartheid. Just take note of it. What

414

did you do in Johannesburg and especially, how is Bartho? Do they all know that things caved in for us? It's so *humiliating*. For you too. For all four of us. My letters sound so *hard* to me. But that isn't really the case. "Ik heb in het gras mijn wapens gelegd / en mijn wapens gaan geuren als gras." Or: Green green I love you green …

Cape Town is flowering and the sea is making a noise in Bantry Bay. All nice things, mysterious. In the lost letter I sent you a copy of my translation of e e cummings's poem "somewhere i have never travelled, gladly beyond".

iewers het ek nooit gereis nie daardie groene verte
verby alle herinnering jou oë dra hul stilte
in jou geringste gebaar is daar iets wat my omsluit
of wat ek nie durf aanraak nie iets te ná

jou oë van landskappe sal my maklik blootlê
al het ek my hart gesluit soos twee hande
jy ontvou my keer op keer soos die lente
bedrewe en heimlik haar eerste roos

en as jy my sou verlaat geslote dan
sou my voorhoof sluit mooi en onmiddellik
soos die hart van 'n blom sou droom
van 'n wit sneeu wat alles oral bedek

niks wat ons in hierdie wêreld kan versin
ewenaar die krag van jou broosheid die tekstuur
van jou oë tref my die groen van sy velde
en bevestig die ewige en die viraltyd met elke sug

ek weet nie wat dit is wat jou laat vou
en óntvou nie ek verstaan net êrens op my reise
die stem van jou oë is dieper as alle rose
nee nie eens die reën nie het sulke klein hande

[somewhere i have never travelled, gladly beyond
any experience, your eyes have their silence:
in your most frail gesture are things which enclose me,
or which i cannot touch because they are too near

your slightest look easily will unclose me
though i have closed myself as fingers,
you open always petal by petal myself as Spring opens
(touching skilfully, mysteriously) her first rose

or if your wish be to close me, i and
my life will shut very beautifully, suddenly,
as when the heart of this flower imagines
the snow carefully everywhere descending;

nothing which we are to perceive in this world equals
the power of your intense fragility: whose texture
compels me with the colour of its countries,
rendering death and forever with each breathing

(i do not know what it is about you that closes
and opens; only something in me understands
the voice of your eyes is deeper than all roses)
nobody, not even the rain, has such small hands]

A free translation. Nice? Stow myself in the word and especially in your *Stroomgebied*. But it's difficult for me to write you know how tough the going is. And then still a bit pro amico and half devil-may-care. While I believe in the heart of the flower. And why in the name of God were we created so similar? Have I asked you that before? What do you hear from Chris [Barnard] – are they still dying of hunger and motor cars and Paris? I still see Chris Lombard sometimes and he also sometimes asks after his boy. El. is alone again and W. happily settled with family; they live in a big piece of glass and over weekends they go to Lanzerac. The theatre here is dead and I don't want to suffer through Vergelegen. May and Jonty [Driver] are in Roeland Street or Wynberg. (Driver the poet.) Is that now enough news for you, little heart? Because at the moment I can think of nothing else. Opperman asked for "Die Kind" and "Swanger Vrou" ["Pregnant Woman"] for *Groot Verseboek* and I suppose I must write to Bartho now to give permission. Uys is still in Johannesburg and Jack is living alone in his seaside house like the lord of life. I feel sad about him. He even let the servant go and pulled out the phone and locks all his doors. Mostly. I wish the sun would come now. The other day I went for a swim with the children with the same old joy. And climbed Table Mountain all the way to the top.

As always,
Cocoon.

204 Bonne Esperance
Beach Road
Sea Point
Thursday, 17 September 1964

My dearest André,

This very day I have written your name so often, on the foreheads of my friends … But they were also absent! Thank you for your beautiful yellow suns which will make the night bright morning; I'm already impatient to get into bed with them! In an undetectable manner … I thought about you so much today, or rather, felt such a part of you. During the lunch hour I went to visit Anne at Citadel and while she was elsewhere occupied I sat in our cage and god! felt the snows of yesteryear falling upon me again! Now I work in a neat office and everyone addresses me formally and I can now see why the Dutch think we are so *courteous*! Tell your learned German friend that I am very glad he likes my poems and that he's sure to translate them and please give him my address. Tell him also that I have a publisher in Germany, Berlin, that is very interested in publishing *Rook en Oker,* and that "Die Kind" has already been translated into German by Peter Sulzer and is appearing in a German anthology. Tell him also that I cared (and still care) deeply about Berlin, and have several invitations to come and stay there for as long as I wish.

Dear man, it is "nieuwe griffels schone leien" for us. And it is precisely we who can now do so little for one another. While we just had to … you know, say goodbye, and how! Rather, let me try to be practical. Have I described the new flat to you? *Blue* curtains, "the colour of absence". If I had my tape recorder here now I would rather have chatted to you, but Chris [Lombard] borrowed it. And all my own furniture, for a change. I'll soon have a phone too; and I must speak to you about *Orgie*. I have this beautiful thing's bromides here and Freda's coming on Monday to chat about them. I'm worried that a libel action might be brought against us and I must get an opinion; my respectable

418

father is not going to be impressed with it and nor will my sister *or* my sister or brother. Even less my step! Or am I seeing ghosts because I myself sometimes – feel – so – desolate? I can no longer think clearly. Fears barge in everywhere. I need you André, but just forget it …

Further: had a few friends here yesterday, including the Stranger [Jack], who does everything for me so coolly and quietly, makes little tables and tall lamp stands, and goes away … God! if only I had patience for this black life! A picnic with Barnie [Barend] Toerien and his "girl-friend" and the Stranger at windswept desolate Noordhoek, read Dutch poetry round the fire, and then each one disappears, quietly, alone, for long lonely walks …

A new friend, Mr E. Middlemiss, from Rondevlei Bird Sanctuary, praise god! (Husband of the English poet Tania van Zyl.)

Your *90 Days* sounds helluva interesting. Send the MS as you write and don't you lose confidence too, now! One of us is enough!

Paris … Paris … Paris … *Every* gesture, every word, every caress, every sigh is so bright, blinding. When, that first night, you fell asleep in my arms, tired and content, at the Seine, and said "My treasure …"; didn't I realise *then* already? That we will never truly be free of one another.

And I thank you gratefully, and I greet you, yours as you touched me, in Barcelona –

Your Cocoon.

My dearest yellow-and-purple penguin doll,

Thank you for all the telegrams and the banknotes (that fell out of the
yellow nightie and which the servant later picked up and put on my
agenda) and with which I bought a white bikini with little frills and a
white-and-red blouse with little frills that hang from the top down the
middle. And the irises (why are you grieving?) and the daffodils and
carnations that again arrived at such a critical time when the world's
gossipmongers were congregating at Bonne Separance. Freda brought
me three cups of wine and Jack made a lamp and a little table and an adult
tea set (bought) and Marjorie and Jan gave me Etienne's new book and
two watercolours. Too beautiful. So you see how spoilt I am. Was just
dead scared of Uys whom I've not yet seen (he arrived back yesterday
and if he hears about – he probably already has – the Paris-Barcelona-
business he'll eat me alive). I phoned him and he sounded perfectly
friendly and excited about himself so I hope it carries on like that. He'll
definitely be disappointed, at least because I returned so quickly to this
lot. About you I will say no comment if I can.

Tomorrow evening there's a party at Bakoven for Marjorie's birthday and all the Cape Circle Artists will be present so you can imagine
how much gossip there'll be. And you, lief-ste-tjie, how are you holi-
daying? On Saturday we were at the Darling show (veld flowers) and
then Barend Toerien's car went and broke down and we had to be scan-
dalously towed back to town and spent the rest of the day there buggering around in the veld among the flowers and things. Afterwards,
like a crushed veld flower myself, I fell into bed and slept for ten solid
hours. You should see the new flat. Living in the centre of a highly
polished saucer. Shiny and clean. Shiny and clean like life should be
and sometimes actually is, in these half-spring days. But what can equal

that Tuesday morning in Paris? It's actually terrible, the way I carry the Paris days around with me and "the sun in my eyes now forever covered / with black butterflies". End of my most recent poem.

Sorry that I'm typing this letter, but I've wanted to write to you from home every night since Saturday and every evening people come around and stay till late. So now I'm writing quickly during work hours, and my dear little boy, I'm probably not even telling much. There is, in any case, so little news since I last wrote to you – everything is just the same. Tonight Freda's coming and then we're going to discuss *Orgie.* (On Monday night she was there with Anne Fischer, nice person.) I hardly ever go out at night because of Simone and the servant lives too far away to stay in. Probably better that way because sometimes I feel too wild to be let loose and I walk around the flat like a caged and wounded animal. Frustrated, my boy. Can it carry on like this? And you?

On Wednesday afternoons I run to my class. The psychiatrist says goo-goo. French I'll have to learn from the beginning again because while I was doctoring (just after I got back) I was "on call" in the evenings and fell behind. Still can't see when I'll go to Paris, but I WILL. And I WILL need money! I think about you lots these radiant thoughts and memories and wonder how strangely you live there so far away.

Much love for you,
Always,
Cocoon.
COCOON FROM BARCELONA.

Grahamstown
Thursday, 1 October 1964

Darling Cocoon, my most special one, my very own,

Thank you for your two precious letters – one of them has only just arrived, via Potchefstroom. I'm already feeling cornered, there's not a second to write in peace, especially during a vacation week. I had a "social" holiday – addressed the Women's Association in Klerksdorp and the students in Potch. This last event was a fantastic encounter – first the audience was hellishly antagonistic, along with questions based on Biblical texts, followed by an *ovation*, with incredible enthusiasm. The Enlightenment arrives in the Transvaal?! (Rather presumptuous, hey!)

Bought a new car. Had to, as the old one suddenly gave up the ghost. With all its memories: Hout Bay, Gordon's Bay, Franschhoek, Stellenbosch, Green Point – Green Point. And that first Sunday morning, driving back from Bantry Bay. Everything, however, moves forward. Yet the heart remains, it *lingers*. My darling, my dazzling thing: without you my days are empty, all monotone. At night I sleep in my study, among many books, alone. Roaming, role-play, often unconcealed venom.

In ten days' time (Tuesday 13th until Friday 16th) it's off to Johannesburg for *The Ambassador*. Alone. I suddenly began to wonder – madness, I know – if you couldn't, perhaps? To sleep, to sleep, perchance to dream.

You're really funny: how would notes have fallen out of your parcel when I sent you a cheque? God is a god of surprises. How do you look in your pale-yellow piece, my chick-with-the-kontjie? And the white bikini. And *you*. It's cold and wet and miserable here. Summer won't be coming back in a hurry. But my heart, full of compassion and admiration, carries memories of Paris, of Montmartre, of the sun on the Seine.

I'm struggling with *90 Dae*. Should the main character be coloured? I hope to finish it off this summer. And the book about Spain that I'm not looking forward to at all because the memories are so impersonal. And just a little youth thing for John Malherbe.

Don't be worried about *Orgie*! It's impossible for anyone to recognise your father: in the story he isn't even married to the girl (I can make it more explicit if you like), and she was his only child; I'll shift the country town, with river and all, to the coast. I want John to release it on 29 May. As I turn 30. Let us fuck and cry and be human. Tomorrow a new decade begins.

Please send me your new poem with its beautiful closing lines. One of these days you'll have a new volume of poems. Next week, with the third-years, I'll be doing Ingrid Jonker. And my heart dare not break.

Don't take too long with French, with Paris.

A silly girl in Uys's *Twaalfde Nag* [translation of Shakespeare's *Twelfth Night*] (a female prompt) writes extremely embarrassing letters – about how she takes a photo of me with her to the bathroom, etc. Why can't *you* and *I* take a bath again, standing in the heavy rain of *grace*?

You are so lovely: and you fill my eyes "with light and restlessness". Love, always,

Ever your André.

Friday, 9 October 1964

AIR COACH SABOTAGING US STOP CONGRATULATIONS PUBLICATION THE AMBASSADOR LOVE = COCOON

Sea Point
Friday, 16 October 1964

My dearest André,

Where is your letter that follows the mysterious telegram? I did in fact receive a *beautiful* letter from you and thanks a lot for that, but it's *this* one that was written last Thursday *before* my telegram: you ask (stupid) whether I can't come up to Grahamstown with John [Malherbe]: but how is that possible if you're working? Remember the Cape Divisional Council, 6 Dorp Street, as translator, with a group of prim people; and your week in Johannesburg I'll be working too: are you serious? And what did you "ask me last time" that I must remember? Dearest little hell!

No. I don't think you should swop around the two roles: X and he. You wouldn't be able to swop the roles of the ambassador and Stephen. Why is this possible in *Orgie*? So do you see, my pet, you must still work on the role that "he" plays. One doesn't really ever gain sympathy for *him*, even less so for X, but I want you to round them off a little and certainly to bring *him* even *more* into the foreground. Let me count your moesies again! Let me hold you in my arms again, heavy and tired, like in Paris, that first night. This is how you'll enable him to gain more form: remember "Where will I hide from the speckles that peck?"

We're already touching summer here: even have a tan already: took Simone to the bioscope this afternoon to see the hateful Elvis Presley, who she's crazy about.

Jack and Jan went mountain-climbing for ten days – left Wednesday but came back Thursday: the weather was apparently terrible, and they tried to sleep exposed out in the rain on Wednesday night. Last night Jack came to visit, everything is still just as *static* between us: I fell asleep around nine o'clock and when I woke at four this morning he'd clearly been gone for ages already.

I'll probably go to Paris early next year: would have left by now already but Simone ... Further child, I am so *hungry* for love and sex – this

424

is probably the longest chaste period for years! What is one to do? Take portraits to the bath! I am not satisfied with just "remembrance, oh beautiful ship" and want to be right *in* it where life throbs. I don't even *fight* any more! Why are you sleeping in the study with its knobbly bed? I wish you would tell me *everything*! I'd love to come to you in Jhb. Even just for a weekend, but – I am AFRAID. You're probably just as scared, "André". A thing like Barcelona must never be allowed to happen to us again – I wouldn't be able to take it. I saw your beloved portrait in the newspaper the other day about the cute "Koekoek [in Ons Nes]" ["Cuckoo in Our Nest"]. You make it quite hard to forget you! Your dream about you and Jack is quite realistic especially if you take into consideration that I have now applied for a .22 revolver, and the darkness. Maybe I'll never use it, because of Simone, and you and Jack. Paris is perhaps a much better answer.

My little lamb, I have no news and no words.

Have you seen the latest *Contrast* with my "Wiegelied vir die Beminde" – André, why were you so close again today, is it your "evil genius"? God! I miss you! After your open, fearless fervour, your eternal chastity, your fiery submission. I miss your body, and your entire death, and your youth beyond words.

Your Cocoon.

———————

204 Bonne Esperance
Beach Road
Three Anchor Bay
Monday, 9 November 1964

My dearest André,

Thank you for your lekker long fat letter: which upset me for more than one reason – the "Thursday night" is resolved – don't you know, everything sounds worse long range. And when I called you I'd been particularly down that day. Surely you forgive me? I've tried so often to write to you, but words are insufficient, my darling boy. And how must I write now? In a kind of general direction … every now and again I notice with a shock your beloved face in one of the newspapers; yesterday in the *Sunday Times* too and a while ago about the "Koekoek in Ons Nes" which has drawn much attention in Cape Town. I am so glad you had a good time in Johannesburg and that you met Stephen [Etienne Leroux] – he's a lovely guy, I wish he'd come and farm in the Cape, he's cut off from the people he wants to write about and it says much about him as an artist that he can apply himself, solitary as he is the Free State, so seriously … ag God, that sounds rubbishy. Was Renée [le Roux] also there? Anyway, Stephen is sympathetic. Maybe his politics are a little off the mark, like Bartho's …

Yesterday morning Jan and Marjorie arrived here and unexpectedly invited us for lunch. Cosy, reading newspapers and listening to music and I got Jan's book: *Die Groot Anders-maak*: For Ingrid of the Coast from Jan of the Cape. We've got horrible weather here, and you? We also had a thunderstorm during the news of poor [John] Harris – I am deeply upset about all these matters – the liberals are generally seen in a bad light, especially the ones who betrayed their friends.

Darling I read *The Ambassador* again. On Saturday night, with Simone sleeping in my arms. It's a new experience again in English and beautifully translated – you mustn't say "soothingly" so often. You never say "comforted" but always "soothed". And for me it's a slippery word. I noted quite a number of little things I hadn't seen before, probably because we visited all the places and people in Paris. Everything is so rounded off. My neatest little one. Do you think you could exploit that wonderful Keyter–Van Heerden situation more fully? Or would it be too dramatic then? Where did you find the name Keyter?

I also want to write a story about something that I've dreamt. I dreamt I am in love with a beautiful horse with a red mane, but at the end of the dream I discover he is married – to another *girl*. He tosses his mane around and the little brown girl in the white dress leads him away …

426

Further, child, further. Still building little towers and roads and translating the dullest, most innoffensive lot of reports. Amazed, I listen every day to the lives of the bourgeoisie. Lord, but they are self-satisfied … and pathetic. They call me a Sekstiger. Speaking of Sestig, don't let the thing die now. What is it with you? What have we achieved? It's only just begun. Jan thinks just as I do. We'll have to have a council meeting! Convey this to Jan, or John Malherbe.

Oh yes, another reason I was unsettled by your letter – you sound so *desperate*. Is it really so bad, my treasure …? I "more or less firmly" decided that Jack and I cannot go on, not as "friends" and not on any of his terms. It's a difficult decision, we've known one another so long, our whole situation is a way of life.

But God, even if I go through the valley of the shadow of death … definitely no further, not like this. It is in any case never further, it's a painful withdrawal. I am so deeply indebted there that I'll never get out of it. Why did I pursue him with such aggressive energy? But it's a dreary subject.

I call out to you, my little prince. Do you know, I have a maid who cooks wonderfully, you'll never get fried eggs again! I'm fatter already. People say I look "radiant". God!

André, I don't know any more. The whole negative past always comes back and lies between us and gnaws. Gnaws away at everything we tried so carefully and delicately to build. Do you remember, in Paris I told you we have to get to know our enemy. Paris. I can't bear to think of Paris. I get this sharp, blinding visual impression of the whole swarming city in the sun and of us.

Forgive the typing. I don't have a pen here at work. I wrote to you last night too, but it was in my diary. I'm going to write a nice diary. I don't want people one day to believe in some people's bladdy prejudiced opinions! Did you see in *Standpunte* about big Org and little Orgie? They tease you a lot, don't they? Don't you sometimes get the hell-in? Gossip: people here say Chris [Barnard]'s story in *Windroos* lacks talent!

André, do you know how neatly I live now? Extremely *carefully*. As though I am constantly in mortal danger. Even Nasionale Boekhandel says they hear nothing. I think about you so much. But unfortunately it looks as if die Here al klaar die dice geskommel het. Do you think that, just once, the dice will fall right for me? Or for you?

A kiss for your fat papie.

Love, darling,
Your Cocoon.

————————

Ingrid, darling little thing,

I'm sitting here in the heart of a room that's full of music. It's getting dark outside and the Cathedral bell is pealing. There's such an unexpected sense of silence and rest nowadays, the certainty of a creative summer; all the unrest and murkiness is in the process of finding form. A central moment in all of this is simply that I've decided I'm coming to visit you in December, for ten days. I'll probably arrive on Friday the 10th (or the 11th), stay the weekend, the next week, and the following weekend. That's if you want me to come. If I may. If you also believe, as I do, that it will be full of ecstasy and quietude.

My examination work will be completed by the day after tomorrow, but the staff are meant to stay here until 10 December. Rob won't mind me leaving earlier, although two considerations make me think the suggested dates are better: a) Bartho and company, and Stephen and his lot, are only coming down in about the middle of December, and I'd very much like to see everyone while I'm there; b) if I wait until the 10th, I might yet finish my Spanish book. I want to begin on Thursday and then work on it for ten days. Planning, the lot.

Die Trommel [The Trunk] and *Die Tas* [The Suitcase] are both done – in draft form. And they're good. I believe so. I must.

428

But what else would or could I say aside from the fact that tonight in four weeks' time we'll be walking together along the seafront. God, child, most beloved, a new honeymoon, a new "marriage full of whispered, magical meaning" lies ahead.

Go ahead and book one weekend for us at the Van Riebeeck Hotel in Gordon's Bay (maybe the weekend from 11 to 13 December). Or wherever you like. Or should we take a long trip – five hours or so – all the way to Herold's Bay or Knysna or somewhere like that? It doesn't matter. As long as it's with *you*.

I am tired, my dearest. I'm working myself absolutely to death on the scripts of well-meaning but untalented students. Masses of them. And each one is such hell to evaluate, now this way, now that way.

You talk in your last, lovely letter about the sabotage cases. The Stephanie Kemp one was an enormous shock – all of them so young, so inexperienced, so full of promise (and she so lovely, too!); so much idealism that grew bitter – or may yet. From a *human* point of view it was all so very poignant. [Adrian] Leftwich's role so *detestable* – and yet, God knows, he also elicits a certain sympathy. Thank God there's hope of renewal with the minister. But everything remains deeply upsetting. My *90 Dae* took quite a few lessons from it all. Darling, it *has* to be something that's unalloyed, above petty bitterness, luminous and tender in its horrible opening up of human anguish and love and *guilt*. And the need to be liberated. Everything.

We need so many days and nights of conversation. My heart hungers for poetry. (And my body for pussy rather than poesy!) I'll be well-behaved, with a smile on my face, and I'll thoroughly purify myself for our Ten Days.

With love, and tenderness and passion, and a kiss and a touch, full of feeling, for everything that's precious on and in you,

Your André.

204 Bonne Esperance
Beach Road
Three Anchor Bay
Wednesday, 18 November 1964

My darling,

Thank you for your long-awaited letter of Friday which I answered immediately but, tortured by the inadequacy of words, scrapped again – *and* thank you for that mysterious telegram on Monday – you little hell! How did you manage it, what date: I must have all details immediately. Top secret here. You were especially with me on Friday, extremely clear in the early twilight with your little laugh. Tell me precisely what happened on Friday: it feels as though I was telepathically connected to you! My treasure, did you hear me on the radio on Friday: I forgot to tell you about it. And praised you highly. And where is my copy of *Elders* and the beginning of *90 Dae*? God, the News Check could at least have put our photos together. Mean of them! It's quite a good article. Did you see me in the [*Cape*] *Times*? I was on the front page two days running – and I'm sending you a photo taken quite by chance from the Supreme Court during the "Red Drive". Because it seems as if you are missing me a lot again. I was in court almost every day during the sabotage case.

No, I don't think your papie (little lamb) will pine away! Nothing upon which I have bestowed my blessing could possibly pine away! Hell!

Don't know how Nico is. I told you I've not been socialising. But, are you listening? After quite a long break, Chris came around again on Monday. He says it's a nice picture of you with the hand. He and I are going away to Lanzerac for a weekend. SINGLE ROOMS. You surely don't mind, do you? I'm just a little WELL-BEHAVED.

Jack's been away for more than two weeks but no word – as arranged.

I madly want to come to Grahamstown to the sacred wood, André Brink. But first, Cape Town in December. I'll have to subject myself to the sun day after day to get lots of freckles. But my darling, we must be *good* to one another. We will, surely? No, my little sheep, I like "These are private words addressed to you in public". Who says they're ugly? That idiot! Send me *Die Trommel.* I miss you too, after all!

I'm now working on the fourth floor with the translators. Did you hear the municipality wants to get rid of us? One guy who's been working here for 38 years is terribly indignant. After *that* he's told he's *superfluous*! It's the most futile work that one's got to approach with an exceptional sense of humour. They've just brought in a hell of a pile of work for me. I get so FURIOUS when they give me work! Where is my *Sestiger*? What does the new ORGIE look like? Will go round to Freda myself this afternoon. Maybe she knows more than I do. Jan and Marjorie will be passing by East London and then camping. They'll call you from there to come around, so that you can also meet Athol Fugard. It'll be nice for you. Athol is very kind and full of life.

My man, the sun is shining again. God is a god of surprises. I can't WAIT for you to come. I will stand before you undivided and "whiter than snow". ("I have failed in everything. But not in this.")

I also attended the [Wilbur] Smith trial concerning the *When the Lion Feeds* case. Have you read it? Pity there had to be a hearing about a mediocre book that proves nothing. (My boss has warned me that I'll be sitting in court full time one of these days.)

And oh yes how was John [Malherbe]'s visit? And how are Rob and the rest of them? Does that Frieda friend of yours know about your plans? Sorry the letter is so mixed up but I haven't written for so long and everything's bubbling out. And now I must say goodbye:

I greet you
Redhead, who thinks everything up and your
Green eyes that encounter me with the texture of His fields,
And your laughing mouth and
The tooth,
And the dimple in your chin
And the new fat
Under the shower at the Hotel Centraal

And the Paris *you*
And the long hands that hold so well
And the little laugh
And the little lamb.

Your Cocoon.

And the 20 – 30 – 50 moesies! Jesus!
He is a handsome man
How do you like your green-eyed boy
For life?

———————

204 Bonne Esperance
Beach Road
Three Anchor Bay
Friday, 20 November 1964

My dearest André,

Friday, fourth. I've booked for us from Saturday 5th to Monday 7th at the Van Riebeeck Hotel in Gordon's Bay. After that, my heart, we could perhaps spend a few days in my flat and then, where? Maybe a homely "inn" somewhere. Do you have any ideas? We must book now, otherwise they'll be full. Remember, it's December. I don't yet know whether I'll be able to get time off at work but I hope so, otherwise I'll TAKE off. I don't want to ask them yet: seeing as I spent every day last week in court instead of at my post. I'll probably send Simone to Johannesburg on the 1st because it's her birthday. I'm nice and tipsy now after a dinner at the Club with Mrs Bouws – whom I told about *us*. Do you think it's wise to see Bartho and Stephen *together* (us two together)? I won't, at any rate, oppose you – was just wondering! Because until I received your lovely letter I treated the matter as a hot

432

top secret. To date, only Juliana Bouws knows – I *had* to tell someone! Did you tell Frieda? My liefsteling, why don't you tell me how on earth you managed it: I want to know *everything*: and if necessary also *bear the burden*.

Are you bringing the *Trommel* and *Tas* with you and also *Elders*?

Before I forget: APPOINTMENT FOUR O'CLOCK 4 DECEMBER AT MY FLAT. I'll take the afternoon off. Darling boy, this is the way:

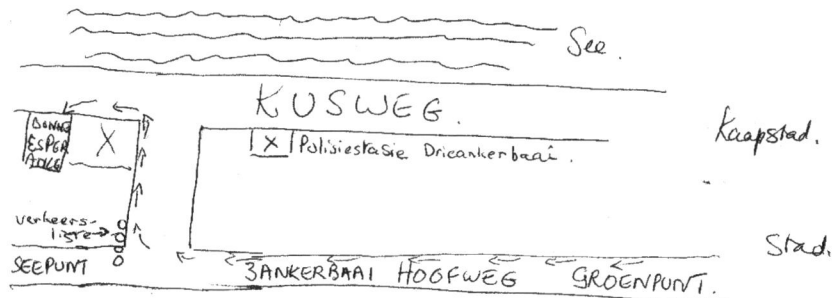

Is it clear? Don't be late, but drive safely! And let me know when exactly you plan to leave.

Little treasure, we mustn't be afraid. Despite everything we've probably, at the very least, *learnt* a lot during these tortured months. And all love, all trust has been affirmed.

Yes, we do have a summer again. Our *deep* summer.

But God, André, what are we going to do about the GODDAMN weather? I so badly want to get tanned for you and now it's raining again in November. I don't know why you want my exact new address, but here it is: Cape Divisional Council: Translation Department 4th Floor, 6 Dorp Street, Cape Town. Phone 41 3266. I'll make sure my home phone is installed by the 4th. They've given me a number already; but I'll have to go and beat them up again on Monday.

Yes, of course I still "have" my tape recorder, *only* Chris borrowed it, *and* – I like guitar music. At the moment, though, I like the rhythm of your body a whole lot more: or the song of your body? Be careful, because I'm going to eat you up! And now I still have thirteen nights to feel desire and to love – and forever –

And now,
Your Cocoon.

———————————

Friday, 27 November 1964

My little André,

All the little Andrés I don't know although I suspect there's one wandering around in the bush in a brown shirt and horns and I know there's one swimming in the Steenbras River he is distinct as a stone, a laughing one in a strange room (though he's only in the mirror) and a rather possessive one right here inside me.

Until: just ONE WEEK CLEAR

THANK YOU FOR DIE YSTERKOEI MOET SWEET [*The Iron Cow Must Sweat*] THANK YOU FOR YOU.

Keep well my little André.

My home telephone number is: 44-9277

Drive safely, don't let anything go wrong, we have a reservation at Cape Hangklip Hotel 8–11 Dec. My week's leave has been granted. I'm waiting, darling, and I can't wait!

COCOON.

Tuesday, 15 December 1964, 2.00 pm

Mine, my darling,

I was born to know you – where are you driving now? Not too hot, I
hope? I am so happy – even though "die oë nog nat van die trane van
gister" and this morning – but I did at least write something for you
while I was sitting on the balcony at four this morning and you were
lying on your side. I can't write you a letter now because it's office time.
I love you.

   The poem "Plant vir My 'n Boom André" ["Plant Me a Tree André"]
is for you and *Sestiger*.

Yours ever *more*,
Cocoon.

ps: The little "rabbit" is you!

----

204 Bonne Esperance
Beach Road
Three Anchor Bay
Wednesday, 16 December 1964

My dearest André Brink,

Just a question of saying good night; I'll "answer" your letter tomorrow – and thank you for it. I was so happy to be able to speak to you
on Wednesday and to hear once again the pure clear ABUNDANCE in my
stomach. There is a lull in the wind here; this morning Simone came
back on the BOEING; glowing and beautiful; and says THANK YOU VERY
MUCH for the doll. I will, of course, take down a letter from her tomorrow; magtig, darling, I wish you could have heard the conversation

435

tonight, she had sand in her pawpaw – we'd been for a swim; and I had to remove it all and put on some ointment:

"Mamma, why does one have a little pawpaw inside your big pawpaw?"

"One is just made like that, angel."

"But Mamma, it is not *necessary*."

"How are you going to wee-wee?"

"Through your bottom?"

"Well, your pawpaw is not *only* made for wee-wee."

"What then?"

"It is part of the different parts in one's body made to have babies."

"Like your tits Ma?"

"Yes darling. I'll make a drawing for you to show you how everything happens, and that everything you are given is necessary."

Etc. Etc. And now fast asleep and Tanya [too].

I walked out of the Divisional Council; why be insulted by a government institution, even if the coward did withdraw his complaint? It was all very calm, a little bit sinister and dramatic.

But liefsteling; who is coming to me, everything is once again good and open, bolstered by your love and the strange *grace* I receive, I'm going to sleep well now with my door open to the benign summer night air. Stay beautiful, for me, and for your own heaven-graced *being*.

Good night, sweet prince.

Love and love,
Your Cocoon.

ps: I'm going to read the first page proofs of *Orgie* on Monday. IJ.

436

Lovely mine,

Do you remember – "when I saw your dear face in the newspaper, the years fell away like cut corn" (?). The report in the Sunday Slimes was unintelligible: who has *Sestiger* and who "produces" it and what was Bartho talking about? Your behaviour was of course entirely *correct*, but Jan and Marjorie and Uys's cousin and I couldn't fathom it. Tell me about it. To hell with it.

   Are you asleep? Yes, this is still no "answer" to your letter – your letter is in any case very dear and does not request an answer; I've had people the whole goddamn day until *now and* beach, and *burnt*.

   And now I once again just want to say hello and goodbye, remember always, I love you; my liberated treasure.

Cocoon.

———————

204 Bonne Esperance
Beach Road
Three Anchor Bay
Monday, 21 December 1964

My darling,

Thank you for your two telegrams and also that you drove so safely – and have you found your cuff links (?) I put them into your suitcase myself, right, front part. I knew you'd forget them and then feel stupid about it! You've been gone almost a week, but close; close; close; after our fullest ten days, and was it 36 times? I love you so much, but [Jorge Carrera] Andrade says it better, so I typed it for you (the poem) ["Second Life of My Mother"]. Do you know it?

And I got our loveliest little puppy Tanya. On the beach yesterday she and I had a lot of admirers, and heavens, did I burn again!

Darling, you must send the Spanish book quickly because I want to work for you. I want to show you how very much I love you (even though you're so slappy!). Ever since you left the days have been a continual stream of people to Esperance and invitations. Tonight I'm going to Bartho and Kita because they're leaving tomorrow specially to get Uys's book out. I visited Uys and Bonnie this weekend, but magtig they can fight. The beach was terribly crowded – Uys says they lie there *"djew upon djew"* [*"djood op djood"*].

I haven't even thanked Jack for his [?], but I'll at least be courteous and send a Christmas telegram. And when do I get a letter from you? Or is it difficult for the boys to talk?

I'm also including my press-ready poem – changes – and the title, if you like, "Plant vir My 'n Boom André".

I forgot to ask, why don't you go to Potchefstroom then? For Christmas. You must think of me a lot on Friday, because I'll be alone, all right? And when do I get my *Sestiger*? Everyone keeps asking about "Mamma", but I haven't seen it in print yet. And then you must send your plays too. And *90 Days* – section by section. (Jan and Marjorie's party was lovely, liefsteling, you really should have been there! It was the best party of the year – just terrible without you!)

Have you developed the photos yet and are they good? I want to see the ones of you. Soon. And now the feathers are starting to grow again and the days absent blue stay beautiful and just till January. All right?

Stay well. Be good. Be you.

Your Cocoon.

{The cheque is for Anton's little gift.}

Wednesday, 23 December 1964

MERRY CHRISTMAS MY DARLING SUNCHILD AND FIRST HONEY OF THE EARTH
= COCOON

———————

Saturday night, 26 December 1964

My darling André,

Thank you for your letter and the cheque for Simone's doll – it wasn't necessary, darling, you're already broke! But I'll write to her and tell her that the doll is also from you. Bartho and Kita eventually took her with them to Johannesburg.

The "Christmas season" is very quiet – was on the beach alone with Tanya yesterday and ate at Jan and Marjorie's yesterday evening. Today just walked around in the sun and tried to translate *Orgie's* poetry – an impossible job – send all your translations to me, maybe I can make a few suggestions. Oh yes, you left your *Katastrofes* [Breyten Breytenbach] here – I'll send it on – I got one from Jan for Christmas.

In heaven's name forget about the tension of that last night. It's not at all important – especially if one weighs it against everything! We must remember to spend the last nights quiet and alone – that's all, really.

Ag, darling – it's so awful that you're not here now – but in fact you are – I know. But let us not hurt or complain!

What "fantastical things" do you dream at night? Tell me? You must sleep *well*, and not get too tired. Ask them for an extension for the translation of *Orgie;* it's impossible for you to finish everything by the end of the year.

André, Tanya is terribly naughty and she needs a garden. Maybe I should send her to the farm for a while – she chews up everything and wants constant attention and *screams* at night when she can't sleep with

439

me. It's a bit of a defeat to send her to the farm, but it's so damn hard! We'll just have to make a little human child, my darling. I was quite upset again when the little death began.

I'll keep vigil and pray and hold fast until January. Because in March I'll have to go; a little scared of our beautiful Paris; but it has to be. But I still have to arrange to borrow money.

Uys and Barnie Toerien have gone to Witsand and apparently he and Bonnie are FINISHED. *Our* few words are low tide compared to *their* tide – EVERY DAY. It was so depressing – especially since I was so happy with you.

What do you mean you're putting "shock-absorbers" between you and LIFE? You're always so "aware".

It's right that you have to go to Pretoria. In god's name, save *Sestiger*. They can't take everything that we built up, it's immoral. I will scream very loudly.

I'll write more tomorrow. Meanwhile, you're here in any case; you've just gone out for a walk in that bright sun and blue sky outside.

My *darling*.

Sunday, 27 December 1964

Nothing; except for the conversation with *you*. Made changes to *Orgie*; there comes my father, etc; soon, the MADMAN WILL RETURN.

Burnt sore; full of love; lonely in the absent blue.

Sleep sweetly, dear prince.

Your Cocoon.

ps: Use poem as you *want* to remember it just SQUIRRELS instead of rabbits; also; still the title: "Plant vir My 'n Boom André".

Your Cocoon.

440

Sunday, 27 December 1964

My André,

What are you making what are you thinking what are you doing do you see me do you hear me, you are not lonelier than a leaf in a tree, than a bird in the wind, or a declared treasure. I'm spending a quiet weekend with friends in Bellville, of all places. They have four cats and a dog Tanya can play with. Darling, I've decided. I'm going to Johannesburg. At the end of January I'll give notice at work and I'll write to Bartho today to ask if he can create a post for me at APB. I know, it's my climate this, but after the unexpected anxiety of Wednesday I want to get away. Do you agree that it is best? I have quite a few good friends in Jhb. I'll probably share a flat with Bonnie – and in that way not be so very lonely. I don't want to become a burden to you – I want to remain your "light".

Listen, I still don't know when I'll be going to Paris because I got a hell of a shock at the bank on Tuesday. I am so sorry about everything, liefsteling, I was so happy with you and around you – Freda said the *Standpunte* meeting is at the end of January. She doesn't yet know about *Orgie* – but she doesn't think the proofs will be ready this month.

Did I tell you that I saw Nico and Mel and the baby? They came and had a meal with me one evening. Nico still speaks with a bit of a slur, that's all. Otherwise they all look completely healthy and happy. André Brink, if you *again* bring up that last night's tiny bit of tension I'll have to call you to account when I see you again. Please believe me, I don't regard it as in any way important. I didn't go to Marjorie's party on Friday after all. Apparently she's livid. But for God's sake, I've at least got a little bit of loyalty towards Jack. They didn't want to invite him because they'd asked me. The audacity! Barnie then said I was wrong and so I hurled my glass and it broke and then *he* did too – and now I've had enough, although it is all rather comical.

The weekend was very calm, puppies playing in the background, reading the Sunday paper, missing you. Phone again soon, darling? Or tell me when I can phone. As Bartho says: a day without you is a foot-slog through the Sahara.

And how are things otherwise? I often try to think myself into the situation there, but it's simply inconceivable. Are you still sleeping in your study? Do you sleep with me? Do you walk in the bush? Does the Southeaster blow there too?

Love to everything of you; stay with me, and no, darling, you will never have empty hands. Your hands are *always* full of dreams and sometimes vague reality.

I love you; look after yourself well; and forgive me the anxiety I caused you.

Your Cocoon.

Sunday night, 3 January 1965

My dearest,

I take a long time writing just one letter to you, don't I, and it is wonderfully quiet!

Thank you for your New Year telegram. I *understand* the silence, because I am quiet too – after the replenishment.

Tanya is running around and growling and barking; was at Jan and Marjorie's again this evening and drank some punch with Erik Laubscher, but you don't have to worry, I drink very little, and that's my New Year's resolution.

Was at quite a decadent party last night – but I was a well-behaved spectator. But when the Nats attacked me about "Jare" ["Years"] and "Die Kind" – and it was an advocate! – I totally out-argued him!

I miss you, my darling, I want to hold you so tenderly and God!

never let you go! I am happy, I swim in the sun, and hear your familiar footsteps around me. (Look after youself well, André, I call you by the name you are mine.)

All hail, all love, all trust – confirmed,

Yours always,
Cocoon.

Thursday, 7 January 1965

UNFORTUNATELY NO BUTTERFLY ONLY ANGST ALL MY LOVE = COCOON

---

204 Bonne Esperance
Beach Road
Three Anchor Bay
Friday, 8 January 1965

My dearest André,

Thank you for your letter of "frustrations", which at *last* arrived. Sorry to hear about the boil – where did you get it and have you seen a doctor? No, I still have Tanya, who is sometimes very cute but she *demands* attention and makes me tired sometimes. Well, sorry, liefsteling, about the call. I so often wished you would call and then …

And at that moment you phoned again. Many thanks, my own, that changes so *much*. I've just told you what happened. I don't want you to take it too seriously. It was an anxiety attack, which is not unusual; a coma, which can happen easily to *imaginative* people when they want to avoid something and they withdraw from reality. And it is not just a "fear" of Jack, but also a "fear" of loneliness. In the nursing home they just let me rest – and now I will get better again. And keep hoping that circumstances will one day change so that I can live like an ordinary person and be somewhere, with you. Belong.

I was so worried about you and your worry the whole time. I just hope now that *Standpunte* and *Orgie* happen, so that you can come back again this month. Till then I will wait nicely and not be afraid of the great gloom (night). Or of Jack, or of the gossip. Will probably go to the party tonight, just to show them!

God, but these Cape Town people are busybodies. Marjorie would have known nothing about the incident if that stupid lot at work hadn't phoned her. But enough of that! I'll get over it soon. "Vitality shows … in the ability to start over …" says Fitzgerald, and on Monday I'm going back to work.

I'm sorry to hear about all the frustrations there. We'll have to make a plan. We need one another. See how easily you'd be able to dictate your Spain book to me! And hundreds of other things. I didn't realise I was so defenceless. I just want to say to you, my love, that I only went to the nursing home because there is no one here who can look after me when I am unwell. One also doesn't want to be a bladdy *burden* to your friends.

Otherwise well and no news. I haven't written another poem again, you'll first have to come and sleep wrathfully and well before I am inspired enough. Or should I write a nice one like "Vergange Winter" ["Bygone Winter"]:

Jou hande het geruik
Na angeliere en die dood
Vergange winter.

Oh and Jan says his short story was accepted by *Standpunte* and so it can't go to *Sestiger*.

Are you sorry that no butterfly arrived? I was sorry, to put it mildly. It would make such a hell of a difference, and it would be beautiful like your tooth. Write soon, you hear, immediately. And I'm glad to hear your unromantic illness is over. You must take multi-life-pills. It's because of a vitamin shortage, though I don't know how you manage that.

Darling, André, don't draw "conclusions" about my anxiety, you hear? I love you more than ever. But that you know, of course?

Your own,
Cocoon.

———————

204 Bonne Esperance
Beach Road
Three Anchor Bay
Wednesday, 20 January 1965

My dearest André,

Many thanks for your letter today, which sounds so jolly and for the one beautiful colour slide of IJ. (What other uterine miscarriage slipped in with it?) In any case, I am somewhat comforted by the one of me arching back on our green blankets. Could you have it developed as a photo – I don't know who to ask here to do it – and you surely wouldn't want Desmond to see it? Anne Fischer is also a friend of mine and [Desmond] Bowes Taylor I do indeed know, and the redhead photographer at Clifton (who has a mother complex.) "Push anything past me in a wheel-chair …!" I can't remember his name now.

Sorry I gave away my bank information – now what? Work, and borrow from somewhere. Laurens [van der Post] will probably lend me R700; he'd already offered it a while ago. You will understand that I was VERY upset about this: "then your poverty arrives like an armed man". But especially about the aborted trip – mostly a result of my own stupidity.

I'm still using the French paper you bought me in Paris – one really tiny sheet to write to Jack – so you can see for yourself the shocks I've been exposed to; to hell with the Divisional Council's kak work that I didn't want in any case – Bonnie wrote to say that she has her eyes on a six-storey – (sorry! a six-room house) in which she and I and two other students might stay. Haven't heard from Bartho again, except that the post is highly probable and that the letter will follow.

And you, darling, and you? I am so sorry that the photos I took of you are black. Still, you could at least let me see them …! I have such a need to SEE. God, when you come again – soon-soon, end January to beginning February – I am just going to LOOK and LOOK.

Otherwise, everything good; Tanya healthy, Simone too; Anne is keeping a watchful eye; life is loyal to me – and my blood is surging through my veins …

I was at Maynardville last night to see Shakespeare's *The Taming of the Shrew*. (Oh God, student humour!) Was a little disappointed with the production. But Maynardville is lovely!

Congratulations on all the completed work. But you must also rest. PLEASE my darling, come and lie here against my heart, my lamb. Thank you for the lovely [Frederico Garciá] Lorca translation. Your Spanish is good, hey? You can go ahead and write the horse story; I don't know how, really. I began at full throttle, but it's difficult material.

I see you have the same trouble. I could DIE from all the guests. I am NEVER alone any more, and yet so terribly alone! They gobble you up.

I love you. I miss you. I need you. Do you know, my dearest boy, that you are well on your way to becoming *indispensable*?

Come to our healing waters, come to me, come to Cape Town, which will always be mine, and to me, who will always be yours,

Cocoon.

Grahamstown
Wednesday, 10 February 1965

Dearest only Con,

A long silence, again! But I fell so heavily back into work when I got back – dealing with overdue stuff, and then immediately launching into exam duties. Meanwhile, I'm reworking *Elders* and trying to get into the "spirit" of *Die Meisie* [The Girl]. Now, just as I've more or less readied myself for work, Christie and company are coming to visit, luckily only until tomorrow. As a result, I probably won't be able to start *writing* again until Friday. But it's not a real frustration, because, love, my love, I'm living so fully and beautifully nowadays. The week with you was such a restful, positive invigoration, and it ended so ecstatically, so full of enchantment, that I'll have to come back *soon*.

Meanwhile I've had another huge fight with Chris Barnard. He wrote to me again about his latest creations – including one that takes place during a "night of heathen feasting". Man, I've been fed-up with his thievery for a long time now. So I made him a little list: girl in the window across the way that he steals in *Pa Maak vir My 'n Vlieër* [translated as *Tomorrow and Tomorrow and Tomorrow*], with my trunk in there, too; Sumerian mythology in *Dwaal* [Wandering] – and now this, too. I made a friendly request that he find himself another pasture. Piece of shit! If he never writes back, then good. And if he does write back, I'll give him hell. (Gentle Neelsie?!)

John [Malherbe] phoned last night to say Molly Reinhardt will be devoting an entire column to *Orgie*; Stanley Uys will write a review; and Maish [Levin] will see to a "story".

Of course, the latter phoned me once again about the De Beer conference, but I shook him off. I have a lot to say about this stupid, sanctimonious bunch. *But* if I am invited to the conference, I can say what I want to there; and if I *don't* get invited, it'd be impertinent to talk to the press. It was in any case notable that, according to his report, the conference was actually sparked by Stephen [Etienne Leroux]'s work

447

and mine – and yet we're the only two who haven't yet made any comment! Some of the others' comments weren't too bad. Yours were very neat, and funny. Jack's also good. Adam's were good in parts. Jan's comments were ridiculous.

But these are all side issues. The main thing is the heart that is still here. And this time it's beating so steadily and happily that life has gained new meaning. "May it continue many days, Lord, may it continue many days." Reading for today.

Bye-bye for now; a *deep* bye-bye, with a little sleep in the crook of my arm, and a heart that talks to mine, full of bliss, during all the long hours that the body sleeps.

Always yours, always love,
André.

Friday, 12 February 1965

FORGIVE SILENCE CONFUSED AMAZED LIKELY BUTTERFLY LOVE = COCOON

Thursday, 18 February 1965

I LOVED THEM THOSE LITTLE TOWNS THAT NOW TUMBLE FROM THE MICRO-PHONE DEIRDRE ANDREA NICOLETTE = COCOON

Thursday, 18 February 1965

TELEGRAM SENT I LOVED THEM THOSE LITTLE TOWNS THAT NOW TUMBLE
FROM A MICROPHONE DEIRDRE ANDREA NICOLETTE STOP THERE IS NOTHING
ANDRE = COCOON

———

Tuesday, 2 March 1965

REST ASSURED LIEFSTELING DIFFICULT CIRCUMSTANCES NOW CLEAR AGAIN
STOP DID YOU RECEIVE LETTER STOP ANSWER LOVE AND TRUST = YOUR
COCOON

———

204 Bonne Esperance
Three Anchor Bay
Wednesday, 3 March 1965

My liefsteling,

I heard your voice and your laugh for no reason the most beautiful fruit
of the earth – and received your letter of "complaint" – and don't think
I ever abandoned you. You must have received the previous letter by
now – or who is having a giggle about my pudding now?

Funnily enough, Laurens didn't get my letter either; I'm expecting
him back in SA by the end of this month; and hope to go along on the
Kalahari expedition. Wrote again yesterday, but lack ⅓ [?] to send the
letter! RIDICULOUS. This lot will never know what that is.

You little hell, it was so wonderful to speak to you after all the
stormy weather. As I said; it was a terrible blow for me – the child –
paralysing. And as I said: I seriously considered getting married; and
to heal *this* deep wound once and for all. But your *face* – everywhere.

And: "men moet zo zonder gestalte zijn / om lief te kunnen hebben."
And *that* I am, my darling, my *own* salvation though without form.
And I love you. In between everything else here: parties, work, living,
socialising, Simone and all her little friends who constantly need seeing
to; and the Grey Pit I'd once crept out of. The worry about you, my
certain "faithlessness" – but what is one to do in such a confused and
difficult world?

On Friday I'm going to the Sunday Slimes again – they're going to
phone you; and then we can talk again.

Functions, functions, parties, openings – [?], god, but he is sometimes sentimental – Jan and Marjorie have gone away for a while; to
Waenhuiskrans; on Saturday Jack went and bought me, after a long
silence, a R40 dress; what could this mean? Ag darling, so much news
and so many questions. But one of these beautiful days of clear light
you will be here, and then for once it will probably be necessary not to
ask questions. I am *sorry* that I left you in silence for so long and that
my one letter also had to get lost and that you had to weather all the
criticism on your own. Alone? At least there is still Estelle who can
LAUGH about my panties. "Op hierdie verspotte plein is jy nie alleniger
nie / As 'n blaar in 'n boom as 'n voël in die wind / Of 'n bevryde skat."

And what's the matter with this bladdy Uncle Wyk? He's been getting *far* too cheeky, *Tristia* or no *Tristia*.

Thank you for *Sestiger*: the title is wrong: it's: PLANT VIR MY 'N BOOM
ANDRÉ! You can see here of course that so far I have only looked at my
own poem! And the witticisms at the back.

Tonight is a tiny spot of silence, praise god, in between the hubbub
of the day. An evening for reflection and Walt Whitman and thinking
about you. I'm seeing *Orgie* through all the stages of publication and
even *blush* a bit when other people look at it. The cover is lovely: you
don't have to worry at all – but you've probably received it by now?

And now I am waiting sedately for you.

Till then, my Prince, all love, in anticipation, of *everything*,

Your Cocoon.

Grahamstown
Thursday morning, 4 March 1965

Loveliest darling,

Thank you for your clarifying voice yesterday; if it hadn't been *your* voice, I'd have been totally taken aback, because when the exchange told me Maish was going to phone at five-thirty, I just *knew* you'd be on the other end of the line.

You're so close and warm and alive; at night you sleep snugly against me on the small divan in my study; and in the afternoons you walk with me in the bush of surprises.

I've been feeling such dazzling *respect* for you lately. I lie on my little bed at night and think – about your love, your thoughtfulness, the manner in which you pour *everything* into your love. It makes me feel almost overwhelmed, unworthy of so much beauty, such vulnerability.

My darling, was it *hard* to make a decision about the painter [Herman van Nazareth]? I had no *specific* suspicions, of course; but still, I "knew" someone was trying to take you away from me. Ag God, I *want* you so badly. I want so badly to see you *happy*. I dare not be selfish. But how can it be otherwise when it comes to you?

I'm sending you another little cheque to fill a small gap; things will be better from August onwards, when I get royalties for *Bakkies* [*en Sy Maats*] [Bakkies and His Friends] and *Orgie*.

Our little moesie-girl – sometimes it's difficult to wake up and suddenly realise: No, she hasn't arrived. I'll just have to dedicate *Die Meisie* to Nicolette, Deirdre and Andrea. (You can imagine how people will try to *guess*!)

Ag, this Pretoria thunder makes my head feel confused. And Maish is also driving me crazy, phoning me every other minute. (He's phoning again on Friday – tell him you're coming along, again. Sorry, dammit, I've just realised you'll only be getting this letter on Saturday!)

Right now I'm translating *Alice in Wonderland*; surprisingly enough, the poems are working out quite well. But on Monday I want to start working on the novel. And then, in just 23 days, I'll be with you; it's *so* close now. Then we can celebrate *our* book. *Thank you* also for your inspiration with the cover. I'm getting my copy today and can't wait to see you with your little horns.

If people have anything akin to a "mating season" – then mine is right now. I'm really "on heat"! Sorry! But it's appalling. I don't know *what*'s going to happen to you when I get there. Just make sure the flat's *immediately* available!

And, along with this lust, my love has become so very tender; because you're more precious and wonderful and exquisite than ever.

Live in light, my darling. I'm sending you four kisses: one for your beloved mouth, one for each nipple, and one for your beloved gooseberry.

With endless love,
Your André.

———————

[incomplete letter]
Grahamstown
Thursday night, 11 March 1965

Dearest Kontjie,

I long for you. But tonight in three weeks' time I'll be in your arms. And therefore I'm *happy*. You should've been with me today: I didn't have classes, so I drove to the coast early this morning and stayed there the whole, long, holy day: it's a beach with miles and miles of sand and dunes; with a slight breeze all the time, and not a living soul in sight – so I roamed around the whole day in primitive nudity, running across dunes, cavorting in the water – and getting badly burnt, *everywhere*, without a single bit of protected white. (Not even R. Schutte would have been able to criticise me!)

452

Wouldn't it be wonderful if you could come and visit me here? Roam around in the bush and live primitively in sun and sea, just us! In fact, from the 26th I'll be all alone here.

I actually need to start working on the novel tomorrow, but I'm feeling *lazy*. And especially: it's been just mine for so long now that that it's going to be a heavy struggle to

––––––––––

204 Bonne Esperance
Beach Road
Three Anchor Bay
Thursday, 11 March 1965

Liefsteling,

Thank you for the very handy R10 cheque and the letter, and the moan-letter of Monday morning early before you received my speed-post one. I know – I left you in silence and it's terrible – by now you should have received my other letter though. WHERE were you on Friday afternoon? I had to endure Maish's company and wait for the phone call and then *you* were out and I was in a state of rebellion! Monday morning and surprised by the report in the Slimes – huge hell at work, I almost lost my wretched little post because they saw me on Friday in the company of the newspaper people. There was a phone call from Johannesburg (headquarters) and talk about stopping the printing of *Orgie*. But John [Malherbe] reassured them very diplomatically and I can see daily how he is progressing. Was at John's on Tuesday – he has TWINS and every-thing now peaceful and quiet again. He himself told the *Sunday Times* that Citadel is printing – but that they mustn't let the cat out of the bag. But all that's nothing at all – just work news.

You ask so many questions, darling. In your last letter whether it was DIFFICULT to decide: just one thing, I neither WANT to nor CAN I struggle on alone forever. *That* is difficult. You talk so lightly about going to France – WHAT will become of me? Can you see my heart is rebelling? The humiliating financial struggle too – my landlady is contantly asking for the rent, and if she arrives here this evening I'm giving notice! And the Grey Pit – and everything – on top of it all I had to subject myself to a dental inspection. I'm not even as scared of Jack as I am of the dentist – no, there is nothing worse than the shiny chair with the headrest! (Jack, by the way, went to Johannesburg today, without saying goodbye, because I don't want to see him any more.) No, my pet, the post (for me) in Johannesburg is not available. But this flat has been far too expensive ever since I got fired from the Divisional Council – and I will have to move again. Far away, maybe to one of those little old houses in Wynberg. My maid is pregnant (nearly nine months) and when she's had her baby they'll throw her out of that room I found for her in Mouille Point – that's for sure – so I will *have* to get a house with a servant's quarters. If I can just see light this year, then next year I can send Simone to boarding school and move into a single room.

Do you see, my silly man, in the real world it is dark; and that I may now live only from day to day; "step by step, oh lord". Today's reading. And with all these really old problems I didn't want to come to you – but now, like [?], I have to COMPLAIN. And André, 1 April is too late, child! 26 March, as the date was set earlier, suits me. As far as I can see it today, you must stick to our meeting of 26 March. It is just right. And *Die Meisie* must be dedicated to DEIRDRE.

There is a possibility – just a possibility – that Laurens van der Post will take me back to England later this year. And that I will apply for a bursary for Belgium. I went to see Prof. Malherbe, he is on the board, and was enthusiastic about IJ. Of course, it's all vague; and darling, not even impossible that we, with me far gone, will meet in Paris!

Or is it?

O Star of France

Miserable! Yet for thy errors, vanities, sins, I will not now rebuke thee;

454

Thy unexampled woes and pangs have quell'd them all,
And left thee sacred.

In that amid thy many faults, thou ever aimedst highly
…
In that thou couldst not, wouldst not, wear the usual chains,

O star! O ship of France, beat back and baffled long!
Bear up, O smitten orb! O ship continue on!
…
Again thy star, O France – fair, lustrous star,
In heavenly peace, clearer, more bright than ever,
Shall rise immortal.
(Walt Whitman)

(Simone just said to Anne: "Mummy is busy with a writing competition." Anne: "Seems to me André is meeting his match tonight.")

Orgie: I'm glad you like the cover so much. I think it's beautiful. I've hidden the first galleys and I'll smuggle them out of the factory. (They're already yellow.)

Time to say goodbye: and liefsteling mine, much love and light and hope; I'll phone you shortly from Maish's. Even better: I'll try to pay my telephone account, then you can call me again.

Come on the 26th, whatever happens, or *may* happen; I feel her knocking *in* you at me.

Darling,
Cocoon.

ps: Answer with a little tape? IJ.

Grahamstown
Monday morning, 15 March 1965

Quiet, beloved child,

Such a Blue Monday feeling, unilluminated by your voice or your hands. And thanks to my consistent attempts – I have quite a knack for persistence! – I know that your phone account hasn't been paid. Unless it's been taken off the hook so the Painter won't be disturbed. I'm absolutely the most *jealous* person on earth.

I just can't get working. On the one hand there's all the anticipation for *Orgie*; also, it's murderously hot; third, I'm having sleepless nights with Anton. Because Estelle just doesn't wake up, even when she's lying right next to him – so each time I've got to get up and leave the study to lend a hand. Whooping cough or something at the moment.

But my soul is healthy, whole, and full of love; as summer slowly tilts into autumn, I feel I have in fact achieved something, that I can believe in something and be secure in that knowledge, my little Namaqualand daisy.

I'm counting off the days quietly, like petals ("She loves me – she loves me not"!?), waiting patiently for the time ahead. I've made all kinds of smart plans with my lecture schedule so I'll be able to leave on Wednesday the 31st – but only after finishing my morning classes. I'll thus be in your sleeping arms by midnight; or an hour or so before.

That's if you still want me; and if your silence betokens hope and not aloofness.

Tell me, tell me, *tell* me where your love lies!

John says – you probably know this already – that he's inviting mainly press people to his party, but also Uys and Jan and that crowd; it goes without saying that you'll be coming with me. Sorry that social things will have to intervene, and that I'll have to go to St'bosch on the Friday, too, but we *are* going to have an island of happiness for ourselves, too, unclouded, quiet, and without any seaweed-tangles.

Do you still get out into the sun? Are you tanned and beautiful?

456

(Are you still able to pull up your zips?!) Is your hair growing? Is the little tortoise lonely?

What's *going on* with you? It's such an awful silence this, and at times quite terrifying. I lie awake many nights thinking about you, about your happiness, your everything. I feel longing and worry and love.

Write. Write *everything*. And believe in your wholeness.

With love and tenderness,
André, yours.

––––––––––

Thursday, 25 March 1965

CONGRATULATIONS ON ORGIE LIEFSTELING STOP THANK YOU CHEQUE LET-
TER TREASURE STOP WHEN ARE YOU COMING COME MINE = COCOON

––––––––––

204 Bonne Esperance
Tuesday evening, April 1965

My liefsteling,

Just a goodnight kiss and a little bit very happy about our few days together. I am very close to you, and I love you very much.

Was on the beach all day today and am absolutely the most burnt. Tonight Roger took me to France Hotel [?] to fetch Simone. She's sleeping nicely here with me again – tomorrow school starts – the search for a maid continues – but now I am going to sleep with you.

How are things with you, all alone there, are you also missing me? How's it going with *Die Meisie*? Don't overexert yourself. About eating I don't have to scold you but in heaven's name sleep enough and well.

Between all the rushing around and the goings-on here I have almost finished *The Blood of Others* which I bought on Monday (Simone de Beauvoir). You *must* read it if you don't know it.

Good night, my treasure, you are actually sleeping here on the little mound.

Yours, always,
Cocoon.

———————

Wednesday night, April 1965

My dearest André,

It was an endless day – the heat wave continues. I found a maid, a beautiful little black mother with glasses and a round affectionate face. I am beginning to feel embarrassed that I always have such luck. Her "madam" is away on holiday for a month. My Anne had her baby, a little girl. I want to give her a name myself, but don't want to part with Deirdre or Andrea, or Nicolette. You really must dedicate *Die Meisie* to them. Will you my darling?

I also finished reading *The Blood of Others* today and parts of it over and over and am suffering a little from a lump in the throat, and am missing you. Listen:

> I let you go off alone through the festive streets, I set off on my way, thinking that I too was still alone, and, after my fashion, nursing a vague regret. As if all the kisses which I did not give you had not bound us to each other as surely as the most ardent embraces, as surely as the kisses which I shall give no more, as the words which I shall no more say to you and which bind me to you for ever ... There is no salvation. Not even the intoxication of despair and blind resolve, since you are there, on that bed, in the fierce light of your own death.

458

(So bladdy simple!)

> That good which saves each man from all the others and from myself
> – Freedom – then my passion will not have been in vain. You have
> not given me peace; but why should I desire peace? You have given
> me the courage to accept for ever the risk and the anguish, to bear
> my crimes and my guilt …

If you haven't yet read it I'll send you a copy. Let me know, okay?
And tomorrow I'm going to buy the wool in the most beautiful white
and black you've ever seen. Remember, send me your measurements
urgently and don't be shy, fatty!

I saw your publicity in *Die Landstem* – quite good, for them!

Tomorrow I am going back to the Grey Pit, to give notice. Of course
I still need time to find a job – I don't think Johan Cilliers's one will
come off. But one never knows. Most of all, don't worry, I still have a
little money to get by.

Darling, you didn't sign the Van Ostaijens. Did I ever thank you
properly? By the way, did you perhaps take the others? I've just given
the bookshelf a quick glance, but I still have a suitcase full of books.

I am well-behaved and busy and introverted. You must work well
and sleep well and be happy. I hope this letter reaches you before you
go to Potchefstroom.

Love, love and a kiss for every bright moesie. Come and dream with
me, you hear?

Your Cocoon.

204 Bonne Esperance
Beach Road
Three Anchor Bay. Sunday. Two-year-existence.
18 April 1965

Liefsteling André,

Don't get a fright that I'm typing to you, but as I type I sometimes think better and I've just got this rattletrap and I'm practising. Two birds with one stone. Thank you for your rushed letter before you left for Potchefstroom and for the telegram on the way to Johannesburg and for the telegram yesterday to commemorate our two-year-long existence. I don't know how long you're staying in Potch and I hope this letter reaches you. When are you going to write, you little hell. How was Johannesburg and did you go and visit my rival? What does Van Wyk say? In your letter you said you were going to stay with them. They have a swimming pool, don't they? And did Uncle Wyk sit in his leather armchair and talk literature?

And how are you spending Easter? It's the one long weekend I cannot bear. One's never certain of the weather, so you don't make appointments. On top of it all Jan and them have gone camping and took my artist [Herman van Nazareth] with them and left me behind! Don't worry, darling, he's not actually mine, you hear, though he is trying very hard to marry me. But you're not allowed to tell anyone, because he's quite sensitive and this steadfast refusal of mine is probably not very flattering. He's made this triptych now – The Child – The Poem (in my handwriting on a canvas the same size) – and The Poet – which he wants to exhibit together in July and later in Belgium. And while I'm talking about rivals like this, I must tell you that Jack managed to see me again on the strength of Charles Eglington and [Christopher] Hope who are visiting him at the moment. I popped in there yesterday evening (wearing your pretty satin dress) and apparently I am now being appointed to the editorial board of *Contrast*. I gave notice at the Grey Pit last Monday and start selling *Contrast* on Wednesday and loans and

460

advertisements [?]. I don't know how it will go but it is, in any case, worthwhile. In the meantime, I'm looking for a permanent post. Damn Johan Cilliers just upped and left for Johannesburg and I hear he's appointed Desmond Windell in his absence. He could at least have let me know. He says *Orgie* is very nice – typographically – but he hasn't read it yet. What do others say?

I'm working on a short story called "Die Pop" ["The Doll"], but it's so sad that on this blue day I can't see my way clear to continuing. Other than that, I'm devouring books and keeping my heart pure of sin. Do you know what, 28 days like clockwork on Wednesday. And Anne's baby is so cute. But oh God, my darling, I'm beginning to feel I am long past grief. "Ik heb in het gras mijn wapens gelegd / en mijn wapens gaan geuren als gras." And perhaps today especially we should remember that two years ago we had no thought other than the fire of our loins. The following Monday I walked into Freda's office and said: I slept with André Brink. I cut your photo out of *Pot-Pourri* and put it in my diary. Tell me the old tale again.

Your jersey is coming along, but send your measurements soon, my love, I want to start with the sleeve. I'm knitting it a bit bigger than the red one, because you're fatter now, aren't you, and I am not knitting squares, because then you'll look like a chequerboard, and not diamonds either, because then you'll look like a clown, especially with the smiling mouth, and not stripes because then you'll look like a zebra. But it will be charcoal black and white, you'll see. Pitch black is too harsh for your fair skin. Where do you get your funny ideas about clothes, my darling little idiot?

Now I'm going to go and walk by the sea because today really is a lost summer's day in the middle of winter, and I had to accompany Simone all morning in front of the cameras for advertisements. She enjoys it so much and considers it part of her career as an actress. And I'll think of a face, a beloved face, your face …

Be good with all our secrets,
Your Cocoon.

Grahamstown
Tuesday night, 27 April 1965

Dear child,

Finally back again after my long silence. My apologies. I spent the whole time rushing about, back and forth between Potch, Pretoria and Johannesburg.

Thank you for your letter that was waiting for me here, so mature and so lovely; and yet also a bit strange, suddenly, in the semi-formal voice of a typewriter. Easter weekends, unless one could be in Paris, hiding away in Notre Dame during Mass, are always so lonely, so melancholy.

My lectures went off well; the one for the students especially was a major success. The evening talk before the Academy's working community was a chilly thing: an icy wet night, 100 people in a hall that holds 200, cold chrome chairs, "and every coat with its face". The party afterwards at Van Wyk Louw's was an improvement; but also not without the irritations of *social* people. Would have loved to talk to him more; but the precious times when it was indeed possible, were unforgettable. He's such a *human* being, so *wise*. Some people have an aura of wisdom that they hide behind: he's so *human*, so *wise*.

You've probably also seen the recent while's vicious reviews of *Orgie* – Bill and the rest. Funny, a while ago this kind of thing would've upset me enormously. Now, not at all. A smile, at most. It's not out of a sense of feeling superior – just a feeling that if I've done something that for *me* was truly imperative and honest, then people can make as much noise as they like. I don't care.

Send your story. I *must* have it for the final *Sestiger* (copy must arrive by June).

Is *Contrast* paying you? Or is it a "service of love"?! How are you getting *by*? For my part, I thought things were going better, before the holiday, but then I had to pay R120 for Estelle's two weeks at her mother's, and now I'm terribly broke.

462

Two years.

Yes, two years. Praise the Lord, my soul; all my inmost being, praise his holy name.

But:

April is the cruellest month, breeding
Lilacs out of the dead land, mixing
Memory and desire, stirring
Dull roots with spring rain.

April.

Dear child, sit with me now and listen. And try to understand that it's the hardest thing I've ever had to say to anyone, *ever*. I want to do it in the fewest words possible, because you're a woman – and you would have known it already: a month ago, *before* me, you knew it.

Yes. I was with her [Salomi Louw]. And we slept together.

I stand naked before you; I don't *want* to retain any clothing or protection. I dare not even ask for forgiveness, because that implies guilt – and as little as I can ever feel guilt about me and you, can I feel it about *this*.

All I know is that it's a terrible thing to do – to have to say this, to *you*, *now*. More than that I don't know. Just that you're irreplaceable in my heart. And that I always carry the burden of your happiness.

I am in the hands of the living God.

And I say farewell to you, my Cocoon. With tears.

And with love.

André.

Three months before his death, André Brink offered his correspondence with Ingrid Jonker to Penguin Random House for publication. It consisted of some two hundred original letters written over a period of almost two years, from April 1963 to April 1965. The project to collate, edit and translate the letters was launched soon after Brink died in February 2015. A core team was assembled, consisting of Francis Galloway (editor and overall project adviser), Lynda Gilfillan (English copy-editor), Karin Schimke (translator of Jonker's letters into English), and Leon de Kock (translator of Brink's letters), with Fourie Botha acting as project manager, while further assistance was provided by Willie Burger (professor of Afrikaans literature at the University of Pretoria), Karina Brink (writer, critic, and André Brink's widow), the Ingrid Jonker Trust under the curatorship of Greg Marsh, and Erika Viljoen.

Flame in the Snow contains all the letters preserved by Brink. They are published here in full. Brink kept carbon copies of his typed and handwritten letters; Jonker occasionally typed hers, but most of them were handwritten. The letters were duly arranged in chronological order and scanned. Thereafter, the letters were re-typed, and the typed textual record so produced was checked against the original letters, creating a working manuscript. A decision was made to publish an exact version of the correspondence.

This record of correspondence, which Brink preserved for fifty years in brown envelopes in his study, is, however, incomplete. A handful of letters are missing as a result of mail not reaching its destination, or because in certain cases a carbon copy was not made of a particular missive. In addition, several letters that Brink wrote to Jonker during her travels in Europe in 1964 do not appear here, though Jonker refers to them in her own letters. In the inventory of documentation on Ingrid Jonker that Jack Cope handed over to the National English Literary Museum (NELM) in 1979, nineteen letters are listed as issuing from Brink between 23 March 1964 and 3 June 1964. Sixteen of them do not appear in Brink's collection. These original letters (some

464

"torn into fragments", some with their "fragments taped together, fragile", according to the NELM inventory) are currently in Portugal in the archive of the late Dutch writer Gerrit Komrij, who bought the Jonker documentation, consisting of diaries, clippings, and letters. It was not possible to secure copies of Brink's letters from the Komrij archive.

The original collection of letters on which *Flame in the Snow* is based will be made available for consultation by researchers after the appearance of this book.

Flame in the Snow is intended for a general readership and it therefore does not contain explanatory annotations, although this (English) version of the letters does contain limited annotations in the form of square-bracket references after some Afrikaans titles, for the sake of clarity (see explanation under "Translation" below). The writing style of the correspondents has been respected, and so the text includes language that might be perceived as salacious, as well as critical comments about fellow writers.

Obvious errors and cases of mistyping were corrected, and occasionally a word or phrase has been added in square brackets for the sake of clarity. Words that are unreadable in the original letters are indicated by way of a question mark within square brackets. Brink and Jonker's use of punctuation and paragraph divisions has mostly been kept unchanged in the Afrikaans version of this book, and is similarly respected in these translations. (Exclamation marks, however, have been reduced significantly.) In certain cases it proved necessary, for the sake of typographical consistency, to make small adjustments (such as the addition of commas and periods in postal addresses, and in the opening and closing of the letters). On occasion, paragraphs have been indented for the sake of readability.

Where the correspondents underlined certain words, these have been italicised. Words and phrases in foreign languages have not been italicised unless Jonker and Brink themselves underlined such words or phrases in their original letters. Words written entirely in capital letters have been retained as such. Longer quotations have been indented. Telegrams are given in capital letters. The first text on p. 404 has been replicated from a postcard. Wherever possible, words or sentences that were crossed out by the correspondents in their original letters have been retained as such in the translations. Author additions to the letters by way of marginalia – whether in pen or pencil on typed letters, or added onto the writing sheets in handwritten letters – are given between curly brackets.

The sources of quotations used by the correspondents are not provided, except in cases where Brink and Jonker themselves identify the authors. Only these references have been included in the Index of Persons. Obvious errors and identifiable mistakes in quotations have been corrected.

Translation

In rendering the letters into English, we have assumed a mainly South African audience, given this book's predominantly regional distribution and probable range of circulation. In view of such a readership, we have retained certain key Afrikaans terms that are all but untranslatable and are likely to be understood by most South Africans, including those who are not mother-tongue speakers of Afrikaans. At the same time, non-South African readers should be able to deduce the meanings and connotative range of such terms from the context of the letters themselves. Examples include Jonker's frequent term of endearment, "liefsteling" (literally "dearestling", a play on the term "darling"), and both correspondents' frequent play on the word "Kontjie" (a derivation from "Kokon" or "Cocoon", their term of endearment for Jonker; "kontjie" translates literally as "little vagina"). Brink and Jonker frequently use the term "moesie" (a mole or beauty spot) in a playful manner, referring to their oft-imagined baby daughter as their "moesie-girl". The translators and editors decided, after much deliberation, to retain the term "moesie" in the English version of these letters, as it is a word in fairly common use in South African English, and even more so in the early 1960s, when these letters were written. Of course, the "moesiemeisie" that Jonker and Brink repeatedly claim so ardently to wish for in these letters would never be conceived.

The letters abound with literary quotations from the work of Afrikaans, Dutch, English, Italian, German, and other foreign-language writers – mostly poets. Some of these intertextual additions in the letters consist of whole poems or extracts that are longer than just one or two lines, and these are presented as indented quotations, while others are short excerpts or fragments, and we have rendered these in quotation marks in the text of the letters themselves. Brink and Jonker took each other to be highly literate mutual "audiences", and Brink's act of preserving, and then handing over for publication, carbon copies of most of his letters suggests that he meant them to be read by a wide range of equally cosmopolitan readers. In view of this, the project team decided not to translate (and thereby possibly diminish the power of) original quotations. They are presented here as they were in the letters, in Afrikaans, Dutch, German, Italian, and so on. This rule has been observed in all cases where the quoted excerpts and fragments are identifiably taken from published, existing literary work. In cases where Jonker and Brink versify to each other in the course of their correspondence (that is, the verse so produced exists nowhere as literary artifacts except in these letters), we have generally translated such versification into English for the sake of readability and flow. In a few cases, where one of the authors copies out in a letter a fuller poem, recently composed (but otherwise unpublished), we have given the Afrikaans original, followed by a translation in square brackets.

In cases where Jonker and Brink mention the titles of existing, published literary works (including their own), the original (Afrikaans or otherwise) title is given in italics, followed by an English translation of the title in ordinary type within square brackets at the first instance. Afrikaans poem titles, and their published English translations, are in quotation marks, following the usual convention. In rare cases where Brink's *English* titles are referred to, they are given as such (*The Ambassador* in its life as a published English translation of the Afrikaans novel *Die Ambassadeur* gets a mention or two late in the correspondence), that is, when reference is made to the already existing English translation of the book. In such cases we give the English title in italics, as this English book did actually exist at the moment of its being mentioned in the correspondence. Elsewhere, when the Afrikaans version of the book is being referred to, it is called *Die Ambassadeur* [The Ambassador] – the translation in square brackets given at first mention only.

In cases where one of the correspondents translates from a foreign language into Afrikaans, we have rendered the Afrikaans translation in English (an example is Brink's rendering of Jacques Prévert's poem "Alicante" in his letter dated 30 May 1963). In some cases, the correspondents quote a foreign-language poem and translate it, as Brink does for Salvatore Quasimodo in his letter of 24 June 1963; here we provide the original quoted text and we translate the Afrikaans translation into English. In one case, Jonker provides her own translation of E.E. Cummings's "somewhere i have never travelled, gladly beyond", and here we retain Jonker's Afrikaans translation for the sake of its originality, as published in her *Versamelde Werke* [Collected Works]. For the sake of interest, in this case, we add the English version so that readers can compare her translation to her source material. In cases where informal Afrikaans versification is used, such as the "words of a wise old lady" that Brink quotes in his letter of 2 June 1963, we have reproduced the Afrikaans, along with a literal English rendering in square brackets, for the sake of content comprehension. Occasionally, when an important refrain in the letters, consisting of a foreign-language fragment, is repeatedly accentuated in the correspondence, we have worked an explanatory translation into the text, without quote marks, such as "Good daayyy Fish! *Daaag visselijn mijn*!" which occurs in Brink's letter of 26 June 1963, referring back to Dutch poet Paul van Ostaijen's "Marc Groet 's Morgens de Dingen". In such cases, the aim was both comprehensibility and preservation of the original literary allusion, which is most directly legible from the foreign-language phrase. Where Jonker's poems have been rendered in English, the translations have been taken from *Black Butterflies, Selected Poems by Ingrid Jonker* (Human & Rousseau, 2007). These poems were translated by André Brink and Antjie Krog. The translations do not always follow to the letter earlier versions of Jonker's Afrikaans poems, as presented in the correspondence, though ultimately they represent the most refined translation available in English of these poems.